The History of Herodotus Vol. 2

Translated into English by G. C. Macaulay

Table of Contents

The History of Herodotus Vol. 2..1

Translated into English by G. C. Macaulay...1

BOOK V. THE FIFTH BOOK OF THE HISTORIES, CALLED
TERPSICHORE...1

BOOK VI. THE SIXTH BOOK OF THE HISTORIES, CALLED ERATO......54

BOOK VII. THE SEVENTH BOOK OF THE HISTORIES, CALLED
POLYMNIA..109

BOOK VIII. THE EIGHTH BOOK OF THE HISTORIES, CALLED
URANIA...207

BOOK IX. THE NINTH BOOK OF THE HISTORIES, CALLED
CALLIOPE...262

The History of Herodotus Vol. 2

Translated into English by G. C. Macaulay

- BOOK V. THE FIFTH BOOK OF THE HISTORIES, CALLED TERPSICHORE
- BOOK VI. THE SIXTH BOOK OF THE HISTORIES, CALLED ERATO
- BOOK VII. THE SEVENTH BOOK OF THE HISTORIES, CALLED POLYMNIA
- BOOK VIII. THE EIGHTH BOOK OF THE HISTORIES, CALLED URANIA
- BOOK IX. THE NINTH BOOK OF THE HISTORIES, CALLED CALLIOPE

e Herodotou diathesis en apasin epieikes, kai tois men agathois sunedomene, tois de kakois sunalgousa.—Dion. Halic.

PREPARER'S NOTE

This text was prepared from the third edition, printed in 1914, by MacMillan and Co., Limited, St. Martin's Street, London.

Greek text has been transliterated and marked with brackets, as in the opening citation above.

THE HISTORY OF HERODOTUS

BOOK V. THE FIFTH BOOK OF THE HISTORIES, CALLED TERPSICHORE

1. In the meantime those of the Persians who had been left behind in Europe by Dareios, of whom Megabazos was the commander, had subdued the people of Perinthos first of the Hellespontians, since they refused to be subject to Dareios. These had in former times also been hardly dealt with by the Paionians: for the Paionians from the Strymon had been commanded by an oracle of their god to march against the Perinthians; and if the Perinthians, when encamped opposite to them, should shout aloud and call to them by their name, they were to attack them; but if they should not shout to them, they were not to attack them: and thus the Paionians proceeded to do. Now when the Perinthians were encamped opposite to them in the suburb of their city, a challenge was made and a single combat took place in three different forms; for they matched a man against a man, and a horse against a horse, and a dog against a dog. Then, as the Perinthians were getting the better in two of the three, in their exultation they raised a shout of paion,[1] and the Paionians conjectured that this was the very thing which was spoken of in the oracle, and said doubtless to one another, "Now surely the oracle is being accomplished for us, now it is time for us to act." So the Paionians attacked the Perinthians when they had raised the shout of paion, and they had much the better in the fight, and left but few of them alive. 2. Thus it happened with respect to those things which had been done to them in former times by the Paionians; and at this time, although the Perinthians proved themselves brave men in defence of their freedom, the Persians and Megabazos got the better of them by numbers. Then after Perinthos had been conquered, Megabazos marched his army through the length of Thracia, forcing every city and every race of those who dwell there to submit to the king, for so it had been commanded him by Dareios, to subdue Thracia.

3. Now the Thracian race is the most numerous, except the Indians, in all the world: and if it should come to be ruled over by one man, or to agree together in one, it would be irresistible in fight and the strongest by far of all nations, in my opinion. Since however this is impossible for them and cannot ever come to pass among them,[2] they are in fact weak for that reason. They have many names, belonging to their various tribes in different places; but they all follow customs which are nearly the same in all respects, except the Getai and Trausians and those who dwell above the Crestonians. 4. Of these the practices of the Getai, who believe themselves to be immortal, have been spoken of by me already:[3] and the Trausians perform everything else in the same manner as the other Thracians, but in regard to those who are born and die among them they do as follows:—when a child has been born, the nearest of kin sit round it and

make lamentation for all the evils of which he must fulfil the measure, now that he is born,[3a] enumerating the whole number of human ills; but when a man is dead, they cover him up in the earth with sport and rejoicing, saying at the same time from what great evils he has escaped and is now in perfect bliss. 5. Those who dwell above the Crestonians do as follows:—each man has many wives, and when any man of them is dead, a great competition takes place among his wives, with much exertion on the part of their friends, about the question of which of them was most loved by their husband; and she who is preferred by the decision and so honoured, is first praised by both men and women, then her throat is cut over the tomb by her nearest of kin, and afterwards she is buried together with her husband; and the others are exceedingly grieved at it, for this is counted as the greatest reproach to them. 6. Of the other Thracians the custom is to sell their children to be carried away out of the country; and over their maidens they do not keep watch, but allow them to have commerce with whatever men they please, but over their wives they keep very great watch; and they buy their wives for great sums of money from their parents. To be pricked with figures is accounted a mark of noble rank, and not to be so marked is a sign of low birth.[4] Not to work is counted most honourable, and to be a worker of the soil is above all things dishonourable: to live on war and plunder is the most honourable thing. 7. These are their most remarkable customs; and of the gods they worship only Ares and Dionysos and Artemis. Their kings, however, apart from the rest of the people, worship Hermes more than all gods, and swear by him alone; and they say that they are descended from Hermes. 8. The manner of burial for the rich among them is this:—for three days they expose the corpse to view, and they slay all kinds of victims and feast, having first made lamentation. Then they perform the burial rites, either consuming the body with fire or covering it up in the earth without burning; and afterwards when they have heaped up a mound they celebrate games with every kind of contest, in which reasonably the greatest prizes are assigned for single combat.[5] This is the manner of burial among the Thracians.

9. Of the region lying further on towards the North of this country no one can declare accurately who the men are who dwell in it; but the parts which lie immediately beyond the Ister are known to be uninhabited and vast in extent. The only men of whom I can hear who dwell beyond the Ister are those who are said to be called Sigynnai, and who use the Median fashion of dress. Their horses, it is said, have shaggy hair all over their bodies, as much as five fingers long; and these are small and flat-nosed and too weak to carry men, but when yoked in chariots they are very

high−spirited; therefore the natives of the country drive chariots. The boundaries of this people extend, it is said, to the parts near the Enetoi, who live on the Adriatic; and people say that they are colonists from the Medes. In what way however these have come to be colonists from the Medes I am not able for my part to conceive, but everything is possible in the long course of ages. However that may be, the Ligurians who dwell in the region inland above Massalia call traders sigynnai, and the men of Cyprus give the same name to spears. 10. Now the Thracians say that the other side of the Ister is occupied by bees, and that by reason of them it is not possible to pass through and proceed further: but to me it seems that when they so speak, they say that which is not probable; for these creatures are known to be intolerant of cold, and to me it seems that the regions which go up towards the pole are uninhabitable by reason of the cold climate. These then are the tales reported about this country; and however that may be, Megabazos was then making the coast−regions of it subject to the Persians.

11. Meanwhile Dareios, so soon as he had crossed over the Hellespont and come to Sardis, called to mind the service rendered to him by Histiaios the Milesian and also the advice of the Mytilenian Coës, and having sent for them to come to Sardis he offered them a choice of rewards. Histiaios then, being despot of Miletos, did not make request for any government in addition to that, but he asked for the district of Myrkinos which belonged to the Edonians, desiring there to found a city. Histiaios chose this for himself; but Coës, not being a despot but a man of the people, asked to be made despot of Mitylene. 12. After the desires of both had been fulfilled, they betook themselves to that which they had chosen: and at this same time it chanced that Dareios saw a certain thing which made him desire to command Megabazos to conquer the Paionians and remove them forcibly from Europe into Asia: and the thing was this:—There were certain Paionians named Pigres and Mantyas, who when Dareios had crossed over into Asia, came to Sardis, because they desired themselves to have rule over the Paionians, and with them they brought their sister, who was tall and comely. Then having watched for a time when Dareios took his seat publicly in the suburb of the Lydian city, they dressed up their sister in the best way they could, and sent her to fetch water, having a water−jar upon her head and leading a horse after her by a bridle round her arm, and at the same time spinning flax. Now when the woman passed out of the city by him, Dareios paid attention to the matter, for that which was done by the woman was not of Persian nor yet of Lydian fashion, nor indeed after the manner of any people of Asia. He sent therefore some of his spearmen, bidding them watch what the woman would do with the horse. They accordingly followed after her; and she having

arrived at the river watered the horse, and having watered him and filled her jar with the water, she passed along by the same way, bearing the water upon her head, leading the horse after her by a bridle round her arm, and at the same time turning the spindle. 13. Then Dareios, marvelling both at that which he heard from those who went to observe and also at that which he saw himself, bade them bring her into his presence: and when she was brought, her brothers also came, who had been watching these things at no great distance off. So then when Dareios asked of what country she was, the young men said that they were Paionians and that she was their sister; and he replied: "Who then are these Paionians, and where upon the earth do they dwell?" and he asked them also what they desired, that they had come to Sardis. They declared to him that they had come to give themselves up to him, and that Paionia was a country situated upon the river Strymon, and that the Strymon was not far from the Hellespont, and finally that they were colonists from the Teucrians of Troy. All these things severally they told him; and he asked whether all the women of that land were as industrious as their sister; and they very readily replied to this also, saying that it was so, for it was with a view to that very thing that they had been doing this. 14. Then Dareios wrote a letter to Megabazos, whom he had left to command his army in Thrace, bidding him remove the Paionians from their place of habitation and bring them to the king, both themselves and their children and their wives. Then forthwith a horseman set forth to ride in haste bearing the message to the Hellespont, and having passed over to the other side he gave the paper to Megabazos. So he having read it and having obtained guides from Thrace, set forth to march upon Paionia: 15, and the Paionians, being informed that the Persians were coming against them, gathered all their powers together and marched out in the direction of the sea, supposing that the Persians when they invaded them would make their attack on that side. The Paionians then were prepared, as I say, to drive off the army of Megabazos when it came against them; but the Persians hearing that the Paionians had gathered their powers and were guarding the entrance which lay towards the sea, directed their course with guides along the upper road; and passing unperceived by the Paionians they fell upon their cities, which were left without men, and finding them without defenders they easily took possession of them. The Paionians when they heard that their cities were in the hands of the enemy, at once dispersed, each tribe to its own place of abode, and proceeded to deliver themselves up to the Persians. Thus then it happened that these tribes of the Paionians, namely the Siropaionians,[6] the Paioplians and all up to the lake Prasias, were removed from their place of habitation and brought to Asia; 16, but those who dwell about mount Pangaion, and about the Doberians and Agrianians and

Odomantians,[7] and about the lake Prasias itself, were not conquered at all by Megabazos. He tried however to remove even those who lived in the lake and who had their dwellings in the following manner:—a platform fastened together and resting upon lofty piles stood in the middle of the water of the lake, with a narrow approach to it from the mainland by a single bridge. The piles which supported the platform were no doubt originally set there by all the members of the community working together, but since that time they continue to set them by observance of this rule, that is to say, every man who marries brings from the mountain called Orbelos three piles for each wife and sets them as supports; and each man takes to himself many wives. And they have their dwelling thus, that is each man has possession of a hut upon the platform in which he lives and of a trap–door[8] leading through the platform down to the lake: and their infant children they tie with a rope by the foot, for fear that they should roll into the water. To their horses and beasts of burden they give fish for fodder; and of fish there is so great quantity that if a man open the trap–door and let down an empty basket by a cord into the lake, after waiting quite a short time he draws it up again full of fish. Of the fish there are two kinds, and they call them paprax and tilon.

17. So then those of the Paionians who had been conquered were being brought to Asia: and Megabazos meanwhile, after he had conquered the Paionians, sent as envoys to Macedonia seven Persians, who after himself were the men of most repute in the army. These were being sent to Amyntas to demand of him earth and water for Dareios the king. Now from lake Prasias there is a very short way into Macedonia; for first, quite close to the lake, there is the mine from which after this time there came in regularly a talent of silver every day to Alexander; and after the mine, when you have passed over the mountain called Dysoron, you are in Macedonia. 18. These Persians then, who had been sent to Amyntas, having arrived came into the presence of Amyntas and proceeded to demand earth and water for king Dareios. This he was willing to give, and also he invited them to be his guests; and he prepared a magnificent dinner and received the Persians with friendly hospitality. Then when dinner was over, the Persians while drinking pledges to one another[9] said thus: "Macedonian guest–friend, it is the custom among us Persians, when we set forth a great dinner, then to bring in also our concubines and lawful wives to sit beside us. Do thou then, since thou didst readily receive us and dost now entertain us magnificently as thy guests, and since thou art willing to give to king Dareios earth and water, consent to follow our custom." To this Amyntas replied: "Persians, among us the custom is not so, but that men should be separate from women. Since however ye

being our masters make this request in addition, this also shall be given you." Having so said Amyntas proceeded to send for the women; and when they came being summoned, they sat down in order opposite to the Persians. Then the Persians, seeing women of comely form, spoke to Amyntas and said that this which had been done was by no means well devised; for it was better that the women should not come at all, than that they should come and should not seat themselves by their side, but sit opposite and be a pain to their eyes. So Amyntas being compelled bade them sit by the side of the Persians; and when the women obeyed, forthwith the Persians, being much intoxicated, began to touch their breasts, and some no doubt also tried to kiss them. 19. Amyntas seeing this kept quiet, notwithstanding that he felt anger, because he excessively feared the Persians; but Alexander the son of Amyntas, who was present and saw this, being young and without experience of calamity was not able to endure any longer; but being impatient of it he said to Amyntas: "My father, do thou grant that which thy age demands, and go away to rest, nor persevere longer in the drinking; but I will remain here and give to our guests all that is convenient." On this Amyntas, understanding that Alexander was intending to do some violence, said: "My son, I think that I understand thy words, as the heat of anger moves thee, namely that thou desirest to send me away and then do some deed of violence: therefore I ask of thee not to do violence to these men, that it may not be our ruin, but endure to see that which is being done: as to my departure, however, in that I will do as thou sayest." 20. When Amyntas after having made of him this request had departed, Alexander said to the Persians: "With these women ye have perfect freedom, guests, to have commerce with all, if ye so desire, or with as many of them as ye will. About this matter ye shall be they who give the word; but now, since already the hour is approaching for you to go to bed and I see that ye have well drunk, let these women go away, if so it is pleasing to you, to bathe themselves; and when they have bathed, then receive them back into your company." Having so said, since the Persians readily agreed, he dismissed the women, when they had gone out, to the women's chambers; and Alexander himself equipped men equal in number to the women and smooth-faced, in the dress of the women, and giving them daggers he led them into the banqueting-room; and as he led them in, he said thus to the Persians: "Persians, it seems to me that ye have been entertained with a feast to which nothing was wanting; for other things, as many as we had, and moreover such as we were able to find out and furnish, are all supplied to you, and there is this especially besides, which is the chief thing of all, that is, we give you freely in addition our mothers and our sisters, in order that ye may perceive fully that ye are honoured by us with that treatment which ye deserve, and also in order that ye may report to the king who sent you that a man of Hellas, ruler under him of the Macedonians, entertained you well at board and bed." Having thus said Alexander caused a Macedonian man in the guise of a woman to sit by each Persian, and they, when the Persians attempted to lay hands on them, slew them. 21. So these perished by this fate, both they themselves and their company of servants; for there came with them carriages and servants and all the usual pomp of equipage, and this was all made away with at the same time as they. Afterwards in no long time a great search was made by the Persians for these men, and Alexander stopped them with cunning by giving large sums of money and his own sister, whose name was Gygaia; —by giving, I say, these things to Bubares a Persian, commander of those who were searching for the men who had been killed, Alexander stopped their search. 22. Thus the death of these Persians was kept concealed. And that these descendants of Perdiccas are Hellenes, as they themselves say, I happen to know myself, and not only so, but I will prove in the succeeding history that they are Hellenes.[10] Moreover the Hellanodicai, who manage the games at Olympia, decided that they were so: for when Alexander wished to contend in the games and had descended for this purpose into the arena, the Hellenes who were to run against him tried to exclude him, saying that the contest was not for Barbarians to contend in but for Hellenes: since however Alexander proved that he was of Argos, he was judged to be a Hellene, and when he entered the contest of the foot-race his lot came out with that of the first.[11]

23. Thus then it happened with regard to these things: and at the same time Megabazos had arrived at the Hellespont bringing with him the Paionians; and thence after passing over the straits he came to Sardis. Then, since Histiaios the Milesian was already engaged in fortifying with a wall the place which he had asked and obtained from Dareios as a reward for keeping safe the bridge of boats (this place being that which is called Myrkinos, lying along the bank of the river Strymon), Megabazos, having perceived that which was being done by Histiaios, as soon as he came to Sardis bringing the Paionians, said thus to Dareios: "O king, what a thing is this that thou hast done, granting permission to a Hellene who is skilful and cunning to found a city in Thracia in a place where there is forest for shipbuilding in abundance and great quantity of wood for oars and mines of silver and great numbers both of Hellenes and Barbarians living round, who when they have obtained a leader will do that which he shall command them both by day and by night. Therefore stop this man from doing so, that thou be not involved in a domestic war: and stop him by sending for him in a courteous manner; but when thou hast got him in thy hands, then cause that he shall

never again return to the land of the Hellenes. 24. Thus saying Megabazos easily persuaded Dareios, who thought that he was a true prophet of that which was likely to come to pass: and upon that Dareios sent a messenger to Myrkinos and said as follows: "Hisiaios, king Dareios saith these things:—By taking thought I find that there is no one more sincerely well disposed than thou art to me and to my power; and this I know having learnt by deeds not words. Now therefore, since I have it in my mind to accomplish great matters, come hither to me by all means, that I may communicate them to thee." Histiaios therefore, trusting to these sayings and at the same time accounting it a great thing to become a counsellor of the king, came to Sardis; and when he had come Dareios spoke to him as follows: "Histiaios, I sent for thee for this reason, namely because when I had returned from the Scythians and thou wert gone away out of the sight of my eyes, never did I desire to see anything again within so short a time as I desired then both to see thee and that thou shouldst come to speech with me; since I perceived that the most valuable of all possessions is a friend who is a man of understanding and also sincerely well–disposed, both which qualities I know exist in thee, and I am able to bear witness of them in regard to my affairs. Now therefore (for thou didst well in that thou camest hither) this is that which I propose to thee:—leave Miletos alone and also thy newly– founded city in Thracia, and coming with me to Susa, have whatsoever things I have, eating at my table and being my counseller." 25. Thus said Dareios, and having appointed Artaphrenes[12] his own brother and the son of his father to be governor of Sardis, he marched away to Susa taking with him Histiaios, after he had first named Otanes to be commander of those who dwelt along the sea coasts. This man's father Sisamnes, who had been made one of the Royal Judges, king Cambyses slew, because he had judged a cause unjustly for money, and flayed off all his skin: then after he had torn away the skin he cut leathern thongs out of it and stretched them across the seat where Sisamnes had been wont to sit to give judgment; and having stretched them in the seat, Cambyses appointed the son of that Sisamnes whom he had slain and flayed, to be judge instead of his father, enjoining him to remember in what seat he was sitting to give judgment. 26. This Otanes then, who was made to sit in that seat, had now become the successor of Megabazos in the command: and he conquered the Byzantians and Calchedonians, and he conquered Antandros in the land of Troas, and Lamponion; and having received ships from the Lesbians he conquered Lemnos and Imbros, which were both at that time still inhabited by Pelasgians. 27. Of these the Lemnians fought well, and defending themselves for a long time were at length brought to ruin;[13] and over those of them who survived the Persians set as governor Lycaretos the brother of that

Maiandrios who had been king of Samos. This Lycaretos ruled in Lemnos till his death. And the cause of it[14] was this:—he continued to reduce all to slavery and subdue them, accusing some of desertion to the Scythians and others of doing damage to the army of Dareios as it was coming back from Scythia.

28. Otanes then effected so much when he was made commander: and after this for a short time there was an abatement[15] of evils; and then again evils began a second time to fall upon the Ionians, arising from Naxos and Miletos. For Naxos was superior to all the other islands in wealth, and Miletos at the same time had just then come to the very height of its prosperity and was the ornament[16] of Ionia; but before these events for two generations of men it had been afflicted most violently by faction until the Parians reformed it; for these the Milesians chose of all the Hellenes to be reformers of their State. 29. Now the Parians thus reconciled their factions:—the best men of them came to Miletos, and seeing that the Milesians were in a grievously ruined state, they said that they desired to go over their land: and while doing this and passing through the whole territory of Miletos, whenever they saw in the desolation of the land any field that was well cultivated, they wrote down the name of the owner of that field. Then when they had passed through the whole land and had found but few of such men, as soon as they returned to the city they called a general gathering and appointed these men to manage the State, whose fields they had found well cultivated; for they said that they thought these men would take care of the public affairs as they had taken care of their own: and the rest of the Milesians, who before had been divided by factions, they commanded to be obedient to these men.

30. The Parians then had thus reformed the Milesians; but at the time of which I speak evils began to come to Ionia from these States[17] in the following manner:—From Naxos certain men of the wealthier class[18] were driven into exile by the people, and having gone into exile they arrived at Miletos. Now of Miletos it happened that Aristagoras son of Molpagoras was ruler in charge, being both a son-in-law and also a cousin of Histiaios the son of Lysagoras, whom Dareios was keeping at Susa: for Histiaios was despot of Miletos, and it happened that he was at Susa at this time when the Naxians came, who had been in former times guest-friends of Histiaios. So when the Naxians arrived, they made request of Aristagoras, to see if perchance he would supply them with a force, and so they might return from exile to their own land: and he, thinking that if by his means they should return to their own State, he would be ruler of Naxos, but at the same time making a pretext of the guest-friendship of

Histiaios, made proposal to them thus: "I am not able to engage that I can supply you with sufficient force to bring you back from exile against the will of those Naxians who have control of the State; for I hear that the Naxians have an army which is eight thousand shields strong and many ships of war: but I will use every endeavour to devise a means; and my plan is this:—it chances that Artaphrenes is my friend: now Artaphrenes, ye must know,[18a] is a son of Hystaspes and brother of Dareios the king; and he is ruler of all the people of the sea-coasts in Asia, with a great army and many ships. This man then I think will do whatsoever we shall request of him." Hearing this the Naxians gave over the matter to Aristagoras to manage as best he could, and they bade him promise gifts and the expenses of the expedition, saying that they would pay them; for they had full expectation that when they should appear at Naxos, the Naxians would do all their bidding, and likewise also the other islanders. For of these islands, that is the Cyclades, not one was as yet subject to Dareios. 31. Aristagoras accordingly having arrived at Sardis, said to Artaphrenes that Naxos was an island not indeed large in size, but fair nevertheless and of fertile soil, as well as near to Ionia, and that there was in it much wealth and many slaves: "Do thou therefore send an expedition against this land, and restore it to those who are now exiles from it: and if thou shalt do this, first I have ready for thee large sums of money apart from the expenses incurred for the expedition (which it is fair that we who conduct it should supply), and next thou wilt gain for the king not only Naxos itself but also the islands which are dependent upon it, Paros and Andros and the others which are called Cyclades; and setting out from these thou wilt easily attack Eubœa, an island which is large and wealth, as large indeed as Cyprus, and very easy to conquer. To subdue all these a hundred ships are sufficient." He made answer in these words: "Thou makest thyself a reporter of good things to the house of the king; and in all these things thou advisest well, except as to the number of the ships: for instead of one hundred there shall be prepared for thee two hundred by the beginning of the spring. And it is right that the king himself also should join in approving this matter." 32. So Aristagoras hearing this went back to Miletos greatly rejoiced; and Artaphrenes meanwhile, when he had sent to Susa and communicated that which was said by Aristagoras, and Dareios himself also had joined in approving it, made ready two hundred triremes and a very great multitude both of Persians and their allies, and appointed to be commander of these Megabates a Persian, one of the Achaimenidai and a cousin to himself and to Dareios, to whose daughter afterwards Pausanias the son of Cleombrotus the Lacedaemonian (at least if the story be true) betrothed himself, having formed a desire to become a despot of Hellas. Having appointed Megabates, I say, to be commander,

Artaphrenes sent away the armament to Aristagoras. 33. So when Megabates had taken force together with the Naxians, he sailed with the pretence of going to the Hellespont; but when he came to Chios, he directed his ships to Caucasa, in order that he might from thence pass them over to Naxos with a North Wind. Then, since it was not fated that the Naxians should be destroyed by this expedition, there happened an event which I shall narrate. As Megabates was going round to visit the guards set in the several ships, it chanced that in a ship of Myndos there was no one on guard; and he being very angry bade his spearmen find out the commander of the ship, whose name was Skylax, and bind him in an oar–hole of his ship in such a manner[19] that his head should be outside and his body within. When Skylax was thus bound, some one reported to Aristagoras that Megabates had bound his guest–friend of Myndos and was doing to him shameful outrage. He accordingly came and asked the Persian for his release, and as he did not obtain anything of that which he requested, he went himself and let him loose. Being informed of this Megabates was exceedingly angry and broke out in rage against Aristagoras; and he replied: "What hast thou to do with these matters? Did not Artaphrenes send thee to obey me, and to sail whithersoever I should order? Why dost thou meddle with things which concern thee not?" Thus said Aristagoras; and the other being enraged at this, when night came on sent men in a ship to Naxos to declare to the Naxians all the danger that threatened them. 34. For the Naxians were not at all expecting that this expedition would be against them: but when they were informed of it, forthwith they brought within the wall the property which was in the fields, and provided for themselves food and drink as for a siege, and strengthened their wall.[20] These then were making preparations as for war to come upon them; and the others meanwhile having passed their ships over from Chios to Naxos, found them well defended when they made their attack, and besieged them for four months. Then when the money which the Persians had brought with them had all been consumed by them, and not only that, but Aristagoras himself had spent much in addition, and the siege demanded ever more and more, they built walls for the Naxian exiles and departed to the mainland again with ill success. 35. And so Aristagoras was not able to fulfil his promise to Artaphrenes; and at the same time he was hard pressed by the demand made to him for the expenses of the expedition, and had fears because of the ill success of the armament and because he had become an enemy of Megabates; and he supposed that he would be deprived of his rule over Miletos. Having all these various fears he began to make plans of revolt: for it happened also that just at this time the man who had been marked upon the head had come from Hisiaios who was at Susa, signifying that Aristagoras should revolt from the king. For Histiaios, desiring to signify to Aristagoras that he should revolt, was not able to do it safely in any other way, because the roads were guarded, but shaved off the hair of the most faithful of his slaves, and having marked his head by pricking it, waited till the hair had grown again; and as soon as it was grown, he sent him away to Miletos, giving him no other charge but this, namely that when he should have arrived at Miletos he should bid Aristagoras shave his hair and look at his head: and the marks, as I have said before, signified revolt. This thing Histiaios was doing, because he was greatly vexed by being detained at Susa. He had great hopes then that if a revolt occurred he would be let go to the sea−coast; but if no change was made at Miletos[20a] he had no expectation of ever returning thither again.

36. Accordingly Hisiaios with this intention was sending the messenger; and it chanced that all these things happened to Aristagoras together at the same time. He took counsel therefore with his partisans, declaring to them both his own opinion and the message from Hisiaios; and while all the rest expressed an opinion to the same effect, urging him namely to make revolt, Hecataios the historian urged first that they should not undertake war with the king of the Persians, enumerating all the nations over whom Dareios was ruler, and his power: and when he did not succeed in persuading him, he counselled next that they should manage to make themselves masters of the sea. Now this, he continued, could not come to pass in any other way, so far as he could see, for he knew that the force of the Milesians was weak, but if the treasures should be taken[21] which were in the temple at Branchidai, which Crœsus the Lydian dedicated as offerings, he had great hopes that they might become masters of the sea; and by this means they would not only themselves have wealth at their disposal, but the enemy would not be able to carry the things off as plunder. Now these treasures were of great value, as I have shown in the first part of the history.[22] This opinion did not prevail; but nevertheless it was resolved to make revolt, and that one of them should sail to Myus, to make the force which had returned from Naxos and was then there, and endeavour to seize the commanders who sailed in the ships. 37. So Iatragoras was sent for this purpose and seized by craft Oliatos the son of Ibanollis of Mylasa, and Histiaios the son of Tymnes of Termera, and Coës the son of Erxander, to whom Dareios had given Mytilene as a gift, and Aristagoras the son of Heracleides of Kyme, and many others; and then Aristagoras openly made revolt and devised all that he could to the hurt of Dareios. And first he pretended to resign the despotic power and give to Miletos equality,[23] in order that the Milesians might be willing to revolt with him: then afterwards he proceeded to do this same thing in the rest of Ionia also; and

some of the despots he drove out, but those whom he had taken from the ships which had sailed with him to Naxis, these he surrendered, because he desired to do a pleasure to their cities, delivering them over severally to that city from which each one came. 38. Now the men of Mitylene, so soon as they received Coës into their hands, brought him out and stoned him to death; but the men of Kyme let their despot go, and so also most of the others let them go. Thus then the despots were deposed in the various cities; and Aristagoras the Milesian, after having deposed the despots, bade each people appoint commanders in their several cities, and then himself set forth as an envoy to Lacedemon; for in truth it was necessary that he should find out some powerful alliance.

39. Now at Sparta Anaxandrides the son of Leon was no longer surviving as king, but had brought his life to an end; and Cleomenes the son of Anaxandrides was holding the royal power, not having obtained it by merit but by right of birth. For Anaxandrides had to wife his own sister's daughter and she was by him much beloved, but no children were born to him by her. This being so, the Ephors summoned him before them and said: "If thou dost not for thyself take thought in time, yet we cannot suffer this to happen, that the race of Eurysthenes should become extinct. Do thou therefore put away from thee the wife whom thou now hast, since, as thou knowest, she bears thee no children, and marry another: and in doing so thou wilt please the Spartans." He made answer saying that he would do neither of these two things, and that they did not give him honourable counsel, in that they advised him to send away the wife whom he had, though she had done him no wrong, and to take to his house another; and in short he would not follow their advice. 40. Upon this the Ephors and the Senators deliberated together and proposed to Anaxandrides as follows: "Since then we perceive that thou art firmly attached to the wife whom thou now hast, consent to do this, and set not thyself against it, lest the Spartans take some counsel about thee other than might be wished. We do not ask of thee the putting away of the wife whom thou hast; but do thou give to her all that thou givest now and at the same time take to thy house another wife in addition to this one, to bear thee children." When they spoke to him after this manner, Anaxandrides consented, having two wives, a thing which was not by any means after the Spartan fashion. 41. Then when no long time had elapsed, the wife who had come in afterwards bore this Cleomenes of whom we spoke; and just when she was bringing to the light an heir to the kingdom of the Spartans, the former wife, who had during the time before been childless, then by some means conceived, chancing to do so just at that time: and though she was in truth with child, the kinsfolk

of the wife who had come in afterwards, when they heard of it cried out against her and said that she was making a vain boast, and that she meant to pass off another child as her own. Since then they made a great show of indignation, as the time was fast drawing near, the Ephors being incredulous sat round and watched the woman during the birth of her child: and she bore Dorieos and then straightway conceived Leonidas and after him at once Cleombrotos,—nay, some even say that Cleombrotos and Leonidas were twins. The wife however who had born Cleomenes and had come in after the first wife, being the daughter of Primetades the son of Demarmenos, did not bear a child again. 42. Now Cleomenes, it is said, was not quite in his right senses but on the verge of madness,[24] while Dorieos was of all his equals in age the first, and felt assured that he would obtain the kingdom by merit. Seeing then that he had this opinion, when Anaxandrides died and the Lacedemonians followed the usual custom established the eldest, namely Cleomenes, upon the throne, Dorieos being indignant and not thinking it fit that he should be a subject of Cleomenes, asked the Spartans to give him a company of followers and led them out to found a colony, without either inquiring of the Oracle at Delphi to what land he should go to make a settlement, or doing any of the things which are usually done; but being vexed he sailed away with his ships to Libya, and the Theraians were his guides thither. Then having come to Kinyps[25] he made a settlement in the fairest spot of all Libya, along the banks of the river; but afterwards in the third year he was driven out from thence by the Macai and the Libyans[26] and the Carthaginians, and returned to Peloponnesus. 43. Then Antichares a man of Eleon gave him counsel out of the oracles of Laïos to make a settlement at Heracleia[27] in Sicily, saying that the whole land of Eryx belonged to the Heracleidai, since Heracles himself had won it: and hearing this he went forthwith to Delphi to inquire of the Oracle whether he would be able to conquer the land to which he was setting forth; and the Pythian prophetess replied to him that he would conquer it. Dorieos therefore took with him the armament which he conducted before to Libya, and voyaged along the coast of Italy.[28] 44. Now at this time, the men of Sybaris say that they and their king Telys were about to make an expedition against Croton, and the men of Croton being exceedingly alarmed asked Dorieos to help them and obtained their request. So Dorieos joined them in an expedition against Sybaris and helped them to conquer Sybaris. This is what the men of Sybaris say of the doings of Dorieos and his followers; but those of Croton say that no stranger helped them in the war against the Sybarites except Callias alone, a diviner of Elis and one of the descendants of Iamos, and he in the following manner:—he ran away, they say, from Telys the despot of the Sybarites, when the sacrifices did not prove favourable, as he was sacrificing for the expedition against Croton, and so he came to them. 45. Such, I say, are the tales which these tell, and they severally produce as evidence of them the following facts:—the Sybarites point to a sacred enclosure and temple by the side of the dried-up bed of the Crathis,[29] which they say that Dorieos, after he had joined in the capture of the city, set up to Athene surnamed "of the Crathis"; and besides they consider the death of Dorieos himself to be a very strong evidence, thinking that he perished because he acted contrary to the oracle which was given to him; for if he had not done anything by the way but had continued to do that for which he was sent, he would have conquered the land of Eryx and having conquered it would have become possessor of it, and he and his army would not have perished. On the other hand the men of Croton declare that many things were granted in the territory of Croton as special gifts to Callias the Eleisan, of which the descendants of Callias were still in possession down to my time, and that nothing was granted to Dorieos or the descendants of Dorieos: but if Dorieos had in fact helped them in the way with Sybaris, many times as much, they say, would have been given to him as to Callias. These then are the evidences which the two sides produce, and we may assent to whichever of them we think credible. 46. Now there sailed with Dorieos others also of the Spartans, to be joint-founders with him of the colony, namely Thessalos and Paraibates and Keleas and Euryleon; and these when they had reached Sicily with all their armament, were slain, being defeated in battle by the Phenicians and the men of Egesta; and Euryleon only of the joint-founders survived this disaster. This man then having collected the survivors of the expedition, took possession of Minoa the colony of Selinus, and he helped to free the men of Selinus from their despot Peithagoras. Afterwards, when he had deposed him, he laid hands himself upon the despotism in Selinus and became sole ruler there, though but for a short time; for the men of Selinus rose in revolt against him and slew him, notwithstanding that he had fled for refuge to the altar of Zeus Agoraios.[30]

47. There had accompanied Dorieos also and died with him Philip the son of Butakides, a man of Croton, who having betrothed himself to the daughter of Telys the Sybarite, became an exile from Croton; and then being disappointed of this marriage he sailed away to Kyrene, whence he set forth and accompanied Dorieos with a trireme of his own, himself supplying the expenses of the crew. Now this man had been a victor at the Olympic games, and he was the most beautiful of the Hellenes who lived in his time; and on account of his beauty he obtained from the men of Egesta that which none else ever obtained from them, for they established a hero-temple over his

tomb, and they propitiate him still with sacrifices.

48. In this manner Dorieos ended his life: but if he had endured to be a subject of Cleomenes and had remained in Sparta, he would have been king of Lacedemon; for Cleomenes reigned no very long time, and died leaving no son to succeed him but a daughter only, whose name was Gorgo.

49. However, Aristagoras the despot of Miletos arrived at Sparta while Cleomenes was reigning: and accordingly with him he came to speech, having, as the Lacedemonians say, a tablet of bronze, on which was engraved a map[31] of the whole Earth, with all the sea and all the rivers. And when he came to speech with Cleomenes he said to him as follows: "Marvel not, Cleomenes, at my earnestness in coming hither, for the case is this.—That the sons of the Ionians should be slaves instead of free is a reproach and a grief most of all indeed to ourselves, but of all others most to you, inasmuch as ye are the leaders of Hellas. Now therefore I entreat you by the gods of Hellas to rescue from slavery the Ionians, who are your own kinsmen: and ye may easily achieve this, for the Barbarians are not valiant in fight, whereas ye have attained to the highest point of valour in that which relates to war: and their fighting is of this fashion, namely with bows and arrows and a short spear, and they go into battle wearing trousers and with caps[32] on their heads. Thus they are easily conquered. Then again they who occupy that continent have good things in such quantity as not all the other nations of the world together possess; first gold, then silver and bronze and embroidered garments and beasts of burden and slaves; all which ye might have for yourselves, if ye so desired. And the nations moreover dwell in such order one after the other as I shall declare:—the Ionians here; and next to them the Lydians, who not only dwell in a fertile land, but are also exceedingly rich in gold and silver,"[33]—and as he said this he pointed to the map of the Earth, which he carried with him engraved upon the tablet,—"and here next to the Lydians," continued Aristagoras, "are the Eastern Phrygians, who have both the greatest number of sheep and cattle[34] of any people that I know, and also the most abundant crops. Next to the Phrygians are the Cappadokians, whom we call Syrians; and bordering upon them are the Kilikians, coming down to this[35] sea, in which lies the island of Cyprus here; and these pay five hundred talents to the king for their yearly tribute. Next to these Kilikians are the Armenians, whom thou mayest see here, and these also have great numbers of sheep and cattle. Next to the Armenians are the Matienians occupying this country here; and next to them is the land of Kissia here, in which land by the banks of this river

Choaspes is situated that city of Susa where the great king has his residence, and where the money is laid up in treasuries. After ye have taken this city ye may then with good courage enter into a contest with Zeus in the matter of wealth. Nay, but can it be that ye feel yourselves bound to take upon you the risk of[36] battles against Messenians and Arcadians and Argives, who are equally matched against you, for the sake of land which is not much in extent nor very fertile, and for confines which are but small, though these peoples have neither gold nor silver at all, for the sake of which desire incites one to fight and to die,—can this be, I say, and will ye choose some other way now, when it is possible for you easily to have the rule over all Asia?" Aristagoras spoke thus, and Cleomenes answered him saying: "Guest–friend from Miletos, I defer my answer to thee until the day after to–morrow."[37] 50. Thus far then they advanced at that time; and when the appointed day arrived for the answer, and they had come to the place agreed upon, Cleomenes asked Aristagoras how many days' journey it was from the sea of the Ionians to the residence of the king. Now Aristagoras, who in other respects acted cleverly and imposed upon him well, in this point made a mistake: for whereas he ought not to have told him the truth, at least if he desired to bring the Spartans out to Asia, he said in fact that it was a journey up from the sea of three months: and the other cutting short the rest of the account which Aristagoras had begun to give of the way, said: "Guest–friend from Miletos, get thee away from Sparta before the sun has set; for thou speakest a word which sounds not well in the ears of the Lacedemonians, desiring to take them a journey of three months from the sea." 51. Cleomenes accordingly having so said went away to his house: but Aristagoras took the suppliant's branch and went to the house of Cleomenes; and having entered in as a suppliant, he bade Cleomenes send away the child and listen to him; for the daughter of Cleomenes was standing by him, whose name was Gorgo, and this as it chanced was his only child, being of the age now of eight or nine years. Cleomenes however bade him say that which he desired to say, and not to stop on account of the child. Then Aristagoras proceeded to promise him money, beginning with ten talents, if he would accomplish for him that for which he was asking; and when Cleomenes refused, Aristagoras went on increasing the sums of money offered, until at last he had promised fifty talents, and at that moment the child cried out: "Father, the stranger will do thee hurt,[38] if thou do not leave him and go." Cleomenes, then, pleased by the counsel of the child, departed into another room, and Aristagoras went away from Sparta altogether, and had no opportunity of explaining any further about the way up from the sea to the residence of the king.

52. As regards this road the truth is as follows.—Everywhere there are royal stages[39] and excellent resting–places, and the whole road runs through country which is inhabited and safe. Through Lydia and Phrygia there extend twenty stages, amounting to ninety–four and a half leagues;[40] and after Phrygia succeeds the river Halys, at which there is a gate[40a] which one must needs pass through in order to cross the river, and a strong guard–post is established there. Then after crossing over into Cappadokia it is twenty–eight stages, being a hundred and four leagues, by this way to the borders of Kilikia; and on the borders of the Kilikians you will pass through two several gates and go by two several guard–posts: then after passing through these it is three stages, amounting to fifteen and a half leagues, to journey through Kilikia; and the boundary of Kilikia and Armenia is a navigable river called Euphrates. In Armenia the number of stages with resting–places is fifteen, and of leagues fifty–six and a half, and there is a guard–post on the way: then from Armenia, when one enters the land of Matiene,[41] there are thirty–four stages, amounting to a hundred and thirty–seven leagues; and through this land flow four navigable rivers, which cannot be crossed but by ferries, first the Tigris, then a second and third called both by the same name,[42] though they are not the same river nor do they flow from the same region (for the first–mentioned of them flows from the Armenian land and the other[43] from that of the Matienians), and the fourth of the rivers is called Gyndes, the same which once Cyrus divided into three hundred and sixty channels.[44] Passing thence into the Kissian land, there are eleven stages, forty–two and a half leagues, to the river Choaspes, which is also a navigable stream; and upon this is built the city of Susa. The number of these stages amounts in all to one hundred and eleven. 53. This is the number of stages with resting–places, as one goes up from Sardis to Susa: and if the royal road has been rightly measured as regards leagues, and if the league[45] is equal to thirty furlongs,[46] (as undoubtedly it is), the number of furlongs from Sardis to that which is called the palace of Memnon is thirteen thousand five hundred, the number of leagues being four hundred and fifty. So if one travels a hundred and fifty furlongs each day, just ninety days are spent on the journey.[47] 54. Thus the Milesian Aristagoras, when he told Cleomenes the Lacedemonian that the journey up from the sea to the residence of the king was one of three months, spoke correctly: but if any one demands a more exact statement yet than this, I will give him that also: for we ought to reckon in addition to this the length of the road from Ephesos to Sardis; and I say accordingly that the whole number of furlongs from the sea of Hellas to Susa (for by that name the city of Memnon is known) is fourteen thousand and forty; for the number of furlongs from Ephesos to Sardis is five hundred and forty: thus the three

months' journey is lengthened by three days added.

55. Aristagoras then being driven out of Sparta proceeded to Athens; which had been set free from the rule of despots in the way which I shall tell.—When Hipparchos the son of Peisistratos and brother of the despot Hippias, after seeing a vision of a dream which signified it to him plainly,[48] had been slain by Aristogeiton and Harmodios, who were originally by descent Gephyraians, the Athenians continued for four years after this to be despotically governed no less than formerly,—nay, even more. 56. Now the vision of a dream which Hipparchos had was this:—in the night before the Panathenaia it seemed to Hipparchos that a man came and stood by him, tall and of fair form, and riddling spoke to him these verses:

"With enduring soul as a lion endure unendurable evil: No one of men who doth wrong shall escape from the judgment appointed."

These verses, as soon as it was day, he publicly communicated to the interpreters of dreams; but afterwards he put away thought of the vision[49] and began to take part in that procession during which he lost his life.

57. Now the Gephyraians, of whom were those who murdered Hipparchos, according to their own account were originally descended from Eretria; but as I find by carrying inquiries back, they were Phenicians of those who came with Cadmos to the land which is now called Bœotia, and they dwelt in the district of Tanagra, which they had had allotted to them in that land. Then after the Cadmeians had first been driven out by the Argives, these Gephyraians next were driven out by the Bœotians and turned then towards Athens: and the Athenians received them on certain fixed conditions to be citizens of their State, laying down rules that they should be excluded from a number of things not worth mentioning here. 58. Now these Phenicians who came with Cadmos, of whom were the Gephyraians, brought in among the Hellenes many arts when they settled in this land of Bœotia, and especially letters, which did not exist, as it appears to me, among the Hellenes before this time; and at first they brought in those which are used by the Phenician race generally, but afterwards, as time went on, they changed with their speech the form of the letters also. During this time the Ionians were the race of Hellenes who dwelt near them in most of the places where they were; and these, having received letters by instruction of the Phenicians, changed their form slightly and so made use of them, and in doing so they declared them to be called

"phenicians," as was just, seeing that the Phenicians had introduced them into Hellas. Also the Ionians from ancient time call paper "skins," because formerly, paper being scarce, they used skins of goat and sheep; nay, even in my own time many of the Barbarians write on such skins. 59. I myself too once saw Cadmeian characters in the temple of Ismenian Apollo at Thebes of the Bœotians, engraved on certain[49a] tripods, and in most respects resembling the Ionic letters: one of these tripods has the inscription,

"Me Amphitryon offered from land Teleboian returning:"[50]

this inscription would be of an age contemporary with Laïos the son of Labdacos, the son of Polydoros, the son of Cadmos. 60. Another tripod says thus in hexameter rhythm:

"Me did Scaios offer to thee, far-darting Apollo, Victor in contest of boxing, a gift most fair in thine honour:"

now Scaios would be the son of Hippocoön (at least if it were really he who offered it, and not another with the same name as the son of Hippocoön), being of an age contemporary with Œdipus the son of Laïos: 61, and the third tripod, also in hexameter rhythm, says:

"Me Laodamas offered to thee, fair-aiming Apollo, He, of his wealth,[51] being king, as a gift most fair in thine honor:"

now it was in the reign of this very Laodamas the son of Eteocles that the Cadmeians were driven out by the Argives and turned to go to the Enchelians; and the Gephyraians being then left behind were afterwards forced by the Bœotians to retire to Athens. Moreover they have temples established in Athens, in which the other Athenians have no part, and besides others which are different from the rest, there is especially a temple of Demeter Achaia and a celebration of her mysteries.

62. I have told now of the vision of a dream seen by Hipparchos, and also whence the Gephrynians were descended, of which race were the murderers of Hipparchos; and in addition to this I must resume and continue the story which I was about to tell at first, how the Athenians were freed from despots. When Hippias was despot and was

dealing harshly with the Athenians because of the death of Hipparchos, the Alcmaionidai, who were of Athenian race and were fugitives from the sons of Peisistratos,[52] as they did not succeed in their attempt made together with the other Athenian exiles to return by force, but met with great disaster when they attempted to return and set Athens free, after they had fortified Leipsydrion which is above Paionia,— these Alomaionidai after that, still devising every means against the sons of Peisistratos, accepted the contract to build and complete the temple at Delphi, that namely which now exists but then did not as yet: and being wealthy and men of repute already from ancient time, they completed the temple in a manner more beautiful than the plan required, and especially in this respect, that having agreed to make the temple of common limestone,[53] they built the front parts of it in Parian marble. 63. So then, as the Athenians say, these men being settled at Delphi persuaded the Pythian prophetess by gifts of money, that whenever men of the Spartans should come to inquire of the Oracle, either privately or publicly sent, she should propose to them to set Athens free. The Lacedemonians therefore, since the same utterance was delivered to them on all occasions, sent Anchimolios the son of Aster, who was of repute among their citizens, with an army to drive out the sons of Peisistratos from Athens, although these were very closely connected with them by guest-friendship; for they held that the concerns of the god[53a] should be preferred to those of men: and this force they sent by sea in ships. He therefore, having put in to shore at Phaleron, disembarked his army; but the sons of Peisistratos being informed of this beforehand called in to their aid an auxiliary force from Thessaly, for they had made an alliance with the Thessalians; and the Thessalians at their request sent by public resolution a body of a thousand horse and also their king Kineas, a man of Conion.[54] So having obtained these as allies, the sons of Peisistratos contrived as follows:—they cut down the trees in the plain of Phaleron and made this district fit for horsemen to ride over, and after that they sent the cavalry to attack the enemy's camp, who falling upon it slew (besides many others of the Lacedemonians) Anchimolios himself also: and the survivors of them they shut up in their ships. Such was the issue of the first expedition from Lacedemon: and the burial-place of Anchimolios is at Alopecai in Attica, near the temple of Heracles which is at Kynosarges. 64. After this the Lacedemonians equipped a larger expedition and sent it forth against Athens; and they appointed to be commander of the army their king Cleomenes the son of Anaxandrides, and sent it this time not by sea but by land. With these, when they had invaded the land of Attica, first the Thessalian horse engaged battle; and in no long time they were routed and there fell of them more than forty men; so the survivors departed without more ado and went straight back to Thessaly. Then Cleomenes came to the city together with those of the Athenians who desired to be free, and began to besiege the despots shut up in the Pelasgian wall. 64. And the Lacedemonians would never have captured the sons of Peisistratos at all; for they on their side had no design to make a long blockade, and the others were well provided with food and drink; so that they would have gone away back to Sparta after besieging them for a few days only: but as it was, a thing happened just at this time which was unfortunate for those, and at the same time of assistance to these; for the children of the sons of Peisistratos were captured, while being secretly removed out of the country: and when this happened, all their matters were thereby cast into confusion, and they surrendered receiving back their children on the terms which the Athenians desired, namely that they should depart out of Attica within five days. After this they departed out of the country and went to Sigeion on the Scamander, after their family had ruled over the Athenians for six–and–thirty years. These also[54a] were originally Pylians and sons of Neleus, descended from the same ancestors as the family of Codros and Melanthos, who had formerly become kings of Athens being settlers from abroad. Hence too Hippocrates had given to his son the name of Peisistratos as a memorial, calling him after Peisistratos the son of Nestor.

Thus the Athenians were freed from despots; and the things worthy to be narrated which they did or suffered after they were liberated, up to the time when Ionia revolted from Dareios and Aristagoras the Milesian came to Athens and asked them to help him, these I will set forth first before I proceed further.

66. Athens, which even before that time was great, then, after having been freed from despots, became gradually yet greater; and in it two men exercised power, namely Cleisthenes a descendant of Alcmaion, the same who is reported to have bribed the Pythian prophetess, and Isagoras, the son of Tisander, of a family which was highly reputed, but of his original descent I am not able to declare; his kinsmen however offer sacrifices to the Carian Zeus. These men came to party strife for power; and then Cleisthenes was being worsted in the struggle, he made common cause with the people. After this he caused the Athenians to be in ten tribes, who were formerly in four; and he changed the names by which they were called after the sons of Ion, namely Geleon, Aigicoreus, Argades, and Hoples, and invented for them names taken from other heroes, all native Athenians except Ajax, whom he added as a neighbour and ally, although he was no Athenian.

67. Now in these things it seems to me that this Cleisthenes was imitating his mother's father Cleisthenes the despot of Sikyon: for Cleisthenes when he went to war with Argos first caused to cease in Sikyon the contests of rhapsodists, which were concerned with the poems of Homer, because Argives and Argos are celebrated in them almost everywhere; then secondly, since there was (as still there is) in the market-place itself of the Sikyonians a hero-temple of Adrastos the son of Talaos, Cleisthenes had a desire to cast him forth out of the land, because he was an Argive. So having come to Delphi he consulted the Oracle as to whether he should cast out Adrastos; and the Pythian prophetess answered him saying that Adrastos was king of the Sikyonians, whereas he was a stoner[55] of them. So since the god did not permit him to do this, he went away home and considered means by which Adrastos should be brought to depart of his own accord: and when he thought that he had discovered them, he sent to Thebes in Bœotia and said that he desired to introduce into his city Melanippos the son of Astacos, and the Thebans gave him leave. So Cleisthenes introduced Melanippos into his city, and appointed for him a sacred enclosure within the precincts of the City Hall[56] itself, and established him there in the strongest position. Now Cleisthenes introduced Melanippos (for I must relate this also) because he was the greatest enemy of Adrastos, seeing that he had killed both his brother Mekisteus and his son-in-law Tydeus: and when he had appointed the sacred enclosure for him, he took away the sacrifices and festivals of Adrastos and gave them to Melanippos. Now the Sikyonians were accustomed to honour Adrastos with very great honours; for this land was formerly the land of Polybos, and Adrastos was daughter's son to Polybos, and Polybos dying without sons gave his kingdom to Adrastos: the Sikyonians then not only gave other honours to Adrastos, but also with reference to his sufferings they specially honoured him with tragic choruses, not paying the honour to Dionysos but to Adrastos. Cleisthenes however gave back the choruses to Dionysos, and the other rites besides this he gave to Melannipos. 68. Thus he had done to Adrastos; and he also changed the names of the Dorian tribes, in order that the Sikyonians might not have the same tribes as the Argives; in which matter he showed great contempt of the Sikyonians, for the names he gave were taken from the names of a pig and an ass by changing only the endings, except in the case of his own tribe, to which he gave a name from his own rule. These last then were called Archelaoi,[57] while of the rest those of one tribe were called Hyatai,[58] of another Oneatai,[59] and of the remaining tribe Choireatai.[60] These names of tribes were used by the men of Sikyon not only in the reign of Cleisthenes, but also beyond that for sixty years after his death; then however they considered the matter and changed them

into Hylleis, Pamphyloi, and Dymanatai, adding to these a fourth, to which they gave the name Aigialeis after Aigialeus the son of Adrastos.

69. Thus had the Cleisthenes of Sikyon done: and the Athenian Cleisthenes, who was his daughter's son and was called after him, despising, as I suppose, the Ionians, as he the Dorians, imitated his namesake Cleisthenes in order that the Athenians might not have the same tribes as the Ionians: for when at the time of which we speak he added to his own party the whole body of the common people of the Athenians, which in former time he had despised,[61] he changed the names of the tribes and made them more in number than they had been; he made in fact ten rulers of tribes instead of four, and by tens also he distributed the demes in the tribes; and having added the common people to his party he was much superior to his opponents. 70. Then Isagoras, as he was being worsted in his turn, contrived a plan in opposition to him, that is to say, he called in Cleomenes the Lacedemonian to help him, who had been a guest-friend to himself since the siege of the sons of Peisistratos; moreover Cleomenes was accused of being intimate with the wife of Isagoras. First then Cleomenes sent a herald to Athens demanding the expulsion of Cleisthenes and with him many others of the Athenians, calling them the men who were under the curse:[62] this message he sent by instruction of Isagoras, for the Alcmaionidai and their party were accused of the murder to which reference was thus made, while he and his friends had no part in it. 71. Now the men of the Athenians who were "under the curse" got this name as follows:—there was one Kylon among the Athenians, a man who had gained the victory at the Olympic games: this man behaved with arrogance, wishing to make himself despot; and having formed for himself an association of men of his own age, he endeavoured to seize the Acropolis: but not being able to get possession of it, he sat down as a suppliant before the image of the goddess.[63] These men were taken from their place as suppliants by the presidents of the naucraries, who then administered affairs at Athens, on the condition that they should be liable to any penalty short of death; and the Alcmaionidai are accused of having put them to death. This had occurred before the time of Peisistratos. 72. Now when Cleomenes sent demanding the expulsion of Cleisthenes and of those under the curse, Cleisthenes himself retired secretly; but after that nevertheless Cleomenes appeared in Athens with no very large force, and having arrived he proceeded to expel as accursed seven hundred Athenian families, of which Isagoras had suggested to him the names. Having done this he next endeavoured to dissolve the Senate, and he put the offices of the State into the hands of three hundred, who were the partisans of Isagoras. The Senate however making

opposition, and not being willing to submit, Cleomenes with Isagoras and his partisans seized the Acropolis. Then the rest of the Athenians joined together by common consent and besieged them for two days; and on the third day so many of them as were Lacedemonians departed out of the country under a truce. Thus was accomplished for Cleomenes the ominous saying which was uttered to him: for when he had ascended the Acropolis with the design of taking possession of it, he was going to the sanctuary of the goddess, as to address her in prayer; but the priestess stood up from her seat before he had passed through the door, and said, "Lacedemonian stranger, go back and enter not into the temple, for it is not lawful for Dorians to pass in hither." He said: "Woman, I am not a Dorian, but an Achaian." So then, paying no attention to the ominous speech, he made his attempt and then was expelled again with the Lacedemonians; but the rest of the men the Athenians laid in bonds to be put to death, and among them Timesitheos the Delphian, with regard to whom I might mention very great deeds of strength and courage which he performed. 73. These then having been thus laid in bonds were put to death; and the Athenians after this sent for Cleisthenes to return, and also for the seven hundred families which had been driven out by Cleomenes: and then they sent envoys to Sardis, desiring to make an alliance with the Persians; for they were well assured that the Lacedemonians and Cleomenes had been utterly made their foes. So when these envoys had arrived at Sardis and were saying that which they had been commanded to say, Artaphrenes the son of Hystaspes, the governor of Sardis, asked what men these were who requested to be allies of the Persians, and where upon the earth they dwelt; and having heard this from the envoys, he summed up his answer to them thus, saying that if the Athenians were willing to give earth and water to Dareios, he was willing to make alliance with them, but if not, he bade them begone: and the envoys taking the matter upon themselves said that they were willing to do so, because they desired to make the alliance. 74. These, when they returned to their own land, were highly censured: and Cleomenes meanwhile, conceiving that he had been outrageously dealt with by the Athenians both with words and with deeds, was gathering together an army from the whole of the Peloponnese, not declaring the purpose for which he was gathering it, but desiring to take vengeance on the people of the Athenians, and intending to make Isagoras despot; for he too had come out of the Acropolis together with Cleomenes. Cleomenes then with a large army entered Eleusis, while at the same time the Bœotians by agreement with him captured Oinoe and Hysiai, the demes which lay upon the extreme borders of Attica, and the Chalkidians on the other side invaded and began to ravage various districts of Attica. The Athenians then, though attacked on more sides than one, thought that they would remember the Bœotians and Chalkidians afterwards, and arrayed themselves against the Peloponnesians who were in Eleusis. 75. Then as the armies were just about the join battle, the Corinthians first, considering with themselves that they were not acting rightly, changed their minds and departed; and after that Demaratos the son of Ariston did the same, who was king of the Spartans as well as Cleomenes, though he had joined with him in leading the army out from Lacedemon and had not been before this at variance with Cleomenes. In consequence of this dissension a law was laid down at Sparta that it should not be permitted, when an army went out, that both the kings should go with it, for up to this time both used to go with it, and that as one of the kings was set free from service, so one of the sons of Tyndareus[64] also should be left behind; for before this time both of these two were called upon by them for help and went with the armies. 76. At this time then in Eleusis the rest of the allies, seeing that the kings of the Lacedemonians did not agree and also that the Corinthians had deserted their place in the ranks, themselves too departed and got them away quickly. And this was the fourth time that the Dorians had come to Attica, twice having invaded it to make war against it, and twice to help the mass of the Athenian people,—first when they at the same time colonised Megara (this expedition may rightly be designated as taking place when Codros was king of the Athenians), for the second and third times when they came making expeditions from Sparta to drive out the sons of Peisistratos, and fourthly on this occasion, when Cleomenes at the head of the Peloponnesians invaded Eleusis: thus the Dorians invaded Athens then for the fourth time.

77. This army then having been ingloriously broken up, the Athenians after that, desiring to avenge themselves, made expedition first against the Chalkidians; and the Bœotians came to the Euripos to help the Chalkidians. The Athenians, therefore, seeing those who had come to help,[64a] resolved first to attack the Bœotians before the Chalkidians. Accordingly they engaged battle with the Bœotians, and had much the better of them, and after having slain very many they took seven hundred of them captive. On this very same day the Athenians passed over into Eubœa and engaged battle with the Chalkidians as well; and having conquered these also, they left four thousand holders of allotments in the land belonging to the "Breeders of Horses":[65] now the wealthier of the Chalkidians were called the Breeders of Horses. And as many of them as they took captive, they kept in confinement together with the Bœotians who had been captured, bound with fetters; and then after a time they let them go, having fixed their ransom at two pounds of silver apiece:[66] but their fetters, in which they

had been bound, they hung up on the Acropolis; and these were still existing even to my time hanging on walls which had been scorched with fire by the Mede,[67] and just opposite the sanctuary which lies towards the West. The tenth part of the ransom also they dedicated for an offering, and made of it a four-horse chariot of bronze, which stands on the left hand as you enter the Propylaia in the Acropolis, and on it is the following inscription:

"Matched in the deeds of war with the tribes of Bœotia and Chalkis The sons of Athens prevailed, conquered and tamed them in fight: In chains of iron and darkness they quenched their insolent spirit; And to Athene present these, of their ransom a tithe."

78. The Athenians accordingly increased in power; and it is evident, not by one instance only but in every way, that Equality[68] is an excellent thing, since the Athenians while they were ruled by despots were not better in war that any of those who dwelt about them, whereas after they had got rid of despots they became far the first. This proves that when they were kept down they were wilfully slack, because they were working for a master, whereas when they had been set free each one was eager to achieve something for himself.

79. These then were faring thus: and the Thebans after this sent to the god, desiring to be avenged on the Athenians; the Pythian prophetess however said that vengeance was not possible for them by their own strength alone, but bade them report the matter to the "many-voiced" and ask help of those who were "nearest" to them. So when those who were sent to consult the Oracle returned, they made a general assembly and reported the oracle; and then the Thebans heard them say that they were to ask help of those who were nearest to them, they said: "Surely those who dwell nearest to us are the men of Tanagra and Coroneia and Thespiai; and these always fight zealously on our side and endure the war with us to the end: what need is there that we ask of these? Rather perhaps that is not the meaning of the oracle." 80. While they commented upon it thus, at length one perceived that which the oracle means to tell us. Asopos is said to have had two daughters born to him, Thebe and Egina; and as these are sisters, I think that the god gave us for answer that we should ask the men of Egina to become our helpers." Then as there seemed to be no opinion expressed which was better than this, they sent forthwith and asked the men of Egina to help them, calling upon them in accordance with the oracle; and they, when these made request, said that they sent with them the sons of Aiacos to help them. 81. After that the Thebans, having made an

attempt with the alliance of the sons of Aiacos and having been roughly handled by the Athenians, sent again and gave them back the sons of Aiacos and asked them for men. So the Eginetans, exalted by great prosperity and calling to mind an ancient grudge against the Athenians, then on the request of the Thebans commenced a war against the Athenians without notice: for while the Athenians were intent on the Bœotians, they sailed against them to Attica with ships of war, and they devastated Phaleron and also many demes in the remainder of the coast region, and so doing they deeply stirred the resentment of the Athenians.[69]

82. Now the grudge which was due beforehand from the Eginetans to the Athenians came about from a beginning which was as follows:—The land of the Epidaurians yielded to its inhabitants no fruit; and accordingly with reference to this calamity the Epidaurians went to inquire at Delphi, and the Pythian prophetess bade them set up images of Damia and Auxesia, and said that when they had set up these, they would meet with better fortune. The Epidaurians then asked further whether they should make images of bronze or of stone; and the prophetess bade them not use either of these, but make them of the wood of a cultivated olive-tree. The Epidaurians therefore asked the Athenians to allow them to cut for themselves an olive-tree, since they thought that their olives were the most sacred; nay some say that at that time there were no olives in any part of the earth except at Athens. The Athenians said that they would allow them on condition that they should every year bring due offerings to Athene Polias[70] and to Erechtheus. The Epidaurians, then, having agreed to these terms, obtained that which they asked, and they made images out of these olive-trees and set them up: and their land bore fruit and they continued to fulfil towards the Athenians that which they had agreed to do. 83. Now during this time and also before this the Eginetans were subject to the Epidaurians, and besides other things they were wont to pass over to Epidauros to have their disputes with one another settled by law:[71] but after this time they built for themselves ships and made revolt from the Epidaurians, moved thereto by wilfulness. So as they were at variance with them, they continued to inflict damage on them, since in fact they had command of the sea, and especially they stole away from them these images of Damia and Auxesia, and they brought them and set them up in the inland part of their country at a place called Oia, which is about twenty furlongs distant from their city. Having set them up in this spot they worshipped them with sacrifices and choruses of women accompanied with scurrilous jesting, ten men being appointed for each of the deities to provide the choruses: and the choruses spoke evil of no man, but only of the women of the place. Now the Epidaurians also had the same

rites; and they have also rites which may not be divulged. 84. These images then having been stolen, the Epidaurians no longer continued to fulfil towards the Athenians that which they had agreed. The Athenians accordingly sent and expressed displeasure to the Epidaurians; and they declared saying that they were doing no wrong; for during the time when they had the images in their country they continued to fulfil that which they had agreed upon, but since they had been deprived of them, it was not just that they should make the offerings any more; and they bade them demand these from the men of Egina, who had the images. So the Athenians sent to Egina and demanded the images back; but the Eginetans said that they had nothing to do with the Athenians.

85. The Athenians then report that in one single trireme were despatched those of their citizens who were sent by the State after this demand; who having come to Egina, attempted to tear up from off their pedestals the images, (alleging that they were made of wood which belonged to the Athenians), in order to carry them back with them: but not being able to get hold of them in this manner (say the Athenians) they threw ropes round them and were pulling them, when suddenly, as they pulled, thunder came on and an earthquake at the same time with the thunder; and the crew of the trireme who were pulling were made beside themselves by these, and being brought to this condition they killed one another as if they were enemies, until at last but one of the whole number was left; and he returned alone to Phaleron. 86. Thus the Athenians report that it came to pass: but the Eginetans say that it was not with a single ship that the Athenians came; for a single ship, and even a few more than one, they could have easily repelled, even if they had not happened to have ships of their own: but they say that the Athenians sailed upon their country with a large fleet of ships, and they gave way before them and did not fight a sea–battle. They cannot however declare with certainty whether they gave way thus because they admitted that they were not strong enough to fight the battle by sea, or because they intended to do something of the kind which they actually did. The Athenians then, they say, as no one met them in fight, landed from their ships and made for the images; but not being able to tear them up from their pedestals, at last they threw ropes round them and began to pull, until the images, as they were being pulled, did both the same thing (and here they report something which I cannot believe, but some other man may), for they say that the images fell upon their knees to them and that they continue to be in that position ever since this time. The Athenians, they say, were doing thus; and meanwhile they themselves (say the Eginetans), being informed that the Athenians were about to make an expedition against them, got the Argives to help them; and just when the Athenians

had disembarked upon the Eginetan land, the Argives had come to their rescue, and not having been perceived when they passed over from Epidauros to the island, they fell upon the Athenians before these had heard anything of the matter, cutting them off secretly from the way to their ships; and at this moment it was that the thunder and the earthquake came upon them. 87. This is the report which is given by the Argives and Eginetans both, and it is admitted by the Athenians also that but one alone of them survived and came back to Attica: only the Argives say that this one remained alive from destruction wrought by them upon the army of Athens, while the Athenians say that the divine power was the destroyer. However, even this one man did not remain alive, but perished, they say, in the following manner:—when he returned to Athens he reported the calamity which had happened; and the wives of the men who had gone on the expedition to Egina, hearing it and being very indignant that he alone of all had survived, came round this man and proceeded to stab him with the brooches of their mantles, each one of them asking of him where her husband was. Thus he was slain; and to the Athenians it seemed that the deed of the women was a much more terrible thing even than the calamity which had happened; and not knowing, it is said, how they should punish the women in any other way, they changed their fashion of dress to that of Ionia,—for before this the women of the Athenians wore Dorian dress, very like that of Corinth,—they changed it therefore to the linen tunic, in order that they might not have use for brooches. 88. In truth however this fashion of dress is not Ionian originally but Carian, for the old Hellenic fashion of dress for women was universally the same as that which we now call Dorian. Moreover it is said that with reference to these events the Argives and Eginetans made it a custom among themselves in both countries[72] to have the brooches made half as large again as the size which was then established in use, and that their women should offer brooches especially in the temple of these goddesses,[73] and also that they should carry neither pottery of Athens nor anything else of Athenian make to the temple, but that it should be the custom for the future to drink there from pitchers made in the lands themselves.

89. The women of the Argives and Eginetans from this time onwards because of the quarrel with the Athenians continued to wear brooches larger than before, and still do so even to my time; and the origin of the enmity of the Athenians towards the Eginetans came in the manner which has been said. So at this time, when the Thebans invaded them, the Eginetans readily came to the assistance of the Bœotians, calling to mind what occurred about the images. The Eginetans then were laying waste, as I have said, the coast regions of Attica; and when the Athenians were resolved to make an

expedition against the Eginetans, an oracle came to them from Delphi bidding them stay for thirty years reckoned from the time of the wrong done by the Eginetans, and in the one−and−thirtieth year to appoint a sacred enclosure for Aiacos and then to begin the war against the Eginetans, and they would succeed as they desired; but if they should make an expedition against them at once, they would suffer in the meantime very much evil and also inflict very much, but at last they would subdue them. When the Athenians heard the report of this, they appointed a sacred enclosure for Aiacos, namely that which is now established close to the market− place, but they could not endure to hear that they must stay for thirty years, when they had suffered injuries from the Eginetans. 90. While however they were preparing to take vengeance, a matter arose from the Lacedemonians which provided a hindrance to them: for the Lacedemonians, having learnt that which had been contrived by the Alcmaionidai with respect to the Pythian prophetess, and that which had been contrived by the Pythian prophetess against themselves and the sons of Peisistratos, were doubly grieved, not only because they had driven out into exile men who were their guest−friends, but also because after they had done this no gratitude was shown to them by the Athenians. Moreover in addition to this, they were urged on by the oracles which said that many injuries would be suffered by them from the Athenians; of which oracles they had not been aware of before, but they had come to know them, since Cleomenes had brought them to Sparta. In fact Cleomenes had obtained from the Acropolis of the Athenians those oracles which the sons of Peisistratos possessed before and had left in the temple when they were driven out; and Cleomenes recovered them after they had been left behind. 91. At this time, then, when the Lacedemonians had recovered the oracles and when they saw that the Athenians were increasing in power and were not at all willing to submit to them, observing that the Athenian race now that it was free was becoming[74] a match for their own, whereas when held down by despots it was weak and ready to be ruled,—perceiving, I say, all these things, they sent for Hippias the son of Peisistratos to come from Sigeion on the Hellespont, whither the family of Peisistratos go for refuge;[75] and when Hippias had come upon the summons, the Spartans sent also for envoys to come from their other allies and spoke to them as follows: "Allies, we are conscious within ourselves that we have not acted rightly; for incited by counterfeit oracles we drove out into exile men who were very closely united with us as guest−friends and who undertook the task of rendering Athens submissive to us, and then after having done this we delivered over the State to a thankless populace, which so soon as it had raised its head, having been freed by our means drove out us and our king with wanton outrage; and now exalted with pride[76] it is increasing in power, so that the neighbours of these men first of all, that is the Bœotians and Chalkidians, have already learnt, and perhaps some others also will afterwards learn, that they committed an error.[76a] As however we erred in doing those things of which we have spoken, we will try now to take vengeance on them, going thither together with you;[77] since it was for this very purpose that we sent for Hippias, whom ye see here, and for you also, to come from your cities, in order that with common counsel and a common force we might conduct him to Athens and render back to him that which we formerly took away."

92. Thus they spoke; but the majority of the allies did not approve of their words. The rest however kept silence, but the Corinthian Socles[78] spoke as follows: (a) "Surely now the heaven shall be below the earth, and the earth raised up on high above the heaven, and men shall have their dwelling in the sea, and fishes shall have that habitation which men had before, seeing that ye, Lacedemonians, are doing away with free governments[79] and are preparing to bring back despotism again into our cities, than which there is no more unjust or more murderous thing among men. For if in truth this seems to you to be good, namely that the cities should be ruled by despots, do ye yourselves first set up a despot in your own State, and then endeavour to establish them also for others: but as it is, ye are acting unfairly towards your allies, seeing that ye have had no experience of despots yourselves and provide with the greatest care at Sparta that this may never come to pass. If however ye had had experience of it, as we have had, ye would be able to contribute juster opinions of it than at present. (b) For the established order of the Corinthian State was this:—the government was an oligarchy, and the oligarchs, who were called Bacchiadai, had control over the State and made marriages among themselves.[80] Now one of these men, named Amphion, had a daughter born to him who was lame, and her name was Labda. This daughter, since none of the Bacchiadai wished to marry her, was taken to wife by Aëtion the son of Echecrates, who was of the deme of Petra, but by original descent a Lapith and of the race of Caineus. Neither from this wife nor from another were children born to him, therefore he set out to Delphi to inquire about offspring; and as he entered, forthwith the prophetess addressed him in these lines:

"'Much to be honoured art thou, yet none doth render thee honour.[81] Labda conceives, and a rolling rock will she bear, which shall ruin Down on the heads of the kings, and with chastisement visit Corinthos.'

This answer given to Aëtion was by some means reported to the Bacchiadai, to whom the oracle which had come to Corinth before this was not intelligible, an oracle which had reference to the same thing as that of Aëtion and said thus:

"'An eagle conceives in the rocks[82] and shall bear a ravening lion, Strong and fierce to devour, who the knees of many shall loosen. Ponder this well in your minds, I bid you, Corinthians, whose dwelling Lies about fair Peirene's spring and in craggy Corinthos.'

(c) This oracle, I say, having come before to the Bacchiadai was obscure; but afterwards when they heard that which had come to Aëtion, forthwith they understood the former also, that it was in accord with that of Aëtion; and understanding this one also they kept quiet, desiring to destroy the offspring which should be born to Aëtion. Then, so soon as his wife bore a child, they sent ten of their own number to the deme in which Aëtion had his dwelling, to slay the child; and when these had come to Petra and had passed into the court of Aëtion's house, they asked for the child; and Labda, not knowing anything of the purpose for which they had come, and supposing them to be asking for the child on account of friendly feeling towards its father, brought it and placed it in the hands of one of them. Now they, it seems, had resolved by the way that the first of them who received the child should dash it upon the ground. However, when Labda brought and gave it, it happened by divine providence that the child smiled at the man who had received it; and when he perceived this, a feeling of compassion prevented him from killing it, and having this compassion he delivered it to the next man, and he to the third. Thus it passed through the hands of all the ten, delivered from one to another, since none of them could bring himself to destroy its life. So they gave the child back to its mother and went out; and then standing by the doors they abused and found fault with one another, laying blame especially on the one who had first received the child, because he had not done according to that which had been resolved; until at last after some time they determined again to enter and all to take a share in the murder. (d) From the offspring of Aëtion however it was destined that evils should spring up for Corinth: for Labda was listening to all this as she stood close by the door, and fearing lest they should change their mind and take the child a second time and kill it, she carried it and concealed it in the place which seemed to her the least likely to be discovered, that is to say a corn-chest,[84] feeling sure that if they should return and come to a search, they were likely to examine everything: and this in fact happened. So when they had come, and searching had failed to find it, they thought it best to return and say to those who had sent them that they had done all that which they had been charged by them to do. (e) They then having departed said this; and after this the son of Aëtion grew, and because he had escaped this danger, the name of Kypselos was given him as a surname derived from the corn–chest. Then when Kypselos had grown to manhood and was seeking divination, a two–edged[85] answer was given him at Delphi, placing trust in which he made an attempt upon Corinth and obtained possession of it. Now the answer was as follows:

"'Happy is this man's lot of a truth, who enters my dwelling, Offspring of Aëtion, he shall rule in famous Corinthos, Kypselos, he and his sons, but his children's children no longer.'

Such was the oracle: and Kypselos when he became despot was a man of this character,—many of the Corinthians he drove into exile, many he deprived of their wealth, and very many more of their lives. (f) And when he had reigned for thirty years and had brought his life to a prosperous end, his son Periander became his successor in the despotism. Now Periander at first was milder than his father; but after he had had dealings through messengers with Thrasybulos the despot of Miletos, he became far more murderous even than Kypselos. For he sent a messenger to Thrasybulos and asked what settlement of affairs was the safest for him to make, in order that he might best govern his State: and Thrasybulos led forth the messenger who had come from Periander out of the city, and entered into a field of growing corn: and as he passed through the crop of corn, while inquiring and asking questions repeatedly[86] of the messenger about the occasion of his coming from Corinth, he kept cutting off the heads of those ears of corn which he saw higher than the rest: and as he cut off their heads he cast them away, until he had destroyed in this manner the finest and richest part of the crop. So having passed through the place and having suggested no word of counsel, he dismissed the messenger. When the messenger returned to Corinth, Periander was anxious to hear the counsel which had been given; but he said that Thrasybulos had given him no counsel, and added that he wondered at the deed of Periander in sending him to such a man, for the man was out of his senses and a waster of his own goods,—relating at the same time that which he had seen Thrasybulos do. (g) So Periander, understanding that which had been done and perceiving that Thrasybulos counselled him to put to death those who were eminent among his subjects, began then to display all manner of evil treatment to the citizens of the State; for whatsoever Kypselos had left undone in killing and driving into exile, this

Periander completed. And in one day he stripped all the wives of the Corinthians of their clothing on account of his own wife Melissa. For when he had sent messengers to the Thesprotians on the river Acheron to ask the Oracle of the dead about a deposit made with him by a guest–friend, Melissa appeared and said she would not tell in what place the deposit was laid, for she was cold and had no clothes, since those which he had buried with her were of no use to her, not having been burnt; and this, she said, would be an evidence to him that she was speaking the truth, namely that when the oven was cold, Periander had put his loaves into it. When the report of this was brought back to Periander, the token made him believe, because he had had commerce with Melissa after she was dead; and straightway after receiving the message he caused proclamation to be made that all the wives of the Corinthians should come out to the temple of Hera. They accordingly went as to a festival in their fairest adornment; and he having set the spearmen of his guard in ambush, stripped them all alike, both the free women and their attendant; and having gathered together all their clothes in a place dug out, he set fire to them, praying at the same time to Melissa. Then after he had done this and had sent a second time, the apparition of Melissa told him in what spot he had laid the deposit entrusted to him by his guest–friend.

"Such a thing, ye must know, Lacedemonians, is despotism, and such are its deeds: and we Corinthians marvelled much at first when we saw that ye were sending for Hippias, and now we marvel even more because ye say these things; and we adjure you, calling upon the gods of Hellas, not to establish despotisms in the cities. If however ye will not cease from your design, but endeavour to restore Hippias contrary to that which is just, know that the Corinthians at least do not give their consent to that which ye do."

93. Socles being the envoy of Corinth thus spoke, and Hippias made answer to him, calling to witness the same gods as he, that assuredly the Corinthians would more than all others regret the loss of the sons of Peisistratos, when the appointed days should have come for them to be troubled by the Athenians. Thus Hippias made answer, being acquainted with the oracles more exactly than any other man: but the rest of the allies, who for a time had restrained themselves and kept silence, when they heard Socles speak freely, gave utterance every one of them to that which they felt, and adopted the opinion of the Corinthian envoy, adjuring the Lacedemonians not to do any violence to a city of Hellas.

94. Thus was this brought to an end: and Hippias being dismissed from thence had Anthemus offered to him by Amyntas king of the Macedonians and Iolcos by the Thessalians. He however accepted neither of these, but retired again to Sigeion; which city Peisistratos had taken by force of arms from the Mytilenians, and having got possession of it, had appointed his own natural son Hegesistratos, born of an Argive woman, to be despot of it: he however did not without a struggle keep possession of that which he received from Peisistratos; for the Mytilenians and Athenians carried on war for a long time, having their strongholds respectively at Achilleion and at Sigeion, the one side demanding that the place be restored to them, and the Athenians on the other hand not admitting this demand, but proving by argument that the Aiolians had no better claim to the territory of Ilion than they and the rest of the Hellenes, as many as joined with Menelaos in exacting vengeance for the rape of Helen. 95. Now while these carried on the war, besides many other things of various kinds which occurred in the battles, once when a fight took place and the Athenians were conquering, Alcaios the poet, taking to flight, escaped indeed himself, but the Athenians retained possession of his arms and hung them up on the walls of the temple of Athene which is at Sigeion. About this matter Alcaios composed a song and sent it to Mytilene, reporting therein his misadventure to one Melanippos, who was his friend. Finally Periander the son of Kypselos made peace between the Athenians and the Mytilenians,[87] for to him they referred the matter as arbitrator; and he made peace between them on the condition that each should continue to occupy that territory which they then possessed. 96. Sigeion then in this matter had come under the rule of the Athenians. And when Hippias had returned to Asia from Lacedemon, he set everything in motion, stirring up enmity between the Athenians and Artaphrenes, and using every means to secure that Athens should come under the rule of himself and of Dareios. Hippias, I say, was thus engaged; and the Athenians meanwhile hearing of these things sent envoys to Sardis, and endeavoured to prevent the Persians from following the suggestions of the exiled Athenians. Artaphrenes however commanded them, if they desired to be preserved from ruin, to receive Hippias back again. This proposal the Athenians were not by any means disposed to accept when it was reported; and as they did not accept this, it became at once a commonly received opinion among them that they were enemies of the Persians.

97. While they had these thoughts and had been set at enmity with the Persians, at this very time Aristagoras the Milesian, ordered away from Sparta by Cleomenes the Lacedemonian, arrived at Athens; for this was the city which had most power of all the

rest besides Sparta. And Aristagoras came forward before the assembly of the people and said the same things as he had said at Sparta about the wealth which there was in Asia, and about the Persian manner of making war, how they used neither shield nor spear and were easy to overcome. Thus I say he said, and also he added this, namely that the Milesians were colonists from the Athenians, and that it was reasonable that the Athenians should rescue them, since they had such great power; and there was nothing which he did not promise, being very urgent in his request, until at last he persuaded them: for it would seem that it is easier to deceive many than one, seeing that, though he did not prove able to deceive Cleomenes the Lacedemonian by himself, yet he did this to thirty thousand Athenians. The Athenians then, I say, being persuaded, voted a resolution to despatch twenty ships to help the Ionians, and appointed to command them Melanthios one of their citizens, who was in all things highly reputed. These ships proved to be the beginning of evils for the Hellenes and the Barbarians.

98. Aristagoras however sailed on before and came to Miletos; and then having devised a plan from which no advantage was likely to come for the Ionians (nor indeed was he doing what he did with a view to that, but in order to vex king Dareios), he sent a man to Phrygia to the Piaonians who had been taken captive by Megabazos from the river Strymon, and who were dwelling in a district and village of Phrygia apart by themselves; and when the messenger came to the Paionians he spoke these words: "Paionians, Aristagoras the despot of Miletos sent me to offer to you salvation, if ye shall be willing to do as he says; for now all Ionia has revolted from the king and ye have an opportunity of coming safe to your own land: to reach the sea shall be your concern, and after this it shall be thenceforth ours." The Paionians hearing this received it as a most welcome proposal, and taking with them their children and their women they began a flight to the sea; some of them however were struck with fear and remained in the place where they were. Having come to the coast the Paionians crossed over thence to Chios, and when they were already in Chios there arrived in their track a large body of Persian horsemen pursuing the Paionians. These, as they did not overtake them, sent over to Chios to bid the Paionians return back: the Paionians however did not accept their proposal, but the men of Chios conveyed them from Chios to Lesbos, and the Lesbians brought them to Doriscos, and thence they proceeded by land and came to Paionia.

99. Aristagoras meanwhile, when the Athenians had arrived with twenty ships, bringing with them also five triremes of the Eretrians, he joined the expedition not for the sake of the Athenians but of the Milesians themselves, to repay them a debt which they owed (for the Milesians in former times had borne with the Eretrians the burden of all that war which they had with the Chalkidians at the time when the Chalkidians on their side were helped by the Samians against the Eretrians and Milesians),—when these, I say, had arrived and the other allies were on the spot, Aristagoras proceeded to make a march upon Sardis. On this march he did not go himself, but remained at Miletos and appointed others to be in command of the Milesians, namely his brother Charopinos and of the other citizens one Hermophantos.[87a] 100. With this force then the Ionians came to Ephesos, and leaving their ships at Coresos in the land of Ephesos, went up themselves in a large body, taking Ephesians to guide them in their march. So they marched along by the river Caÿster, and then when they arrived after crossing the range of Tmolos, they took Sardis without any resistance, all except the citadel, but the citadel Artaphrenes himself saved from capture, having with him a considerable force of men. 101. From plundering this city after they had taken it they were prevented by this:—the houses in Sardis were mostly built of reeds, and even those of them which were of brick had their roofs thatched with reeds: of these houses one was set on fire by a soldier, and forthwith the fire going on from house to house began to spread over the whole town. So then as the town was on fire, the Lydians and all the Persians who were in the city being cut off from escape, since the fire was prevailing in the extremities round about them, and not having any way out of the town, flowed together to the market−place and to the river Pactolos, which brings down gold−dust for them from Tmolos, flowing through the middle of their market−place, and then runs out into the river Hermos, and this into the sea;—to this Pactolos, I say, and to the market−place the Lydians and Persians gathered themselves together, and were compelled to defend themselves. The Ionians then, seeing some of the enemy standing on their defence and others in great numbers coming on to the attack, were struck with fear and retired to the mountain called Tmolos, and after that at nightfall departed to go to their ships.

102. Sardis was then destroyed by fire, and in it also the temple of the native goddess Hybebe; which the Persians alleged afterwards as a reason for setting on fire in return the temples in the land of the Hellenes. However at the time of which I speak the Persians who occupied districts within the river Halys, informed beforehand of this movement, were gathering together and coming to the help of the Lydians; and, as it

chanced, they found when they came that the Ionians no longer were in Sardis; but they followed closely in their track and came up with them at Ephesos: and the Ionians stood indeed against them in array, but when they joined battle they had very much the worse; and besides other persons of note whom the Persians slaughtered, there fell also Eualkides commander of the Eretrians, a man who had won wreaths in contests of the games and who was much celebrated by Simonides of Keos: and those of them who survived the battle dispersed to their various cities.

103. Thus then they fought at that time; and after the battle the Athenians left the Ionians together, and when Aristagoras was urgent in calling upon them by messengers for assistance, they said that they would not help them: the Ionians, however, though deprived of the alliance of the Athenians, none the less continued to prepare for the war with the king, so great had been the offences already committed by them against Dareios. They sailed moreover to the Hellespont and brought under their power Byzantion and all the other cities which are in those parts; and then having sailed forth out of the Hellespont, they gained in addition the most part of Caria to be in alliance with them: for even Caunos, which before was not willing to be their ally, then, after they had burnt Sardis, was added to them also. 104. The Cyprians too, excepting those of Amathus, were added voluntarily to their alliance; for these also had revolted from the Medes in the following manner:—there was one Onesilos, younger brother of Gorgos king of Salamis, and son of Chersis, the son of Siromos, the son of Euelthon. This man in former times too had been wont often to advise Gorgos to make revolt from the king, and at this time, when he heard that the Ionians had revolted, he pressed him very hard and endeavoured to urge him to it. Since however he could not persuade Gorgos, Onesilos watched for a time when he had gone forth out of the city of Salamis, and then together with the men of his own faction he shut him out of the gates. Gorgos accordingly being robbed of the city went for refuge to the Medes, and Onesilos was ruler of Salamis and endeavoured to persuade all the men of Cyprus to join him in revolt. The others then he persuaded; but since those of Amathus were not willing to do as he desired, he sat down before their city and besieged it.

105. Onesilos then was besieging Amathus; and meanwhile, when it was reported to king Dareios that Sardis had been captured and burnt by the Athenians and the Ionians together, and that the leader of the league for being about these things[88] was the Milesian Aristagoras, it is said that at first being informed of this he made no account of the Ionians, because he knew that they at all events would not escape unpunished for

their revolt, but he inquired into who the Athenians were; and when he had been informed, he asked for his bow, and having received it and placed an arrow upon the string, he discharged it upwards towards heaven, and as he shot into the air he said: "Zeus, that it may be granted me to take vengeance upon the Athenians!" Having so said he charged one of his attendants, that when dinner was set before the king he should say always three times: "Master, remember the Athenians.' 106. When he had given this charge, he called into his presence Histiaios the Milesian, whom Dareios had now been keeping with him for a long time, and said: "I am informed, Histiaios, that thy deputy, to whom thou didst depute the government of Miletos, has made rebellion against me; for he brought in men against me from the other continent and persuaded the Ionians also,—who shall pay the penalty to me for that which they did,—these, I say, he persuaded to go together with them, and thus he robbed me of Sardis. Now therefore how thinkest thou that this is well? and how without thy counsels was anything of this kind done? Take heed lest thou afterwards find reason to blame thyself for this." Histiaios replied: "O king, what manner of speech is this that thou hast uttered, saying that I counselled a matter from which it was likely that any vexation would grow for thee, either great or small? What have I to seek for in addition to that which I have, that I should do these things; and of what am I in want? for I have everything that thou hast, and I am thought worthy by thee to hear all thy counsels. Nay, but if my deputy is indeed acting in any such manner as thou hast said, be assured that he has done it merely on his own account. I however, for my part, do not even admit the report to be true, that the Milesians and my deputy are acting in any rebellious fashion against thy power: but if it prove that they are indeed doing anything of that kind, and if that which thou hast heard, O king, be the truth, learn then what a thing thou didst in removing me away from the sea–coast; for it seems that the Ionians, when I had gone out of the sight of their eyes, did that which they had long had a desire to do; whereas if I had been in Ionia, not a city would have made the least movement. Now therefore as quickly as possible let me set forth to go to Ionia, that I may order all these matters for thee as they were before, and deliver into thy hands this deputy of Miletos who contrived these things: and when I have done this after thy mind, I swear by the gods of the royal house that I will not put off from me the tunic which I wear when I go down to Ionia, until I have made Sardinia tributary to thee, which is the largest of all islands." 107. Thus saying Histiaios endeavoured to deceive the king, and Dareios was persuaded and let him go, charging him, when he should have accomplished that which he had promised, to return to him again at Susa.

108. In the meantime, while the news about Sardis was going up to the king, and while Dareios, after doing that which he did with the bow, came to speech with Histiaios, and Histiaios having been let go by Dareios was making his journey to the sea-coast,—during all that time the events were happening which here follow.—As Onesilos of Salamis was besieging those of Amathus, it was reported to him that Artybios a Persian, bringing with him in ships a large Persian army, was to be expected shortly to arrive in Cyprus. Being informed of this, Onesilos sent heralds to different places in Ionia to summon the Ionians to his assistance; and they took counsel together and came without delay with a large force. Now the Ionians arrived in Cyprus just at the time when the Persians having crossed over in ships from Kilikia were proceeding by land to attack Salamis, while the Phenicians with the ships were sailing round the headland which is called the "Keys of Cyprus." 109. This being the case, the despots of Cyprus called together the commanders of the Ionians and said: "Ionians, we of Cyprus give you a choice which enemy ye will rather fight with, the Persians or the Phenicians: for if ye will rather array yourselves on land and make trial of the Persians in fight, it is time now for you to disembark from your ships and array yourselves on the land, and for us to embark in your ships to contend against the Phenicians; but if on the other hand ye will rather make trial of the Phenicians,—whichever of these two ye shall choose, ye must endeavour that, so far as it rests with you, both Ionia and Cyprus shall be free." To this the Ionians replied: "We were sent out by the common authority of the Ionians to guard the sea, and not to deliver our ships to the Cyprians and ourselves fight with the Persians on land. We therefore will endeavour to do good service in that place to which we were appointed; and ye must call to mind all the evils which ye suffered from the Medes, when ye were in slavery to them, and prove yourselves good men." 110. The Ionians made answer in these words; and afterwards, when the Persians had come to the plain of Salamis, the kings of the Cyprians set in order their array, choosing the best part of the troops of Salamis and of Soloi to be arrayed against the Persians and setting the other Cyprians against the rest of the enemy's troops; and against Artybios, the commander of the Persians, Onesilos took up his place in the array by his own free choice.

111. Now Artybios was riding a horse which had been trained to rear up against a hoplite. Onesilos accordingly being informed of this, and having a shield-bearer, by race of Caria, who was of very good repute as a soldier and full of courage besides,[89] said to this man: "I am informed that the horse of Artybios rears upright and works both with his feet and his mouth against any whom he is brought to attack. Do thou

therefore consider the matter, and tell me forthwith which of the two thou wilt rather watch for and strike, the horse or Artybios himself." To this his attendant replied: "O king, I am ready to do both or either of these two things, and in every case to do that which thou shalt appoint for me; but I will declare to thee the way in which I think it will be most suitable[90] for thy condition. I say that it is right for one who is king and commander to fight with a king and commander; for if thou shalt slay the commander of the enemy, it turns to great glory for thee; and again, if he shall slay thee, which heaven forbid, even death when it is at the hands of a worthy foe is but half to be lamented: but for us who are under thy command it is suitable to fight with the others who are under his command and with his horse: and of the tricks of the horse have thou no fear at all, for I engage to thee that after this at least he shall never stand against any man more." Thus he spoke; and shortly afterwards the opposed forces joined battle both on land and with their ships. 112. On that day the Ionians for their part greatly distinguished themselves and overcame the Phenicians, and of them the Samians were best: and meanwhile on land, when the armies met, they came to close quarters and fought; and as regards the two commanders, what happened was this:—when Artybios came to fight with Onesilos sitting upon his horse, Onesilos, as he had concerted with his shield–bearer, struck at Artybios himself, when he came to fight with him; and when the horse put its hoofs against the shield of Onesilos, then the Carian struck with a falchion[91] and smote off the horse's feet. 113 So Artybios the commander of the Persians fell there on the spot together with his horse: and while the others also were fighting, Stesenor the despot of Curion deserted them, having with him a large force of men,—now these Curians are said to be settlers from Argos,—and when the Curians had deserted, forthwith also the war–chariots of the men of Salamis proceeded to do the same as the Curians. When these things took place, the Persians had the advantage over the Cyprians; and after their army had been put to rout, many others fell and among them Onesilos the son of Chersis, he who brought about the revolt of the Cyprians, and also the king of the Solians, Aristokypros the son of Philokypros,—that Philokypros whom Solon the Athenian, when he came to Cyprus, commended in verse above all other despots. 114. So the men of Amathus cut off the head of Onesilos, because he had besieged them; and having brought it to Amathus they hung it over the gate of the city: and as the head hung there, when it had now become a hollow, a swarm of bees entered into it and filled it with honeycomb. This having so come to pass, the Amathusians consulted an Oracle about the head, and they received an answer bidding them take it down and bury it and sacrifice to Onesilos every year as a hero; and if they did this, it would go better with them. 115. The

Amathusians accordingly continued to do so even to my time. But the Ionians who had fought the sea–fight in Cyprus, when they perceived that the fortunes of Onesilos were ruined and that the cities of the Cyprians were besieged, except Salamis, and that this city had been delivered over by the Salaminians to Gorgos the former king,—as soon as they perceived this, the Ionians sailed away back to Ionia. Now of the cities in Cyprus Soloi held out for the longest time under the siege; and the Persians took it in the fifth month by undermining the wall round.

116. The Cyprians then, after they had made themselves free for one year, had again been reduced to slavery afresh: and meanwhile Daurises, who was married to a daughter of Dareios, and Hymaies and Otanes, who were also Persian commanders and were married also to daughters of Dareios, after they had pursued those Ionians who had made the expedition to Sardis and defeating them in battle had driven them by force to their ships,—after this distributed the cities amongst themselves and proceeded to sack them. 117. Daurises directed his march to the cities on the Hellespont, and he took Dardanos and Abydos and Percote and Lampsacos and Paisos, of these he took on each day one; and as he was marching from Paisos against the city of Parion, the report came that the Carians had made common cause with the Ionians and were in revolt from the Persians. He turned back therefore from the Hellespont and marched his army upon Caria. 118. And, as it chanced, a report of this was brought to the Carians before Daurises arrived; and the Carians being informed of it gathered together at the place which is called the "White Pillars" and at the river Marsyas, which flows from the region of Idrias and runs out into the Maiander. When the Carians had been gathered together there, among many other counsels which were given, the best, as it seems to me, was that of Pixodaros the son of Mausolos, a man of Kindye, who was married to the daughter of the king of the Kilikians, Syennesis. The opinion of this man was to the effect that the Carians should cross over the Maiander and engage battle with the Persians having the river at their backs, in order that the Carians, not being able to fly backwards and being compelled to remain where they were, might prove themselves even better men in fight than they naturally would. This opinion did not prevail; but they resolved that the Persians rather than themselves should have the Maiander at their backs, evidently[92] in order that if there should be a flight of the Persians and they should be worsted in the battle, they might never return home, but might fall into the river. 119. After this, when the Persians had come and had crossed the Maiander, the Carians engaged with the Persians on the river Marsyas and fought a battle which was obstinately contested and lasted long; but at length they were worsted by superior

numbers: and of the Persians there fell as many as two thousand, but of the Carians ten thousand. Then those of them who escaped were shut up in Labraunda[93] within the sanctuary of Zeus Stratios, which is a large sacred grove of plane–trees; now the Carians are the only men we know who offer sacrifices to Zeus Stratios. These men then, being shut up there, were taking counsel together about their safety, whether they would fare better if they delivered themselves over to the Persians or if they left Asia altogether. 120. And while they were thus taking counsel, there came to their aid the Milesians and their allies. Then the Carians dismissed the plans which they were before considering and prepared to renew the war again from the beginning: and when the Persians came to attack them, they engaged with them and fought a battle, and they were worsted yet more completely than before; and while many were slain of all parties,[94] the Milesians suffered most. 121. Then afterwards the Carians repaired this loss and retrieved their defeat; for being informed that the Persians had set forth to march upon their cities, they laid an ambush on the road which is by Pedasos,[95] and the Persians falling into it by night were destroyed both they and their commanders, namely Daurises and Amorges and Sisimakes; and with them died also Myrsos the son of Gyges. Of this ambush the leader was Heracleides the son of Ibanollis, a man of Mylasa.

122. These then of the Persians were thus destroyed; and meanwhile Hymaies, who was another of those who pursued after the Ionians that had made the expedition to Sardis, directed his march to the Propontis and took Kios in Mysia; and having conquered this city, when he was informed that Daurises had left the Hellespont and was marching towards Caria, he left the Propontis and led his army to the Hellespont: and he conquered all the Aiolians who occupy the district of Ilion, and also the Gergithes, who were left behind as a remnant of the ancient Teucrians. While conquering these tribes Hymaies himself ended his life by sickness in the land of Troas. 123. He thus brought his life to an end; and Artaphrenes the governor of the province of Sardis was appointed with Otanes the third of the commanders to make the expedition against Ionia and that part of Aiolia which bordered upon it. Of Ionia these took the city of Clazomenai, and of the Aiolians Kyme.

124. While the cities were thus being taken, Aristagoras the Milesian, being, as he proved in this instance, not of very distinguished courage, since after having disturbed Ionia and made preparation of great matters[96] he counselled running away when he saw these things, (moreover it had become clear to him that it was impossible to

overcome king Dareios),—he, I say, having regard to these things, called together those of his own party and took counsel with them, saying that it was better that there should be a refuge prepared for them, in case that they should after all be driven out from Miletos, and proposing the question whether he should lead them from thence to Sardinia, to form a colony there, or to Myrkinos in the land of the Edonians, which Histiaios had been fortifying, having received it as a gift from Dareios. This was the question proposed by Aristagoras. 125. Now the opinion of Hecataios the son of Hegesander the historian[97] was that he should not take a colony to either of these places, but build a wall of defence for himself in the island of Leros and keep still, if he should be forced to leave Miletos; and afterwards with this for his starting point he would be able to return to Miletos. 126. This was the counsel of Hecataios; but Aristagoras was most inclined to go forth to Myrkinos. He therefore entrusted the government of Miletos to Pythagoras, a man of repute among the citizens, and he himself sailed away to Thrace, taking with him every one who desired to go; and he took possession of the region for which he had set out. But starting from this to make war, he perished by the hands of the Thracians, that is both Aristagoras himself and his army, when he was encamped about a certain city and the Thracians desired to go out from it under a truce. ——————

NOTES TO BOOK V

1. *ie paion* (or *paian*), as the burden of a song of triumph.

2. *eggenetai*: many MSS. and some Editors read *en genetai*, "and the race can never become united."

3. iv. 93.

3a. Or "from the time that he was born."

4. *to astikton* is probably for *to me estikhthai*: but possibly the meaning may be, "those who are not so marked are of low birth."

5. "the greatest prizes are assigned for single combat in proportion" (as it is more difficult).

6. Or "Siriopaionians."

7. The words "and about the Doberians and Agrianians and Odomantians" are marked by Stein as an interpolation, on the ground that the two tribes first mentioned are themselves Paionian; but Doberians are distinguished from Paionians in vii. 113.

8. *theres katarraktes*: the MSS. have *thures katapaktes* (which can hardly be right, since the Ionic form would be *katapektes*), meaning "fastened down." Stein suggests *thures katepaktes* (from *katepago*), which might mean "a door closed downwards," but the word is not found. (The Medicean MS. has *e* written over the last *a* of *katapaktes*.)

9. *diapinontes*: or perhaps, "drinking against one another."

10. See viii. 137.

11. i.e. "he was drawn to run in the first pair."

12. The best MSS. give this form throughout, which is also used by Æschylus: cp. iii. 70, note 60.

13. *ekakothesan*.

14. *toutou*: it is doubtful whether this means his power or his death. Perhaps something has dropped out after *teleuta*.

15. *anesis*: a conjectural emendation of *aneos*. (Perhaps however, the word was rather *ananeosis*, "after a short time there was a renewal of evils"). Grote wishes to translate this clause, "after a short time there was an abatement of evils," being of opinion that the *anesis kakon* lasted about eight years. However the expression *ou pollon khronon* is so loose that it might well cover the required period of time.

16. *praskhema*.

17. i.e. Miletos and Naxos.

18. *ton pakheon*.

18a. *umin*: omitted in some MSS. and editions.

19. Lit. "dividing him in such a manner."

20. *kai to teikhos esaxanto*: *esaxanto* from *satto*, which generally means "load." Various conjectures have been made, e.g. *kai to teikhos ephraxanto*, or *kata takhos esaxanto*, the comma after *pota* being removed.

20a. *me de neoteron ti poieuses tes Miletou*, "if Miletos made no change (i.e. rebellion)."

21. *katairetheie*, "taken down" from their place (cp. *anetheke* below).

22. *en to peoto ton logon*. The reference is to i. 92.

23. *isonomien*: cp. iii. 80.

24. *akromantes*: cp. *akrakholos*. It may mean "somewhat mad," so *akrozumos*, "slightly leavened," and other words.

25. *Kinupa*: for this Stein reads by conjecture *Aibuen* and afterwards *para Kinupa potamon* for *para potamon*: but Kinyps was the name of the district about the river (iv. 198), and the name of the river is easily supplied from this.

26. *Makeon te kai Libuon*. The Macai were of course Libyans, therefore perhaps we should read (with Niebuhr) *Makeon te Libuon*: or *Makeon te kai allon Libuon*.

27. Stein thinks that Heracleia Minoa on the S. coast of Sicily cannot be meant, because too distant to be considered part of the "land of Eryx." Evidently however this expression is very vague, and there seems no need to correct the text as he proposes.

28. *para ten Italion*: the name applied anciently only to the South– West of the peninsula.

29. *Krathin*, the MSS. give *krastin* here, and *krastie* below for *Krathie*. Sybaris was situated between the rivers Crathis and Sybaris.

30. i.e. "of the Market–place."

31. *periodos.*

32. *kurbasias*: see vii. 64.

33. *poluargurotatoi*: this seems to include gold also, for which Lydia was famous.

34. *poluprobatotatoi.*

35. *tende*, pointing to it in the map.

36. If *anaballesthai* is the true reading here, it cannot mean, "put off to another time," as Stein translates it; for the form of the sentence proves that it is to be taken as a question, co–ordinate with that which follows: *peri men khores ara ou polles khreon esti umeas makhas anaballesthai, parekhon de tes Asies arkhein alio ti airesesthe*; the first clause being in sense subordinate to the second.

37. *es triten emeren.*

38. *diaphthereei se*. It is impossible to reproduce the double meaning of *diaphtheirein*, "to destroy," and "to corrupt with bribes." The child was apparently alarmed by the vehement gestures of Aristagoras and supposed that he was going to kill her father. Cleomenes accepts the omen.

39. *stathmoi*: "stations," the distance between them averaging here about 120 stades.

40. *parasaggai*: the "parasang," as estimated at 30 stades, would be nearly 3½ English miles.

40a. i.e. a narrow pass; so also below in speaking of the passes into Kilikia.

41. In the MSS. this clause follows the account of the four rivers, and the distance through Matiene is given as "four stages" with no number of leagues added. By transposing the clause we avoid placing the rivers in Armenia instead of Matiene; and by making the number of stages thirty–four, with a corresponding number of leagues,

we make the total right at the end and give the proper extension to Matiene.

42. i.e. Zabatos: the name has perhaps fallen out of the text.

43. *o d' usteron*: "the one mentioned afterwards." Stein reads *o d' usteros*.

44. See i. 189.

45. *parasagges*.

46. *stadia*: the stade being equal to 606¾ English feet.

47. Reckoned for the march of an army.

48. Omitting *to eoutou pathei* which stands in the MSS. before *enargestaten*. If the words are retained, we must translate "which clearly pointed to his fate."

49. *apeipamenos ten opsin*, which some translate "he made offerings to avert the dream."

49a. *tisi*: many Editors adopt the conjecture *trisi*, three.

50. *anetheken eon*: various conjectures have been made here, e.g. *anetheken elon*, *anetheken ion*, *anetheke theo*, *anetheken eont*, *anetheke neon*: the last, which is Bentley's, is perhaps the best; but it is doubtful whether the active form of the verb is admissible.

51. *autos*: the MSS. have *auton*. If *autos* is right, the meaning is "from his own property."

52. The expression *Peisistratidai* is used loosely for the family in general.

53. *porinou lithou*, "tufa."

53a. Or "of God."

54. *Koniaion*. There is no such place as Conion known in Thessaly, but we cannot correct the text with any certainty.

55. There is perhaps a play of words in *basileus* and *leuster*.

56. *prutaneio*.

57. "Rulers of the people."

58. "Swine—ites."

59. "Ass—ites."

60. "Pig—ites."

61. *proteron aposmenon, tote panta*: most of the MSS. read *panton* for *panta*. The Editors propose various corrections, e.g. *proteron apospenon panton, tote k.t.l.*, "which before were excluded from everything," or *proteron apospenon, tote panton metadidous*, "giving the people, which before he had despised, a share of all rights": or *panton* is corrected to *epanion*, "on his return from exile," temporary exile being supposed as the result of the defeat mentioned in ch. 66.

62. *tous enageas*.

63. i.e. of Athene Polias in the Erechtheion.

64. Cp. iv. 145.

64a. *tous boethous*: most of the MSS. have *tous Boiotous*.

65. *ippobotai*.

66. *dimneos apotimesamenoi*.

67. See viii. 53.

68. *isegorin*: probably not "equal freedom of speech," but practically the same as *isonomie*, ch. 37.

69. Lit. "penetrated the Athenian greatly": most MSS. and Editors read *esineonto* (or *esinonto*) for *esikneonto*, which is given by the first hand in at least two good MSS.

70. i.e. "Athene (protectress) of the city," who shared with Erechtheus the temple on the Acropolis called the "Erechtheion"; see viii. 55.

71. More lit. "to give and receive from one another satisfaction."

72. *eti tode poiesai nomon einai, para sphisi ekateroisi k.t.l.* The Editors punctuate variously, and alterations have been proposed in the text.

73. i.e. Damia and Auxesia.

74. *ginoito*: some MSS. read *an ginoito*, "would become": so Stein and many other Editors.

75. Some Editors omit this clause, "whither—refuge."

76. "having grown a good opinion of itself."

76a. Or, altering *oste* to *os ge* or *osper*, "as the neighbours of these men first of all, that is the Bœotians and Chalkidians, have already learnt, and perhaps some others will afterwards learn that they have committed an error." The word *amarton* would thus be added as an afterthought, with reference primarily to the Corinthians, see ch. 75.

77. *peiresometha spheas ama umin apikomenoi tisasthai*: some MSS. read *akeomenoi* and omit *tisasthai*. Hence it has been proposed to read *peisesometha sphea ama umin akeomenoi*, "we will endeavour to remedy this with your help," which may be right.

78. So the name is given by the better class of MSS. Others, followed by most Editors, make it "Sosicles."

79. *isokratias*.

80. Lit. "gave and took (in marriage) from one another."

81. *Eetion, outis se tiei polutiton eonta*: the play upon *Eetion* and *tio* can hardly be rendered. The "rolling rock" in the next line is an allusion to Petra, the name of the deme.

82. *aietos en petresi kuei*, with a play upon the names *Eetion* (*Aeton*) and *Petre* again.

83. *ophruoenta*, "situated on a brow or edge," the regular descriptive epithet of Corinth.

84. *kupselen*: cp. Aristoph. Pax, 631.

85. *amphidexion*: commonly translated "ambiguous," but in fact the oracle is of the clearest, so much so that Abicht cuts the knot by inserting *ouk*. Stein explains it to mean "doubly favourable," *amphoterothen dexion*. I understand it to mean "two-edged" (cp. *amphekes*), in the sense that while promising success to Kypselos and his sons, it prophesies also the deposition of the family in the generation after, and so acts (or cuts) both ways.

86. *anapodizon*, "calling him back over the same ground again."

87. Evidently the war must be dated earlier than the time of Peisistratos.

87a. Or (according to some MSS.), "another of the citizens, named Hermophantos."

88. *tes sulloges oste tauta sunuphanthenai*, "the assembling together so that these things were woven."

89. *kai allos lematos pleos.*

90. *plospheresteron*, or perhaps *plopheresteron*, "to be preferred"; so one MS.: *plospheres* ordinarily means "like."

91. *drepano*, cp. vii. 93.

92. *delade*, ironical.

93. Or, "Labranda."

94. i.e. Carians, Persians, and Ionians.

95. *en Pedaso*: the MSS. vary between *en Pidaso, epi daso*, and *epi lasoisi*, and Valla's translation has "in viam quae in Mylassa fert." Some Editors read *epi Mulasoisi*, others *epi Pedaso*.

96. *egkerasamenos pregmata megala*.

97. *andros logopoiou*.

BOOK VI. THE SIXTH BOOK OF THE HISTORIES, CALLED ERATO

1. Aristagoras accordingly, after having caused Ionia to revolt, thus brought his life to an end; and meanwhile Histiaios the despot of Miletos, having been let go by Dareios had arrived at Sardis: and when he came from Susa, Artaphrenes the governor of Sardis asked him for what reason he supposed the Ionians had revolted; and he said that he could not tell, and moreover he expressed wonder at that which had happened, pretending that he knew nothing of the state of affairs. Then Artaphrenes seeing that he was using dissimulation said, having knowledge of the truth about the revolt: "Thus it is with thee, Histiaios, about these matters,—this shoe was stitched by thee, and put on by Aristagoras." 2. Thus said Artaphrenes with reference to the revolt; and Histiaios fearing Artaphrenes because he understood the matter, ran away the next night at nightfall and went to the sea– coast, having deceived king Dareios, seeing that he had engaged to subdue Sardinia the largest of islands, and instead of that he was endeavouring to take upon himself leadership of the Ionians in the war against Dareios. Then having crossed over to Chios he was put in bonds by the Chians, being accused by them of working for a change of their State by suggestion of Dareios. When however the Chians learnt the whole story and heard that he was an enemy to the king, they released him. 3. Then Histiaios, being asked by the Ionians for what reason he had so urgently charged Aristagoras to revolt from the king and had wrought so great an

evil for the Ionians, did not by any means declare to them that which had been in truth the cause, but reported to them that king Dareios had resolved to remove the Phenicians from their land and to settle them in Ionia, and the Ionians in Phenicia; and for this reason, he said, he had given the charge. Thus he attempted to alarm the Ionians, although the king had never resolved to do so at all.

4. After this Histiaios acting through a messenger, namely Hermippos a man of Atarneus, sent papers to the Persians who were at Sardis, implying that he had already talked matters over with them about a revolt: and Hermippos did not deliver them to those to whom he was sent, but bore the papers and put them into the hands of Artaphrenes. He then, perceiving all that was being done, bade Hermippos bear the papers sent by Histiaios and deliver them to those to whom he was sent to bear them, and to deliver to him the replies sent back by the Persians to Histiaios. These things having been discovered, Artaphrenes upon that put to death many of the Persians.

5. As regards Sardis therefore there was confusion of the design; and when Histiaios had been disappointed of this hope, the Chians attempted to restore him to Miletos at the request of Histiaios himself. The Milesians, however, who had been rejoiced before to be rid of Aristagoras, were by no means eager to receive another despot into their land, seeing that they had tasted of liberty: and in fact Histiaios, attempting to return to Miletos by force and under cover of night, was wounded in the thigh by one of the Milesians. He then, being repulsed from his own city, returned to Chios; and thence, as he could not persuade the Chians to give him ships, he crossed over to Mytilene and endeavoured to persuade the Lesbians to give him ships. So they manned eight triremes and sailed with Histiaios to Byzantion, and stationing themselves there they captured the ships which sailed out of the Pontus, excepting where the crews of them said that they were ready to do the bidding of Histiaios.

6. While Histiaios and the men of Mytilene were acting thus, a large army both of sea and land forces was threatening to attack Miletos itself; for the commanders of the Persians had joined together to form one single army and were marching upon Miletos, considering the other towns of less account. Of their naval force the most zealous were the Phenicians, and with them also served the Cyprians, who had just been subdued, and the Kilikians and Egyptians. 7. These, I say, were advancing upon Miletos and the rest of Ionia; and meanwhile the Ionians being informed of this were sending deputies[1] chosen from themselves to the Panionion.[2] When these had arrived at

that place and took counsel together, they resolved not to gather a land—army to oppose the Persians, but that the Milesians should defend their walls by themselves, and that the Ionians should man their fleet, leaving out not one of their ships, and having done so should assemble as soon as possible at Lade, to fight a sea—battle in defence of Miletos. Now Lade is a small island lying opposite the city of the Milesians. 8. Then the Ionians manned their ships and came thither, and with them also those Aiolians who inhabit Lesbos; and they were drawn up in order thus:—the extremity of the line towards the East was held by the Milesians themselves, who furnished eighty ships; next to them were the Prienians with twelve ships and the men of Myus with three; next to those of Myus were the Teians with seventeen ships, and after the Teians the Chians with a hundred; after these were stationed the men of Erythrai and of Phocaia, the former furnishing eight ships and the latter three; next to the Phocaians were the Lesbians with seventy ships, and last, holding the extremity of the line towards the West, were stationed the Samians with sixty ships. Of all these the total number proved to be three hundred and fifty—three triremes. 9. These were the ships of the Ionians; and of the Barbarians the number of ships was six hundred. When these too were come to the Milesian coast and their whole land—army was also there, then the commanders of the Persians, being informed of the number of the Ionian ships, were struck with fear lest they should be unable to overcome them, and thus on the one hand should not be able to conquer Miletos from not having command of the sea, and at the same time should run a risk of being punished by Dareios. Reflecting upon these things they gathered together the despots of the Ionians who were exiles with the Medes, having been deposed from their governments by Aristagoras the Milesian, and who chanced to be then joining in the expedition against Miletos,—of these men they called together those who were present and spoke to them as follows: "Ionians, now let each one of you show himself a benefactor of the king's house, that is to say, let each one of you endeavour to detach his own countrymen from the body of the alliance: and make your proposals promising at the same time that they shall suffer nothing unpleasant on account of the revolt, and neither their temples nor their private houses shall be burnt, nor shall they have any worse treatment than they had before this; but if they will not do so, but will by all means enter into a contest with us, threaten them and tell them this, which in truth shall happen to them, namely that if they are worsted in the fight they shall be reduced to slavery, and we shall make their sons eunuchs, and their maidens we shall remove to Bactria, and deliver their land to others." 10. They thus spoke; and the despots of Ionia sent each one by night to his own people announcing to them this. The Ionians however, that is those to whom these messages came, continued obstinate and would not accept the thought of treason to their cause; and each people thought that to them alone the Persians were sending this message.

11. This happened as soon as the Persians came to Miletos; and after this the Ionians being gathered together at Lade held meetings; and others no doubt also made speeches to them, but especially the Phocaian commander Dionysios, who said as follows: "Seeing that our affairs are set upon the razor's edge, Ionians, whether we shall be free or slaves, and slaves too to be dealt with as runaways, now therefore if ye shall be willing to take upon yourselves hardships, ye will have labour for the time being, but ye will be able to overcome the enemy and be free; whereas if ye continue to be self-indulgent and without discipline, I have no hope for you that ye will not pay the penalty to the king for your revolt. Nay, but do as I say, and deliver yourselves over to me; and I engage, if the gods grant equal conditions, that either the enemy will not fight with us, or that fighting he shall be greatly discomfited." 12. Hearing this the Ionians delivered themselves to Dionysios; and he used to bring the ships out every day in single file,[3] that he might practise the rowers by making the ships break through one another's line,[4] and that he might get the fighting-men in the ships under arms; an then for the rest of the day he would keep the ships at anchor; and thus he gave the Ionians work to do during the whole day. For seven days then they submitted and did that which he commanded; but on the day after these the Ionians, being unaccustomed to such toils and being exhausted with hard work and hot sun, spoke to one another thus: "Against which of the deities have we offended, that we thus fill up the measure of evil? for surely we have delivered ourselves to a Phocaian, an impostor, who furnishes but three ships: and he has taken us into his hands and maltreats us with evil dealing from which we can never recover; and many of us in fact have fallen into sicknesses, and many others, it may be expected, will suffer the same thing shortly; and for us it is better to endure anything else in the world rather than these ills, and to undergo the slavery which will come upon us, whatever that shall be, rather than to be oppressed by that which we have now. Come, let us not obey him after this any more." So they said, and forthwith after this every one refused to obey him, and they pitched their tents in the island like an army, and kept in the shade, and would not go on board their ships or practise any exercises.

13. Perceiving this which was being done by the Ionians, the commanders of the Samians then at length accepted from Aiakes the son of Syloson those proposals which Aiakes sent before at the bidding of the Persians, asking them to leave the alliance of

the Ionians; the Samians, I say, accepted these proposals, perceiving that there was great want of discipline on the part of the Ionians, while at the same time it was clear to them that it was impossible to overcome the power of the king; and they well knew also that even if they should overcome the present naval force of Dareios,[5] another would be upon them five times as large. Having found an occasion[6] then, so soon as they saw that the Ionians refused to be serviceable, they counted it gain for themselves to save their temples and their private property. Now Aiakes, from whom the Samians accepted the proposals, was the son of Syloson, the son of Aiakes, and being despot of Samos he had been deprived of his rule by Aristagoras the Milesian, like the other despots of Ionia. 14. So when the Phenicians sailed to the attack, the Ionians also put out their ships from shore against them, sailing in single file:[3] and when they came near and engaged battle with one another, as regards what followed I am not able exactly to record which of the Ionians showed themselves cowards or good men in this sea-fight, for they throw blame upon one another. The Samians however, it is said, according to their agreement with Aiakes put up their sails then and set forth from their place in the line to sail back to Samos, excepting only eleven ships: of these the captains stayed in their places and took part in the sea-fight, refusing to obey the commanders of their division; and the public authority of the Samians granted them on account of this to have their names written up on a pillar with their fathers' names also,[6a] as having proved themselves good men; and this pillar exists still in the market-place. Then the Lesbians also, when they saw that those next them in order were taking to flight, did the same things as the Samians had done, and so also most of the Ionians did the very same thing. 15. Of those which remained in their places in the sea-fight the Chians suffered very severely,[7] since they displayed brilliant deeds of valour and refused to play the coward. These furnished, as was before said, a hundred ships and in each of them forty picked men of their citizens served as fighting-men:[8] and when they saw the greater number of their allies deserting them, they did not think fit to behave like the cowards among them, but left along with a few only of their allies they continued to fight and kept breaking through the enemy's line; until at last, after they had conquered many ships of the enemy, they lost the greater number of their own. 16. The Chians then with the remainder of their ships fled away to their own land; but those of the Chians whose ships were disabled by the damage which they had received, being pursued fled for refuge to Mycale; and their ships they ran ashore there and left them behind, while the men proceeded over the mainland on foot: and when the Chians had entered the Ephesian territory on their way, then since[8a] they came into it by night and at a time when a festival of Thesmophoria was being celebrated by the women of the place, the Ephesians, not having heard beforehand how it was with the Chians and seeing that an armed body had entered their land, supposed certainly that they were robbers and had a design upon the women; so they came out to the rescue in a body and slew the Chians.

17. Such was the fortune which befell these men: but Dionysios the Phocaian, when he perceived that the cause of the Ionians was ruined, after having taken three ships of the enemy sailed away, not to Pocaia any more, for he knew well that it would be reduced to slavery together with the rest of Ionia, and he sailed forthwith straight to Phenicia; and having there sunk merchant ships and taken a great quantity of goods, he sailed thence to Sicily. Then with that for his starting–point he became a freebooter, not plundering any Hellenes, but Carthaginians and Tyrsenians only.

18. The Persians, then, being conquerors of the Ionians in the sea– fight, besieged Miletos by land and sea, undermining the walls and bringing against it all manner of engines; and they took it completely[9] in the sixth year from the revolt of Aristagoras, and reduced the people to slavery; so that the disaster agreed with the oracle which had been uttered with reference to Miletos. 19. For when the Argives were inquiring at Delphi about the safety of their city, there was given to them an oracle which applied to both, that is to say, part of it had reference to the Argives themselves, while that which was added afterwards referred to the Milesians. The part of it which had reference to the Argives I will record when I reach that place in the history,[10] but that which the Oracle uttered with reference to the Milesians, who were not there present, is as follows:

"And at that time, O Miletos, of evil deeds the contriver, Thou shalt be made for many a glorious gift and a banquet: Then shall thy wives be compelled to wash the feet of the long–haired, And in Didyma then my shrine shall be tended by others."

At the time of which I speak these things came upon the Milesians, since most of the men were killed by the Persians, who are long– haired, and the women and children were dealt with as slaves; and the temple at Didyma, with the sacred building and the sanctuary of the Oracle, was first plundered and then burnt. Of the things in this temple I have made mention frequently in other parts of the history.[11] 20. After this the Milesians who had been taken prisoner were conducted to Susa; and king Dareios did to them no other evil, but settled them upon the Sea called Erythraian, in the city of

Ampe, by which the Tigris flows when it runs out into the sea. Of the Milesian land the Persians themselves kept the surroundings of the city and the plain, but the heights they gave to the Carians of Pedasa for a possession.

21. When the Milesians suffered this treatment from the Persians, the men of Sybaris, who were dwelling in Laos and Skidros, being deprived of their own city, did not repay like with like: for when Sybaris was taken by the men of Croton, the Milesians all from youth upwards shaved their heads and put on great mourning: for these cities were more than all others of which we know bound together by ties of friendship. Not like the Sybarites were the Athenians; for these made it clear that they were grieved at the capture of Miletos, both in many other ways and also by this, that when Phrynichos had composed a drama called the "Capture of Miletos" and had put it on the stage, the body of spectators fell to weeping, and the Athenians moreover fined the poet a thousand drachmas on the ground that he had reminded them of their own calamities; and they ordered also that no one in future should represent this drama.

22. Miletos then had been stripped bare of its former inhabitants: but of the Samians they who had substance were by no means satisfied with that which had been concerted by the commanders of their fleet with the Medes; and taking counsel forthwith after the sea–fight it seemed good to them, before their despot Aiakes arrived in the country, to sail away and make a colony, and not to stay behind and be slaves of the Medes and of Aiakes: for just at this time the people of Zancle in Sicily were sending messengers to Ionia and inviting the Ionians to come to the "Fair Strand,"[11a] desiring there to found a city of Ionians. Now this which is called the Fair Strand is in the land of the Sikelians and on that side of Sicily which lies towards Tyrsenia. So when these gave the invitation, the Samians alone of all the Ionians set forth, having with them those of the Milesians who had escaped: and in the course of this matter it happened as follows:—23. The Samians as they made their way towards Sicily reached Locroi Epizephyroi, and at the same time the people of Zancle, both themselves and their king, whose name was Skythes, were encamped about a city of the Sikelians, desiring to conquer it. Perceiving these things, Anaxilaos the despot of Rhegion, being then at variance with those of Zancle, communicated with the Samians and persuaded them that they ought to leave the Fair Strand alone, to which they were sailing, and take possession of Zancle instead, since it was left now without men to defend it. The Samians accordingly did as he said and took possession of Zancle; and upon this the men of Zancle, being informed that their city was possessed by an enemy, set out to

rescue it, and invited Hippocrates the despot of Gela to help them, for he was their ally. When however Hippocrates also with his army had come up to their rescue, first he put Skythes the ruler of the Zanclaians in fetters, on the ground that he had been the cause of the city being lost, and together with him his brother Pythogenes, and sent them away to the town of Incyos;[12] then he betrayed the cause of the remaining Zanclaians by coming to terms with the Samians and exchanging oaths with them; and in return for this it had been promised by the Samians that Hippocrates should receive as his share the half of all the movable goods in the city and of the slaves, and the whole of the property in the fields round. So the greater number of the Zanclaians he put in bonds and kept himself as slaves, but the chief men of them, three hundred in number, he gave to the Samians to put to death; which however the Samians did not do. 24. Now Skythes the ruler of the Zanclaians escaped from Incyos to Himera, and thence he came to Asia and went up to the court of Dareios: and Dareios accounted him the most righteous of all the men who had come up to him from Hellas; for he obtained leave of the king and went away to Sicily, and again came back from Sicily to the king; and at last he brought his life to an end among the Persians in old age and possessing great wealth. The Samians then, having got rid of the rule of the Medes, had gained for themselves without labour the fair city of Zancle.

25. After the sea–battle which was fought for Miletos, the Phenicians by the command of the Persians restored to Samos Aiakes the son of Syloson, since he had been to them of much service and had done for them great things; and the Samians alone of all who revolted from Dareios, because of the desertion of their ships which were in the sea–fight,[13] had neither their city nor their temples burnt. Then after the capture of Miletos the Persians forthwith got possession of Caria, some of the cities having submitted to their power voluntarily, while others of them they brought over by force.

26. Thus it came to pass as regards these matters: and meanwhile Histiaios the Milesian, who was at Byzantion and was seizing the merchant vessels of the Ionians as they sailed forth out of the Pontus, received the report of that which had happened about Miletos. Upon that he entrusted the matters which had to do with the Hellespont to Bisaltes the son of Apollophanes, a man of Abydos, while he himself with the Lesbians sailed to Chios; and when a body of the Chians who were on guard did not allow him to approach, he fought with them at that spot in the Chian land which is called the "Hollows."[14] Histiaios then not only slew many of these, but also, taking Polichne of the Chians as his base, he conquered with the help of the Lesbians the

remainder of the Chians as well, since they had suffered great loss by the sea–fight. 27. And heaven is wont perhaps to give signs beforehand whenever great evils are about to happen to a city or a race of men; for to the Chians also before these events remarkable signs had come. In the first place when they had sent to Delphi a chorus of a hundred youths, two only returned home, the remaining ninety–eight of them having been seized by a plague and carried off; and then secondly in their city about the same time, that is shortly before the sea–fight, as some children were being taught[15] in school the roof fell in upon them, so that of a hundred and twenty children only one escaped. These signs God showed to them beforehand; and after this the sea–fight came upon them and brought their State down upon its knees; and as the Chians had suffered great loss, he without difficulty effected the conquest of them.

28. Thence Histiaios made an expedition against Thasos, taking with him a large force of Ionians and Aiolians; and while he was encamped about the town of Thasos, a report came to him that the Phenicians were sailing up from Miletos to conquer the rest of Ionia. Being informed of this he left Thasos unconquered and himself hastened to Lesbos, taking with him his whole army. Then, as his army was in want of food,[16] he crossed over from Lesbos to reap the corn in Atarneus and also that in the plain of the Caïcos, which belonged to the Mysians. In these parts there chanced to be a Persian named Harpagos commanding a considerable force; and this man fought a battle with him after he had landed, and he took Histiaios himself prisoner and destroyed the greater part of his army. 29. And Histiaios was taken prisoner in the following manner:—As the Hellenes were fighting with the Persians at Malene in the district of Atarneus, after they had been engaged in close combat for a long time, the cavalry at length charged and fell upon the Hellenes; and the cavalry in fact decided the battle.[17] So when the Hellenes had been turned to flight, Histiaios trusting that he would not be put to death by the king on account of his present fault, conceived a love of life, so that when he was being caught in his flight by a Persian and was about to be run through by him in the moment of his capture, he spoke in Persian and made himself known, saying that he was Histiaios the Milesian. 30. If then upon being taken prisoner he had been brought to king Dareios, he would not, as I think, have suffered any harm, but Dareios would have forgiven the crime with which he was charged; as it was, however, for this very reason and in order that he might not escape from punishment and again become powerful with the king, Artaphrenes the governor of Sardis and Harpagos who had captured him, when he had reached Sardis on his way to the king, put him to death there and then, and his body they impaled, but embalmed his

head and brought it up to Dareios at Susa. Dareios having been informed of this, found fault with those who had done so, because they had not brought him up to his presence alive; and he bade wash the head of Histiaios and bestow upon it proper care, and then bury it, as that of one who had been greatly a benefactor both of the king himself and of the Persians.

31. Thus it happened about Histiaios; and meanwhile the Persian fleet, after wintering near Miletos, when it put to sea again in the following year conquered without difficulty the islands lying near the mainland, Chios, Lesbos, and Tenedos; and whenever they took one of the islands, the Barbarians, as each was conquered, swept the inhabitants off it;[18] and this they do in the following manner:— they extend themselves from the sea on the North to the sea on the South, each man having hold of the hand of the next, and then they pass through the whole island hunting the people out of it. They took also the Ionian cities on the mainland in the same manner, except that they did not sweep off the inhabitants thus, for it was not possible. 32. Then the commanders of the Persians proved not false to the threats with which they had threatened the Ionians when these were encamped opposite to them: for in fact when they conquered the cities, they chose out the most comely of the boys and castrated them, making eunuchs of them, and the fairest of the maidens they carried off by force to the king; and not only this, but they also burnt the cities together with the temples. Thus for the third time had the Ionians been reduced to slavery, first by the Lydians and then twice in succession by the Persians.

33. Departing from Ionia the fleet proceeded to conquer all the places of the Hellespont on the left as one sails in, for those on the right had been subdued already by the Persians themselves, approaching them by land. Now the cities of the Hellespont in Europe are these:—first comes the Chersonese, in which there are many cities, then Perinthos, the strongholds of the Thracian border, Selymbria, and Byzantion. The people of Byzantion and those of Calchedon opposite did not even wait for the coming of the Persian ships, but had left their own land first and departed, going within the Euxine; and there they settled in the city of Mesambria.[19] So the Phenicians, having burnt these places which have been mentioned, directed their course next to Proconnesos and Artake; and when they had delivered these also to the flames, they sailed back to the Chersonese to destroy the remaining cities which they had not sacked when they touched there before: but against Kyzicos they did not sail at all; for the men of Kyzicos even before the time when the Phenicians sailed in had submitted

to the king of their own accord, and had made terms with Oibares the son of Megabazos, the Persian governor at Daskyleion.[20] 34. In the Chersonese then the Phenicians made themselves masters of all the other cities except the city of Cardia. Of these cities up to that time Miltiades the son of Kimon, the son of Stesagoras, had been despot, Miltiades the son of Kypselos having obtained this government in the manner which here follows:—The inhabitants of this Chersonese were Dolonkian Thracians; and these Dolonkians, being hard pressed in war by the Apsinthians, sent their kings to Delphi to consult the Oracle about the war. And the Pythian prophetess answered them that they must bring into their land as founder of a settlement the man who should first offer them hospitality as they returned from the temple. The Dolonkians then passed along the Sacred Road through the land of the Phokians and of the Bœotians, and as no man invited them, they turned aside and came to Athens. 35. Now at that time in Athens the government was held by Peisistratos, but Miltiades also the son of Kypselos had some power, who belonged to a family which kept four– horse chariot teams, and who was descended originally from Aiacos and Egina, though in more recent times his family was Athenian, Philaios the son of Ajax having been the first of his house who became an Athenian. This Miltiades was sitting in the entrance of his own dwelling, and seeing the Dolonkians going by with dress that was not of the native Athenian fashion and with spears, he shouted to them; and when they approached, he offered them lodging and hospitality. They then having accepted and having been entertained by him, proceeded to declare all the utterances of the Oracle; and having declared it they asked him to do as the god had said: and Miltiades when he heard it was at once disposed to agree, because he was vexed by the rule of Peisistratos and desired to be removed out of the way. He set out therefore forthwith to Delphi to inquire of the Oracle whether he should do that which the Dolonkians asked of him: 36, and as the Pythian prophetess also bade him do so, Miltiades the son of Kypselos, who had before this been victor at Olympia with a four–horse chariot, now taking with him of the Athenians everyone who desired to share in the expedition, sailed with the Dolonkians and took possession of the land: and they who had invited him to come to them made him despot over them. First then he made a wall across the isthmus of the Chersonese from the city of Cardia to Pactye, in order that the Apsinthians might not be able to invade the land and do them damage. Now the number of furlongs[21] across the isthmus at this place is six–and–thirty, and from this isthmus the Chersonese within is altogether four hundred and twenty furlongs in length. 37. Having made a wall then across the neck of the Chersonese and having in this manner repelled the Apsinthians, Miltiades made war upon the people of Lampsacos first of all others; and the people of

Lampsacos laid an ambush and took him prisoner. Now Miltiades had come to be a friend[22] of Crœsus the Lydian; and Crœsus accordingly, being informed of this event, sent and commanded the people of Lampsacos to let Miltiades go; otherwise he threatened to destroy them utterly like a pine-tree.[23] Then when the people of Lampsacos were perplexed in their counsels as to what that saying should mean with which Crœsus had threatened them, namely that he would destroy them utterly like a pine-tree, at length one of the elder men with difficulty perceived the truth, and said that a pine alone of all trees when it has been cut down does not put forth any further growth but perishes, being utterly destroyed. The people of Lampsacos therefore fearing Crœsus loosed Miltiades and let him go. 38. He then escaped by means of Crœsus, but afterwards he brought his life to an end leaving no son to succeed him, but passing over his rule and his possessions to Stesagoras, who was the son of Kimon, his brother on the mother's side:[24] and the people of the Chersonese still offer sacrifices to him after his death as it is usual to do to a founder, and hold in his honour a contest of horse-races and athletic exercises, in which none of the men of Lampsacos are allowed to contend. After this there was war with those of Lampsacos; and it happened to Stesagoras also that he died without leaving a son, having been struck on the head with an axe in the City Hall by a man who pretended to be a deserter, but who proved himself to be in fact an enemy and a rather hot one moreover. 39. Then after Stesagoras also had ended his life in this manner, Miltiades son of Kimon and brother of that Stesagoras who was dead, was sent in a trireme to the Chersonese to take possession of the government by the sons of Peisistratos, who had dealt well with him at Athens also, pretending that they had had no share in the death of his father Kimon, of which in another part of the history I will set forth how it came to pass.[25] Now Miltiades, when he came to the Chersonese, kept himself within his house, paying honours in all appearance[26] to the memory of his brother Stesagoras; and the chief men of the inhabitants of the Chersonese in every place, being informed of this, gathered themselves together from all the cities and came in a body to condole with him, and when they had come they were laid in bonds by him. Miltiades then was in possession of the Chersonese, supporting a body of five hundred mercenary troops; and he married the daughter of Oloros the king of the Thracians, who was named Hegesipyle.

40. Now this Miltiades son of Kimon had at the time of which we speak but lately returned[27] to the Chersonese; and after he had returned, there befell him other misfortunes worse than those which had befallen him already; for two years before this

he had been a fugitive out of the land from the Scythians, since the nomad Scythians provoked by king Dareios had joined all in a body and marched as far as this Chersonese, and Miltiades had not awaited their attack but had become a fugitive from the Chersonese, until at last the Scythians departed and the Dolonkians brought him back again. These things happened two years before the calamities which now oppressed him: 41, and now, being informed that the Phenicians were at Tenedos, he filled five triremes with the property which he had at hand and sailed away for Athens. And having set out from the city of Cardia he was sailing through the gulf of Melas; and as he passed along by the shore of the Chersonese, the Phenicians fell in with his ships, and while Miltiades himself with four of his ships escaped to Imbros, the fifth of his ships was captured in the pursuit by the Phenicians. Of this ship it chanced that Metiochos the eldest of the sons of Miltiades was in command, not born of the daughter of Oloros the Thracian, but of another woman. Him the Phenicians captured together with his ship; and being informed about him, that he was the son of Miltiades, they brought him up to the king, supposing that they would lay up for themselves a great obligation; because it was Miltiades who had declared as his opinion to the Ionians that they should do as the Scythians said, at that time when the Scythians requested them to break up the bridge of boats and sail away to their own land. Dareios however, when the Phenicians brought up to him Metiochos the son of Miltiades, did Metiochos no harm but on the contrary very much good; for he gave him a house and possessions and a Persian wife, by whom he had children born who have been ranked as Persians. Miltiades meanwhile came from Imbros to Athens.

42. In the course of this year there was done by the Persians nothing more which tended to strife with the Ionians, but these things which follow were done in this year very much to their advantage.— Artaphrenes the governor of Sardis sent for envoys from all the cities and compelled the Ionians to make agreements among themselves, so that they might give satisfaction for wrongs and not plunder one another's land. This he compelled them to do, and also he measured their territories by parasangs,—that is the name which the Persians give to the length of thirty furlongs,[28]—he measured, I say, by these, and appointed a certain amount of tribute for each people, which continues still unaltered from that time even to my own days, as it was appointed by Artaphrenes; and the tribute was appointed to be nearly of the same amount for each as it had been before. 43. These were things which tended to peace for the Ionians; but at the beginning of the spring, the other commanders having all been removed by the king, Mardonios the son of Gobryas came down to the sea, bringing with him a very

large land–army and a very large naval force, being a young man and lately married to Artozostra daughter of king Dareios. When Mardonios leading this army came to Kilikia, he embarked on board a ship himself and proceeded together with the other ships, while other leaders led the land–army to the Hellespont. Mardonios however sailing along the coast of Asia came to Ionia: and here I shall relate a thing which will be a great marvel to those of the Hellenes who do not believe that to the seven men of the Persians Otanes declared as his opinion that the Persians ought to have popular rule;[29] for Mardonios deposed all the despots of the Ionians and established popular governments in the cities. Having so done he hastened on to the Hellespont; and when there was collected a vast number of ships and a large land–army, they crossed over the Hellespont in the ships and began to make their way through Europe, and their way was directed against Eretria and Athens. 44. These, I say, furnished them the pretence for the expedition, but they had it in their minds to subdue as many as they could of the Hellenic cities; and in the first place they subdued with their ships the Thasians, who did not even raise a hand to defend themselves: then with the land–army they gained the Macedonians to be their servants in addition to those whom they had already; for all the nations on the East of the Macedonians[30] had become subject to them already before this. Crossing over then from Thasos to the opposite coast, they proceeded on their way near the land as far as Acanthos, and then starting from Acanthos they attempted to get round Mount Athos; but as they sailed round, there fell upon them a violent North Wind, against which they could do nothing, and handled them very roughly, casting away very many of their ships on Mount Athos. It is said indeed that the number of the ships destroyed was three hundred,[30a], and more than twenty thousand men; for as this sea which is about Athos is very full of sea monsters, some were seized by these and so perished, while others were dashed against the rocks; and some of them did not know how to swim and perished for that cause, others again by reason of cold. 45. Thus fared the fleet; and meanwhile Mardonios and the land–army while encamping in Macedonia were attacked in the night by the Brygian Thracians, and many of them were slain by the Brygians and Mardonios himself was wounded. However not even these escaped being enslaved by the Persians, for Mardonios did not depart from that region until he had made them subject. But when he had subdued these, he proceeded to lead his army back, since he had suffered great loss with his land– army in fighting against the Brygians and with his fleet in going round Athos. So this expedition departed back to Asia having gained no honour by its contests.

46. In the next year after this Dareios first sent a messenger to the men of Thasos, who had been accused by their neighbours of planning revolt, and bade them take away the wall around their town and bring their ships to Abdera. The Thasians in fact, as they had been besieged by Histiaios the Milesian and at the same time had large revenues coming in, were using their money in building ships of war and in surrounding their city with a stronger wall. Now the revenues came to them from the mainland and from the mines: from the gold–mines in Scapte Hyle[31] there came in generally eighty talents a year, and from those in Thasos itself a smaller amount than this but so much that in general the Thasians, without taxes upon the produce of their soil, had a revenue from the mainland and from the mines amounting yearly to two hundred talents, and when the amount was highest, to three hundred. 47. I myself saw these mines, and by much the most marvellous of them were those which the Phenicians discovered, who made the first settlement in this island in company with Thasos; and the island had the name which it now has from this Thasos the Phenician. These Phenician mines are in that part of Thasos which is between the places called Ainyra and Koinyra and opposite Samothrake, where there is a great mountain which has been all turned up in the search for metal. Thus it is with this matter: and the Thasians on the command of the king both razed their walls and brought all their ships to Abdera.

48. After this Dareios began to make trial of the Hellenes, what they meant to do, whether to make war with him or to deliver themselves up. He sent abroad heralds therefore, and appointed them to go some to one place and others to another throughout Hellas, bidding them demand earth and water for the king. These, I say, he sent to Hellas; and meanwhile he was sending abroad other heralds to his own tributary cities which lay upon the sea–coast, and he bade them have ships of war built and also vessels to carry horses. 49. They then were engaged in preparing these things; and meanwhile when the heralds had come to Hellas, many of those who dwelt upon the mainland gave that for which the Persian made demand,[32] and all those who dwelt in the islands did so, to whomsoever they came to make their demand. The islanders, I say, gave earth and water to Dareios, and among them also those of Egina, and when these had done so, the Athenians went forthwith urgent against them, supposing that the Eginetans had given with hostile purpose against themselves, in order to make an expedition against them in combination with the Persians; and also they were glad to get hold of an occasion against them. Accordingly they went backward and forwards to Sparta and accused the Eginetans of that which they had done, as having proved themselves traitors to Hellas. 50. In consequence of this accusation Cleomenes the son

of Anaxandrides, king of the Spartans, crossed over to Egina meaning to seize those of the Eginetans who were the most guilty; but as he was attempting to seize them, certain of the Eginetans opposed him, and among them especially Crios the son of Polycritos, who said that he should not with impunity carry off a single Eginetan, for he was doing this (said he) without authority from the Spartan State, having been persuaded to it by the Athenians with money; otherwise he would have come and seized them in company with the other king: and this he said by reason of a message received from Demaratos. Cleomenes then as he departed from Egina, asked Crios[33] what was his name, and he told him the truth; and Cleomenes said to him: "Surely now, O Ram, thou must cover over thy horns with bronze for thou wilt shortly have a great trouble to contend with."

51. Meanwhile Demaratos the son of Ariston was staying behind in Sparta and bringing charges against Cleomenes, he also being king of the Spartans but of the inferior house; which however is inferior in no other way (for it is descended from the same ancestor), but the house of Eurysthenes has always been honoured more, apparently because he was the elder brother. 52. For the Lacedemonians, who herein agree with none of the poets, say that Aristodemos the son of Aristomachos, the son of Cleodaios, the son of Hyllos, being their king, led them himself (and not the sons of Aristodemos) to this land which they now possess. Then after no long time the wife of Aristodemos, whose name was Argeia,—she was the daughter, they say, of Autesion, the son of Tisamenes, the son of Thersander, the son of Polyneikes,—she, it is said, brought forth twins; and Aristodemos lived but to see his children and then ended his life by sickness. So the Lacedemonians of that time resolved according to established custom to make the elder of the children their king; but they did not know which of them they should take, because they were like one another and of equal size; and when they were not able to make out, or even before this, they inquired of their mother; and she said that even she herself did not know one from the other. She said this, although she knew in truth very well, because she desired that by some means both might be made kings. The Lacedemonians then were in a strait; and being in a strait they sent to Delphi to inquire what they should do in the matter. And the Pythian prophetess bade them regard both children as their kings, but honour most the first in age.[34] The prophetess, they say, thus gave answer to them; and when the Lacedemonians were at a loss none the less how to find out the elder of them, a Messenian whose name was Panites made a suggestion to them: this Panites, I say, suggested to the Lacedemonians that they should watch the mother and see which of the children she washed and fed

before the other; and if she was seen to do this always in the same order, then they would have all that they were seeking and desiring to find out, but if she too was uncertain and did it in a different order at different times, it would be plain to them that even she had no more knowledge than any other, and they must turn to some other way. Then the Spartans following the suggestion of the Messenian watched the mother of the sons of Aristodemos and found that she gave honour thus to the first−born both in feeding and in washing; for she did not know with that design she was being watched. They took therefore the child which was honoured by its mother and brought it up as the first−born in the public hall,[35] and to it was given the name of Eurysthenes, while the other was called Procles. These, when they had grown up, both themselves were at variance, they say, with one another, though they were brothers, throughout the whole time of their lives, and their descendants also continued after the same manner.

53. This is the report given by the Lacedemonians alone of all the Hellenes; but this which follows I write in accordance with that which is reported by the Hellenes generally,—I mean that the names of these kings of the Dorians are rightly enumerated by the Hellenes up to Perseus the son of Danae (leaving the god out of account),[36] and proved to be of Hellenic race; for even from that time they were reckoned as Hellenes. I said "up to Perseus" and did not take the descent from a yet higher point, because there is no name mentioned of a mortal father for Perseus, as Amphitryon is for Heracles. Therefore with reason, as is evident, I have said "rightly up to Perseus"; but if one enumerates their ancestors in succession going back from Danae the daughter of Acrisios, the rulers of the Dorians will prove to be Egyptians by direct descent. 54. Thus I have traced the descent according to the account given by the Hellenes; but as the story is reported which the Persians tell, Perseus himself was an Assyrian and became a Hellene, whereas the ancestors of Perseus were not Hellenes; and as for the ancestors of Acrisios, who (according to this account) belonged not to Perseus in any way by kinship, they say that these were, as the Hellenes report, Egyptians. 55. Let it suffice to have said so much about these matters; and as to the question how and by what exploits being Egyptians they received the sceptres of royalty over the Dorians, we will omit these things, since others have told about them; but the things with which other narrators have not dealt, of these I will make mention.

56. These are the royal rights which have been given by the Spartans to their kings, namely, two priesthoods, of Zeus Lakedaimon and Zeus Uranios;[37] and the right of

70

making war against whatsoever land they please, and that no man of the Spartans shall hinder this right, or if he do, he shall be subject to the curse; and that when they go on expeditions the kings shall go out first and return last; that a hundred picked men shall be their guard upon expeditions; and that they shall use in their goings forth to war as many cattle as they desire, and take both the hides and the backs of all that are sacrificed. 57. These are their privileges in war; and in peace moreover things have been assigned to them as follows:—if any sacrifice is performed at the public charge, it is the privilege of the kings to sit down at the feast before all others, and that the attendants shall begin with them first, and serve to each of them a portion of everything double of that which is given to the other guests, and that they shall have the first pouring of libations and the hides of the animals slain in sacrifice; that on every new moon and seventh day of the month there shall be delivered at the public charge to each one of these a full-grown victim in the temple of Apollo, and a measure[38] of barley-groats and a Laconian "quarter"[39] of wine; and that at all the games they shall have seats of honour specially set apart for them: moreover it is their privilege to appoint as protectors of strangers[40] whomsoever they will of the citizens, and to choose each two "Pythians:" now the Pythians are men sent to consult the god at Delphi, and they eat with the kings at the public charge. And if the kings do not come to the dinner, it is the rule that there shall be sent out for them to their houses two quarts[41] of barley-groats for each one and half a pint[42] of wine; but if they are present, double shares of everything shall be given them, and moreover they shall be honoured in this same manner when they have been invited to dinner by private persons. The kings also, it is ordained, shall have charge of the oracles which are given, but the Pythians also shall have knowledge of them. It is the rule moreover that the kings alone give decision on the following cases only, that is to say, about the maiden who inherits her father's property, namely who ought to have her, if her father have not betrothed her to any one, and about public ways; also if any man desires to adopt a son, he must do it in presence of the kings: and it is ordained that they shall sit in council with the Senators, who are in number eight-and-twenty, and if they do not come, those of the Senators who are most closely related to them shall have the privileges of the kings and give two votes besides their own, making three in all.[42a] 58. These rights have been assigned to the kings for their lifetime by the Spartan State; and after they are dead these which follow:—horsemen go round and announce that which has happened throughout the whole of the Laconian land, and in the city women go about and strike upon a copper kettle. Whenever this happens so, two free persons of each household must go into mourning, a man and a woman, and for those who fail to do this great penalties are appointed. Now the custom of the Lacedemonians about the deaths of their kings is the same as that of the Barbarians who dwell in Asia, for most of the Barbarians practise the same customs as regards the death of their kings. Whensoever a king of the Lacedemonians is dead, then from the whole territory of Lacedemon, not reckoning the Spartans, a certain fixed number of the "dwellers round"[43] are compelled to go to the funeral ceremony: and when there have been gathered together of these and of the Helots and of the Spartans themselves many thousands in the same place, with their women intermingled, they beat their foreheads with a good will and make lamentation without stint, saying that this one who has died last of their kings was the best of all: and whenever any of their kings has been killed in war, they prepare an image to represent him, laid upon a couch with fair coverings, and carry it out to be buried. Then after they have buried him, no assembly is held among them for ten days, nor is there any meeting for choice of magistrates, but they have mourning during these days. In another respect too these resemble the Persians; that is to say, when the king is dead and another is appointed king, this king who is newly coming in sets free any man of the Spartans who was a debtor to the king or to the State; while among the Persians the king who comes to the throne remits to all the cities the arrears of tribute which are due. 60. In the following point also the Lacedemonians resemble the Egyptians; that is to say, their heralds and fluteplayers and cooks inherit the crafts of their fathers, and a fluteplayer is the son of a fluteplayer, a cook of a cook, and a herald of a herald; other men do not lay hands upon the office because they have loud and clear voices, and so shut them out of it, but they practise their craft by inheritance from their fathers.

61. Thus are these things done: and at this time of which we speak,[44] while Cleomenes was in Egina doing deeds[45] which were for the common service of Hellas, Demaratos brought charges against him, not so much because he cared for the Eginetans as because he felt envy and jealousy of him. Then Cleomenes, after he returned from Egina, planned to depose Demaratos from being king, making an attempt upon him on account of this matter which follows:—Ariston being king in Sparta and having married two wives, yet had no children born to him; and since he did not acknowledge that he himself was the cause of this, he married a third wife; and he married her thus:—he had a friend, a man of the Spartans, to whom of all the citizens Ariston was most inclined; and it chanced that this man had a wife who was of all the women in Sparta the fairest by far, and one too who had become the fairest from having been the foulest. For as she was mean in her aspect, her nurse, considering that

she was the daughter of wealthy persons and was of uncomely aspect, and seeing moreover that her parents were troubled by it,—perceiving I say these things, her nurse devised as follows:—every day she bore her to the temple of Helen, which is in the place called Therapne, lying above the temple of Phoebus; and whenever the nurse bore her thither, she placed her before the image and prayed the goddess to deliver the child from her unshapeliness. And once as the nurse was going away out of the temple, it is said that a woman appeared to her, and having appeared asked her what she was bearing in her arms; and she told her that she was bearing a child; upon which the other bade her show the child to her, but she refused, for it had been forbidden to her by the parents to show it to any one: but the woman continued to urge her by all means to show it to her. So then perceiving that the woman earnestly desired to see it, the nurse showed her the child. Then the woman stroking the head of the child said that she should be the fairest of all the women in Sparta; and from that day her aspect was changed. Afterwards when she came to the age for marriage, she was married to Agetos the son of Alkeides, this friend of Ariston of whom we spoke. 62. Now Ariston it seems was ever stung by the desire of this woman, and accordingly he contrived as follows:—he made an engagement himself with his comrade, whose wife this woman was, that he would give him as a gift one thing of his own possessions, whatsoever he should choose, and he bade his comrade make return to him in similar fashion. He therefore, fearing nothing for his wife, because he saw that Ariston also had a wife, agreed to this; and on these terms they imposed oaths on one another. After this Ariston on his part gave that which Agetos had chosen from the treasures of Ariston, whatever the thing was; and he himself, seeking to obtain from him the like return, endeavoured then to take away the wife of his comrade from him: and he said that he consented to give anything else except this one thing only, but at length being compelled by the oath and by the treacherous deception,[46] he allowed her to be taken away from him. 63. Thus had Ariston brought into his house the third wife, having dismissed the second: and this wife, not having fulfilled the ten months[47] but in a shorter period of time, bore him that Demaratos of whom we were speaking; and one of his servants reported to him as he was sitting in council[48] with the Ephors, that a son had been born to him. He then, knowing the time when he took to him his wife, and reckoning the months upon his fingers, said, denying with an oath, "The child would not be mine." This the Ephors heard, but they thought it a matter of no importance at the moment; and the child grew up and Ariston repented of that which he had said, for he thought Demaratos was certainly his own son; and he gave him the name "Demaratos" for this reason, namely because before these things took place the

Spartan people all in a body[49] had made a vow[50] praying that a son might be born to Ariston, as one who was pre−eminent in renown over all the kings who had ever arisen in Sparta. 64. For this reason the name Demaratos[51] was given to him. And as time went on Ariston died, and Demaratos obtained the kingdom: but it was fated apparently that these things should become known and should cause Demaratos to be deposed from the kingdom; and therefore[52] Demaratos came to be at variance greatly with Cleomenes both at the former time when he withdrew his army from Eleusis, and also now especially, when Cleomenes had crossed over to take those of the Eginetans who had gone over to the Medes. 65. Cleomenes then, being anxious to take vengeance on him, concerted matters with Leotychides the son of Menares, the son of Agis, who was of the same house as Demaratos, under condition that if he should set him up as king instead of Demaratos, he would go with him against the Eginetans. Now Leotychides had become a bitter foe of Demaratos on account of this matter which follows:—Leotychides had betrothed himself to Percalos the daughter of Chilon son of Demarmenos; and Demaratos plotted against him and deprived Leotychides of his marriage, carrying off Percalos himself beforehand, and getting her for his wife. Thus had arisen the enmity of Leotychides against Demaratos; and now by the instigation of Cleomenes Leotychides deposed against Demaratos, saying that he was not rightfully reigning over the Spartans, not being a son of Ariston: and after this deposition he prosecuted a suit against him, recalling the old saying which Ariston uttered at the time when his servant reported to him that a son was born to him, and he reckoning up the months denied with an oath, saying that it was not his. Taking his stand upon this utterance, Leotychides proceeded to prove that Demaratos was not born of Ariston nor was rightfully reigning over Sparta; and he produced as witnesses those Ephors who chanced then to have been sitting with Ariston in council and to have heard him say this. 66. At last, as there was contention about those matters, the Spartans resolved to ask the Oracle at Delphi whether Demaratos was the son of Ariston. The question then having been referred by the arrangement of Cleomenes to the Pythian prophetess, thereupon Cleomenes gained over to his side Cobon the son of Aristophantos, who had most power among the Delphians, and Cobin persuaded Perialla the prophetess of the Oracle[53] to say that which Cleomenes desired to have said. Thus the Pythian prophetess, when those who were sent to consult the god asked her their question, gave decision that Demaratos was not the son of Ariston. Afterwards however these things became known, and both Cobon went into exile from Delphi and Perialla the prophetess of the Oracle was removed from her office.

67. With regard to the deposing of Demaratos from the kingdom it happened thus: but Demaratos became an exile from Sparta to the Medes on account of a reproach which here follows:—After he had been deposed from the kingdom Demaratos was holding a public office to which he had been elected. Now it was the time of the Gymnopaidiai; and as Demaratos was a spectator of them, Leotychides, who had now become king himself instead of Demaratos, sent his attendant and asked Demaratos in mockery and insult what kind of a thing it was to be a magistrate after having been king; and he vexed at the question made answer and said that he himself had now had experience of both, but Leotychides had not; this question however, he said, would be the beginning either of countless evil or countless good fortune for the Lacedemonians. Having thus said, he veiled his head and went forth out of the theatre to his own house; and forthwith he made preparations and sacrificed an ox to Zeus, and after having sacrificed he called his mother. 68. Then when his mother had come, he put into her hands some of the inner parts[54] of the victim, and besought her, saying as follows: "Mother, I beseech thee, appealing to the other gods and above all to this Zeus the guardian of the household,[55] to tell me the truth, who is really and truly my father. For Leotychides spoke in his contention with me, saying that thou didst come to Ariston with child by thy former husband; and others besides, reporting that which is doubtless an idle tale,[56] say that thou didst go in to one of the servants, namely the keeper of the asses, and that I am his son. I therefore entreat thee by the gods to tell me the truth; for if thou hast done any of these things which are reported, thou hast not done them alone, but with many other women; and the report is commonly believed in Sparta that there was not in Ariston seed which should beget children; for if so, then his former wives also would have borne children." 69. Thus he spoke, and she made answer as follows: "My son, since thou dost beseech me with entreaties to speak the truth, the whole truth shall be told to thee. When Ariston had brought me into his house, on the third night[57] there came to me an apparition in the likeness of Ariston, and having lain with me it put upon me the garlands which it had on; and the apparition straitway departed, and after this Ariston came; and when he saw me with garlands, he asked who it was who had given me them; and I said that he had given them, but he did not admit it; and I began to take oath of it, saying that he did not well to deny it, for he had come (I said) a short time before and had lain with me and given me the garlands. Then Ariston, seeing that I made oath of it, perceived that the matter was of the gods; and first the garlands were found to be from the hero–temple which stands by the outer door of the house, which they call the temple of Astrabacos,[58] and secondly the diviners gave answer that it was this same hero. Thus, my son, thou

hast all, as much as thou desirest to learn; for either thou art begotten of this hero and the hero Astrabacos is thy father, or Ariston is thy father, for on that night I conceived thee: but as to that wherein thy foes most take hold of thee, saying that Ariston himself, when thy birth was announced to him, in the hearing of many declared that thou wert not his son, because the time, the ten months namely, had not yet been fulfilled, in ignorance of such matters he cast forth that saying; for women bring forth children both at the ninth month and also at the seventh, and not all after they have completed ten months; and I bore thee, my son, at the seventh month: and Ariston himself also perceived after no long time that he had uttered this saying in folly. Do not thou then accept any other reports about thy begetting, for thou hast heard in all the full truth; but to Leotychides and to those who report these things may their wives bear children by keepers of asses!" 70. Thus she spoke; and he, having learnt that which he desired to learn, took supplies for travelling and set forth to go to Elis, pretending that he was going to Delphi to consult the Oracle: but the Lacedemonians, suspecting that he was attempting to escape, pursued after him; and it chanced that before they came Demaratos had passed over to Zakynthos from Elis; and the Lacedemonians crossing over after him laid hands on his person and carried away his attendants from him. Afterwards however, since those of Zakynthos refused to give him up, he passed over from thence to Asia, to the presence of king Dareios; and Dareios both received him with great honour as a guest, and also gave him land and cities. Thus Demaratos had come to Asia, and such was the fortune which he had had, having been distinguished in the estimation of the Lacedemonians[59] in many other ways both by deeds and by counsels, and especially having gained for them an Olympic victory with the four-horse chariot, being the only one who achieved this of all the kings who ever arose in Sparta.

71. Demaratos being deposed, Leotychides the son of Menares succeeded to the kingdom; and he had born to him a son Zeuxidemos, whom some of the Spartans called Kyniscos. This Zeuxidemos did not become king of Sparta, for he died before Leotychides, leaving a son Archidemos: and Leotychides having lost Zeuxidemos married a second wife Eurydame, the sister of Menios and daughter of Diactorides, by whom he had no male issue, but a daughter Lampito, whom Archidemos the son of Zeuxidemos took in marriage, she being given to him by Leotychides. 72. Leotychides however did not himself[60] live to old age in Sparta, but paid a retribution for Demaratos as follows:—he went as commander of the Lacedemonians to invade Thessaly, and when he might have reduced all to subjection, he accepted gifts of

money amounting to a large sum; and being taken in the act there in the camp, as he was sitting upon a glove full of money, he was brought to trial and banished from Sparta, and his house was razed to the ground. So he went into exile to Tegea and ended his life there. 73. These things happened later; but at this time, when Cleomenes had brought to a successful issue the affair which concerned Demaratos, forthwith he took with him Leotychides and went against the Eginetans, being very greatly enraged with them because of their insults towards him. So the Eginetans on their part, since both the kings had come against them, thought fit no longer to resist; and the Spartans selected ten men who were the most considerable among the Eginetans both by wealth and by birth, and took them away as prisoners, and among others also Crios[61] the son of Polycritos and Casambos the son of Aristocrates, who had the greatest power among them; and having taken these away to the land of Attica, they deposited them as a charge with the Athenians, who were the bitterest enemies of the Eginetans.

74. After this Cleomenes, since it had become known that he had devised evil against Demaratos, was seized by fear of the Spartans and retired to Thessaly. Thence he came to Arcadia, and began to make mischief[62] and to combine the Arcadians against Sparta; and besides other oaths with which he caused them to swear that they would assuredly follow him whithersoever he should lead them, he was very desirous also to bring the chiefs of the Arcadians to the city of Nonacris and cause them to swear by the water of Styx; for near this city it is said by the Arcadians[63] that there is the water of Styx, and there is in fact something of this kind: a small stream of water is seen to trickle down from a rock into a hollow ravine, and round the ravine runs a wall of rough stones. Now Nonacris, where it happens that this spring is situated, is a city of Arcadia near Pheneos. 75. The Lacedemonians, hearing that Cleomenes was acting thus, were afraid, and proceeded to bring him back to Sparta to rule on the same terms as before: but when he had come back, forthwith a disease of madness seized him (who had been even before this somewhat insane[64]), and whenever he met any of the Spartans, he dashed his staff against the man's face. And as he continued to do this and had gone quite out of his senses, his kinsmen bound him in stocks. Then being so bound, and seeing his warder left alone by the rest, he asked him for a knife; and the warder not being at first willing to give it, he threatened him with that which he would do to him afterwards if he did not; until at last the warder fearing the threats, for he was one of the Helots, gave him a knife. Then Cleomenes, when he had received the steel, began to maltreat himself from the legs upwards: for he went on cutting his flesh lengthways from the legs to the thighs and from the thighs to the loins and flanks, until

at last he came to the belly; and cutting this into strips he died in that manner. And this happened, as most of the Hellenes report, because he persuaded the Pythian prophetess to advise that which was done about Demaratos; but as the Athenians alone report, it was because when he invaded Eleusis he laid waste the sacred enclosure of the goddesses;[65] and according to the report of the Argives, because from their sanctuary dedicated to Argos he caused to come down those of the Argives who had fled for refuge from the battle and slew them, and also set fire to the grove itself, holding it in no regard. 76. For when Cleomenes was consulting the Oracle at Delphi, the answer was given him that he should conquer Argos; so he led the Spartans and came to the river Erasinos, which is said to flow from the Stymphalian lake; for this lake, they say, running out into a viewless chasm, appears again above ground in the land of Argos; and from thence onwards this water is called by the Argives Erasinos: having come, I say, to this river, Cleomenes did sacrifice to it; and since the sacrifices were not at all favourable for him to cross over, he said that he admired the Erasinos for not betraying the men of its country, but the Argives should not even so escape. After this he retired back from thence and led his army down to Thyrea; and having done sacrifice to the Sea by slaying a bull, he brought them in ships to the land of Tiryns and Nauplia. 77. Being informed of this, the Argives came to the rescue towards the sea; and when they had got near Tiryns and were at the place which is called Hesipeia,[66] they encamped opposite to the Lacedemonians leaving no very wide space between the armies. There the Argives were not afraid of the open fighting, but only lest they should be conquered by craft; for to this they thought referred the oracle which the Pythian prophetess gave in common to these and to the Milesians,[67] saying as follows:

"But when the female at length shall conquer the male in the battle, Conquer and drive him forth, and glory shall gain among Argives, Then many wives of the Argives shall tear both cheeks in their mourning; So that a man shall say some time, of the men that came after, 'Quelled by the spear it perished, the three–coiled terrible serpent,'

The conjunction of all these things caused fear to the Argives, and with a view to this they resolved to make use of the enemy's herald; and having so resolved they proceeded to do as follows:—whenever the Spartan herald proclaimed anything to the Lacedemonians, the Argives also did that same thing. 78. So Cleomenes, perceiving that the Argives were doing whatever the herald of the Lacedemonians proclaimed, passed the word to the Lacedemonians that when the herald should proclaim that they were to get breakfast, then they should take up their arms and go to attack the Argives. This was carried out even so by the Lacedemonians; for as the Argives were getting breakfast according to the herald's proclamation, they attacked them; and many of them they slew, but many more yet took refuge in the sacred grove of Argos, and upon these they kept watch, sitting round about the place. Then Cleomenes did this which follows:—79. He had with him deserters, and getting information by inquiring of these, he sent a herald and summoned forth those of the Argives who were shut up in the sanctuary, mentioning each by name; and he summoned them forth saying that he had received their ransom. Now among the Peloponnesians ransom is two pounds weight of silver[68] appointed to be paid for each prisoner. So Cleomenes summoned forth about fifty of the Argives one by one and slew them; and it chanced that the rest who were in the enclosure did not perceive that this was being done; for since the grove was thick, those within did not see how it fared with those who were without, at least until one of them climbed up a tree and saw from above that which was being done. Accordingly they then no longer came forth when they were called. 80. So Cleomenes thereupon ordered all the Helots to pile up brushwood round the sacred grove; and they obeying, he set fire to the grove. And when it was now burning, he asked one of the deserters to what god the grove was sacred, and the man replied that it was sacred to Argos. When he heard that, he groaned aloud and said, "Apollo who utterest oracles, surely thou hast greatly deceived me, saying that I should conquer Argos: I conjecture that the oracle has had its fulfilment for me already." 81. After this Cleomenes sent away the greater part of his army to go back to Sparta, but he himself took a thousand of the best men and went to the temple of Hera to sacrifice: and when he wished to sacrifice upon the altar, the priest forbade him, saying that it was not permitted by religious rule for a stranger to sacrifice in that place. Cleomenes however bade the Helots take away the priest from the altar and scourge him, and he himself offered the sacrifice. Having so done he returned back to Sparta; 82, and after his return his opponents brought him up before the Ephors, saying that he had received gifts and therefore had not conquered Argos, when he might easily have conquered it. He said to them,—but whether he was speaking falsely or whether truly I am not able with certainty to say,—however that may be, he spoke and said that when he had conquered the sanctuary of Argos, it seemed to him that the oracle of the god had had its fulfilment for him; therefore he did not think it right to make an attempt on the city, at least until he should have had recourse to sacrifice, and should have learnt whether the deity[69] permitted him or whether she stood opposed to him: and as he was sacrificing for augury[70] in the temple of Hera, a flame of fire blazed forth from the breasts of the image; and thus he knew the certainty of the matter, namely that he would not conquer Argos: for if fire had blazed forth from the head of the image, he would have been conqueror of the city from top to bottom,[71] but since it blazed from the breasts, everything had been accomplished for him which the god desired should come to pass. Thus speaking he seemed to the Spartans to speak credibly and reasonably, and he easily escaped his pursuers.[72]

83. Argos however was so bereft of men that their slaves took possession of all the State, ruling and managing it until the sons of those who had perished grew to be men. Then these, endeavouring to gain Argos back to themselves, cast them out; and the slaves being driven forth gained possession of Tiryns by fighting. Now for a time these two parties had friendly relations with one another; but afterwards there came to the slaves a prophet named Cleander, by race a Phigalian from Arcadia: this man persuaded the slaves to attack their masters, and in consequence of this there was war between them for a long time, until at last with difficulty the Argives overcame them.

84. The Argives then say that this was the reason why Cleomenes went mad and had an evil end: but the Spartans themselves say that Cleomenes was not driven mad by any divine power, but that he had become a drinker of unmixed wine from having associated with Scythians, and that he went mad in consequence of this: for the nomad Scythians, they say, when Dareios had made invasion of their land, desired eagerly after this to take vengeance upon him; and they sent to Sparta and tried to make an alliance, and to arrange that while the Scythians themselves attempted an invasion of Media by the way of the river Phasis, the Spartans should set forth from Ephesos and go up inland, and then that they should meet in one place: and they say that Cleomenes when the Scythians had come for this purpose, associated with them largely, and that thus associating more than was fit, he learnt the practice of drinking wine unmixed with water; and for this cause (as the Spartans think) he went mad. Thenceforth, as they say themselves, when they desire to drink stronger wine, they say "Fill up in Scythian fashion."[73] Thus the Spartans report about Cleomenes; but to me it seems that this was a retribution which Cleomenes paid for Demaratos.

85. Now when the Eginetans heard that Cleomenes had met his end, they sent messengers to Sparta to denounce Leotychides for the matter of the hostages which were being kept at Athens: and the Lacedemonians caused a court to assemble and judged that the Eginetans had been dealt with outrageously by Leotychides; and they

condemned him to be taken to Egina and delivered up in place of the men who were being kept at Athens. Then when the Eginetans were about to take Leotychides, Theasides the son of Leoprepes, a man of repute in Sparta, said to them: "What are ye proposing[74] to do, men of Egina? Do ye mean to take away the king of the Spartans, thus delivered up to you by his fellow–citizens? If the Spartans now being in anger have decided so, beware lest at some future time, if ye do this, they bring an evil upon your land which may destroy it." Hearing this the Eginetans abstained from taking him; but they came to an agreement that Leotychides should accompany them to Athens and restore the men to the Eginetans.

86. When however Leotychides came to Athens and asked for the deposit back, the Athenians, not being willing to give up the hostages, produced pretexts for refusing, and alleged that two kings had deposited them and they did not think it right to give them back to the one without the other: so since the Athenians said that they would not give them back, Leotychides spoke to them as follows:

(a) "Athenians, do whichever thing ye yourselves desire; for ye know that if ye give them up, ye do that which religion commands, and if ye refuse to give them up, ye do the opposite of this: but I desire to tell you what kind of a thing came to pass once in Sparta about a deposit. We Spartans report that there was in Lacedemon about two generations before my time one Glaucos the son of Epikydes. This man we say attained the highest merit in all things besides, and especially he was well reported of by all who at that time dwelt in Lacedemon for his uprightness: and we relate that in due time[75] it happened to him thus:—a man of Miletos came to Sparta and desired to have speech with him, alleging the reasons which follow: 'I am a Milesian,' he said, 'and I am come hither desiring to have benefit from thy uprightness, Glaucos; for as there was much report of thy uprightness throughout all the rest of Hellas and also in Ionia, I considered with myself that Ionia is ever in danger, whereas Peloponnesus is safely established, and also that we never see wealth continue in the possession of the same persons long;—reflecting, I say, on these things and taking counsel with myself, I resolved to turn into money the half of my possessions, and to place it with thee, being well assured that if it were placed with thee I should have it safe. Do thou therefore, I pray thee, receive the money, and take and keep these tallies; and whosoever shall ask for the money back having the tokens answering to these, to him do thou restore it.' (b) The stranger who had come from Miletos said so much; and Glaucos accepted the deposit on the terms proposed. Then after a long time had gone by, there came to

Sparta the sons of him who had deposited the money with Glaucos; and they came to speech with Glaucos, and producing the tokens asked for the money to be given back: but he repulsed them answering them again thus: 'I do not remember the matter, nor does my mind bring back to me any knowledge of those things whereof ye speak; but I desire to recollect and do all that is just; for if I received it, I desire to restore it honestly; and if on the other hand I did not receive it at all, I will act towards you in accordance with the customs of the Hellenes:[76] therefore I defer the settling of the matter with you for three months from now.' (c) The Milesians accordingly went away grieved, for they supposed that they had been robbed of the money; but Glaucos set forth to Delphi to consult the Oracle: and when he inquired of the Oracle whether he should rob them of the money by an oath, the Pythian prophetess rebuked him with these lines:

"'Glaucos, thou, Epikydes' son, yea, this for the moment, This, to conquer their word by an oath and to rob, is more gainful. Swear, since the lot of death waits also for him who swears truly. But know thou that Oath has a son, one nameless and handless and footless, Yet without feet he pursues, without hands he seizes, and wholly He shall destroy the race and the house of the man who offendeth. But for the man who swears truly his race is the better hereafter.'

Having heard this Glaucos entreated that the god would pardon him for that which he had said, but the prophetess said that to make trial of the god and to do the deed were things equivalent. (d) Glaucos then, having sent for the Milesians, gave back to them the money: but the reason for which, O Athenians, I set forth to relate to you this story, shall now be told. At the present time there is no descendant of Glaucos existing, nor any hearth which is esteemed to be that of Glaucos, but he has been utterly destroyed and rooted up out of Sparta. Thus it is good not even to entertain a thought about a deposit other than that of restoring it, when they who made it ask for it again."

87. When Leotychides had thus spoken, since not even so were the Athenians willing to listen to him, he departed back; and the Eginetans, before paying the penalty for their former wrongs wherein they did outrage to the Athenians to please the Thebans,[77] acted as follows:—complaining of the conduct of the Athenians and thinking that they were being wronged, they made preparations to avenge themselves upon the Athenians; and since the Athenians were celebrating a four-yearly festival[78] at Sunion, they lay in wait for the sacred ship which was sent to it and took

it, the vessel being full of men who were the first among the Athenians; and having taken it they laid the men in bonds. 88. The Athenians after they had suffered this wrong from the Eginetans no longer delayed to contrive all things possible to their hurt. And there was[79] in Egina a man of repute, one Nicodromos the son of Cnithos:[80] this man had cause of complaint against the Eginetans for having before this driven him forth out of the island; and hearing now that the Athenians had resolved to do mischief to the Eginetans, he agreed with the Athenians to deliver up Egina to them, telling them on what day he would make his attempt and by what day it would be necessary for them to come to his assistance. 89. After this Nicodromos, according as he had agreed with the Athenians, seized that which is called the old city, but the Athenians did not come to his support at the proper time; for, as it chanced, they had not ships sufficient to fight with the Eginetans; so while they were asking the Corinthians to lend them ships, during this time their cause went to ruin. The Corinthians however, being at this time exceedingly friendly with them, gave the Athenians twenty ships at their request; and these they gave by selling them at five drachmas apiece, for by the law it was not permitted to give them as a free gift. Having taken these ships of which I speak and also their own, the Athenians with seventy ships manned in all sailed to Egina, and they were later by one day than the time agreed. 90. Nicodromos meanwhile, as the Athenians did not come to his support at the proper time, embarked in a ship and escaped from Egina, and with him also went others of the Eginetans; and the Athenians gave them Sunion to dwell in, starting from whence these men continued to plunder the Eginetans who were in the island. 91. This happened afterwards: but at the time of which we speak the well-to-do class among the Eginetans prevailed over the men of the people, who had risen against them in combination with Nicodromos, and then having got them into their power they were bringing their prisoners forth to execution. From this there came upon them a curse which they were not able to expiate by sacrifice, though they devised against it all they could; but they were driven forth from the island before the goddess became propitious to them. For they had taken as prisoners seven hundred of the men of the people and were bringing them forth to execution, when one of them escaped from his bonds and fled for refuge to the entrance of the temple of Demeter the Giver of Laws,[81] and he took hold of the latch of the door and clung to it; and when they found that they could not drag him from it by pulling him away, they cut off his hands and so carried him off, and those hands remained clinging to the latch of the door. 92. Thus did the Eginetans to one another: and when the Athenians came, they fought against them with seventy ships, and being worsted in the sea-fight they called to their assistance the same whom they had summoned before, namely the Argives. These would no longer come to their help, having cause of complaint because the ships of Egina compelled by Cleomenes had put in to the land of Argos and their crews had landed with the Lacedemonians; with whom also had landed men from ships of Sikyon in this same invasion: and as a penalty for this there was laid upon them by the Argives a fine of a thousand talents, five hundred for each State. The Sikyonians accordingly, acknowledging that they had committed a wrong, had made an agreement to pay a hundred talents and be free from the penalty; the Eginetans however did not acknowledge their wrong, but were more stubborn. For this reason then, when they made request, none of the Argives now came to their help at the charge of the State, but volunteers came to the number of a thousand; and their leader was a commander named Eurybates, a man who had practised the five contests.[82] Of these men the greater number never returned back, but were slain by the Athenians in Egina; and the commander himself, Eurybates, fighting in single combat[83] killed in this manner three men and was himself slain by the fourth, Sophanes namely of Dekeleia. 93. The Eginetans however engaged in contest with the Athenians in ships, when these were in disorder, and defeated them; and they took of them four ships together with their crews.

94. So the Athenians were at war with the Eginetans; and meanwhile the Persian was carrying forward his design, since he was put in mind ever by his servant to remember the Athenians, and also because of the sons of Peisistratos were near at hand and brought charges continually against the Athenians, while at the same time Dareios himself wished to take hold of this pretext and subdue those nations of Hellas which had not given him earth and water. Mardonios then, since he had fared miserably in his expedition, he removed from his command; and appointing other generals to command he despatched them against Eretria and Athens, namely Datis, who was a Mede by race, and Artaphrenes the son of Artaphrenes, a nephew of the king: and he sent them forth with the charge to reduce Athens and Eretria to slavery and to bring the slaves back into his presence. 95. When these who had been appointed to command came in their march from the king to the Aleïan plain in Kilikia, taking with them a large and well-equipped land-army, then while they were encamping there, the whole naval armament came up, which had been appointed for several nations to furnish; and there came to them also the ships for carrying horses, which in the year before Dareios had ordered his tributaries to make ready. In these they placed their horses, and having embarked the land-army in the ships they sailed for Ionia with six hundred triremes.

After this they did not keep their ships coasting along the mainland towards the Hellespont and Thrace, but they started from Samos and made their voyage by the Icarian Sea[84] and between the islands; because, as I think, they feared more than all else the voyage round Athos, seeing that in the former year[85] while making the passage by this way they had come to great disaster. Moreover also Naxos compelled them, since it had not been conquered at the former time.[86] 96. And when they had arrived at Naxos, coming against it from the Icarian Sea (for it was against Naxos first that the Persians intended to make expedition, remembering the former events), the Naxians departed forthwith fleeing to the mountains, and did not await their attack; but the Persians made slaves of those of them whom they caught and set fire to both the temples and the town. Having so done they put out to sea to attack the other islands.

97. While these were doing thus, the Delians also had left Delos and fled away to Tenos; and when the armament was sailing in thither, Datis sailed on before and did not allow the ships to anchor at the island of Delos, but at Rhenaia on the other side of the channel; and he himself, having found out by inquiry where the men of Delos were, sent a herald and addressed them thus: "Holy men, why are ye fled away and departed, having judged of me that which is not convenient? for even I of myself have wisdom at least so far, and moreover it has been thus commanded me by the king, not to harm at all that land in which the two divinities were born, neither the land itself nor the inhabitants of it. Now therefore return to your own possessions and dwell in your island." Thus he proclaimed by a herald to the Delians; and after this he piled up and burned upon the altar three hundred talents' weight of frankincense. 98. Datis having done these things sailed away with his army to fight against Eretria first, taking with him both Ionians and Aiolians; and after he had put out to sea from thence, Delos was moved, not having been shaken (as the Delians reported to me) either before that time or since that down to my own time; and this no doubt the god[86a] manifested as a portent to men of the evils that were about to be; for in the time of Dareios the son of Hystaspes and Xerxes the son of Dareios and Artoxerxes the son of Xerxes, three generations following upon one another, there happened more evils to Hellas than during the twenty other generations which came before Dareios, some of the evils coming to it from the Persians, and others from the leaders themselves of Hellas warring together for supremacy. Thus it was not unreasonable that Delos should be moved, which was before unmoved. [And in an oracle it was thus written about it:

"Delos too will I move, unmoved though it hath been aforetime. '][87]

Now in the Hellenic tongue the names which have been mentioned have this meaning—Dareios means "compeller,"[88] Xerxes "warrior,"[89] Artoxerxes "great warrior."[90] Thus then might the Hellenes rightly call these kings in their own tongue.

99. The Barbarians then, when they had departed from Delos, touched at the islands as they went, and from them received additional forces and took sons of the islanders as hostages: and when in sailing round about the islands they put in also to Carystos, seeing that the Carystians would neither give them hostages nor consent to join in an expedition against cities that were their neighbours, meaning Eretria and Athens, they began to besiege them and to ravage their land; until at last the Carystians also came over to the will of the Persians. 100. The Eretrians meanwhile being informed that the armament of the Persians was sailing to attack them, requested the Athenians to help them; and the Athenians did not refuse their support, but gave as helpers those four thousand to whom had been allotted the land of the wealthy[91] Chalkidians. The Eretrians however, as it turned out, had no sound plan of action, for while they sent for the Athenians, they had in their minds two different designs: some of them, that is, proposed to leave the city and go to the heights of Eubœa; while others of them, expecting to win gain for themselves from the Persian, were preparing to surrender the place. Having got knowledge of how things were as regards both these plans, Aischines the son of Nothon, one of the leaders of the Eretrians, told the whole condition of their affairs to those of the Athenians who had come, and entreated them to depart and go to their own land, that they might not also perish. So the Athenians did according to this counsel given to them by Aischines. 101. And while these passed over to Oropos and saved themselves, the Persians sailed on and brought their ships to land about Temenos and Chioreai and Aigilea in the Eretrian territory; and having taken possession of these places,[91a] forthwith they began to disembark their horses and prepared to advance against the enemy. The Eretrians however did not intend to come forth against them and fight; but their endeavour was if possible to hold out by defending their walls, since the counsel prevailed not to leave the city. Then a violent assault was made upon the wall, and for six days there fell many on both sides; but on the seventh day Euphorbos the son of Alkimachos and Philagros the son of Kyneos, men of repute among the citizens, gave up the city to the Persians. These having entered the city plundered and set fire to the temples in retribution for the temples which were burned at Sardis, and also reduced the people to slavery according to the commands of Dareios.

102. Having got Eretria into their power, they stayed a few days and then sailed for the land of Attica, pressing on[92] hard and supposing that the Athenians would do the same as the Eretrians had done. And since Marathon was the most convenient place in Attica for horsemen to act and was also very near to Eretria, therefore Hippias the son of Peisistratos was guiding them thither. 103. When the Athenians had information of this, they too went to Marathon to the rescue of their land; and they were led by ten generals, of whom the tenth was Miltiades, whose father Kimon of Stesagoras had been compelled to go into exile from Athens because of Peisistratos the son of Hippocrates: and while he was in exile it was his fortune to win a victory at the Olympic games with a four–horse chariot, wherein, as it happened, he did the same thing as his half–brother Miltiades[93] had done, who had the same mother as he. Then afterwards in the next succeeding Olympic games he gained a victory with the same mares and allowed Peisistratos to be proclaimed as victor; and having resigned to him the victory he returned to his own native land under an agreement for peace. Then after he had won with the same mares at another Olympic festival, it was his hap to be slain by the sons of Peisistratos, Peisistratos himself being no longer alive. These killed him near the City Hall, having set men to lie in wait for him by night; and the burial–place of Kimon is in the outskirts of the city, on the other side of the road which is called the way through Coile, and just opposite him those mares are buried which won in three Olympic games. This same thing was done also by the mares belonging to Euagoras the Laconian, but besides these by none others. Now the elder of the sons of Kimon, Stesagoras, was at that time being brought up in the house of his father's brother Miltiades in the Chersonese, while the younger son was being brought up at Athens with Kimon himself, having been named Miltiades after Miltiades the settler of the Chersonese. 104. This Miltiades then at the time of which we speak had come from the Chersonese and was a general of the Athenians, after escaping death in two forms; for not only did the Phenicians, who had pursued after him as far as Imbros, endeavour earnestly to take him and bring him up to the presence of the king, but also after this, when he had escaped from these and had come to his own native land and seemed to be in safety from that time forth, his opponents, who had laid wait for him there, brought him up before a court and prosecuted him for his despotism in the Chersonese. Having escaped these also, he had then been appointed a general of the Athenians, being elected by the people.

105. First of all, while they were still in the city, the generals sent off to Sparta a herald, namely Pheidippides[94] an Athenian and for the rest a runner of long

day-courses and one who practised this as his profession. With this man, as Pheidippides himself said and as he made report to the Athenians, Pan chanced to meet by mount Parthenion, which is above Tegea; and calling aloud the name of Pheidippides, Pan bade him report to the Athenians and ask for what reason they had no care of him, though he was well disposed to the Athenians and had been serviceable to them on many occasions before that time, and would be so also yet again. Believing that this tale was true, the Athenians, when their affairs had been now prosperously settled, established under the Acropolis a temple of Pan; and in consequence of this message they propitiate him with sacrifice offered every year and with a torch-race. 106. However at that time, the time namely when he said that Pan appeared to him, this Pheidippides having been sent by the generals was in Sparta on the next day after that on which he left the city of the Athenians; and when he had come to the magistrates he said: "Lacedemonians, the Athenians make request of you to come to their help and not to allow a city most anciently established among the Hellenes to fall into slavery by the means of Barbarians; for even now Eretria has been enslaved, and Hellas has become the weaker by a city of renown." He, as I say, reported to them that with which he had been charged, and it pleased them well to come to help the Athenians; but it was impossible for them to do so at once, since they did not desire to break their law; for it was the ninth day of the month, and on the ninth day they said they would not go forth, nor until the circle of the moon should be full.[95]

107. These men were waiting for the full moon: and meanwhile Hippias the son of Peisistratos was guiding the Barbarians in to Marathon, after having seen on the night that was just past a vision in his sleep of this kind,—it seemed to Hippias that he lay with his own mother. He conjectured then from the dream that he should return to Athens and recover his rule, and then bring his life to an end in old age in his own land. From the dream, I say, he conjectured this; and after this, as he guided them in, first he disembarked the slaves from Eretria on the island belonging to the Styrians, called Aigleia;[96] and then, as the ships came in to shore at Marathon, he moored them there, and after the Barbarians had come from their ships to land, he was engaged in disposing them in their places. While he was ordering these things, it came upon him to sneeze and cough more violently than was his wont. Then since he was advanced in years, most of his teeth were shaken thereby, and one of these teeth he cast forth by the violence of the cough:[97] and the tooth having fallen from him upon the sand, he was very desirous to find it; since however the tooth was not to be found when he searched, he groaned aloud and said to those who were by him: "This land is not

ours, nor shall we be able to make it subject to us; but so much part in it as belonged to me the tooth possesses."

108. Hippias then conjectured that his vision had been thus fulfilled: and meanwhile, after the Athenians had been drawn up in the sacred enclosure of Heracles, there joined them the Plataians coming to their help in a body: for the Plataians had given themselves to the Athenians, and the Athenians before this time undertook many toils on behalf of them; and this was the manner in which they gave themselves: —Being oppressed by the Thebans, the Plataians at first desired to give themselves to Cleomenes the son of Anaxandrides and to the Lacedemonians, who chanced to come thither; but these did not accept them, and said to them as follows: "We dwell too far off, and such support as ours would be to you but cold comfort; for ye might many times be reduced to slavery before any of us had information of it: but we counsel you rather to give yourselves to the Athenians, who are both neighbours and also not bad helpers." Thus the Lacedemonians counselled, not so much on account of their goodwill to the Plataians as because they desired that the Athenians should have trouble by being involved in a conflict with the Bœtians. The Lacedemonians, I say, thus counselled the men of Plataia; and they did not fail to follow their counsel, but when the Athenians were doing sacrifice to the twelve gods, they sat down as suppliants at the altar and so gave themselves. Then the Thebans having been informed of these things marched against the Plataians, and the Athenians came to their assistance: and as they were about to join battle, the Corinthians did not permit them to do so, but being by chance there, they reconciled their strife; and both parties having put the matter into their hands, they laid down boundaries for the land, with the condition that the Thebans should leave those of the Bœotians alone who did not desire to be reckoned with the other Bœotians. The Corinthians having given this decision departed; but as the Athenians were going back, the Bœotians attacked them, and having attacked them they were worsted in the fight. Upon that the Athenians passed beyond the boundaries which the Corinthians had set to be for the Plataians, and they made the river Asopos itself to be the boundary of the Thebans towards the land of Plataia and towards the district of Hysiai. The Plataians then had given themselves to the Athenians in the manner which has been said, and at this time they came to Marathon to bring them help.

109. Now the opinions of the generals of the Athenians were divided, and the one party urged that they should not fight a battle, seeing that they were too few to fight with the

army of the Medes, while the others, and among them Miltiades, advised that they should do so: and when they were divided and the worse opinion was like to prevail, then, since he who had been chosen by lot[98] to be polemarch of the Athenians had a vote in addition to the ten (for in old times the Athenians gave the polemarch an equal vote with the generals) and at that time the polemarch was Callimachos of the deme of Aphidnai, to him came Miltiades and said as follows: "With thee now it rests, Callimachos, either to bring Athens under slavery, or by making her free to leave behind thee for all the time that men shall live a memorial such as not even Harmodios and Aristogeiton have left. For now the Athenians have come to a danger the greatest to which they have ever come since they were a people; and on the one hand, if they submit to the Medes, it is determined what they shall suffer, being delivered over to Hippias, while on the other hand, if this city shall gain the victory, it may become the first of the cities of Hellas. How this may happen and how it comes to thee of all men[99] to have the decision of these matters, I am now about to tell. Of us the generals, who are ten in number, the opinions are divided, the one party urging that we fight a battle and the others that we do not fight. Now if we do not, I expect that some great spirit of discord will fall upon the minds of the Athenians and so shake them that they shall go over to the Medes; but if we fight a battle before any unsoundness appear in any part of the Athenian people, then we are able to gain the victory in the fight, if the gods grant equal conditions. These things then all belong to thee and depend on thee; for if thou attach thyself to my opinions, thou hast both a fatherland which is free and a native city which shall be the first among the cities of Hellas; but if thou choose the opinion of those who are earnest against fighting, thou shalt have the opposite of those good things of which I told thee." 110. Thus speaking Miltiades gained Callimachos to his side; and the opinion of the polemarch being added, it was thus determined to fight a battle. After this, those generals whose opinion was in favour of fighting, as the turn of each one of them to command for the day[100] came round, gave over their command to Miltiades; and he, accepting it, would not however yet bring about a battle, until his own turn to command had come. 111. And when it came round to him, then the Athenians were drawn up for battle in the order which here follows:— On the right wing the polemarch Callimachos was leader (for the custom of the Athenians then was this, that the polemarch should have the right wing); and he leading, next after him came the tribes in order as they were numbered one after another, and last were drawn up the Plataians occupying the left wing: for[101] ever since this battle, when the Athenians offer sacrifices in the solemn assemblies[102] which are made at the four-yearly festivals,[103] the herald of the Athenians prays thus, "that blessings[104] may come to the Athenians and to the Plataians both." On this occasion however, when the Athenians were being drawn up at Marathon something of this kind was done:—their army being made equal in length of front to that of the Medes, came to drawn up in the middle with a depth of but few ranks, and here their army was weakest, while each wing was strengthened with numbers. 112. And when they had been arranged in their places and the sacrifices proved favourable, then the Athenians were let go, and they set forth at a run to attack the Barbarians. Now the space between the armies was not less than eight furlongs:[105] and the Persians seeing them advancing to the attack at a run, made preparations to receive them; and in their minds they charged the Athenians with madness which must be fatal, seeing that they were few and yet were pressing forwards at a run, having neither cavalry nor archers.[106] Such was the thought of the Barbarians; but the Athenians when all in a body they had joined in combat with the Barbarians, fought in a memorable fashion: for they were the first of all the Hellenes about whom we know who went to attack the enemy at a run, and they were the first also who endured to face the Median garments and the men who wore them, whereas up to this time the very name of the Medes was to the Hellenes a terror to hear. 113. Now while they fought in Marathon, much time passed by; and in the centre of the army, where the Persians themselves and the Sacans were drawn up, the Barbarians were winning, —here, I say, the Barbarians had broken the ranks of their opponents and were pursuing them inland, but on both wings the Athenians and the Plataians severally were winning the victory; and being victorious they left that part of the Barbarians which had been routed to fly without molestation, and bringing together the two wings they fought with those who had broken their centre, and the Athenians were victorious. So they followed after the Persians as they fled, slaughtering them, until they came to the sea; and then they called for fire and began to take hold of the ships. 114. In this part of the work was slain the polemarch Callimachos after having proved himself a good man, and also one of the generals, Stesilaos the son of Thrasylaos, was killed; and besides this Kynegeiros the son of Euphorion while taking hold[107] there of the ornament at the stern of a ship had his hand cut off with an axe and fell; and many others also of the Athenians who were men of note were killed. 115. Seven of the ships the Athenians got possession of in this manner, but with the rest the Barbarians pushed off from land, and after taking the captives from Eretria off the island where they had left them, they sailed round Sunion, purposing to arrive at the city before the Athenians. And an accusation became current among the Athenians to the effect that they formed this design by contrivance of the Alcmaionidai; for these, it was said, having concerted matters with the Persians, displayed to them a shield when they had now embarked in their ships. 116. These then, I say, were sailing round Sunion; and meanwhile the Athenians came to the rescue back to the city as speedily as they could, and they arrived there before the Barbarians came; and having arrived from the temple of Heracles at Marathon they encamped at another temple of Heracles, namely that which is in Kynosarges. The Barbarians however came and lay with their ships in the sea which is off Phaleron, (for this was then the seaport of the Athenians), they anchored their ships, I say, off this place, and then proceeded to sail back to Asia.

117. In this fight at Marathon there were slain of the Barbarians about six thousand four hundred men, and of the Athenians a hundred and ninety and two. Such was the number which fell on both sides; and it happened also that a marvel occurred there of this kind:—an Athenian, Epizelos the son of Cuphagoras, while fighting in the close combat and proving himself a good man, was deprived of the sight of his eyes, neither having received a blow in any part of his body nor having been hit with a missile, and for the rest of his life from this time he continued to be blind: and I was informed that he used to tell about that which had happened to him a tale of this kind, namely that it seemed to him that a tall man in full armour stood against him, whose beard overshadowed his whole shield; and this apparition passed him by, but killed his comrade who stood next to him. Thus, as I was informed, Epizelos told the tale.

118. Datis, however, as he was going with his army to Asia, when he had come to Myconos saw a vision in his sleep; and of what nature the vision was it is not reported, but as soon as day dawned he caused a search to be made of the ships, and finding in a Phenician ship an image of Apollo overlaid with gold, he inquired from whence it had been carried off. Then having been informed from what temple it came, he sailed in his own ship to Delos: and finding that the Delians had returned then to the island, he deposited the image in the temple and charged the men of Delos to convey it back to Delion in the territory of the Thebans, which is situated by the sea-coast just opposite Chalkis. Datis having given this charge sailed away: the Delians however did not convey the statue back, but after an interval of twenty years the Thebans themselves brought it to Delion by reason of an oracle. 119. Now as to those Eretrians who had been reduced to slavery, Datis and Artaphrenes, when they reached Asia in their voyage, brought them up to Susa; and king Dareios, though he had great anger against the Eretrians before they were made captive, because the Eretrians had done wrong to him unprovoked, yet when he saw that they had been brought up to him and were in

his power, he did them no more evil, but established them as settlers in the Kissian land upon one of his own domains, of which the name is Ardericca: and this is distant two hundred and ten furlongs from Susa and forty from the well which produces things of three different kinds; for they draw from it asphalt, salt and oil, in the manner which here follows:—the liquid is drawn with a swipe, to which there is fastened half a skin instead of a bucket, and a man strikes this down into it and draws up, and then pours it into a cistern, from which it runs through into another vessel, taking three separate ways. The asphalt and the salt become solid at once, and the oil[108] which is called by the Persians rhadinake, is black and gives out a disagreeable smell. Here king Dareios established the Eretrians as settlers; and even to my time they continued to occupy this land, keeping still their former language. Thus it happened with regard to the Eretrians.

120. Of the Lacedemonians there came to Athens two thousand after the full moon, making great haste to be in time, so that they arrived in Attica on the third day after leaving Sparta: and though they had come too late for the battle, yet they desired to behold the Medes; and accordingly they went out to Marathon and looked at the bodies of the slain: then afterwards they departed home, commending the Athenians and the work which they had done.

121. Now it is a cause of wonder to me, and I do not accept the report, that the Alcmaionidai could ever have displayed to the Persians a shield by a previous understanding, with the desire that the Athenians should be under the Barbarians and under Hippias; seeing that they are evidently proved to have been haters of despots as much or more than Callias the son of Phainippos and father of Hipponicos, while Callias for his part was the only man of all the Athenians who dared, when Peisistratos was driven out of Athens, to buy his goods offered for sale by the State, and in other ways also he contrived against him everything that was most hostile: [122. Of this Callias it is fitting that every one should have remembrance for many reasons: first because of that which has been before said, namely that he was a man of excellence in freeing his country; and then also for that which he did at the Olympic games, wherein he gained a victory in the horse– race and was second in the chariot–race, and he had before this been a victor at the Pythian games, so that he was distinguished in the sight of all Hellenes by the sums which he expended; and finally because he showed himself a man of such liberality towards his daughters, who were three in number; for when they came to be of ripe age for marriage, he gave them a most magnificent dowry and

also indulged their inclinations; for whomsoever of all the Athenians each one of them desired to choose as a husband for herself, to that man he gave her.][109] 123, and similarly,[110] the Alcmaionidai were haters of despots equally or more[111] than he. Therefore this is a cause of wonder to me, and I do not admit the accusation that these they were who displayed the shield; seeing that they were in exile from the despots during their whole time, and that by their contrivance the sons of Peisistratos gave up their rule. Thus it follows that they were the men who set Athens free much more than Harmodios and Aristogeiton, as I judge: for these my slaying Hipparchos exasperated the rest of the family of Peisistratos, and did not at all cause the others to cease from their despotism; but the Alcmaionidai did evidently set Athens free, at least if these were in truth the men who persuaded the Pythian prophetess to signify to the Lacedemonians that they should set Athens free, as I have set forth before. 124. It may be said however that they had some cause of complaint against the people of the Athenians, and therefore endeavoured to betray their native city. But on the contrary there were no men in greater repute than they, among the Athenians at least, nor who had been more highly honoured. Thus it is not reasonable to suppose that by them a shield should have been displayed for any such purpose. A shield was displayed, however; that cannot be denied, for it was done: but as to who it was who displayed it, I am not able to say more than this.

125. Now the family of Alcmaionidai was distinguished in Athens in the earliest times also, and from the time of Alcmaion and of Megacles after him they became very greatly distinguished. For first Alcmaion the son of Megacles showed himself a helper of the Lydians from Sardis who came from Crœsus to the Oracle at Delphi, and assisted them with zeal; and Crœsus having heard from the Lydians who went to the Oracle that this man did him service, sent for him to Sardis; and when he came, he offered to give him a gift of as much gold as he could carry away at once upon his own person. With a view to this gift, its nature being such, Alcmaion made preparations and used appliances as follows: —he put on a large tunic leaving a deep fold in the tunic to hang down in front, and he draw on his feet the widest boots which he could find, and so went to the treasury to which they conducted him. Then he fell upon a heap of gold−dust, and first he packed in by the side of his legs so much of the gold as his boots would contain, and then he filled the whole fold of the tunic with the gold and sprinkled some of the gold dust on the hair of his head and took some into his mouth, and having so done he came forth out of the treasury, with difficulty dragging along his boots and resembling anything in the world rather than a man; for his mouth was

stuffed full, and every part of him was swelled out: and upon Crœsus came laughter when he saw him, and he not only gave him all that, but also presented him in addition with more not inferior in value to that. Thus this house became exceedingly wealthy, and thus the Alcmaion of whom I speak became a breeder of chariot-horses and won a victory at Olympia. 126. Then in the next generation after this, Cleisthenes the despot of Sikyon exalted the family, so that it became of much more note among the Hellenes than it had been formerly. For Cleisthenes the son of Arisonymos, the son of Myron, the son of Andreas, had a daughter whose name was Agariste; and as to her he formed a desire to find out the best man of all the Hellenes and to assign her to him in marriage. So when the Olympic games were being held and Cleisthenes was victor in them with a four- horse chariot, he caused a proclamation to be made, that whosoever of the Hellenes thought himself worthy to be the son-in-law of Cleisthenes should come on the sixtieth day, or before that if he would, to Sikyon; for Cleisthenes intended to conclude the marriage within a year, reckoning from the sixtieth day. Then all those of the Hellenes who had pride either in themselves or in their high descent,[112] came as wooers, and for them Cleisthenes had a running- course and a wrestling-place made and kept them expressly for their use. 127. From Italy came Smindyrides the son of Hippocrates of Sybaris, who of all men on earth reached the highest point of luxury (now Sybaris at this time was in the height of its prosperity), and Damasos of Siris, the son of that Amyris who was called the Wise; these came from Italy: from the Ionian gulf came Amphimnestos the son of Epistrophos of Epidamnos, this man from the Ionian gulf: from Aitolia came Males, the brother of that Titormos who surpassed all the Hellenes in strength and who fled from the presence of men to the furthest extremities of the Aitolian land: from Peloponnesus, Leokedes the son of Pheidon the despot of the Argives, that Pheidon who established for the Peloponnesians the measures which they use, and who went beyond all other Hellenes in wanton insolence, since he removed from their place the presidents of the games appointed by the Eleians and himself presided over the games at Olympia,—his son, I say, and Amiantos the son of Lycurgos an Arcadian from Trapezus, and Laphanes an Azanian from the city of Paios, son of that Euphorion who (according to the story told in Arcadia) received the Dioscuroi as guests in his house and from thenceforth was wont to entertain all men who came, and Onomastos the son of Agaios of Elis; these, I say, came from Peloponnesus itself: from Athens came Megacles the son of that Alcmaion who went to Crœsus, and besides him Hippocleides the son of Tisander, one who surpassed the other Athenians in wealth and in comeliness of form: from Eretria, which at that time was flourishing, came Lysanias, he alone from Eubœa: from

Thessalia came Diactorides of Crannon, one of the family of the Scopadai: and from the Molossians, Alcon. 128. So many in number did the wooers prove to be: and when these had come by the appointed day, Cleisthenes first inquired of their native countries and of the descent of each one, and then keeping them for a year he made trial continually both of their manly virtue and of their disposition, training and temper, associating both with each one separately and with the whole number together: and he made trial of them both by bringing out to bodily exercises those of them who were younger, and also especially in the common feast: for during all the time that he kept them he did everything that could be done, and at the same time he entertained them magnificently. Now it chanced that those of the wooers pleased him most who had come from Athens, and of these Hippocleides the son of Tisander was rather preferred, both by reason of manly virtues and also because he was connected by descent with the family of Kypselos at Corinth. 129. Then when the appointed day came for the marriage banquet and for Cleisthenes himself to declare whom he selected from the whole number, Cleisthenes sacrificed a hundred oxen and feasted both the wooers themselves and all the people of Sikyon; and when the dinner was over, the wooers began to vie with one another both in music and in speeches for the entertainment of the company;[113] and as the drinking went forward and Hippocleides was very much holding the attention of the others,[114] he bade the flute—player play for him a dance—measure; and when the flute—player did so, he danced: and it so befell that he pleased himself in his dancing, but Cleisthenes looked on at the whole matter with suspicion. Then Hippocleides after a certain time bade one bring in a table; and when the table came in, first he danced upon it Laconian figures, and then also Attic, and thirdly he planted his head upon the table and gesticulated with his legs. Cleisthenes meanwhile, when he was dancing the first and the second time, though he abhorred the thought that Hippocleides should now become his son—in—law, because of his dancing and his shamelessness, yet restrained himself, not desiring to break out in anger against him; but when he saw that he thus gesticulated with his legs, he was no longer able to restrain himself, but said: "Thou hast danced away thy marriage however,[115] son of Tisander!" and Hippocleides answered and said: "Hippocleides cares not!" 130, and hence comes this saying. Then Cleisthenes caused silence to be made, and spoke to the company as follows: "Men who are wooers of my daughter, I commend you all, and if it were possible I would gratify you all, neither selecting one of you to be preferred, nor rejecting the remainder. Since however it is not possible, as I am deliberating about one maiden only, to act so as to please all, therefore to those of you who are rejected from this marriage I give as a gift a talent of silver to each one for the worthy estimation ye had of me, in that ye desired to marry from my house. and for the time of absence from your homes; and to the son of Alcmaion, Megacles, I offer my daughter Agariste in betrothal according to the customs of the Athenians." Thereupon Megacles said that he accepted the betrothal, and so the marriage was determined by Cleisthenes.

131. Thus it happened as regards the judgment of the wooers, and thus the Alcmaionidai got renown over all Hellas. And these having been married, there was born to them that Cleisthenes who established the tribes and the democracy for the Athenians, he being called after the Sikyonian Cleisthenes, his mother's father; this son, I say, was born to Megacles, and also Hippocrates: and of Hippocrates came another Megacles and another Agariste, called after Agariste, the daughter of Cleisthenes, who having been married to Xanthippos the son of Ariphron and being with child, saw a vision in her sleep, and it seemed to her that she had brought forth a lion: then after a few days she bore to Xanthippos Pericles.

132. After the defeat at Marathon, Miltiades, who even before was well reputed with the Athenians, came then to be in much higher estimation: and when he asked the Athenians for seventy ships and an army with supplies of money, not declaring to them against what land he was intending to make an expedition, but saying that he would enrich them greatly if they would go with him, for he would lead them to a land of such a kind that they would easily get from it gold in abundance,— thus saying he asked for the ships; and the Athenians, elated by these words, delivered them over to him. 133. Then Miltiades, when he had received the army, proceeded to sail to Paris with the pretence that the Parians had first attacked Athens by making expedition with triremes to Marathon in company with the Persian: this was the pretext which he put forward, but he had also a grudge against the Parians on account of Lysagoras the son of Tisias, who was by race of Paros, for having accused him to Hydarnes the Persian. So when Miltiades had arrived at the place to which he was sailing, he began to besiege the Parians with his army, first having shut them up within their wall; and sending in to them a herald he asked for a hundred talents, saying that if they refused to give them, his army should not return back[116] until it had conquered them completely. The Parians however had no design of giving any money to Miltiades, but contrived only how they might defend their city, devising various things besides and also this,—wherever at any time the wall proved to be open to attack, that point was raised when night came on to double its former height. 134. So much of the story is reported by all the Hellenes, but as to what followed the Parians alone report, and they

say that it happened thus: —When Miltiades was at a loss, it is said, there came a woman to speech with him, who had been taken prisoner, a Parian by race whose name was Timo, an under–priestess[117] of the Earth goddesses;[118] she, they say, came into the presence of Miltiades and counselled him that if he considered it a matter of much moment to conquer Paros, he could do that which she should suggest to him; and upon that she told him her meaning. He accordingly passed through to the hill which is before the city and leapt over the fence of the temple of Demeter Giver of Laws,[119] not being able to open the door; and then having leapt over he went on towards the sanctuary[120] with the design of doing something within, whether it were that he meant to lay hands on some of the things which should not be touched, or whatever else he intended to do; and when he had reached the door, forthwith a shuddering fear came over him and he set off to go back the same way as he came, and as he leapt down from the wall of rough stones his thigh was dislocated, or, as others say, he struck his knee against the wall. 135. Miltiades accordingly, being in a wretched case, set forth to sail homewards, neither bringing wealth to the Athenians nor having added to them the possession of Paros, but having besieged the city for six–and–twenty days and laid waste the island: and the Parians being informed that Timo the under–priestess of the goddesses had acted as a guide to Miltiades, desired to take vengeance upon her for this, and they sent messengers to Delphi to consult the god, so soon as they had leisure from the siege; and these messengers they sent to ask whether they should put to death the under–priestess of the goddesses, who had been a guide to their enemies for the capture of her native city and had revealed to Miltiades the mysteries which might not be uttered to a male person. The Pythian prophetess however forbade them, saying that Timo was not the true author of these things, but since it was destined that Miltiades should end his life not well, she had appeared to guide him to his evil fate. 136. Thus the Pythian prophetess replied to the Parians: and the Athenians, when Miltiades had returned back from Paros, began to talk of him, and among the rest especially Xanthippos the son of Ariphron, who brought Miltiades up before the people claiming the penalty of death and prosecuted him for his deception of the Athenians: and Miltiades did not himself make his own defence, although he was present, for he was unable to do so because his thigh was mortifying; but he lay in public view upon a bed, while his friends made a defence for him, making mention much both of the battle which had been fought at Marathon and of the conquest of Lemnos, namely how he had conquered Lemnos and taken vengeance on the Pelasgians, and had delivered it over to the Athenians: and the people came over to his part as regards the acquittal from the penalty of death, but they imposed a fine of fifty talents for the wrong committed: and after this Miltiades died, his thigh having gangrened and mortified, and the fifty talents were paid by his son Kimon.

137. Now Miltiades son of Kimon had thus taken possession of the Lemnos:—After the Pelasgians had been cast out of Attica by the Athenians, whether justly or unjustly,—for about this I cannot tell except the things reported, which are these:—Hecataois on the one hand, the son of Hegesander, said in his history that it was done unjustly; for he said that when the Athenians saw the land which extends below Hymettos, which they had themselves given them[121] to dwell in, as payment for the wall built round the Acropolis in former times, when the Athenians, I say, saw that this land was made good by cultivation, which before was bad and worthless, they were seized with jealousy and with longing to possess the land, and so drove them out, not alleging any other pretext: but according to the report of the Athenians themselves they drove them out justly; for the Pelasgians being settled under Hymettos made this a starting–point and committed wrong against them as follows:—the daughters and sons of the Athenians were wont ever to go for water to the spring of Enneacrunos; for at that time neither they nor the other Hellenes as yet had household servants; and when these girls came, the Pelasgians in wantonness and contempt of the Athenians would offer them violence; and it was not enough for them even to do this, but at last they were found in the act of plotting an attack upon the city: and the narrators say that they herein proved themselves better men than the Pelasgians, inasmuch as when they might have slain the Pelasgians, who had been caught plotting against them, they did not choose to do so, but ordered them merely to depart out of the land: and thus having departed out of the land, the Pelasgians took possession of several older places and especially of Lemnos. The former story is that which was reported by Hecataios, while the latter is that which is told by the Athenians. 138. These Pelasgians then, dwelling after that in Lemnos, desired to take vengeance on the Athenians; and having full knowledge also of the festivals of the Athenians, they got[122] fifty– oared galleys and laid wait for the women of the Athenians when they were keeping festival to Artemis in Brauron; and having carried off a number of them from thence, they departed and sailed away home, and taking the women to Lemnos they kept them as concubines. Now when these women had children gradually more and more, they made it their practice to teach their sons both the Attic tongue and the manners of the Athenians. And these were not willing to associate with the sons of the Pelasgian women, and moreover if any of them were struck by any one of those, they all in a body came to the rescue and helped one another. Moreover the boys claimed to have authority over the

other boys and got the better of them easily. Perceiving these things the Pelasgians considered the matter; and when they took counsel together, a fear came over them and they thought, if the boys were indeed resolved now to help one another against the sons of the legitimate wives, and were endeavouring already from the first to have authority over them, what would they do when they were grown up to be men? Then they determined to put to death the sons of the Athenian women, and this they actually did; and in addition to them they slew their mothers also. From this deed and from that which was done before this, which the women did when they killed Thoas and the rest, who were their own husbands, it has become a custom in Hellas that all deeds of great cruelty should be called "Lemnian deeds." 139. After the Pelasgians had killed their own sons and wives, the earth did not bear fruit for them, nor did their women or their cattle bring forth young as they did before; and being hard pressed by famine and by childlessness, they sent to Delphi to ask for a release from the evils which were upon them; and the Pythian prophetess bade them pay such penalty to the Athenians as the Athenians themselves should appoint. The Pelasgians came accordingly to Athens and professed that they were willing to pay the penalty for all the wrong which they had done: and the Athenians laid a couch in the fairest possible manner in the City Hall, and having set by it a table covered with all good things, they bade the Pelasgians deliver up to them their land in that condition. Then the Pelasgians answered and said: "When with a North Wind in one single day a ship shall accomplish the voyage from your land to ours, then we will deliver it up," feeling assured that it was impossible for this to happen, since Attica lies far away to the South of Lemnos. 140. Such were the events which happened then: and very many years later, after the Chersonese which is by the Hellespont had come to be under the Athenians, Miltiades the son of Kimon, when the Etesian Winds blew steadily, accomplished the voyage in a ship from Elaius in the Chersonese to Lemnos, and proclaimed to the Pelasgians that they should depart out of the island, reminding them of the oracle, which the Pelasgians had never expected would be accomplished for them. The men of Hephaistia accordingly obeyed; but those of Myrina, not admitting that the Chersonese was Attica, suffered a siege, until at last these also submitted. Thus it was that the Athenians and Miltiades took possession of Lemnos. ——————

NOTES TO BOOK VI

1. *proboulous.*

2. See i. 148.

3. *epi keras.*

4. *diekploon poieumenos tesi neusi di alleleon.*

5. *tou Dareiou*: a conjecture based upon Valla's translation. The MSS. have *ton Dareion.*

6. *prophasios epilabomenoi.*

6a. *en stele anagraphenai patrothen.*

7. "were very roughly handled."

8. *epibateuontas.*

8a. *nuktos te gar*: so Stein for *nuktos te.*

9. *kat akres*, lit. "from the top downwards," i.e. town and citadel both.

10. See ch. 77.

11. See i. 92 and v. 36.

11a. *Kalen akten.*

12. Possibly the reading should be *Inuka*, "Inyx."

13. *ton en te naumakhie*: perhaps we should read *ten en te naumakhin*, "which took place in the sea–fight."

14. *en Koiloisi kaleomenoisi.*

15. *grammata didaskomenoisi.*

16. *limainouses*: a conjectural reading for *deimainouses*.

17. Lit. "and it became in fact the work of the cavalry."

18. *esagenouon*.

19. Or (according to some good MSS.) "Thelymbria."

20. Cp. iii. 120.

21. *stadioi*: the distances here mentioned are equal to a little more than four and a little less than fifty miles respectively.

22. *en gnome gegonos*.

23. *pituos tropon*: the old name of the town was Pityussa.

24. That is to say, Kimon was his half–brother, and Stesagoras and the younger Miltiades his nephews.

25. See ch. 103.

26. *delade*.

27. *eleuthee*, but the meaning must be this, and it is explained by the clause, *trito men gar etei k.t.l.*

28. *stadia*: see v. 52, note 40.

29. See iii. 80.

30. *entos Makedonon*, "on their side of the Macedonians."

30a. Or (according to some MSS.) "about three hundred."

31. Or "Scaptesyle." (The Medicean MS. however has *skaptes ules*, not *skaptesules*, as reported by Stein.)

32. *ta proiskheto aiteon*, "that which he put forward demanding it."

33. i.e. "ram."

34. *ton geraiteron*.

35. *en to demosio*.

36. This is commonly understood to mean, leaving out of account the god who was father of Perseus; but the reason for stopping short at Perseus is given afterwards, and the expression *tou theou apeontos* refers perhaps rather to the case of Heracles, the legend of whose birth is rejected by Herodotus (see ii. 43), and rejected also by this genealogy, which passes through Amphitryon up to Perseus. I take it that *tou theou apeontos* means "reckoning Heracles" (who is mentioned by name just below in this connexion) "as the son of Amphitryon and not of Zeus."

37. i.e. "of heaven."

38. *medimnon*, the Lacedemonian *medimnos* being equal to rather more than two bushels.

39. *tetarten Lakomiken*, quantity uncertain.

40. *proxeinous*.

41. *khoinikas*. There were 48 *khoinikes* in the *medimnos*.

42. *kotulen*.

42a. The loose manner in which this is expressed, leaving it uncertain whether each king was supposed by the writer to have two votes given for him (cp. Thuc. i. 20), or whether the double vote was one for each king, must of course be reproduced in the translation.

43. *perioikon.*

44. See ch. 51.

45. *proergazomenon*: a conjectural emendation of *prosergazomenon.*

46. *tes apates te paragoge,* "by the misleading of the deception."

47. i.e. lunar months.

48. *en thoko katemeno.*

49. *pandemei.*

50. *aren.*

51. i.e. "prayed for by the people."

52. *di a*: a conjectural emendation of *dia ta.* Some Editors suppose that other words have dropped out.

53. *promantin*: cp. vii. III.

54. *ton splagkhnon.*

55. *tou erkeiou.*

56. *ton mataioteron logon legontes.*

57. Lit. "on the third night after the first," but the meaning is as given.

58. Most of the MSS. have "Astrobacos," which may be right.

59. Or "to the honour of the Lacedemonians."

60. i.e. any more than his predecessor.

61. See ch. 50.

62. *neotera epresse pregmata.*

63. *up Arkadon*: several good MSS. have *ton Arkadon*, which is adopted by some Editors. The meaning would be "near this city it is said that there is the Styx water of the Arcadians."

64. *upomargoteron.*

65. Demeter and Core.

66. The MSS. give also "Sepeia" and "Sipeia." The place is not elsewhere mentioned.

67. See ch. 19.

68. *duo mneai*: cp. v. 77.

69. *o theos*, i.e. Hera: cp. i. 105.

70. *kalliereumeno.*

71. *kat akres*: cp. ch. 18.

72. i.e. was acquitted of the charge brought against him.

73. *episkuthison.*

74. *bouleuesthe*: some MSS. and editions have *boulesthe*, "desiring."

75. *en khrono ikneumeno.*

76. i.e. take an oath to that effect.

77. See v. 80.

78. *penteteris*. The reading *penteres*, which is given by most of the MSS. and by several Editors, can hardly be defended.

79. *kai en gar*, "and since there was."

80. *Knoithou kaleomenos*: cp. vii. 143.

81. *thesmophorou*.

82. *pentaethlon epaskesas*.

83. *mounomakhien epaskeon*, "practising single combat," as if training for the games.

84. *para te Ikarion*: the use of *para* and the absence of the article may justify the conjecture *para te Ikarion* (or *Ikaron*) "by Icaria" (or "Icaros"), the island from which the Icarian Sea had its name.

85. This perhaps should be emended, for the event referred to occurred two years before, cp. ch. 46 and 48. The reading *trito proteron etei* has been proposed.

86. See v. 33 ff.

86a. i.e. Apollo: or perhaps more generally, "God," as in ch. 27.

87. This in brackets is probably an interpolation. It is omitted by some of the best MSS. Some Editors suspect the genuineness of the next four lines also, on internal grounds.

88. *erxies*, perhaps meaning "worker."

89. *areios*.

90. *megas areios*.

91. *ippoboteon*, lit. "horse–breeding": see v. 77.

91a. Or (according to some MSS.), "having come to shore at these places."

92. *katergontes*: the word is not elsewhere found intransitive, yet it is rather difficult to supply *tous Athenaious*. Some alterations have been proposed, but none probable.

93. Lit. "and it happened that in winning this victory he won the same victory as his half–brother Miltiades." See ch. 36.

94. Or, according to some authorities, "Philippides."

95. Lit. "except the circle were full."

96. Or "Aigileia."

97. Lit. "by violence, having coughed."

98. "by the bean."

99. *es se toi*, a conjectural emendation of *es se ti*.

100. *prutaneie tes emeres*.

101. Some Editors propose to omit *gar* or alter it. If it be allowed to stand, the meaning must be that the importance of the place is testified by the commemoration mentioned.

102. *es tas panegurias*, some MSS. have *kai panegurias*, "hold sacrifices and solemn assemblies."

103. *penteterisi*.

104. Lit. "the good things."

105. *stadioi*: the distance would be rather over 1600 yards.

106. Whether this is thrown in here by the historian as an explanation of the rapid advance, or as an additional source of wonder on the part of the Persians at the

boldness of the Athenians, is not clear.

107. Or (according to some MSS.) "having taken hold."

108. The account of how the oil was dealt with has perhaps dropt out: one MS. and the Aldine edition have "the oil they collect in vessels, and this," etc.

109. This chapter is omitted by several of the best MSS., and is almost certainly an interpolation. (In the Medicean MS. it has been added in the margin by a later hand.)

110. Answering to "Callias for his part" at the end of ch. 121, the connexion being broken by the interpolated passage.

111. *ouden esson.*

112. *patre*, "family," or possibly "country," as in ch. 128.

113. *to legomeno es to meson*: perhaps only "general conversation."

114. *katekhon pollon tous allous.*

115. i.e. "though the dancing may be good."

116. *aponostesein*: some MSS. have *apanastesein*, "he would not take away his army thence."

117. *upozakoron.*

118. *ton khthonion theon*, i.e. Demeter and Persephone: cp. vii. 153.

119. *thesmophorou.*

120. *to megaron.*

121. *sphi autoi*: a conjectural rendering of *sphisi autoisi*, which can only be taken with *eousan*, meaning "belonging to them" i.e. the Athenians, and involves the insertion of

Pelasgoisi or something equivalent with *edosan*.

122. *ktesamenoi*: some MSS. and editions have *stesamenoi*, "set fifty–oared galleys in place."

BOOK VII. THE SEVENTH BOOK OF THE HISTORIES, CALLED POLYMNIA

1. Now when the report came to Dareios the son of Hystaspes of the battle which was fought at Marathon, the king, who even before this had been greatly exasperated with the Athenians on account of the attack made upon Sardis, then far more than before displayed indignation, and was far more desirous of making a march against Hellas. Accordingly at once he sent messengers to the various cities and ordered that they should get ready a force, appointing to each people to supply much more than at the former time, and not only ships of war, but also horses and provisions and transport vessels;[1] and when these commands were carried round, all Asia was moved for three years, for all the best men were being enlisted for the expedition against Hellas, and were making preparations. In the fourth year however the Egyptians, who had been reduced to subjection by Cambyses, revolted from the Persians; and then he was even more desirous of marching against both these nations.

2. While Dareios was thus preparing to set out against Egypt and against Athens, there arose a great strife among his sons about the supreme power; and they said that he must not make his expeditions until he had designated one of them to be king, according to the custom of the Persians. For to Dareios already before he became king three sons had been born of his former wife the daughter of Gobryas, and after he became king four other sons of Atossa the daughter of Cyrus: of the first the eldest was Artobazanes, and of those who had been born later, Xerxes. These being not of the same mother were at strife with one another, Artobazanes contending that he was the eldest of all the sons, and that it was a custom maintained by all men that the eldest should have the rule, and Xerxes arguing that he was the son of Atossa the daughter of Cyrus, and that Cyrus was he who had won for the Persians their freedom. 3. Now while Dareios did not as yet declare his judgment, it chanced that Demaratos also, the son of Ariston, had come up to Susa at this very same time, having been deprived of the kingdom in Sparta and having laid upon himself a sentence of exile from

Lacedemon. This man, hearing of the difference between the sons of Dareios, came (as it is reported of him) and counselled Xerxes to say in addition to those things which he was wont to say, that he had been born to Dareios at the time when he was already reigning as king and was holding the supreme power over the Persians, while Artobazanes had been born while Dareios was still in a private station: it was not fitting therefore nor just that another should have the honour before him; for even in Sparta, suggested Demaratos, this was the custom, that is to say, if some of the sons had been born first, before their father began to reign, and another came after, born later while he was reigning, the succession of the kingdom belonged to him who had been born later. Xerxes accordingly made use of the suggestion of Demaratos; and Dareios perceiving that he spoke that which was just, designated him to be king. It is my opinion however that even without this suggestion Xerxes would have become king, for Atossa was all–powerful. 4. Then having designated Xerxes to the Persians as their king, Dareios wished to go on his expeditions. However in the next year after this and after the revolt of Egypt, it came to pass that Dareios himself died, having been king in all six–and–thirty years; and thus he did not succeed in taking vengeance either upon the revolted Egyptians or upon the Athenians.

5. Dareios being dead the kingdom passed to his son Xerxes. Now Xerxes at the first was by no means anxious to make a march against Hellas, but against Egypt he continued to gather a force. Mardonios however, the son of Gobryas, who was a cousin of Xerxes, being sister's son to Dareios, was ever at his side, and having power with him more than any other of the Persians, he kept continually to such discourse as this which follows, saying: "Master, it is not fitting that the Athenians, after having done to the Persians very great evil, should not pay the penalty for that which they have done. What if thou shouldest[2] at this present time do that which thou hast in thy hands to do; and when thou hast tamed the land of Egypt, which has broken out insolently against us, then do thou march an army against Athens, that a good report may be made of thee by men, and that in future every one may beware of making expeditions against thy land." Thus far his speech had to do with vengeance,[3] and to this he would make addition as follows, saying that Europe was a very fair land and bore all kinds of trees that are cultivated for fruit, and was of excellent fertility, and such that the king alone of all mortals was worthy to possess it. 6. These things he was wont to say, since he was one who had a desire for perilous enterprise and wished to be himself the governor of Hellas under the king. So in time he prevailed upon Xerxes and persuaded him to do this; for other things also assisted him and proved helpful to him

in persuading Xerxes. In the first place there had come from Thessaly messengers sent by the Aleuadai, who were inviting the king to come against Hellas and were showing great zeal in his cause, (now these Aleuadai were kings of Thessaly): and then secondly those of the sons of Peisistratos who had come up to Susa were inviting him also, holding to the same arguments as the Aleuadai; and moreover they offered him yet more inducement in addition to these; for there was one Onomacritos an Athenian, who both uttered oracles and also had collected and arranged the oracles of Musaios;[4] and with this man they had come up, after they had first reconciled the enmity between them. For Onomacritos had been driven forth from Athens by Hipparchos the son of Peisistratos, having been caught by Lasos of Hermion interpolating in the works of Musaios an oracle to the effect that the islands which lie off Lemnos should disappear[5] under the sea. For this reason Hipparchos drove him forth, having before this time been very much wont to consult him. Now however he had gone up with them; and when he had come into the presence of the king, the sons of Peisistratos spoke of him in magnificent terms, and he repeated some of the oracles; and if there was in them anything which imported disaster to the Barbarians, of this he said nothing; but choosing out of them the most fortunate things he told how it was destined that the Hellespont should be yoked with a bridge by a Persian, and he set forth the manner of the march. He then thus urged Xerxes with oracles, while the sons of Peisistratos and the Aleuadai pressed him with their advice.

7. So when Xerxes had been persuaded to make an expedition against Hellas, then in the next year after the death of Dareios he made a march first against those who had revolted. Having subdued these and having reduced all Egypt to slavery much greater than it had suffered in the reign of Dareios, he entrusted the government of it to Achaimenes his own brother, a son of Dareios. Now this Achaimenes being a governor of Egypt was slain afterwards by Inaros the son of Psammetichos, a Libyan. 8. Xerxes then after the conquest of Egypt, being about to take in hand the expedition against Athens, summoned a chosen assembly of the best men among the Persians, that he might both learn their opinions and himself in the presence of all declare that which he intended to do; and when they were assembled, Xerxes spoke to them as follows: (a) "Persians, I shall not be the first to establish this custom in your nation, but having received it from others I shall follow it: for as I am informed by those who are older than myself, we never yet have kept quiet since we received this supremacy in succession to the Medes, when Cyrus overthrew Astyages; but God thus leads us, and for ourselves tends to good that we are busied about many things. Now about the

nations which Cyrus and Cambyses and my father Dareios subdued and added to their possessions there is no need for me to speak, since ye know well: and as for me, from the day when I received by inheritance this throne upon which I sit[6] I carefully considered always how in this honourable place I might not fall short of those who have been before me, nor add less power to the dominion of the Persians: and thus carefully considering I find a way by which not only glory may be won by us, together with a land not less in extent nor worse than that which we now possess, (and indeed more varied in its productions), but also vengeance and retribution may be brought about. Wherefore I have assembled you together now, in order that I may communicate to you that which I have it in my mind to do. (b) I design to yoke the Hellespont with a bridge, and to march an army through Europe against Hellas, in order that I may take vengeance on the Athenians for all the things which they have done both to the Persians and to my father. Ye saw how my father Dareios also was purposing to make an expedition against these men; but he has ended his life and did not succeed in taking vengeance upon them. I however, on behalf of him and also of the other Persians, will not cease until I have conquered Athens and burnt it with fire; seeing that they did wrong unprovoked to me and to my father. First they went to Sardis, having come with Aristagoras the Milesian our slave, and they set fire to the sacred groves and the temples; and then secondly, what things they did to us when we disembarked in their land, at the time when Datis and Artaphrenes were commanders of our army, ye all know well, as I think.[7] (c) For these reasons[8] I have resolved to make an expedition against them, and reckoning I find in the matter so many good things as ye shall hear:—if we shall subdue these and the neighbours of these, who dwell in the land of Pelops the Phrygian, we shall cause the Persian land to have the same boundaries as the heaven of Zeus; since in truth upon no land will the sun look down which borders ours, but I with your help shall make all the lands into one land, having passed through the whole extent of Europe. For I am informed that things are so, namely that there is no city of men nor any race of human beings remaining, which will be able to come to a contest with us, when those whom I just now mentioned have been removed out of the way. Thus both those who have committed wrong against us will have the yoke of slavery, and also those who have not committed wrong. (d) And ye will please me best if ye do this:— whensoever I shall signify to you the time at which ye ought to come, ye must appear every one of you with zeal for the service; and whosoever shall come with a force best equipped, to him I will give gifts such as are accounted in our land to be the most honourable. Thus must these things be done: but that I may not seem to you to be following my own counsel alone, I propose the matter for discussion, bidding any one of you who desires it, declare his opinion."

Having thus spoken he ceased; 9, and after him Mardonios said: "Master, thou dost surpass not only all the Persians who were before thee, but also those who shall come after, since thou didst not only attain in thy words to that which is best and truest as regards other matters, but also thou wilt not permit the Ionians who dwell in Europe to make a mock of us, having no just right to do so: for a strange thing it would be if, when we have subdued and kept as our servants Sacans, Indians, Ethiopians, Assyrians, and other nations many in number and great, who have done no wrong to the Persians, because we desired to add to our dominions, we should not take vengeance on the Hellenes who committed wrong against us unprovoked. (a) Of what should we be afraid?—what gathering of numbers, or what resources of money? for their manner of fight we know, and as for their resources, we know that they are feeble; and we have moreover subdued already their sons, those I mean who are settled in our land and are called Ionians, Aiolians, and Dorians. Moreover I myself formerly made trial of marching against these men, being commanded thereto by thy father; and although I marched as far as Macedonia, and fell but little short of coming to Athens itself, no man came to oppose me in fight. (b) And yet it is true that the Hellenes make wars, but (as I am informed) very much without wise consideration, by reason of obstinacy and want of skill: for when they have proclaimed war upon one another, they find out first the fairest and smoothest place, and to this they come down and fight; so that even the victors depart from the fight with great loss, and as to the vanquished, of them I make no mention at all, for they are utterly destroyed. They ought however, being men who speak the same language, to make use of heralds and messengers and so to take up their differences and settle them in any way rather than by battles; but if they must absolutely war with one another, they ought to find out each of them that place in which they themselves are hardest to overcome, and here to make their trial. Therefore the Hellenes, since they use no good way, when I had marched as far as the land of Macedonia, did not come to the resolution of fighting with me. (c) Who then is likely to set himself against thee, O king, offering war, when thou art leading both all the multitudes of Asia and the whole number of the ships? I for my part am of opinion that the power of the Hellenes has not attained to such a pitch of boldness: but if after all I should prove to be deceived in my judgment, and they stirred up by inconsiderate folly should come to battle with us, they would learn that we are the best of all men in the matters of war. However that may be, let not anything be left untried; for nothing comes of itself, but from trial all things are wont to come to men."

10. Mardonios having thus smoothed over the resolution expressed by Xerxes had ceased speaking: and when the other Persians were silent and did not venture to declare an opinion contrary to that which had been proposed, then Artabanos the son of Hystaspes, being father's brother to Xerxes and having reliance upon that, spoke as follows: (a) "O king, if opinions opposed to one another be not spoken, it is not possible to select the better in making the choice, but one must accept that which has been spoken; if however opposite opinions be uttered, this is possible; just as we do not distinguish the gold which is free from alloy when it is alone by itself, but when we rub it on the touchstone in comparison with other gold, then we distinguish that which is the better. Now I gave advice to thy father Dareios also, who was my brother, not to march against the Scythians, men who occupied no abiding city in any part of the earth. He however, expecting that he would subdue the Scythians who were nomads, did not listen to me; but he made a march and came back from it with the loss of many good men of his army. But thou, O king, art intending to march against men who are much better than the Scythians, men who are reported to be excellent both by sea and on land: and the thing which is to be feared in this matter it is right that I should declare to thee. (b) Thou sayest that thou wilt yoke the Hellespont with a bridge and march an army through Europe to Hellas. Now supposing it chance that we are[9] worsted either by land or by sea, or even both, for the men are reported to be valiant in fight, (and we may judge for ourselves that it is so, since the Athenians by themselves destroyed that great army which came with Datis and Artaphrenes to the Attic land),—suppose however that they do not succeed in both, yet if they shall attack with their ships and conquer in a sea-fight, and then sail to the Hellespont and break up the bridge, this of itself, O king, will prove to be a great peril. (c) Not however by any native wisdom of my own do I conjecture that this might happen: I am conjecturing only such a misfortune as all but came upon us at the former time, when thy father, having yoked the Bosphorus of Thracia and made a bridge over the river Ister, had crossed over to go against the Scythians. At that time the Scythians used every means of entreaty to persuade the Ionians to break up the passage, to whom it had been entrusted to guard the bridges of the Ister. At that time, if Histiaios the despot of Miletos had followed the opinion of the other despots and had not made opposition to them, the power of the Persians would have been brought to an end. Yet it is a fearful thing even to hear it reported that the whole power of the king had come to depend upon one human creature.[10] (d) Do not thou therefore propose to go into any such danger when there is no need, but do as I say:—at the present time dissolve this assembly; and afterwards at whatever time it shall seem good to thee, when thou hast

considered prudently with thyself, proclaim that which seems to thee best: for good counsel I hold to be a very great gain; since even if anything shall prove adverse, the counsel which has been taken is no less good, though it has been defeated by fortune; while he who took counsel badly at first, if good fortune should go with him has lighted on a prize by chance, but none the less for that his counsel was bad. (e) Thou seest how God strikes with thunderbolts the creatures which stand above the rest and suffers them not to make a proud show; while those which are small do not provoke him to jealousy: thou seest also how he hurls his darts ever at those buildings which are the highest and those trees likewise; for God is wont to cut short all those things which stand out above the rest. Thus also a numerous army is destroyed by one of few men in some such manner as this, namely when God having become jealous of them casts upon them panic or thundering from heaven, then they are destroyed utterly and not as their worth deserves; for God suffers not any other to have high thoughts save only himself. (f) Moreover the hastening of any matter breeds disasters, whence great losses are wont to be produced; but in waiting there are many good things contained, as to which, if they do not appear to be good at first, yet one will find them to be so in course of time. (g) To thee, O king, I give this counsel: but thou son of Gobryas, Mardonios, cease speaking foolish words about the Hellenes, since they in no way deserve to be spoken of with slight; for by uttering slander against the Hellenes thou art stirring the king himself to make an expedition, and it is to this very end that I think thou art straining all thy endeavour. Let not this be so; for slander is a most grievous thing: in it the wrongdoers are two, and the person who suffers wrong is one. The slanderer does a wrong in that he speaks against one who is not present, the other in that he is persuaded of the thing before he gets certain knowledge of it, and he who is not present when the words are spoken suffers wrong in the matter thus,—both because he has been slandered by the one and because he has been believed to be bad by the other. (h) However, if it be absolutely needful to make an expedition against these men, come, let the king himself remain behind in the abodes of the Persians, and let us both set to the wager our sons; and then do thou lead an army by thyself, choosing for thyself the men whom thou desirest, and taking an army as large as thou thinkest good: and if matters turn out for the king as thou sayest, let my sons be slain and let me also be slain in addition to them; but if in the way which I predict, let thy sons suffer this, and with them thyself also, if thou shalt return back. But if thou art not willing to undergo this proof, but wilt by all means lead an army against Hellas, then I say that those who are left behind in this land will hear[11] that Mardonios, after having done a great mischief to the Persians, is torn by dogs and birds, either in the land of the

Athenians, or else perchance thou wilt be in the land of the Lacedemonians (unless indeed this should have come to pass even before that upon the way), and that thou hast at length been made aware against what kind of men thou art persuading the king to march."

11. Artabanos thus spoke; and Xerxes enraged by it made answer as follows: "Artabanos, thou art my father's brother, and this shall save thee from receiving any recompense such as thy foolish words deserve. Yet I attach to thee this dishonour, seeing that thou art a coward and spiritless, namely that thou do not march with me against Hellas, but remain here together with the women; and I, even without thy help, will accomplish all the things which I said: for I would I might not be descended from Dareios, the son of Hystaspes, the son of Arsames, the son of Ariaramnes, the son of Teïspes, or from Cyrus,[12] the son of Cambyses, the son of Teïspes, the son of Achaimenes, if I take not vengeance on the Athenians; since I know well that if we shall keep quiet, yet they will not do so, but will again[13] march against our land, if we may judge by the deeds which have been done by them to begin with, since they both set fire to Sardis and marched upon Asia. It is not possible therefore that either side should retire from the quarrel, but the question before us is whether we shall do or whether we shall suffer; whether all these regions shall come to be under the Hellenes or all those under the Persians: for in our hostility there is no middle course. It follows then now that it is well for us, having suffered wrong first, to take revenge, that I may find out also what is this terrible thing which I shall suffer if I lead an army against these men,—men whom Pelops the Phrygian, who was the slave of my forefathers, so subdued that even to the present day both the men themselves and their land are called after the name of him who subdued them."

12. Thus far was it spoken then; but afterwards when darkness came on, the opinion of Artabanos tormented Xerxes continually; and making night his counsellor he found that it was by no means to his advantage to make the march against Hellas. So when he had thus made a new resolve, he fell asleep, and in the night he saw, as is reported by the Persians, a vision as follows:—Xerxes thought that a man tall and comely of shape came and stood by him and said: "Art thou indeed changing thy counsel, O Persian, of leading an expedition against Hellas, now that thou hast made proclamation that the Persians shall collect an army? Thou dost not well in changing thy counsel, nor will he who is here present with thee excuse thee from it;[13a] but as thou didst take counsel in the day to do, by that way go." 13. After he had said this, Xerxes thought that he

who had spoken flew away; and when day had dawned he made no account of this dream, but gathered together the Persians whom he had assembled also the former time and said to them these words: "Persians, pardon me that I make quick changes in my counsel; for in judgment not yet am I come to my prime, and they who advise me to do the things which I said, do not for any long time leave me to myself. However, although at first when I heard the opinion of Artabanos my youthful impulses burst out,[14] so that I cast out unseemly words[15] against a man older than myself; yet now I acknowledge that he is right, and I shall follow his opinion. Consider then I have changed my resolve to march against Hellas, and do ye remain still." 14. The Persians accordingly when they heard this were rejoiced and made obeisance: but when night had come on, the same dream again came and stood by Xerxes as he lay asleep and said: "Son of Dareios, it is manifest then that thou hast resigned this expedition before the assembly of the Persians, and that thou hast made no account of my words, as if thou hadst heard them from no one at all. Now therefore be well assured of this:—if thou do not make thy march forthwith, there shall thence spring up for thee this result, namely that, as thou didst in short time become great and mighty, so also thou shalt speedily be again brought low." 15. Xerxes then, being very greatly disturbed by fear of the vision, started up from his bed and sent a messenger to summon Artabanos; to whom when he came Xerxes spoke thus: "Artabanos, at the first I was not discreet, when I spoke to thee foolish words on account of thy good counsel; but after no long time I changed my mind and perceived that I ought to do these things which thou didst suggest to me. I am not able however to do them, although I desire it; for indeed, now that I have turned about and changed my mind, a dream appears haunting me and by no means approving that I should do so; and just now it has left me even with a threat. If therefore it is God who sends it to me, and it is his absolute will and pleasure that an army should go against Hellas, this same dream will fly to thee also, laying upon thee a charge such as it has laid upon me; and it occurs to my mind that this might happen thus, namely if thou shouldst take all my attire and put it on, and then seat thyself on my throne, and after that lie down to sleep in my bed." 16. Xerxes spoke to him thus; and Artabanos was not willing to obey the command at first, since he did not think himself worthy to sit upon the royal throne; but at last being urged further he did that which was commanded, first having spoken these words: (a) "It is equally good in my judgment, O king, whether a man has wisdom himself or is willing to follow the counsel of him who speaks well: and thou, who hast attained to both these good things, art caused to err by the communications of evil men; just as they say that the Sea, which is of all things the most useful to men, is by blasts of winds falling upon it prevented from doing according to its own nature. I however, when I was evil spoken of by thee, was not so much stung with pain for this, as because, when two opinions were laid before the Persians, the one tending to increase wanton insolence and the other tending to check it and saying that it was a bad thing to teach the soul to endeavour always to have something more than the present possession,—because, I say, when such opinions as these were laid before us, thou didst choose that one which was the more dangerous both for thyself and for the Persians. (b) And now that thou hast turned to the better counsel, thou sayest that when thou art disposed to let go the expedition against the Hellenes, a dream haunts thee sent by some god, which forbids thee to abandon thy enterprise. Nay, but here too thou dost err, my son, since this is not of the Deity;[16] for the dreams of sleep which come roaming about to men, are of such nature as I shall inform thee, being by many years older than thou. The visions of dreams are wont to hover above us[17] in such form[18] for the most part as the things of which we were thinking during the day; and we in the days preceding were very much occupied with this campaign. (c) If however after all this is not such a thing as I interpret it to be, but is something which is concerned with God, thou hast summed the matter up in that which thou hast said: let it appear, as thou sayest, to me also, as to thee, and give commands. But supposing that it desires to appear to me at all, it is not bound to appear to me any the more if I have thy garments on me than if I have my own, nor any more if I take my rest in thy bed than if I am in thy own; for assuredly this thing, whatever it may be, which appears to thee in thy sleep, is not so foolish as to suppose, when it sees me, that it is thou, judging so because the garments are thine. That however which we must find out now is this, namely if it will hold me in no account, and not think fit to appear to me, whether I have my own garments or whether I have thine, but continue still to haunt thee;[19] for if it shall indeed haunt thee perpetually, I shall myself also be disposed to say that it is of the Deity. But if thou hast resolved that it shall be so, and it is not possible to turn aside this thy resolution, but I must go to sleep in thy bed, then let it appear to me also, when I perform these things: but until then I shall hold to the opinion which I now have." 17. Having thus said Artabanos, expecting that he would prove that Xerxes was speaking folly, did that which was commanded him; and having put on the garments of Xerxes and seated himself in the royal throne, he afterwards went to bed: and when he had fallen asleep, the same dream came to him which used to come to Xerxes, and standing over Artabanos spoke these words: "Art thou indeed he who endeavours to dissuade Xerxes from making a march against Hellas, pretending to have a care of him? However, neither in the future nor now at the present shalt thou escape unpunished for trying to turn away that which is destined to come to pass: and as for Xerxes, that which he must suffer if he disobeys, hath been shown already to the man himself." 18. Thus it seemed to Artabanos that the dream threatened him, and at the same time was just about to burn out his eyes with hot irons; and with a loud cry he started up from his bed, and sitting down beside Xerxes he related to him throughout the vision of the dream, and then said to him as follows: "I, O king, as one who has seen before now many great things brought to their fall by things less, urged thee not to yield in all things to the inclination of thy youth, since I knew that it was evil to have desire after many things; remembering on the one hand the march of Cyrus against the Massagetai, what fortune it had, and also that of Cambyses against the Ethiopians; and being myself one who took part with Dareios in the campaign against the Scythians. Knowing these things I had the opinion that thou wert to be envied of all men, so long as thou shouldest keep still. Since however there comes a divine impulse, and, as it seems, a destruction sent by heaven is taking hold of the Hellenes, I for my part am both changed in myself and also I reverse my opinions; and do thou signify to the Persians the message which is sent to thee from God, bidding them follow the commands which were given by thee at first with regard to the preparations to be made; and endeavour that on thy side nothing may be wanting, since God delivers the matter into thy hands." These things having been said, both were excited to confidence by the vision, and so soon as it became day, Xerxes communicated the matter to the Persians, and Artabanos, who before was the only man who came forward to dissuade him, now came forward to urge on the design.

19. Xerxes being thus desirous to make the expedition, there came to him after this a third vision in his sleep, which the Magians, when they heard it, explained to have reference to the dominion of the whole Earth and to mean that all men should be subject to him; and the vision was this:—Xerxes thought that he had been crowned with a wreath of an olive–branch and that the shoots growing from the olive– tree covered the whole Earth; and after that, the wreath, placed as it was about his head, disappeared. When the Magians had thus interpreted the vision, forthwith every man of the Persians who had been assembled together departed to his own province and was zealous by all means to perform the commands, desiring each one to receive for himself the gifts which had been proposed: and thus Xerxes was gathering his army together, searching every region of the continent. 20. During four full years from the conquest of Egypt he was preparing the army and the things that were of service for the army, and in the course of the fifth year[20] he began his campaign with a host of great multitude. For of all the armies of which we have knowledge this proved to be by far

the greatest; so that neither that led by Dareios against the Scythians appears anything as compared with it, nor the Scythian host, when the Scythians pursuing the Kimmerians made invasion of the Median land and subdued and occupied nearly all the upper parts of Asia, for which invasion afterwards Dareios attempted to take vengeance, nor that led by the sons of Atreus to Ilion, to judge by that which is reported of their expedition, nor that of the Mysians and Teucrians, before the Trojan war, who passed over into Europe by the Bosphorus and not only subdued all the Thracians, but came down also as far as the Ionian Sea[21] and marched southwards to the river Peneios. 21. All these expeditions put together, with others, if there be any, added to them,[22] are not equal to this one alone. For what nation did Xerxes not lead out of Asia against Hellas? and what water was not exhausted, being drunk by his host, except only the great rivers? For some supplied ships, and others were appointed to serve in the land– army; to some it was appointed to furnish cavalry, and to others vessels to carry horses, while they served in the expedition themselves also;[23] others were ordered to furnish ships of war for the bridges, and others again ships with provisions.

22. Then in the first place, since the former fleet had suffered disaster in sailing round Athos, preparations had been going on for about three years past with regard to Athos: for triremes lay at anchor at Elaius in the Chersonese, and with this for their starting point men of all nations belonging to the army worked at digging, compelled by the lash; and the men went to the work regularly in succession: moreover those who dwelt round about Athos worked also at the digging: and Bubares the son of Megabazos and Artachaies the son of Artaios, Persians both, were set over the work. Now Athos is a mountain great and famous, running down to the sea and inhabited by men: and where the mountain ends on the side of the mainland the place is like a peninsula with an isthmus about twelve furlongs[24] across. Here it is plain land or hills of no great size, extending from the sea of the Acanthians to that which lies off Torone; and on this isthmus, where Athos ends, is situated a Hellenic city called Sane: moreover there are others beyond Sane[25] and within the peninsula of Athos, all which at this time the Persian had resolved to make into cities of an island and no longer of the mainland; these are, Dion, Olophyxos, Acrothoon, Thyssos, Cleonai. 23. These are the cities which occupy Athos: and they dug as follows, the country being divided among the Barbarians by nations for the work:—at the city of Sane they drew a straight line across the isthmus, and when the channel became deep, those who stood lowest dug, while others delivered the earth as it was dug out to other men who stood above, as

upon steps, and they again to others when it was received, until they came to those that were highest; and these bore it away and cast it forth. Now the others except the Phenicians had double toil by the breaking down of the steep edges of their excavation; for since they endeavoured to make the opening at the top and that at the bottom both of the same measure, some such thing was likely to result, as they worked: but the Phenicians, who are apt to show ability in their works generally, did so in this work also; for when they had had assigned to them by lot so much as fell to their share, they proceeded to dig, making the opening of the excavation at the top twice as wide as the channel itself was to be; and as the work went forward, they kept contracting the width; so that, when they came to the bottom, their work was made of equal width with that of the others. Now there is a meadow there, in which there was made for them a market and a place for buying and selling; and great quantities of corn came for them regularly from Asia, ready ground. 24. It seems to me, making conjecture of this work, that Xerxes when he ordered this to be dug was moved by a love of magnificence and by a desire to make a display of his power and to leave a memorial behind him; for though they might have drawn the ships across the isthmus with no great labour, he bade them dig a channel for the sea of such breadth that two triremes might sail through, propelled side by side. To these same men to whom the digging had been appointed, it was appointed also to make a bridge over the river Strymon, yoking together the banks.

25. These things were being done by Xerxes thus; and meanwhile he caused ropes also to be prepared for the bridges, made of papyrus and of white flax,[26] appointing this to the Phenicians and Egyptians; and also he was making preparations to store provisions for his army on the way, that neither the army itself nor the baggage animals might suffer from scarcity, as they made their march against Hellas. Accordingly, when he had learnt by inquiry of the various places, he bade them make stores where it was most convenient, carrying supplies to different parts by merchant ships and ferry—boats from all the countries of Asia. So they conveyed the greater part of the corn[27] to the place which is called Leuke Acte in Thrace, while others conveyed stores to Tyrodiza of the Perinthians, others to Doriscos, others to Eïon on the Strymon, and others to Macedonia, the work being distributed between them.

26. During the time that these were working at the task which had been proposed to them, the whole land—army had been assembled together and was marching with Xerxes to Sardis, setting forth from Critalla in Cappadokia; for there it had been

ordered that the whole army should assemble, which was to go with Xerxes himself by the land: but which of the governors of provinces brought the best equipped force and received from the king the gifts proposed, I am not able to say, for I do not know that they even came to a competition in this matter. Then after they had crossed the river Halys and had entered Phrygia, marching through this land they came to Kelainai, where the springs of the river Maiander come up, and also those of another river not less than the Maiander, whose name is Catarractes;[28] this rises in the market—place itself of Kelainai and runs into the Maiander: and here also is hanging up in the city the skin of Marsyas the Silenos, which is said by the Phrygians to have been flayed off and hung up by Apollo. 27. In this city Pythios the son of Atys, a Lydian, was waiting for the king and entertained his whole army, as well as Xerxes himself, with the most magnificent hospitality: moreover he professed himself ready to supply money for the war. So when Pythios offered money, Xerxes asked those of the Persians who were present, who Pythios was and how much money he possessed, that he made this offer. They said: "O king, this is he who presented thy father Dareios with the golden plane—tree and the golden vine; and even now he is in wealth the first of all men of whom we know, excepting thee only." 28. Marvelling at the conclusion of these words Xerxes himself asked of Pythios then, how much money he had; and he said: "O king, I will not conceal the truth from thee, nor will I allege as an excuse that I do not know my own substance, but I will enumerate it to thee exactly, since I know the truth: for as soon as I heard that thou wert coming down to the Sea of Hellas, desiring to give thee money for the war I ascertained the truth, and calculating I found that I had of silver two thousand talents, and of gold four hundred myriads[29] of daric staters[30] all but seven thousand: and with this money I present thee. For myself I have sufficient livelihood from my slaves and from my estates of land." 29. Thus he said; and Xerxes was pleased by the things which he had spoken, and replied: "Lydian host, ever since I went forth from the Persian land I have encountered no man up to this time who was desirous to entertain my army, or who came into my presence and made offer of his own free will to contribute money to me for the war, except only thee: and thou not only didst entertain my army magnificently, but also now dost make offer of great sums of money. To thee therefore in return I give these rewards,—I make thee my guest—friend, and I will complete for thee the four hundred myriads of staters by giving from myself the seven thousand, in order that thy four hundred myriads may not fall short by seven thousand, but thou mayest have a full sum in thy reckoning, completed thus by me. Keep possession of that which thou hast got for thyself, and be sure to act always thus; for if thou doest so, thou wilt have no cause to repent either at the time or afterwards."

30. Having thus said and having accomplished his promise, he continued his march onwards; and passing by a city of the Phrygians called Anaua and a lake whence salt is obtained, he came to Colossai, a great city of Phrygia, where the river Lycos falls into an opening of the earth and disappears from view, and then after an interval of about five furlongs it comes up to view again, and this river also flows into the Maiander. Setting forth from Colossai towards the boundaries of the Phrygians and Lydians, the army arrived at the city of Kydrara, where a pillar[30a] is fixed, set up by Crœsus, which declares by an inscription that the boundaries are there. 31. From Phrygia then he entered Lydia; and here the road parts into two, and that which goes to the left leads towards Caria, while that which goes to the right leads to Sardis; and travelling by this latter road one must needs cross the river Maiander and pass by the city of Callatebos, where men live whose trade it is to make honey of the tamarisk–tree and of wheat–flour. By this road went Xerxes and found a plane–tree, to which for its beauty he gave an adornment of gold, and appointed that some one should have charge of it always in undying succession;[31] and on the next day he came to the city of the Lydians. 32. Having come to Sardis he proceeded first to send heralds to Hellas, to ask for earth and water, and also to give notice beforehand to prepare meals for the king; except that he sent neither to Athens nor Lacedemon to ask for earth, but to all the other States: and the reason why he sent the second time to ask for earth and water was this,—as many as had not given at the former time to Dareios when he sent, these he thought would certainly give now by reason of their fear: this matter it was about which he desired to have certain knowledge, and he sent accordingly.

33. After this he made his preparations intending to march to Abydos: and meanwhile they were bridging over the Hellespont from Asia to Europe. Now there is in the Chersonese of the Hellespont between the city of Sestos and Madytos, a broad foreland[32] running down into the sea right opposite Abydos; this is the place where no long time afterwards the Athenians under the command of Xanthippos the son of Ariphron, having taken Artaÿctes a Persian, who was the governor of Sestos, nailed him alive to a board with hands and feet extended (he was the man who was wont to take women with him to the temple of Protesilaos at Elaius and to do things there which are not lawful). 34. To this foreland they on whom this work was laid were making their bridges, starting from Abydos, the Phenicians constructing the one with ropes of white flax, and the Egyptians the other, which was made with papyrus rope.

Now from Abydos to the opposite shore is a distance of seven furlongs. But when the strait had been bridged over, a great storm came on and dashed together all the work that had been made and broke it up. Then when Xerxes heard it he was exceedingly enraged, and bade them scourge the Hellespont with three hundred strokes of the lash and let down into the sea a pair of fetters. Nay, I have heard further that he sent branders also with them to brand the Hellespont. However this may be, he enjoined them, as they were beating, to say Barbarian and presumptuous words as follows: "Thou bitter water, thy master lays upon thee this penalty, because thou didst wrong him not having suffered any wrong from him: and Xerxes the king will pass over thee whether thou be willing or no; but with right, as it seems, no man doeth sacrifice to thee, seeing that thou art a treacherous[33] and briny stream." The sea he enjoined them to chastise thus, and also he bade them cut off the heads of those who were appointed to have charge over the bridging of the Hellespont. 36. Thus then the men did, to whom this ungracious office belonged; and meanwhile other chief—constructors proceeded to make the bridges; and thus they made them:— They put together fifty—oared galleys and triremes, three hundred and sixty to be under the bridge towards the Euxine Sea, and three hundred and fourteen to be under the other, the vessels lying in the direction of the stream of the Hellespont (though crosswise in respect to the Pontus), to support the tension of the ropes.[34] They placed them together thus, and let down very large anchors, those on the one side[35] towards the Pontus because of the winds which blow from within outwards, and on the other side, towards the West and the Egean, because of the South—East[36] and South Winds. They left also an opening for a passage through, so that any who wished might be able to sail into the Pontus with small vessels, and also from the Pontus outwards. Having thus done, they proceeded to stretch tight the ropes, straining them with wooden windlasses, not now appointing the two kinds of rope to be used apart from one another, but assigning to each bridge two ropes of white flax and four of the papyrus ropes. The thickness and beauty of make was the same for both, but the flaxen ropes were heavier in proportion,[38] and of this rope a cubit weighed one talent. When the passage was bridged over, they sawed up logs of wood, and making them equal in length to the breadth of the bridge they laid them above the stretched ropes, and having set them thus in order they again fastened them above.[39] When this was done, they carried on brushwood, and having set the brushwood also in place, they carried on to it earth; and when they had stamped down the earth firmly, they built a barrier along on each side, so that the baggage— animals and horses might not be frightened by looking out over the sea.

37. When the construction of the bridges had been finished, and the works about Athos, both the embankments about the mouths of the channel, which were made because of the breaking of the sea upon the beach, that the mouths of it might not be filled up, and the channel itself, were reported to be fully completed, then, after they had passed the winter at Sardis, the army set forth from thence fully equipped, at the beginning of spring, to march to Abydos; and when it had just set forth, the Sun left his place in the heaven and was invisible, though there was no gathering of clouds and the sky was perfectly clear; and instead of day it became night. When Xerxes saw and perceived this, it became a matter of concern to him; and he asked the Magians what the appearance meant to portend. These declared that the god was foreshowing to the Hellenes a leaving[40] of their cities, saying that the Sun was the foreshower of events for the Hellenes, but the Moon for the Persians. Having been thus informed, Xerxes proceeded on the march with very great joy. 38. Then as he was leading forth his army on its march, Pythios the Lydian, being alarmed by the appearance in the heavens and elated by the gifts which he had received, came to Xerxes, and said as follows: "Master, I would desire to receive from thee a certain thing at my request, which, as it chances, is for thee an easy thing to grant, but a great thing for me, if I obtain it." Then Xerxes, thinking that his request would be for anything rather than that which he actually asked, said that he would grant it, and bade him speak and say what he desired. He then, when he heard this, was encouraged, and spoke these words: "Master, I have, as it chances, five sons, and it is their fortune to be all going together with thee on the march against Hellas. Do thou, therefore, O king, have compassion upon me, who have come to so great an age, and release from serving in the expedition one of my sons, the eldest, in order that he may be caretaker both of myself and of my wealth: but the other four take with thyself, and after thou hast accomplished that which thou hast in thy mind, mayest thou have a safe return home." 38. Then Xerxes was exceedingly angry and made answer with these words: "Thou wretched man, dost thou dare, when I am going on a march myself against Hellas, and am taking my sons and my brothers and my relations and friends, dost thou dare to make any mention of a son of thine, seeing that thou art my slave, who ought to have been accompanying me thyself with thy whole household and thy wife as well? Now therefore be assured of this, that the passionate spirit of man dwells within the ears; and when it has heard good things, it fills the body with delight, but when it has heard the opposite things to this, it swells up with anger. As then thou canst not boast of having surpassed the king in conferring benefits formerly, when thou didst to us good deeds and madest offer to do more of the same kind, so now that thou hast turned to shamelessness, thou shalt

receive not thy desert but less than thou deservest: for thy gifts of hospitality shall rescue from death thyself and the four others of thy sons, but thou shalt pay the penalty with the life of the one to whom thou dost cling most." Having answered thus, he forthwith commanded those to whom it was appointed to do these things, to find out the eldest of the sons of Pythios and to cut him in two in the middle; and having cut him in two, to dispose the halves, one on the right hand of the road and the other on the left, and that the army should pass between them by this way.

40. When these had so done, the army proceeded to pass between; and first the baggage–bearers led the way together with their horses, and after these the host composed of all kinds of nations mingled together without distinction: and when more than the half had gone by, an interval was left and these were separated from the king. For before him went first a thousand horsemen, chosen out of all the Persians; and after them a thousand spearmen chosen also from all the Persians, having the points of their spears turned down to the ground; and then ten sacred horses, called "Nesaian,"[41] with the fairest possible trappings. Now the horses are called Nesaian for this reason:—there is a wide plain in the land of Media which is called the Nesaian plain, and this plain produces the great horses of which I speak. Behind these ten horses the sacred chariot of Zeus was appointed to go, which was drawn by eight white horses; and behind the horses again followed on foot a charioteer holding the reins, for no human creature mounts upon the seat of that chariot. Then behind this came Xerxes himself in a chariot drawn by Nesaian horses, and by the side of him rode a charioteer, whose name was Patiramphes, son of Otanes a Persian. 41. Thus did Xerxes march forth out of Sardis; and he used to change, whenever he was so disposed, from the chariot to a carriage. And behind him went spearmen, the best and most noble of the Persians, a thousand in number, holding their spear–points in the customary way;[42] and after them another thousand horsemen chosen out from the Persians; and after the horsemen ten thousand men chosen out from the remainder of the Persians. This body went on foot; and of these a thousand had upon their spears pomegranates of gold instead of the spikes at the butt–end, and these enclosed the others round, while the remaining nine thousand were within these and had silver pomegranates. And those also had golden pomegranates who had their spear–points turned towards the earth, while those who followed next after Xerxes had golden apples. Then to follow the ten thousand there was appointed a body of ten thousand Persian cavalry; and after the cavalry there was an interval of as much as two furlongs. Then the rest of the host came marching without distinction.

42. So the army proceeded on its march from Lydia to the river Caïcos and the land of Mysia; and then setting forth from the Caïcos and keeping the mountain of Cane on the left hand, it marched through the region of Atarneus to the city of Carene. From this it went through the plain of Thebe, passing by the cities of Adramytteion and Antandros of the Pelasgians; and taking mount Ida on the left hand, it came on to the land of Ilion. And first, when it had stopped for the night close under mount Ida, thunder and bolts of lightning fell upon it, and destroyed here in this place a very large number of men.[43] 43. Then when the army had come to the river Scamander,—which of all rivers to which they had come, since they set forth from Sardis and undertook their march, was the first of which the stream failed and was not sufficient for the drinking of the army and of the animals with it,—when, I say, Xerxes had come to this river, he went up to the Citadel of Priam,[44] having a desire to see it; and having seen it and learnt by inquiry of all those matters severally, he sacrificed a thousand heifers to Athene of Ilion, and the Magians poured libations in honour of the heroes: and after they had done this, a fear fell upon the army in the night. Then at break of day he set forth from thence, keeping on his left hand the cities of Rhoition and Ophryneion and Dardanos, which last borders upon Abydos, and having on the right hand the Gergith Teucrians.

44. When Xerxes had come into the midst of Abydos,[45] he had a desire to see all the army; and there had been made purposely for him beforehand upon a hill in this place a raised seat of white stone,[46] which the people of Abydos had built at the command of the king given beforehand. There he took his seat, and looking down upon the shore he gazed both upon the land–army and the ships; and gazing upon them he had a longing to see a contest take place between the ships; and when it had taken place and the Phenicians of Sidon were victorious, he was delighted both with the contest and with the whole armament. 45. And seeing all the Hellespont covered over with the ships, and all the shores and the plains of Abydos full of men, then Xerxes pronounced himself a happy man, and after that he fell to weeping. 46. Artabanos his uncle therefore perceiving him,—the same who at first boldly declared his opinion advising Xerxes not to march against Hellas,— this man, I say, having observed that Xerxes wept, asked as follows: "O king, how far different from one another are the things which thou hast done now and a short while before now! for having pronounced thyself a happy man, thou art now shedding tears." He said: "Yea, for after I had reckoned up, it came into my mind to feel pity at the thought how brief was the whole life of man, seeing that of these multitudes not one will be alive when a hundred years have gone by." He then made answer and said: "To another evil more pitiful than this

we are made subject in the course of our life; for in the period of life, short as it is, no man, either of these here or of others, is made by nature so happy, that there will not come to him many times, and not once only, the desire to be dead rather than to live; for misfortunes falling upon us and diseases disturbing our happiness make the time of life, though short indeed, seem long: thus, since life is full of trouble, death has become the most acceptable refuge for man; and God, having given him to taste of the sweetness of life, is discovered in this matter to be full of jealousy." 47. Xerxes made answer saying: "Artabanos, of human life, which is such as thou dost define it to be, let us cease to speak, and do not remember evils when we have good things in hand: but do thou declare to me this:—If the vision of the dream had not appeared with so much evidence, wouldest thou still be holding thy former opinion, endeavouring to prevent me from marching against Hellas, or wouldest thou have changed from it? Come, tell me this exactly." He answered saying: "O king, may the vision of the dream which appeared have such fulfilment as we both desire! but I am even to this moment full of apprehension and cannot contain myself, taking into account many things besides, and also seeing that two things, which are the greatest things of all, are utterly hostile to thee." 48. To this Xerxes made answer in these words: "Thou strangest of men,[47] of what nature are these two things which thou sayest are utterly hostile to me? Is it that the land–army is to be found fault with in the matter of numbers, and that the army of the Hellenes appears to thee likely to be many times as large as ours? or dost thou think that our fleet will fall short of theirs? or even that both of these things together will prove true? For if thou thinkest that in these respects our power is deficient, one might make gathering at once of another force." 49. Then he made answer and said: "O king, neither with this army would any one who has understanding find fault, nor with the number of the ships; and indeed if thou shalt assemble more, the two things of which I speak will be made thereby yet more hostile: and these two things are—the land and the sea. For neither in the sea is there, as I suppose, a harbour anywhere large enough to receive this fleet of thine, if a storm should arise, and to ensure the safety of the ships till it be over; and yet not one alone[48] ought this harbour to be, but there should be such harbours along the whole coast of the continent by which thou sailest; and if there are not harbours to receive thy ships, know that accidents will rule men and not men the accidents. Now having told thee of one of the two things, I am about to tell thee of the other. The land, I say, becomes hostile to thee in this way:—if nothing shall come to oppose thee, the land is hostile to thee by so much the more in proportion as thou shalt advance more, ever stealing on further and further,[49] for there is no satiety of good fortune felt by men: and this I say, that with no one to stand against thee the country traversed, growing more and more as time goes on, will produce for thee famine. Man, however, will be in the best condition, if when he is taking counsel he feels fear, reckoning to suffer everything that can possibly come, but in doing the deed he is bold." 50. Xerxes made answer in these words: "Artabanos, reasonably dost thou set forth these matters; but do not thou fear everything nor reckon equally for everything: for if thou shouldest set thyself with regard to all matters which come on at any time, to reckon for everything equally, thou wouldest never perform any deed. It is better to have good courage about everything and to suffer half the evils which threaten, than to have fear beforehand about everything and not to suffer any evil at all: and if, while contending against everything which is said, thou omit to declare the course which is safe, thou dost incur in these matters the reproach of failure equally with him who says the opposite to this. This then, I say, is evenly balanced: but how should one who is but man know the course which is safe? I think, in no way. To those then who choose to act, for the most part gain is wont to come; but to those who reckon for everything and shrink back, it is not much wont to come. Thou seest the power of the Persians, to what great might it has advanced: if then those who came to be kings before me had had opinions like to thine, or, though not having such opinions, had had such counsellors as thou, thou wouldest never have seen it brought forward to this point. As it is however, by running risks they conducted it on to this: for great power is in general gained by running great risks. We therefore, following their example, are making our march now during the fairest season of the year; and after we have subdued all Europe we shall return back home, neither having met with famine anywhere nor having suffered any other thing which is unpleasant. For first we march bearing with us ourselves great store of food, and secondly we shall possess the corn-crops of all the peoples to whose land and nation we come; and we are making a march now against men who plough the soil, and not against nomad tribes." 51. After this Artabanos said: "O king, since thou dost urge us not to have fear of anything, do thou I pray thee accept a counsel from me; for when speaking of many things it is necessary to extend speech to a greater length. Cyrus the son of Cambyses subdued all Ionia except the Athenians, so that it was tributary to the Persians. These men therefore I counsel thee by no means to lead against their parent stock, seeing that even without these we are able to get the advantage over our enemies. For supposing that they go with us, either they must prove themselves doers of great wrong, if they join in reducing their mother city to slavery, or doers of great right, if they join in freeing her: now if they show themselves doers of great wrong, they bring us no very large gain in addition; but if they show themselves doers of great right, they are able then to cause

much damage to thy army. Therefore lay to heart also the ancient saying, how well it has been said that at the first beginning of things the end does not completely appear."
52. To this Xerxes made answer: "Artabanos, of all the opinions which thou hast uttered, thou art mistaken most of all in this; seeing that thou fearest lest the Ionians should change side, about whom we have a most sure proof, of which thou art a witness thyself and also the rest are witnesses who went with Dareios on his march against the Scythians,— namely this, that the whole Persian army then came to be dependent upon these men, whether they would destroy or whether they would save it, and they displayed righteous dealing and trustworthiness, and nought at all that was unfriendly. Besides this, seeing that they have left children and wives and wealth in our land, we must not even imagine that they will make any rebellion.[50] Fear not then this thing either, but have a good heart and keep safe my house and my government; for to thee of all men I entrust my sceptre of rule."

53. Having thus spoken and having sent Artabanos back to Susa, next Xerxes summoned to his presence the men of most repute among the Persians, and when they were come before him, he spoke to them as follows: "Persians, I assembled you together desiring this of you, that ye should show yourselves good men and should not disgrace the deeds done in former times by the Persians, which are great and glorious; but let us each one of us by himself, and all together also, be zealous in our enterprise; for this which we labour for is a common good for all. And I exhort you that ye preserve in the war without relaxing your efforts, because, as I am informed, we are marching against good men, and if we shall overcome them, there will not be any other army of men which will ever stand against us. Now therefore let us begin the crossing, after having made prayer to those gods who have the Persians[51] for their allotted charge."

54. During this day then they were making preparation to cross over; and on the next day they waited for the Sun, desiring to see him rise, and in the meantime they offered all kinds of incense upon the bridges and strewed the way with branches of myrtle. Then, as the Sun was rising, Xerxes made libation from a golden cup into the sea, and prayed to the Sun, that no accident might befall him such as should cause him to cease from subduing Europe, until he had come to its furthest limits. After having thus prayed he threw the cup into the Hellespont and with it a golden mixing–bowl and a Persian sword, which they call akinakes: but whether he cast them into the sea as an offering dedicated to the Sun, or whether he had repented of his scourging of the

Hellespont and desired to present a gift to the sea as amends for this, I cannot for certain say. 55. When Xerxes had done this, they proceeded to cross over, the whole army both the footmen and the horsemen going by one bridge, namely that which was on the side of the Pontus, while the baggage–animals and the attendants went over the other, which was towards the Egean. First the ten thousand Persians led the way, all with wreaths, and after them came the mixed body of the army made up of all kinds of nations: these on that day; and on the next day, first the horsemen and those who had their spear– points turned downwards, these also wearing wreaths; and after them the sacred horses and the sacred chariot, and then Xerxes himself and the spear–bearers and the thousand horsemen; and after them the rest of the army. In the meantime the ships also put out from shore and went over to the opposite side. I have heard however another account which says that the king crossed over the very last of all.

56. When Xerxes had crossed over into Europe, he gazed upon the army crossing under the lash; and his army crossed over in seven days and seven nights, going on continuously without any pause. Then, it is said, after Xerxes had now crossed over the Hellespont, a man of that coast exclaimed: "Why, O Zeus, in the likeness of a Persian man and taking for thyself the name of Xerxes instead of Zeus, art thou proposing to lay waste Hellas, taking with thee all the nations of men? for it was possible for thee to do so even without the help of these."

57. When all had crossed over, after they had set forth on their way a great portent appeared to them, of which Xerxes made no account, although it was easy to conjecture its meaning,—a mare gave birth to a hare. Now the meaning of this was easy to conjecture in this way, namely that Xerxes was about to march an army against Hellas very proudly and magnificently, but would come back again to the place whence he came, running for his life. There happened also a portent of another kind while he was still at Sardis,—a mule brought forth young and gave birth to a mule which had organs of generation of two kinds, both those of the male and those of the female, and those of the male were above. Xerxes however made no account of either of these portents, but proceeded on his way, and with him the land–army. 58. The fleet meanwhile was sailing out of the Hellespont and coasting along, going in the opposite direction to the land–army; for the fleet was sailing towards the West, making for the promontory of Sarpedon, to which it had been ordered beforehand to go, and there wait for the army; but the land–army meanwhile was making its march towards the East and the sunrising, through the Chersonese, keeping on its right the tomb of Helle the

daughter of Athamas, and on its left the city of Cardia, and marching through the midst of a town the name of which is Agora.[52] Thence bending round the gulf called Melas and having crossed over the river Melas, the stream of which did not suffice at this time for the army but failed,—having crossed, I say, this river, from which the gulf also has its name, it went on Westwards, passing by Ainos a city of the Aiolians, and by the lake Stentoris, until at last it came to Doriscos. [59] Now Doriscos is a sea-beach and plain of great extent in Thrace, and through it flows the great river Hebros: here a royal fortress had been built, the same which is now called Doriscos, and a garrison of Persians had been established in it by Dareios, ever since the time when he went on his march against the Scythians. It seemed then to Xerxes that the place was convenient to order his army and to number it throughout, and so he proceeded to do. The commanders of the ships at the bidding of Xerxes had brought all their ships, when they arrived at Doriscos, up to the sea-beach which adjoins Doriscos, on which there is situated both Sale a city of the Samothrakians, and also Zone, and of which the extreme point is the promontory of Serreion, which is well known; and the region belonged in ancient time to the Kikonians. To this beach then they had brought in their ships, and having drawn them up on land they were letting them get dry: and during this time he proceeded to number the army at Doriscos.

60. Now of the number which each separate nation supplied I am not able to give certain information, for this is not reported by any persons; but of the whole land-army taken together the number proved to be one hundred and seventy myriads:[53] and they numbered them throughout in the following manner:—they gathered together in one place a body of ten thousand men, and packing them together[54] as closely as they could, they drew a circle round outside: and thus having drawn a circle round and having let the ten thousand men go from it, they built a wall of rough stones round the circumference of the circle, rising to the height of a man's navel. Having made this, they caused others to go into the space which had been built round, until they had in this manner numbered them all throughout: and after they had numbered them, they ordered them separately by nations.

61. Now those who served were as follows:—The Persians with this equipment:—about their heads they had soft[55] felt caps called tiaras, and about their body tunics of various colours with sleeves, presenting the appearance of iron scales like those of a fish,[56] and about the legs trousers; and instead of the ordinary shields they had shields of wicker-work,[57] under which hung quivers; and they had short

spears and large bows and arrows of reed, and moreover daggers hanging by the right thigh from the girdle: and they acknowledged as their commander Otanes the father of Amestris the wife of Xerxes. Now these were called by the Hellenes in ancient time Kephenes; by themselves however and by their neighbours they were called Artaians: but when Perseus, the son of Danae and Zeus, came to Kepheus the son of Belos[58] and took to wife his daughter Andromeda, there was born to them a son to whom he gave the name Perses, and this son he left behind there, for it chanced that Kepheus had no male offspring: after him therefore this race was named. 62. The Medes served in the expedition equipped in precisely the same manner; for this equipment is in fact Median and not Persian: and the Medes acknowledged as their commander Tigranes an Achaimenid. These in ancient time used to be generally called Arians; but when Medea the Colchian came from Athens to these Arians, they also changed their name. Thus the Medes themselves report about themselves. The Kissians served with equipment in other respects like that of the Persians, but instead of the felt caps they wore fillets:[59] and of the Kissians Anaphes the son of Otanes was commander. The Hyrcanians were armed like the Persians, acknowledging as their leader Megapanos, the same who after these events became governor of Babylon. 63. The Assyrians served with helmets about their heads made of bronze or plaited in a Barbarian style which it is not easy to describe; and they had shields and spears, and daggers like the Egyptian knives,[60] and moreover they had wooden clubs with knobs of iron, and corslets of linen. These are by the Hellenes called Syrians, but by the Barbarians they have been called always[61] Assyrians: [among these were the Chaldeans]:[62] and the commander of them was Otaspes the son of Artachaies. 64. The Bactrians served wearing about their heads nearly the same covering as the Medes, and having native bows of reed and short spears. The Scaran Scythians had about their heads caps[63] which were carried up to a point and set upright and stiff; and they wore trousers, and carried native bows and daggers, and besides this axes of the kind called sagaris. These were called Amyrgian Sacans, being in fact Scythians; for the Persians call all the Scythians Sacans: and of the Bactrians and Sacans the commander was Hystaspes, the son of Dareios and of Atossa the daughter of Cyrus. 65. The Indians wore garments made of tree−wool, and they had bows of reed and arrows of reed with iron points. Thus were the Indians equipped; and serving with the rest they had been assigned to Pharnazathres the son of Artabates. 66. The Arians[64] were equipped with Median bows, and in other respects like the Bactrians: and of the Arians Sisamnes the son of Hydarnes was in command. The Parthians and Chorasmians and Sogdians and Gandarians and Dadicans served with the same equipment as the Bactrians. Of these the commanders were, Artabazos the son of Pharnakes of the Parthians and Chorasmians, Azanes the son of Artaios of the Sogdians, and Artyphios the son of Artabanos of the Gandarians and Dadicans. [67] The Caspians served wearing coats of skin[65] and having native bows of reed and short swords:[66] thus were these equipped; and they acknowledged as their leader Ariomardos the brother of Artyphios. The Sarangians were conspicuous among the rest by wearing dyed garments; and they had boots reaching up to the knee, and Median bows and spears: of these the commander was Pherendates the son of Megabazos. The Pactyans were wearers of skin coats[67] and had native bows and daggers: these acknowledged as their commander Artaÿntes the son of Ithamitres. 68. The Utians and Mycans and Paricanians were equipped like the Pactyans: of these the commanders were, Arsamenes the son of Dareios of the Utians and Mycans, and of the Paricanians Siromitres the son of Oiobazos. 69. The Arabians wore loose mantles[68] girt up, and they carried at their right side bows that bent backward[69] of great length. The Ethiopians had skins of leopards and lions tied upon them, and bows made of a slip[70] of palm−wood, which were of great length, not less than four cubits, and for them small arrows of reed with a sharpened stone at the head instead of iron, the same stone with which they engrave seals: in addition to this they had spears, and on them was the sharpened horn of a gazelle by way of a spear−head, and they had also clubs with knobs upon them. Of their body they used to smear over half with white,[71] when they went into battle, and the other half with red.[72] Of the Arabians and the Ethiopians who dwelt above Egypt the commander was Arsames, the son of Dareios and of Artystone, the daughter of Cyrus, whom Dareios loved most of all his wives, and had an image made of her of beaten gold. 70. Of the Ethiopians above Egypt and of the Arabians the commander, I say, was Arsames; but the Ethiopians from the direction of the sunrising (for the Ethiopians were in two bodies) had been appointed to serve with the Indians, being in no way different from the other Ethiopians, but in their language and in the nature of their hair only; for the Ethiopians from the East are straight−haired, but those of Libya have hair more thick and woolly than that of any other men. These Ethiopians from Asia were armed for the most part like the Indians, but they had upon their heads the skin of a horse's forehead flayed off with the ears and the mane, and the mane served instead of a crest, while they had the ears of the horse set up straight and stiff: and instead of shields they used to make defences to hold before themselves of the skins of cranes. 71. The Libyans went with equipments of leather, and they used javelins burnt at the point. These acknowledged as their commander Massages the son of Oarizos. 72. The Paphlagonians served with plaited helmets upon their heads, small shields, and spears of no great size, and also javelins and daggers; and about their feet native boots reaching up to the middle of the shin. The Ligyans and Matienians and Mariandynoi and Syrians served with the same equipment as the Paphlagonians: these Syrians are called by the Persians Cappadokians. Of the Paphlagonians and Matienians the commander was Dotos the son of Megasidros, and of the Mariandynoi and Lygians and Syrians, Gobryas, who was the son of Dareios and Artystone. 73. The Phrygians had an equipment very like that of the Paphlagonians with some slight difference. Now the Phrygians, as the Macedonians say, used to be called Brigians during the time that they were natives of Europe and dwelt with the Macedonians; but after they had changed into Asia, with their country they changed also their name and were called Phrygians. The Armenians were armed just like the Phrygians, being settlers from the Phrygians. Of these two together the commander was Artochmes, who was married to a daughter of Dareios. 74. The Lydians had arms very closely resembling those of the Hellenes. Now the Lydians were in old time called Medonians, and they were named again after Lydos the son of Atys, changing their former name. The Mysians had upon their heads native helmets, and they bore small shields and used javelins burnt at the point. These are settlers from the Lydians, and from mount Olympos they are called Olympienoi. Of the Lydians and Mysians the commander was Artaphrenes the son of Artaphrenes, he who invaded Marathon together with Datis. 75. The Thracians served having fox-skins upon their heads and tunics about their body, with loose mantles[68] of various colours thrown round over them; and about their feet and lower part of the leg they wore boots of deer-skin; and besides this they had javelins and round bucklers and small daggers. These when they had crossed over into Asia came to be called Bithynians, but formerly they were called, as they themselves report, Strymonians, since they dwelt upon the river Strymon; and they say that they were driven out of their abode by the Teucrians and Mysians. Of the Thracians who lived in Asia the commander was Bassakes the son of Artabanos. 76. ...[73] and they had small shields of raw ox-hide, and each man carried two hunting-spears of Lykian workmanship.[74] On their heads they wore helmets of bronze, and to the helmets the ears and horns of an ox were attached, in bronze, and upon them also there were crests; and the lower part of their legs was wrapped round with red-coloured strips of cloth. Among these men there is an Oracle of Ares. 77. The Meonian Cabelians, who are called Lasonians, had the same equipment as the Kilikians, and what this was I shall explain when in the course of the catalogue I come to the array of the Kilikians. The Milyans had short spears, and their garments were fastened on with buckles; some of them had Lykian bows, and about their heads they had caps made of leather. Of all these Badres the son of Hystanes was in command. 78. The Moschoi had wooden caps upon their heads, and shields and small spears, on which long points were set. The Tibarenians and Macronians and Mossynoicoi served with equipment like that of the Moschoi, and these were arrayed together under the following commanders,—the Moschoi and Tibarenians under Ariomardos, who was the son of Dareios and of Parmys, the daughter of Smerdis son of Cyrus; the Macronians and Mossynoicoi under Artaÿctes the son of Cherasmis, who was governor of Sestos on the Hellespont. 79. The Mares wore on their heads native helmets of plaited work, and had small shields of hide and javelins; and the Colchians wore wooden helmets about their heads, and had small shields of raw ox–hide and short spears, and also knives. Of the Mares and Colchians the commander was Pharandates the son of Teaspis. The Alarodians and Saspeirians served armed like the Colchians; and of these the commander was Masistios the son of Siromitres. 80. The island tribes which came with the army from the Erythraian Sea, belonging to the islands in which the king settles those who are called the "Removed,"[75] had clothing and arms very like those of the Medes. Of these islanders the commander was Mardontes the son of Bagaios, who in the year after these events was a commander of the army at Mykale and lost his life in the battle.

81. These were the nations which served in the campaign by land and had been appointed to be among the foot–soldiers. Of this army those who have been mentioned were commanders; and they were the men who sit it in order by divisions and numbered it and appointed commanders of thousands and commanders of tens of thousands, but the commanders of hundreds and of tens were appointed by the commanders of ten thousands; and there were others who were leaders of divisions and nations. 82. These, I say, who have been mentioned were commanders of the army; and over these and over the whole army together that went on foot there were in command Mardonios the son of Gobryas, Tritantaichmes the son of that Artabanos who gave the opinion that they should not make the march against Hellas, Smerdomenes the son of Otanes (both these being sons of brothers of Dareios and so cousins of Xerxes),[76] Masistes the son of Dareios and Atossa, Gergis the son of Ariazos, and Megabyzos the son of Zopyros. 83. These were generals of the whole together that went on foot, excepting the ten thousand; and of these ten thousand chosen Persians the general was Hydarnes the son of Hydarnes; and these Persians were called "Immortals," because, if any one of them made the number incomplete, being overcome either by death or disease, another man was chosen to his place, and they were never either more or fewer than ten thousand. Now of all the nations, the

Persians showed the greatest splendour of ornament and were themselves the best men. They had equipment such as has been mentioned, and besides this they were conspicuous among the rest for great quantity of gold freely used; and they took with them carriages, and in them concubines and a multitude of attendants well furnished; and provisions for them apart from the soldiers were borne by camels and beasts of burden.

84. The nations who serve as cavalry are these; not all however supplied cavalry, but only as many as here follow:—the Persians equipped in the same manner as their foot-soldiers, except that upon their heads some of them had beaten-work of metal, either bronze or iron. 85. There are also certain nomads called Sagartians, Persian in race and in language and having a dress which is midway between that of the Persians and that of the Pactyans. These furnished eight thousand horse, and they are not accustomed to have any arms either of bronze or of iron excepting daggers, but they use ropes twisted of thongs, and trust to these when they go into war: and the manner of fighting of these men is as follows:—when they come to conflict with the enemy, they throw the ropes with nooses at the end of them, and whatsoever the man catches by the throw,[77] whether horse or man, he draws to himself, and they being entangled in toils are thus destroyed. 86. This is the manner of fighting of these men, and they were arrayed next to the Persians. The Medes had the same equipment as their men on foot, and the Kissians likewise. The Indians were armed in the same manner as those of them who served on foot, and they both rode horses[78] and drove chariots, in which were harnessed horses or wild asses. The Bactrians were equipped in the same way as those who served on foot, and the Caspians likewise. The Libyans too were equipped like those who served on foot, and these also all drove chariots. So too the Caspians[79] and Paricanians were equipped like those who served on foot, and they all rode on camels, which in swiftness were not inferior to horses. 87. These nations alone served[80] as cavalry, and the number of the cavalry proved to be eight myriads,[81] apart from the camels and the chariots. Now the rest of the cavalry was arrayed in squadrons, but the Arabians were placed after them and last of all, for the horses could not endure the camels, and therefore they were placed last, in order that the horses might not be frightened. 88. The commanders of the cavalry were Harmamithras and Tithaios sons of Datis, but the third, Pharnuches, who was in command of the horse with them, had been left behind at Sardis sick: for as they were setting forth from Sardis, an accident befell him of an unwished-for kind,—as he was riding, a dog ran up under his horse's feet, and the horse not having seen it beforehand

was frightened, and rearing up he threw Pharnuches off his back, who falling vomited blood, and his sickness turned to a consumption. To the horse however they forthwith at the first did as he commanded, that is to say, the servants led him away to the place where he had thrown his master and cut off his legs at the knees. Thus was Pharnuches removed from his command.

89. Of the triremes the number proved to be one thousand two hundred and seven, and these were they who furnished them:—the Phenicians, together with the Syrians[82] who dwell in Palestine furnished three hundred; and they were equipped thus, that is to say, they had about their heads leathern caps made very nearly in the Hellenic fashion, and they wore corslets of linen, and had shields without rims and javelins. These Phenicians dwelt in ancient time, as they themselves report, upon the Erythraian Sea, and thence they passed over and dwell in the country along the sea coast of Syria; and this part of Syria and all as far as Egypt is called Palestine. The Egyptians furnished two hundred ships: these men had about their heads helmets of plaited work, and they had hollow shields with the rims large, and spears for sea–fighting, and large axes:[83] the greater number of them wore corslets, and they had large knives. 90. These men were thus equipped; and the Cyprians furnished a hundred and fifty ships, being themselves equipped as follows,—their kings had their heads wound round with fillets,[84] and the rest had tunics,[85] but in other respects they were like the Hellenes. Among these there are various races as follows,—some of them are from Salamis and Athens, others from Arcadia, others from Kythnos, others again from Phenicia and others from Ethiopia, as the Cyprians themselves report. 91. The Kilikians furnished a hundred ships; and these again had about their heads native helmets, and for shields they carried targets made of raw ox– hide: they wore tunics[86] of wool and each man had two javelins and a sword, this last being made very like the Egyptian knives. These in old time were called Hypachaians, and they got their later name from Kilix the son of Agenor, a Phenician. The Pamphylians furnished thirty ships and were equipped in Hellenic arms. These Pamphylians are of those who were dispersed from Troy together with Amphilochos and Calchas. 92. The Lykians furnished fifty ships; and they were wearers of corslets and greaves, and had bows of cornel–wood and arrows of reeds without feathers and javelins and a goat–skin hanging over their shoulders, and about their heads felt caps wreathed round with feathers; also they had daggers and falchions.[87] The Lykians were formerly called Termilai, being originally of Crete, and they got their later name from Lycos the son of Pandion, an Athenian. 93. The Dorians of Asia furnished thirty ships; and these had

Hellenic arms and were originally from the Peloponnese. The Carians supplied seventy ships; and they were equipped in other respects like Hellenes but they had also falchions and daggers. What was the former name of these has been told in the first part of the history.[88] 94. The Ionians furnished a hundred ships, and were equipped like Hellenes. Now the Ionians, so long time as they dwelt in the Peloponnese, in the land which is now called Achaia, and before the time when Danaos and Xuthos came to the Peloponnese, were called, as the Hellenes report, Pelasgians of the Coast-land,[89] and then Ionians after Ion the son of Xuthos. 95. The islanders furnished seventeen ships, and were armed like Hellenes, this also being a Pelasgian race, though afterwards it came to be called Ionian by the same rule as the Ionians of the twelve cities, who came from Athens. The Aiolians supplied sixty ships; and these were equipped like Hellenes and used to be called Pelasgians in the old time, as the Hellenes report. The Hellespontians, excepting those of Abydos (for the men of Abydos had been appointed by the king to stay in their place and be guards of the bridges), the rest, I say, of those who served in the expedition from the Pontus furnished a hundred ships, and were equipped like Hellenes: these are colonists of the Ionians and Dorians.

96. In all the ships there served as fighting—men Persians, Medes, or Sacans;: and of the ships, those which sailed best were furnished by the Phenicians, and of the Phenicians the best by the men of Sidon. Over all these men and also over those of them who were appointed to serve in the land—army, there were for each tribe native chieftains, of whom, since I am not compelled by the course of the inquiry,[89a] I make no mention by the way; for in the first place the chieftains of each separate nation were not persons worthy of mention, and then moreover within each nation there were as many chieftains as there were cities. These went with the expedition too not as commanders, but like the others serving as slaves; for the generals who had the absolute power and commanded the various nations, that is to say those who were Persians, having already been mentioned by me. 97. Of the naval force the following were commanders,—Ariabignes the son of Dareios, Prexaspes the son of Aspathines, Megabazos the son of Megabates, and Achaimenes the son of Dareios; that is to say, of the Ionian and Carian force Ariabignes, who was the son of Dareios and of the daughter of Gobryas; of the Egyptians Achaimenes was commander, being brother of Xerxes by both parents; and of the rest of the armament the other two were in command: and galleys of thirty oars and of fifty oars, and light vessels,[90] and long[91] ships to carry horses had been assembled together, as it proved, to the number

of three thousand. 98. Of those who sailed in the ships the men of most note after the commanders were these,—of Sidon, Tetramnestos son of Anysos; of Tyre, Matten[92] son of Siromos; or Arados, Merbalos son of Agbalos; of Kilikia, Syennesis son of Oromedon; of Lykia, Kyberniscos son of Sicas; of Cyprus, Gorgos son of Chersis and Timonax son of Timagoras; of Caria, Histiaios son of Tymnes, Pigres son of Hysseldomos,[93] and Damasithymos son of Candaules. 99. Of the rest of the officers I make no mention by the way (since I am not bound to do so), but only of Artemisia, at whom I marvel most that she joined the expedition against Hellas, being a woman; for after her husband died, she holding the power herself, although she had a son who was a young man, went on the expedition impelled by high spirit and manly courage, no necessity being laid upon her. Now her name, as I said, was Artemisia and she was the daughter of Lygdamis, and by descent she was of Halicarnassos on the side of her father, but of Crete by her mother. She was ruler of the men of Halicarnassos and Cos and Nisyros and Calydna, furnishing five ships; and she furnished ships which were of all the fleet reputed the best after those of the Sidonians, and of all his allies she set forth the best counsels to the king. Of the States of which I said that she was leader I declare the people to be all of Dorian race, those of Halicarnassos being Troizenians, and the rest Epidaurians. So far then I have spoken of the naval force.

100. Then when Xerxes had numbered the army, and it had been arranged in divisions, he had a mind to drive through it himself and inspect it: and afterwards he proceeded so to do; and driving through in a chariot by each nation, he inquired about them and his scribes wrote down the names, until he had gone from end to end both of the horse and of the foot. When he had done this, the ships were drawn down into the sea, and Xerxes changing from his chariot to a ship of Sidon sat down under a golden canopy and sailed along by the prows of the ships, asking of all just as he had done with the land–army, and having the answers written down. And the captains had taken their ships out to a distance of about four hundred feet from the beach and were staying them there, all having turned the prows of the ships towards the shore in an even line[94] and having armed all the fighting–men as for war; and he inspected them sailing within, between the prows of the ships and the beach.

101. Now when he had sailed through these and had disembarked from his ship, he sent for Demaratos the son of Ariston, who was marching with him against Hellas; and having called him he asked as follows: "Demaratos, now it is my pleasure to ask thee somewhat which I desire to know. Thou art not only a Hellene, but also, as I am

informed both by thee and by the other Hellenes who come to speech with me, of a city which is neither the least nor the feeblest of Hellas. Now therefore declare to me this, namely whether the Hellenes will endure to raise hands against me: for, as I suppose, even if all the Hellenes and the remaining nations who dwell towards the West should be gathered together, they are not strong enough in fight to endure my attack, supposing them to be my enemies.[95] I desire however to be informed also of thy opinion, what thou sayest about these matters." He inquired thus, and the other made answer and said: "O king, shall I utter the truth in speaking to thee, or that which will give pleasure?" and he bade him utter the truth, saying that he should suffer nothing unpleasant in consequence of this, any more than he suffered before. 102. When Demaratos heard this, he spoke as follows: "O king, since thou biddest me by all means utter the truth, and so speak as one who shall not be afterwards convicted by thee of having spoken falsely, I say this:—with Hellas poverty is ever an inbred growth, while valour is one that has been brought in, being acquired by intelligence and the force of law; and of it Hellas makes use ever to avert from herself not only poverty but also servitude to a master. Now I commend all the Hellenes who are settled in those Dorian lands, but this which I am about to say has regard not to tall, but to the Lacedemonians alone: of these I say, first that it is not possible that they will ever accept thy terms, which carry with them servitude for Hellas; and next I say that they will stand against thee in fight, even if all the other Hellenes shall be of thy party: and as for numbers, ask now how many they are, that they are able to do this; for whether it chances that a thousand of them have come out into the field, these will fight with thee, or if there be less than this, or again if there be more." 103. Xerxes hearing this laughed, and said: "Demaratos, what a speech is this which thou hast uttered, saying that a thousand men will fight with this vast army! Come tell me this:— thou sayest that thou wert thyself king of these men; wilt thou therefore consent forthwith to fight with ten men? and yet if your State is such throughout as thou dost describe it, thou their king ought by your laws to stand in array against double as many as another man; that is to say, if each of them is a match for ten men of my army, I expect of thee that thou shouldest be a match for twenty. Thus would be confirmed the report which is made by thee: but if ye, who boast thus greatly are such men and in size so great only as the Hellenes who come commonly to speech with me, thyself included, then beware lest this which has been spoken prove but an empty vaunt. For come, let me examine it by all that is probable: how could a thousand or ten thousand or even fifty thousand, at least if they were all equally free and were not ruled by one man, stand against so great an army? since, as thou knowest, we shall be more than a thousand coming about each one of them, supposing them to be in number five thousand. If indeed they were ruled by one man after our fashion, they might perhaps from fear of him become braver than it was their nature to be, or they might go compelled by the lash to fight with greater numbers, being themselves fewer in number; but if left at liberty, they would do neither of these things: and I for my part suppose that, even if equally matched in numbers, the Hellenes would hardly dare to fight with the Persians taken alone. With us however this of which thou speakest is found in single men,[96] not indeed often, but rarely; for there are Persians of my spearmen who will consent to fight with three men of the Hellenes at once: but thou hast had no experience of these things and therefore thou speakest very much at random." 104. To this Demaratos replied: "O king, from the first I was sure that if I uttered the truth I should not speak that which was pleasing to thee; since however thou didst compel me to speak the very truth, I told thee of the matters which concern the Spartans. And yet how I am at this present time attached to them by affection thou knowest better than any; seeing that first they took away from me the rank and privileges which came to me from my fathers, and then also they have caused me to be without native land and an exile; but thy father took me up and gave me livelihood and a house to dwell in. Surely it is not to be supposed likely that the prudent man will thrust aside friendliness which is offered to him, but rather that he will accept it with full contentment.[97] And I do not profess that I am able to fight either with ten men or with two, nay, if I had my will, I would not even fight with one; but if there were necessity or if the cause which urged me to the combat were a great one, I would fight most willingly with one of these men who says that he is a match for three of the Hellenes. So also the Lacedemonians are not inferior to any men when fighting one by one, and they are the best of all men when fighting in a body: for though free, yet they are not free in all things, for over them is set Law as a master, whom they fear much more even than thy people fear thee. It is certain at least that they do whatsoever that master commands; and he commands ever the same thing, that is to say, he bids them not flee out of battle from any multitude of men, but stay in their post and win the victory or lose their life. But if when I say these things I seem to thee to be speaking at random, of other things for the future I prefer to be silent; and at this time I spake only because I was compelled. May it come to pass however according to thy mind, O king."

105. He thus made answer, and Xerxes turned the matter to laughter and felt no anger, but dismissed him with kindness. Then after he had conversed with him, and had appointed Mascames son of Megadostes to be governor at this place Doriscos,

removing the governor who had been appointed by Dareios, Xerxes marched forth his army through Thrace to invade Hellas. 106. And Mascames, whom he left behind here, proved to be a man of such qualities that to him alone Xerxes used to send gifts, considering him the best of all the men whom either he himself or Dareios had appointed to be governors,—he used to send him gifts, I say, every year, and so also did Artaxerxes the son of Xerxes to the descendants of Mascames. For even before this march governors had been appointed in Thrace and everywhere about the Hellespont; and these all, both those in Thrace and in the Hellespont, were conquered by the Hellenes after this expedition, except only the one who was at Doriscos; but Mascames at Doriscos none were ever[98] able to conquer, though many tried. For this reason the gifts are sent continually for him from the king who reigns over the Persians. 107. Of those however who were conquered by the Hellenes Xerxes did not consider any to be a good man except only Boges, who was at Eïon: him he never ceased commending, and he honoured very highly his children who survived him in the land of Persia. For in truth Boges proved himself worthy of great commendation, seeing that when he was besieged by the Athenians under Kimon the son of Miltiades, though he might have gone forth under a truce and so returned home to Asia, he preferred not to do this, for fear that the king should that it was by cowardice that he survived; and he continued to hold out till the last. Then when there was no longer any supply of provisions within the wall, he heaped together a great pyre, and he cut the throats of his children, his wife, his concubines and his servants, and threw them into the fire; and after this he scattered all the gold and silver in the city from the wall into the river Strymon, and having so done he threw himself into the fire. Thus he is justly commended even to this present time by the Persians.

108. Xerxes from Doriscos was proceeding onwards to invade Hellas; and as he went he compelled those who successively came in his way, to join his march: for the whole country as far as Thessaly had been reduced to subjection, as has been set forth by me before, and was tributary under the king, having been subdued by Megabazos and afterwards by Mardonios. And he passed in his march from Doriscos first by the Samothrakian strongholds, of which that which is situated furthest towards the West is a city called Mesambria. Next to this follows Stryme, a city of the Thasians, and midway between them flows the river Lisos, which at this time did not suffice when supplying its water to the army of Xerxes, but the stream failed. This country was in old time called Gallaïke, but now Briantike; however by strict justice this also belongs to the Kikonians. 109. Having crossed over the bed of the river Lisos after it had been

dried up, he passed by these Hellenic cities, namely Maroneia, Dicaia and Abdera. These I say he passed by, and also the following lakes of note lying near them,— the Ismarian lake, lying between Maroneia and Stryme; the Bistonian lake near Dicaia, into which two rivers pour their waters, the Trauos[99] and the Compsantos;[100] and at Abdera no lake indeed of any note was passed by Xerxes, but the river Nestos, which flows there into the sea. Then after passing these places he went by the cities of the mainland,[101] near one of which there is, as it chances, a lake of somewhere about thirty furlongs in circumference, abounding in fish and very brackish; this the baggage–animals alone dried up, being watered at it: and the name of this city is Pistyros.[102] 110. These cities, I say, lying by the sea coast and belonging to Hellenes, he passed by, leaving them on the left hand; and the tribes of Thracians through whose country he marched were as follows, namely the Paitians, Kikonians, Bistonians, Sapaians, Dersaians, Edonians, Satrians. Of these they who were settled along the sea coast accompanied him with their ships, and those of them who dwelt inland and have been enumerated by me, were compelled to accompany him on land, except the Satrians: 111, the Satrians however never yet became obedient to any man, so far as we know, but they remain up to my time still free, alone of all the Thracians; for they dwell in lofty mountains, which are covered with forest of all kinds and with snow, and also they are very skilful in war. These are they who possess the Oracle of Dionysos; which Oracle is on their most lofty mountains. Of the Satrians those who act as prophets[103] of the temple are the Bessians; it is a prophetess[104] who utters the oracles, as at Delphi; and beyond this there is nothing further of a remarkable character.[105]

112. Xerxes having passed over the land which has been spoken of, next after this passed the strongholds of the Pierians, of which the name of the one is Phagres and of the other Pergamos. By this way, I say, he made his march, going close by the walls of these, and keeping Mount Pangaion on the right hand, which is both great and lofty and in which are mines both of gold and of silver possessed by the Pierians and Odomantians, and especially by the Satrians. 113. Thus passing by the Paionians, Doberians and Paioplians, who dwell beyond Pangaion towards the North Wind, he went on Westwards, until at last he came to the river Strymon and the city of Eïon, of which, so long as he lived, Boges was commander, the same about whom I was speaking a short time back. This country about Mount Pangaion is called Phyllis, and it extends Westwards to the river Angites, which flows into the Strymon, and Southwards it stretches to the Strymon itself; and at this river the Magians sacrificed

for good omens, slaying white horses. 114. Having done this and many other things in addition to this, as charms for the river, at the Nine Ways[106] in the land of the Edonians, they proceeded by the bridges, for they had found the Strymon already yoked with bridges; and being informed that this place was called the Nine Ways, they buried alive in it that number of boys and maidens, children of the natives of the place. Now burying alive is a Persian custom; for I am informed that Amestris also, the wife of Xerxes, when she had grown old, made return for her own life to the god who is said to be beneath the earth by burying twice seven children of Persians who were men of renown.

115. As the army proceeded on its march from the Strymon, it found after this a sea-beach stretching towards the setting of the sun, and passed by the Hellenic city, Argilos, which was there placed. This region and that which lies above it is called Bisaltia. Thence, keeping on the left hand the gulf which lies of Posideion, he went through the plain which is called the plain of Syleus, passing by Stageiros a Hellenic city, and so came to Acanthos, taking with him as he went each one of these tribes and also of those who dwell about Mount Pangaion, just as he did those whom I enumerated before, having the men who dwelt along the sea coast to serve in the ships and those who dwelt inland to accompany him on foot. This road by which Xerxes the king marched his army, the Thracians do not disturb nor sow crops over, but pay very great reverence to it down to my own time. 116. Then when he had come to Acanthos, Xerxes proclaimed a guest- friendship with the people of Acanthos and also presented them with the Median dress[107] and commended them, perceiving that they were zealous to serve him in the war and hearing of that which had been dug. 117. And while Xerxes was in Acanthos, it happened that he who had been set over the making of the channel, Artachaies by name, died of sickness, a man who was highly esteemed by Xerxes and belonged to the Achaimenid family; also he was in stature the tallest of all the Persians, falling short by only four fingers of being five royal cubits[108] in height, and he had a voice the loudest of all men; so that Xerxes was greatly grieved at the loss of him, and carried him forth and buried him with great honour, and the whole army joined in throwing up a mound for him. To this Artachaies the Acanthians by the bidding of an oracle do sacrifice as a hero, calling upon his name in worship.

118. King Xerxes, I say, was greatly grieved at the loss of Artachaies: and meanwhile the Hellenes who were entertaining his army and providing Xerxes with dinners had been brought to utter ruin, so that they were being driven from house and home; seeing

that when the Thasians, for example, entertained the army of Xerxes and provided him with a dinner on behalf of their towns upon the mainland, Antipater the son of Orgeus, who had been appointed for this purpose, a man of repute among the citizens equal to the best, reported that four hundred talents of silver had been spent upon the dinner. 119. Just so or nearly so in the other cities also those who were set over the business reported the reckoning to be: for the dinner was given as follows, having been ordered a long time beforehand, and being counted by them a matter of great importance:—In the first place, so soon as they heard of it from the heralds who carried round the proclamation, the citizens in the various cities distributed corn among their several households, and all continued to make wheat and barley meal for many months; then they fed cattle, finding out and obtaining the finest animals for a high price; and they kept birds both of the land and of the water, in cages or in pools, all for the entertainment of the army. Then again they had drinking-cups and mixing-bowls made of gold and of silver, and all the other things which are placed upon the table: these were made for the king himself and for those who ate at his table; but for the rest of the army only the things appointed for food were provided. Then whenever the army came to any place, there was a tent pitched ready wherein Xerxes himself made his stay, while the rest of the army remained out in the open air; and when it came to be time for dinner, then the entertainers had labour; but the others, after they had been satiated with food and had spent the night there, on the next day tore up the tent and taking with them all the movable furniture proceeded on their march, leaving nothing, but carrying all away with them. 120. Then was uttered a word well spoken by Megacreon, a man of Abdera, who advised those of Abdera to go in a body, both themselves and their wives, to their temples, and to sit down as suppliants of the gods, entreating them that for the future also they would ward off from them the half of the evils which threatened; and he bade them feel great thankfulness to the gods for the past events, because king Xerxes had not thought good to take food twice in each day; for if it had been ordered to them beforehand to prepare breakfast also in like manner as the dinner, it would have remained for the men of Abdera either not to await the coming of Xerxes, or if they stayed, to be crushed by misfortune more than any other men upon the Earth.

121. They then, I say, though hard put to it, yet were performing that which was appointed to them; and from Acanthos Xerxes, after having commanded the generals to wait for the fleet at Therma, let the ships take their course apart from himself, (now this Therma is that which is situated on the Thermaic gulf, from which also this gulf

has its name); and thus he did because he was informed that this was the shortest way: for from Doriscos as far as Acanthos the army had been making its march thus:—Xerxes had divided the whole land–army into three divisions, and one of them he had set to go along the sea accompanying the fleet, of which division Mardonios and Masistes were commanders; another third of the army had been appointed to go by the inland way, and of this the generals in command were Tritantaichmes and Gergis; and meanwhile the third of the subdivisions, with which Xerxes himself went, marched in the middle between them, and acknowledged as its commanders Smerdomenes and Megabyzos.

122. The fleet, when it was let go by Xerxes and had sailed right through the channel made in Athos (which went across to the gulf on which are situated the cities of Assa, Piloros, Singos and Sarte), having taken up a contingent from these cities also, sailed thence with a free course to the Thermaïc gulf, and turning round Ampelos the headland of Torone, it left on one side the following Hellenic cities, from which it took up contingents of ships and men, namely Torone, Galepsos, Sermyle, Mekyberna, Olynthos: this region is called Sithonia. 123. And the fleet of Xerxes, cutting across from the headland of Ampelos to that of Canastron,[108a] which runs out furthest to sea of all Pallene, took up there contingents of ships and men from Potidaia, Aphytis, Neapolis, Aige, Therambo, Skione, Mende and Sane, for these are the cities which occupy the region which now is called Pallene, but was formerly called Phlegra. Then sailing along the coast of this country also the fleet continued its course towards the place which has been mentioned before, taking up contingents also from the cities which come next after Pallene and border upon the Thermaïc gulf; and the names of them are these,—Lipaxos, Combreia, Lisai, Gigonos, Campsa, Smila, Aineia; and the region in which these cities are is called even to the present day Crossaia. Then sailing from Aineia, with which name I brought to an end the list of the cities, at once the fleet came into the Thermaïc gulf and to the region of Mygdonia, and so it arrived at the aforesaid Therma and at the cities of Sindos and Chalestra upon the river Axios. This river is the boundary between the land of Mygdonia and Bottiaia, of which district the narrow region which lies on the sea coast is occupied by the cities of Ichnai and Pella.

124. Now while his naval force was encamped about the river Axios an the city of Therma and the cities which lie between these two, waiting for the coming of the king, Xerxes and the land–army were proceeding from Acanthos, cutting through the middle by the shortest way[109] with a view to reaching Therma: and he was proceeding

through Paionia and Crestonia to the river Cheidoros,[110] which beginning from the land of the Crestonians, runs through the region of Mygdonia and comes out alongside of the marsh which is by the river Axios. 125. As he was proceeding by this way, lions attacked the camels which carried his provisions; for the lions used to come down regularly by night, leaving their own haunts, but they touched nothing else, neither beast of burden nor man, but killed the camels only: and I marvel what was the cause, and what was it that impelled the lions to abstain from all else and to attack the camels only, creatures which they had never seen before, and of which they had had no experience. 126. Now there are in these parts both many lions and also wild oxen, those that have the very large horns which are often brought into Hellas: and the limit within which these lions are found is on the one side the river Nestos, which flows through Abdera, and on the other the Achelos, which flows through Acarnania; for neither do the East of the Nestos, in any part of Europe before you come to this, would you see a lion, nor again in the remaining part of the continent to the West of the Acheloos, but they are produced in the middle space between these rivers.

127. When Xerxes had reached Therma he established the army there; and his army encamping there occupied of the land along by the sea no less than this,—beginning from the city of Therma and from Mygdonia it extended as far as the river Lydias and the Haliacmon, which form the boundary between the lands of Bottiaia and Macedonia, mingling their waters together in one and the same stream. The Barbarians, I say, were encamped in these regions; and of the rivers which have been enumerated, only the river Cheidoros flowing from the Crestonian land was insufficient for the drinking of the army and failed in its stream.

128. Then Xerxes seeing from Therma the mountains of Thessaly, Olympos and Ossa, that they were of very great height, and being informed that in the midst between them there was a narrow channel, through which flows the Peneios, and hearing also that by this way there was a good road leading to Thessaly, formed a desire to sail thither and look at the outlet of the Peneios, because he was meaning to march by the upper road, through the land of the Macedonians who dwell inland, until he came to the Perraibians, passing by the city of Gonnos; for by this way he was informed that it was safest to go. And having formed this desire, so also he proceeded to do; that is, he embarked in a Sidonian ship, the same in which he used always to embark when he wished to do anything of this kind, and he displayed a signal for the others to put out to sea also, leaving there the land–army. Then when Xerxes had looked at the outlet of

the Peneios, he was possessed by great wonder, and summoning his guides he asked them whether it was possible to turn the river aside and bring it out to the sea by another way. 129. Now it is said that Thessaly was in old time a lake, being enclosed on all sides by very lofty mountains: for the parts of it which lie towards the East are shut in by the ranges of Pelion and Ossa, which join one another in their lower slopes, the parts towards the North Wind by Olympos, those towards the West by Pindos and those towards the mid–day and the South Wind by Othrys; and the region in the midst, between these mountains which have been named, is Thessaly, forming as it were a hollow. Whereas then many rivers flow into it and among them these five of most note, namely Peneios, Apidanos, Onochonos, Enipeus and Pamisos, these, which collect their waters from the mountains that enclose Thessaly round, and flow into this plain, with names separate each one, having their outflow into the sea by one channel and that a narrow one, first mingling their waters all together in one and the same stream; and so soon as they are mingled together, from that point onwards the Peneios prevails with its name over the rest and causes the others to lose their separate names. And it is said that in ancient time, there not being yet this channel and outflow between the mountains, these rivers, and besides these rivers the lake Boibeïs also, had no names as they have now, but by their waters they made Thessaly to be all sea. The Thessalians themselves say that Poseidon made the channel through which the Peneios flows; and reasonably they report it thus, because whosoever believes that it is Poseidon who shakes the Earth and that the partings asunder produced by earthquake are the work of this god, would say, if he saw this, that it was made by Poseidon; for the parting asunder of the mountains is the work of an earthquake, as is evident to me. 130. So the guides, when Xerxes asked whether there was any other possible outlet to the sea for the Peneios, said with exact knowledge of the truth: "O king, for this river there is no other outgoing which extends to the sea, but this alone; for all Thessaly is circled about with mountains as with a crown." To this Xerxes is said to have replied: "The Thessalians then are prudent men. This it appears was that which they desired to guard against in good time[111] when they changed their counsel,[112] reflecting on this especially besides other things, namely that they had a country which, it appears, is easy to conquer and may quickly be taken: for it would have been necessary only to let the river flow over their land by making an embankment to keep it from going through the narrow channel and so diverting the course by which now it flows, in order to put all Thessaly under water except the mountains." This he said in reference to the sons of Aleuas, because they, being Thessalians, were the first of the Hellenes who gave themselves over to the king; for Xerxes thought that they offered him friendship on behalf of their whole nation. Having said thus and having looked at the place, he sailed back to Therma.

131. He then was staying in the region of Pieria many days, for the road over the mountains of Macedonia was being cut meanwhile by a third part of his army, that all the host might pass over by this way into the land of the Perraibians: and now the heralds returned who had been sent to Hellas to demand the gift of earth, some empty-handed and others bearing earth and water. 132. And among those who gave that which was demanded were the following, namely the Thessalians, Dolopians, Enianians,[113] Perraibians, Locrians, Megnesians, Malians, Achaians of Phthiotis, and Thebans, with the rest of the Bœotians also excepting the Thespians and Plataians. Against these the Hellenes who took up war with the Barbarian made an oath; and the oath was this,— that whosoever being Hellenes had given themselves over to the Persian, not being compelled, these, if their own affairs should come to a good conclusion, they would dedicate as an offering[114] to the god at Delphi. 133. Thus ran the oath which was taken by the Hellenes: Xerxes however had not sent to Athens or to Sparta heralds to demand the gift of earth, and for this reason, namely because at the former time when Dareios had sent for this very purpose, the one people threw the men who made the demand into the pit[115] and the others into a well, and bade them take from thence earth and water and bear them to the king. For this reason Xerxes did not send men to make this demand. And what evil thing[116] came upon the Athenians for having done this to the heralds, I am not able to say, except indeed that their land and city were laid waste; but I do not think that this happened for that cause: 134, on the Lacedemonians however the wrath fell of Talthybios, the herald of Agamemnon; for in Sparta there is a temple of Talthybios, and there are also descendants of Talthybios called Talthybiads, to whom have been given as a right all the missions of heralds which go from Sparta; and after this event it was not possible for the Spartans when they sacrificed to obtain favourable omens. This was the case with them for a long time; and as the Lacedemonians were grieved and regarded it as a great misfortune, and general assemblies were repeatedly gathered together and proclamation made, asking if any one of the Lacedemonians was willing to die for Sparta, at length Sperthias the son of Aneristos and Bulis the son of Nicolaos, Spartans of noble birth and in wealth attaining to the first rank, voluntarily submitted to pay the penalty to Xerxes for the heralds of Dareios which had perished at Sparta. Thus the Spartans sent these to the Medes to be put to death. 135. And not only the courage then shown by these men is worthy of admiration, but also the following sayings in

addition: for as they were on their way to Susa they came to Hydarnes (now Hydarnes was a Persian by race and commander of those who dwelt on the sea coasts of Asia), and he offered them hospitality and entertained them; and while they were his guests he asked them as follows: "Lacedemonians, why is it that ye flee from becoming friends to the king? for ye may see that the king knows how to honour good men, when ye look at me and at my fortunes. So also ye, Lacedemonians, if ye gave yourselves to the king, since ye have the reputation with him already of being good men, would have rule each one of you over Hellenic land by the gift of the king." To this they made answer thus: "Hydarnes, thy counsel with regard to us is not equally balanced,[117] for thou givest counsel having made trial indeed of the one thing, but being without experience of the other: thou knowest well what it is to be a slave, but thou hast never yet made trial of freedom, whether it is pleasant to the taste or no; for if thou shouldest make trial of it, thou wouldest then counsel us to fight for it not with spears only but also with axes." 136. Thus they answered Hydarnes; and then, after they had gone up to Susa and had come into the presence of the king, first when the spearmen of the guard commanded them and endeavoured to compel them by force to do obeisance to the king by falling down before him, they said that they would not do any such deed, though they should be pushed down by them head foremost; for it was not their custom to do obeisance to a man, and it was not for this that they had come. Then when they had resisted this, next they spoke these words or words to this effect: "O king of the Medes, the Lacedemonians sent us in place of the heralds who were slain in Sparta, to pay the penalty for their lives." When they said this, Xerxes moved by a spirit of magnanimity replied that he would not be like the Lacedemonians; for they had violated the rules which prevailed among all men by slaying heralds, but he would not do that himself which he blamed them for having done, nor would he free the Lacedemonians from their guilt by slaying these in return. 137. Thus the wrath of Talthybios ceased for the time being, even though the Spartans had done no more than this and although Sperthias and Bulis returned back to Sparta; but a long time after this it was roused again during the war between the Peloponnesians and Athenians, as the Lacedemonians report. This I perceive to have been most evidently the act of the Deity: for in that the wrath of Talthybios fell upon messengers and did not cease until it had been fully satisfied, so much was but in accordance with justice; but that it happened to come upon the sons of these men who went up to the king on account of the wrath, namely upon Nicolaos the son of Bulis and Aneristos the son of Sperthias (the same who conquered the men of Halieis, who came from Tiryns, by sailing into their harbour with a merchant ship filled with fighting men),—by this it is evident to me that the matter came to pass by the act of the Deity caused by this wrath. For these men, sent by the Lacedemonians as envoys to Asia, having been betrayed by Sitalkes the son of Teres king of the Thracians and by Nymphodoros the son of Pythes a man of Abdera, were captured at Bisanthe on the Hellespont; and then having been carried away to Attica they were put to death by the Athenians, and with them also Aristeas the son of Adeimantos the Corinthian. These things happened many years after the expedition of the king; and I return now to the former narrative.

138. Now the march of the king's army was in name against Athens, but in fact it was going against all Hellas: and the Hellenes being informed of this long before were not all equally affected by it; for some of them having given earth and water to the Persian had confidence, supposing that they would suffer no hurt from the Barbarian; while others not having given were in great terror, seeing that there were not ships existing in Hellas which were capable as regards number of receiving the invader in fight, and seeing that the greater part of the States were not willing to take up the war, but adopted readily the side of the Medes. 139. And here I am compelled by necessity to declare an opinion which in the eyes of most men would seem to be invidious, but nevertheless I will not abstain from saying that which I see evidently to be the truth. If the Athenians had been seized with fear of the danger which threatened them and had left their land,[118] or again, without leaving their land, had stayed and given themselves up to Xerxes, none would have made any attempt by sea to oppose the king. If then none had opposed Xerxes by sea, it would have happened on the land somewhat thus:—even if many tunics of walls[119] had been thrown across the Isthmus by the Peloponnesians, the Lacedemonians would have been deserted by their allies, not voluntarily but of necessity, since these would have been conquered city after city by the naval force of the Barbarian, and so they would have been left alone: and having been left alone and having displayed great deeds of valour, they would have met their death nobly. Either they would have suffered this fate, or before this, seeing the other Hellenes also taking the side of the Medes, they would have made an agreement with Xerxes; and thus in either case Hellas would have come to be under the rule of the Persians: for as to the good to be got from the walls thrown across the Isthmus, I am unable to discover what it would have been, when the king had command of the sea. As it is however, if a man should say that the Athenians proved to be the saviours of Hellas, he would not fail to hit the truth; for to whichever side these turned, to that the balance was likely to incline: and these were they who, preferring that Hellas should continue to exist in freedom, roused up all of Hellas which

remained, so much, that is, as had not gone over to the Medes, and (after the gods at least) these were they who repelled the king. Nor did fearful oracles, which came from Delphi and cast them into dread, induce them to leave Hellas, but they stayed behind and endured to receive the invader of their land. 140. For the Athenians had sent men to Delphi to inquire and were preparing to consult the Oracle; and after these had performed the usual rites in the sacred precincts, when they had entered the sanctuary[120] and were sitting down there, the Pythian prophetess, whose name was Aristonike, uttered to them this oracle:

"Why do ye sit, O ye wretched? Flee thou[121] to the uttermost limits, Leaving thy home and the heights of the wheel–round city behind thee! Lo, there remaineth now nor the head nor the body in safety,— Neither the feet below nor the hands nor the middle are left thee,— All are destroyed[122] together; for fire and the passionate War–god,[123] Urging the Syrian[124] car to speed, doth hurl them[125] to ruin. Not thine alone, he shall cause many more great strongholds to perish. Yes, many temples of gods to the ravening fire shall deliver,— Temples which stand now surely with sweat of their terror down–streaming, Quaking with dread; and lo! from the topmost roof to the pavement Dark blood trickles, forecasting the dire unavoidable evil. Forth with you, forth from the shrine, and steep your soul in the sorrow![126]

141. Hearing this the men who had been sent by the Athenians to consult the Oracle were very greatly distressed; and as they were despairing by reason of the evil which had been prophesied to them, Timon the son of Androbulos, a man of the Delphians in reputation equal to the first, counselled them to take a suppliant's bough and to approach the second time and consult the Oracle as suppliants. The Athenians did as he advised and said: "Lord,[127] we pray thee utter to us some better oracle about our native land, having respect to these suppliant boughs which we have come to thee bearing; otherwise surely we will not depart away from the sanctuary, but will remain here where we are now, even until we bring our lives to an end." When they spoke these words, the prophetess gave them a second oracle as follows:

"Pallas cannot prevail to appease great Zeus in Olympos, Though she with words very many and wiles close–woven entreat him. But I will tell thee this more, and will clench it with steel adamantine: Then when all else shall be taken, whatever the boundary[128] of Kecrops Holdeth within, and the dark ravines of divinest Kithairon, A bulwark of wood at the last Zeus grants to the Trito–born goddess Sole to remain unwasted, which thee and thy children shall profit. Stay thou not there for the horsemen to come and the footmen unnumbered; Stay thou not still for the host from the mainland to come, but retire thee, Turning thy back to the foe, for yet thou shalt face him hereafter. Salamis, thou the divine, thou shalt cause sons of women to perish, Or when the grain[129] is scattered or when it is gathered together."

142. This seemed to them to be (as in truth it was) a milder utterance than the former one; therefore they had it written down and departed with it to Athens: and when the messengers after their return made report to the people, many various opinions were expressed by persons inquiring into the meaning of the oracle, and among them these, standing most in opposition to one another:—some of the elder men said they thought that the god had prophesied to them that the Acropolis should survive; for the Acropolis of the Athenians was in old time fenced with a thorn hedge; and they conjectured accordingly that this saying about the "bulwark of wood" referred to the fence: others on the contrary said that the god meant by this their ships, and they advised to leave all else and get ready these. Now they who said that the ships were the bulwark of wood were shaken in their interpretation by the two last verses which the prophetess uttered:

"Salamis, thou the divine, thou shalt cause sons of women to perish, Or when the grain is scattered or when it is gathered together."

In reference to these verses the opinions of those who said that the ships were the bulwark of wood were disturbed; for the interpreters of oracles took these to mean that it was fated for them, having got ready for a sea–fight, to suffer defeat round about Salamis. 143. Now there was one man of the Athenians who had lately been coming forward to take a place among the first, whose name was Themistocles, called son of Neocles. This man said that the interpreters of oracles did not make right conjecture of the whole, and he spoke as follows, saying that if these words that had been uttered referred really to the Athenians, he did not think it would have been so mildly expressed in the oracle, but rather thus, "Salamis, thou the merciless," instead of "Salamis, thou the divine," at least if its settlers were destined to perish round about it: but in truth the oracle had been spoken by the god with reference to the enemy, if one understood it rightly, and not to the Athenians: therefore he counselled them to get ready to fight a battle by sea, for in this was their bulwark of wood. When Themistocles declared his opinion thus, the Athenians judged that this was to be preferred by them rather than the advice of the interpreters of oracles, who bade them not make ready for a sea–fight, nor in short raise their hands at all in opposition, but leave the land of Attica and settle in some other. 144. Another opinion too of Themistocles before this one proved the best at the right moment, when the Athenians, having got large sums of money in the public treasury, which had come in to them from the mines which are at Laureion, were intending to share it among themselves, taking each in turn the sum of ten drachmas. Then Themistocles persuaded the Athenians to give up this plan of division and to make for themselves with this money two hundred ships for the war, meaning by that the war with the Eginetans: for this war having arisen[130] proved in fact the salvation of Hellas at that time, by compelling the Athenians to become a naval power. And the ships, not having been used for the purpose for which they had been made, thus proved of service at need to Hellas. These ships then, I say, the Athenians had already, having built them beforehand, and it was necessary in addition to these to construct others. They resolved then, when they took counsel after the oracle was given, to receive the Barbarian invading Hellas with their ships in full force, following the commands of the god, in combination with those of the Hellenes who were willing to join them.

145. These oracles had been given before to the Athenians: and when those Hellenes who had the better mind about Hellas[131] came together to one place, and considered their affairs and interchanged assurances with one another, then deliberating together they thought it well first of all things to reconcile the enmities and bring to an end the wars which they had with one another. Now there were wars engaged[132] between others also, and especially between the Athenians and the Eginetans. After this, being informed that Xerxes was with his army at Sardis, they determined to send spies to Asia to make observation of the power of the king; and moreover they resolved to send envoys to Argos to form an alliance against the Persian, and to send others to Sicily to Gelon the son of Deinomenes and also to Corcyra, to urge them to come to the assistance of Hellas, and others again to Crete; for they made it their aim that if possible the Hellenic race might unite in one, and that they might join all together and act towards the same end, since dangers were threatening all the Hellenes equally. Now the power of Gelon was said to be great, far greater than any other Hellenic power.

146. When they had thus resolved, they reconciled their enmities and then sent first three men as spies to Asia. These having come to Sardis and having got knowledge

about the king's army, were discovered, and after having been examined by the generals of the land–army were being led off to die. For these men, I say, death had been determined; but Xerxes, being informed of this, found fault with the decision of the generals and sent some of the spearmen of his guard, enjoining them, if they should find the spies yet alive, to bring them to his presence. So having found them yet surviving they brought them into the presence of the king; and upon that Xerxes, being informed for what purpose they had come, commanded the spearmen to lead them round and to show them the whole army both foot and horse, and when they should have had their fill of looking at these things, to let them go unhurt to whatsoever land they desired. 147. Such was the command which he gave, adding at the same time this saying, namely that if the spies had been put to death, the Hellenes would not have been informed beforehand of his power, how far beyond description it was; while on the other hand by putting to death three men they would not very greatly have damaged the enemy; but when these returned back to Hellas, he thought it likely that the Hellenes, hearing of his power, would deliver up their freedom to him themselves, before the expedition took place which was being set in motion; and thus there would be no need for them to have the labour of marching an army against them. This opinion of his is like his manner of thinking at other times;[133] for when Xerxes was in Abydos, he saw vessels which carried corn from the Pontus sailing out through the Hellespont on their way to Egina and the Peloponnese. Those then who sat by his side, being informed that the ships belonged to the enemy, were prepared to capture them, and were looking to the king to see when he would give the word; but Xerxes asked about them whither the men were sailing, and they replied: "Master, to thy foes, conveying to them corn": he then made answer and said: "Are we not also sailing to the same place as these men, furnished with corn as well as with other things necessary? How then do these wrong us, since they are conveying provisions for our use?"

148. The spies then, having thus looked at everything and after that having been dismissed, returned back to Europe: and meanwhile those of the Hellenes who had sworn alliance against the Persian, after the sending forth of the spies proceeded to send envoys next to Argos. Now the Argives report that the matters concerning themselves took place as follows:—They were informed, they say, at the very first of the movement which was being set on foot by the Barbarian against Hellas; and having been informed of this and perceiving that the Hellenes would endeavour to get their alliance against the Persians, they had sent messengers to inquire of the god at Delphi,

and to ask how they should act in order that it might be best for themselves: because lately there had been slain of them six thousand men by the Lacedemonians and by Cleomenes the son of Anaxandrides,[134] and this in fact was the reason that they were sending to inquire: and when they inquired, the Pythian prophetess made answer to them as follows:

"Thou to thy neighbours a foe, by the gods immortal beloved, Keep thou thy spear[135] within bounds, and sit well-guarded behind it: Guard well the head, and the head shall preserve the limbs and the body."

Thus, they say, the Pythian prophetess had replied to them before this; and afterwards when the messengers of the Hellenes came, as I said, to Argos, they entered the Council-chamber and spoke that which had been enjoined to them; and to that which was said the Council replied that the Argives were ready to do as they were requested, on condition that they got peace made with the Lacedemonians for thirty years and that they had half the leadership of the whole confederacy: and yet by strict right (they said) the whole leadership fell to their share, but nevertheless it was sufficient for them to have half. 149. Thus they report that the Council made answer, although the oracle forbade them to make the alliance with the Hellenes; and they were anxious, they say, that a truce from hostilities for thirty years should be made, although they feared the oracle, in order, as they allege, that their sons might grow to manhood in these years; whereas if a truce did not exist, they had fear that, supposing another disaster should come upon them in fighting against the Persian in addition to that which had befallen them already, they might be for all future time subject to the Lacedemonians. To that which was spoken by the Council those of the envoys who were of Sparta replied, that as to the truce they would refer the matter to their public assembly,[136] but as to the leadership they had themselves been commissioned to make reply, and did in fact say this, namely that they had two kings, while the Argives had one; and it was not possible to remove either of the two who were of Sparta from the leadership, but there was nothing to prevent the Argive king from having an equal vote with each of their two. Then, say the Argives, they could not endure the grasping selfishness of the Spartans, but chose to be ruled by the Barbarians rather than to yield at all to the Lacedemonians; and they gave notice to the envoys to depart out of the territory of the Argives before sunset, or, if not, they would be dealt with as enemies.

150. The Argives themselves report so much about these matters: but there is another story reported in Hellas to the effect that Xerxes sent a herald to Argos before he set forth to make an expedition against Hellas, and this herald, they say, when he had come, spoke as follows: "Men of Argos, king Xerxes says to you these things:—We hold that Perses, from whom we are descended, was the son of Perseus, the son of Danae, and was born of the daughter of Kepheus, Andromeda; and according to this it would seem that we are descended from you. It is not fitting then that we should go forth on an expedition against those from whom we trace our descent, nor that ye should set yourselves in opposition to us by rendering assistance to others; but it is fitting that ye keep still and remain by yourselves: for if things happen according to my mind, I shall not esteem any people to be of greater consequence than you." Having heard this the Argives, it is said, considered it a great matter; and therefore at first they made no offer of help nor did they ask for any share; but afterwards, when the Hellenes tried to get them on their side, then, since they knew well that the Lacedemonians would not give them a share in the command, they asked for this merely in order that they might have a pretext for remaining still. 151. Also some of the Hellenes report that the following event, in agreement with this account, came to pass many years after these things:—there happened, they say, to be in Susa the city of Memnon[137] envoys of the Athenians come about some other matter, namely Callias the son of Hipponicos and the others who went up with him; and the Argives at that very time had also sent envoys to Susa, and these asked Artoxerxes the son of Xerxes, whether the friendship which they had formed with Xerxes still remained unbroken, if they themselves desired to maintain it,[138] or whether they were esteemed by him to be enemies; and king Artoxerxes said that it most certainly remained unbroken, and that there was no city which he considered to be more his friend than Argos. 152. Now whether Xerxes did indeed send a herald to Argos saying that which has been reported, and whether envoys of the Argives who had gone up to Susa inquired of Artoxerxes concerning friendship, I am not able to say for certain; nor do I declare any opinion about the matters in question other than that which the Argives themselves report: but I know this much, that if all the nations of men should bring together into one place the evils which they have suffered themselves, desiring to make exchange with their neighbours, each people of them, when they had examined closely the evils suffered by their fellows, would gladly carry away back with them those which they had brought.[139] Thus it is not the Argives who have acted most basely of all. I however am bound to report that which is reported, though I am not bound altogether to believe it; and let this saying be considered to hold good as regards every narrative in the

history: for I must add that this also is reported, namely that the Argives were actually those who invited the Persian to invade Hellas, because their war with the Lacedemonians had had an evil issue, being willing to suffer anything whatever rather than the trouble which was then upon them.

153. That which concerns the Argives has now been said: and meanwhile envoys had come to Sicily from the allies, to confer with Gelon, among whom was also Syagros from the Lacedemonians. Now the ancestor of this Gelon, he who was at Gela as a settler,[140] was a native of the island of Telos, which lies off Triopion; and when Gela was founded by the Lindians of Rhodes and by Antiphemos, he was not left behind. Then in course of time his descendants became and continued to be priests of the mysteries of the Earth goddesses,[141] an office which was acquired by Telines one of their ancestors in the following manner:— certain of the men of Gela, being worsted in a party struggle, had fled to Mactorion, the city which stands above Gela: these men Telines brought back to Gela from exile with no force of men but only with the sacred rites of these goddesses; but from whom he received them, or whether he obtained them for himself,[142] this I am not able to say; trusting in these however, he brought the men back from exile, on the condition that his descendants should be priests of the mysteries of the goddesses. To me it has caused wonder also that Telines should have been able to perform so great a deed, considering that which I am told; for such deeds, I think, are not apt to proceed from every man, but from one who has a brave spirit and manly vigour, whereas Telines is said by the dwellers in Sicily to have been on the contrary a man of effeminate character and rather poor spirit. 154. He then had thus obtained the privilege of which I speak: and when Cleander the son of Pantares brought his life to an end, having been despot of Gela for seven years and being killed at last by Sabyllos a man of Gela, then Hippocrates succeeded to the monarchy, who was brother of Cleander. And while Hippocrates was despot, Gelon, who was a descendant of Telines the priest of the mysteries, was spearman of the guard[143] to Hippocrates with many others and among them Ainesidemos the son of Pataicos. Then after no long time he was appointed by reason of valour to be commander of the whole cavalry; for when Hippocrates besieged successively the cities of Callipolis, Naxos, Zancle, Leontini, and also Syracuse and many towns of the Barbarians, in these wars Gelon showed himself a most brilliant warrior; and of the cities which I just now mentioned, not one except Syracuse escaped being reduced to subjection by Hippocrates: the Syracusans however, after they had been defeated in battle at the river Eloros, were rescued by the Corinthians and Corcyreans; these

rescued them and brought the quarrel to a settlement on this condition, namely that the Syracusans should deliver up Camarina to Hippocrates. Now Camarina used in ancient time to belong to the men of Syracuse. 155. Then when it was the fate of Hippocrates also, after having been despot for the same number of years as his brother Cleander, to be killed at the city of Hybla, whither he had gone on an expedition against the Sikelians, then Gelon made a pretence of helping the sons of Hippocrates, Eucleides and Cleander, when the citizens were no longer willing to submit; but actually, when he had been victorious in a battle over the men of Gela, he robbed the sons of Hippocrates of the power and was ruler himself. After this stroke of fortune Gelon restored those of the Syracusans who were called "land-holders,"[144] after they had been driven into exile by the common people and by their own slaves, who were called Kyllyrians,[145] these, I say, he restored from the city of Casmene to Syracuse, and so got possession of this last city also, for the common people of Syracuse, when Gelon came against them, delivered up to him their city and themselves. 156. So after he had received Syracuse into his power, he made less account of Gela, of which he was ruler also in addition, and he gave it in charge to Hieron his brother, while he proceeded to strengthen Syracuse. So forthwith that city rose and shot up to prosperity; for in the first place he brought all those of Camarina to Syracuse and made them citizens, and razed to the ground the city of Camarina; then secondly he did the same to more than half of the men of Gela, as he had done to those of Camarina: and as regards the Megarians of Sicily, when they were besieged and had surrendered by capitulation, the well-to-do men[146] of them, though they had stirred up war with him and expected to be put to death for this reason, he brought to Syracuse and made them citizens, but the common people of the Megarians, who had no share in the guilt of this war and did not expect that they would suffer any evil, these also he brought to Syracuse and sold them as slaves to be carried away from Sicily: and the same thing he did moreover to the men of Euboia in Sicily, making a distinction between them: and he dealt thus with these two cities because he thought that a body of commons was a most unpleasant element in the State.

157. In the manner then which has been described Gelon had become a powerful despot; and at this time when the envoys of the Hellenes had arrived at Syracuse, they came to speech with him and said as follows: "The Lacedemonians and their allies sent us to get thee to be on our side against the Barbarian; for we suppose that thou art certainly informed of him who is about to invade Hellas, namely that a Persian is designing to bridge over the Hellespont, and to make an expedition against Hellas,

leading against us out of Asia all the armies of the East, under colour of marching upon Athens, but in fact meaning to bring all Hellas to subjection under him. Do thou therefore, seeing that[147] thou hast attained to a great power and hast no small portion of Hellas for thy share, being the ruler of Sicily, come to the assistance of those who are endeavouring to free Hellas, and join in making her free; for if all Hellas be gathered together in one, it forms a great body, and we are made a match in fight for those who are coming against us; but if some of us go over to the enemy and others are not willing to help, and the sound portion of Hellas is consequently small, there is at once in this a danger that all Hellas may fall to ruin. For do not thou hope that if the Persian shall overcome us in battle he will not come to thee, but guard thyself against this beforehand; for in coming to our assistance thou art helping thyself; and the matter which is wisely planned has for the most part a good issue afterwards." 158. The envoys spoke thus; and Gelon was very vehement with them, speaking to them as follows: "Hellenes, a selfish speech is this, with which ye have ventured to come and invite me to be your ally against the Barbarian; whereas ye yourselves, when I in former time requested of you to join with me in fighting against an army of Barbarians, contention having arisen between me and the Carthaginians, and when I charged you to exact vengeance of the men of Egesta for the death of Dorieos the son of Anaxandrides,[148] while at the same time I offered to help in setting free the trading–places, from which great advantages and gains have been reaped by you,—ye, I say, then neither for my own sake came to my assistance, nor in order to exact vengeance for the death of Dorieos; and, so far as ye are concerned, all these parts are even now under the rule of Barbarians. But since it turned out well for us and came to a better issue, now that the war has come round and reached you, there has at last arisen in your minds a recollection of Gelon. However, though I have met with contempt at your hands, I will not act like you; but I am prepared to come to your assistance, supplying two hundred triremes and twenty thousand hoplites, with two thousand horsemen, two thousand bowmen, two thousand slingers and two thousand light–armed men to run beside the horsemen; and moreover I will undertake to supply corn for the whole army of the Hellenes, until we have finished the war. These things I engage to supply on this condition, namely that I shall be commander and leader of the Hellenes against the Barbarian; but on any other condition I will neither come myself nor will I send others." 159. Hearing this Syagros could not contain himself but spoke these words: "Deeply, I trow, would Agamemnon son of Pelops lament,[149] if he heard that the Spartans had had the leadership taken away from them by Gelon and by the Syracusans. Nay, but make thou no further mention of this condition, namely that we should deliver the leadership to thee; but if thou art desirous to come to the assistance of Hellas, know that thou wilt be under the command of the Lacedemonians; and if thou dost indeed claim not to be under command, come not thou to our help at all."

160. To this Gelon, seeing that the speech of Syagros was adverse, set forth to them his last proposal thus: "Stranger from Sparta, reproaches sinking into the heart of a man are wont to rouse his spirit in anger against them; thou however, though thou hast uttered insults against me in thy speech, wilt not bring me to show myself unseemly in my reply. But whereas ye so strongly lay claim to the leadership, it were fitting that I should lay claim to it more than ye, seeing that I am the leader of an army many times as large and of ships many more. Since however this condition is so distasteful to you,[150] we will recede somewhat from our former proposal. Suppose that ye should be leaders of the land-army and I of the fleet; or if it pleases you to lead the sea-forces, I am willing to be leader of those on land; and either ye must be contented with these terms or go away without the alliance which I have to give." 161. Gelon, I say, made these offers, and the envoy of the Athenians, answering before that of the Lacedemonians, replied to him as follows: "O king of the Syracusans, it was not of a leader that Hellas was in want when it sent us to thee, but of an army. Thou however dost not set before us the hope that thou wilt send an army, except thou have the leadership of Hellas; and thou art striving how thou mayest become commander of the armies of Hellas. So long then as it was thy demand to be leader of the whole army of the Hellenes, it was sufficient for us Athenians to keep silence, knowing that the Lacedemonian would be able to make defence even for us both; but now, since being repulsed from the demand for the whole thou art requesting to be commander of the naval force, we tell that thus it is:—not even if the Lacedemonian shall permit thee to be commander of it, will we permit thee; for this at least is our own, if the Lacedemonians do not themselves desire to have it. With these, if they desire to be the leaders, we do not contend; but none others beside ourselves shall we permit to be in command of the ships: for then to no purpose should we be possessors of a sea-force larger than any other which belongs to the Hellenes, if, being Athenians, we should yield the leadership to Syracusans, we who boast of a race which is the most ancient of all and who are of all the Hellenes the only people who have not changed from one land to another; to whom also belonged a man whom Homer the Epic poet said was the best of all who came to Ilion in drawing up an army and setting it in array.[151] Thus we are not justly to be reproached if we say these things." 162. To this Gelon made

answer thus: "Stranger of Athens, it would seem that ye have the commanders, but that ye will not have the men to be commanded. Since then ye will not at all give way, but desire to have the whole, it were well that ye should depart home as quickly as possible and report to the Hellenes that the spring has been taken out of their year." Now this is the meaning of the saying: —evidently the spring is the noblest part of the year; and so he meant to say that his army was the noblest part of the army of the Hellenes: for Hellas therefore, deprived of his alliance, it was, he said, as if the spring had been taken out of the year.[152]

163. The envoys of the Hellenes, having thus had conference with Gelon, sailed away; and Gelon upon this, fearing on the one hand about the Hellenes, lest they should not be able to overcome the Barbarian, and on the other hand considering it monstrous and not to be endured that he should come to Peloponnesus and be under the command of the Lacedemonians, seeing that he was despot of Sicily, gave up the thought of this way and followed another: for so soon as he was informed that the Persian had crossed over the Hellespont, he sent Cadmos the son of Skythes, a man of Cos, with three fifty−oared galleys to Delphi, bearing large sums of money and friendly proposals, to wait there and see how the battle would fall out: and if the Barbarian should be victorious, he was to give him the money and also to offer him earth and water from those over whom Gelon had rule; but if the Hellenes should be victorious, he was bidden to bring it back. 164. Now this Cadmos before these events, having received from his father in a prosperous state the government[153] of the people of Cos, had voluntarily and with no danger threatening, but moved merely by uprightness of nature, placed the government in the hands of the people of Cos[154] and had departed to Sicily, where he took from[155] the Samians and newly colonised the city of Zancle, which had changed its name to Messene. This same Cadmos, having come thither in such manner as I have said, Gelon was now sending, having selected him on account of the integrity which in other matters he had himself found to be in him; and this man, in addition to the other upright acts which had been done by him, left also this to be remembered, which was not the least of them: for having got into his hands that great sum of money which Gelon entrusted to his charge, though he might have taken possession of it himself he did not choose to do so; but when the Hellenes had got the better in the sea−fight and Xerxes had marched away and departed, he also returned to Sicily bringing back with him the whole sum of money.

165. The story which here follows is also reported by those who dwell in Sicily, namely that, even though he was to be under the command of the Lacedemonians, Gelon would have come to the assistance of the Hellenes, but that Terillos, the son of Crinippos and despot of Himera, having been driven out of Himera by Theron the son of Ainesidemos[156] the ruler of the Agrigentines, was just at this very time bringing in an army of Phenicians, Libyans, Iberians, Ligurians, Elisycans, Sardinians and Corsicans, to the number of thirty myriads,[157] with Amilcas the son of Annon king of the Carthaginians as their commander, whom Terillos had persuaded partly by reason of his own guest−friendship, and especially by the zealous assistance of Anaxilaos the son of Cretines, who was despot of Rhegion, and who to help his father−in−law endeavoured to bring in Amilcas to Sicily, and had given him his sons as hostages; for Anaxilaos was married to the daughter of Terillos, whose name was Kydippe. Thus it was, they say, that Gelon was not able to come to the assistance of the Hellenes, and sent therefore the money to Delphi. 166. In addition to this they report also that, as it happened, Gelon and Theron were victorious over Amilcas the Carthaginian on the very same day when the Hellenes were victorious at Salamis over the Persian. And this Amilcas, who was a Carthaginian on the father's side but on the mother's Syracusan, and who had become king of the Carthaginians by merit, when the engagement took place and he was being worsted in the battle, disappeared, as I am informed; for neither alive nor dead did he appear again anywhere upon the earth, though Gelon used all diligence in the search for him. 167. Moreover there is also this story reported by the Carthaginians themselves, who therein relate that which is probable in itself, namely that while the Barbarians fought with the Hellenes in Sicily from the early morning till late in the afternoon (for to such a length the combat is said to have been protracted), during this time Amilcas was remaining in the camp and was making sacrifices to get good omens of success, offering whole bodies of victims upon a great pyre: and when he saw that there was a rout of his own army, he being then, as it chanced, in the act of pouring a libation over the victims, threw himself into the fire, and thus he was burnt up and disappeared. Amilcas then having disappeared, whether it was in such a manner as this, as it is reported by the Phenicians, or in some other way,[159] the Carthaginians both offer sacrifices to him now, and also they made memorials of him then in all the cities of their colonies, and the greatest in Carthage itself.

168. So far of the affairs of Sicily: and as for the Corcyreans, they made answer to the envoys as follows, afterwards acting as I shall tell: for the same men who had gone to

Sicily endeavoured also to obtain the help of these, saying the same things which they said to Gelon; and the Corcyreans at the time engaged to send a force and to help in the defence, declaring that they must not permit Hellas to be ruined without an effort on their part, for if it should suffer disaster, they would be reduced to subjection from the very first day; but they must give assistance so far as lay in their power. Thus speciously they made reply; but when the time came to send help, they manned sixty ships, having other intentions in their minds, and after making much difficulty they put out to sea and reached Peloponnese; and then near Pylos and Tainaron in the land of the Lacedemonians they kept their ships at anchor, waiting, as Gelon did, to see how the war would turn out: for they did not expect that the Hellenes would overcome, but thought that the Persian would gain the victory over them with ease and be ruler of all Hellas. Accordingly they were acting of set purpose, in order that they might be able to say to the Persian some such words as these: "O king, when the Hellenes endeavoured to obtain our help for this war, we, who have a power which is not the smallest of all, and could have supplied a contingent of ships in number not the smallest, but after the Athenians the largest, did not choose to oppose thee or to do anything which was not to thy mind." By speaking thus they hoped that they would obtain some advantage over the rest, and so it would have happened, as I am of opinion: while they had for the Hellenes an excuse ready made, that namely of which they actually made use: for when the Hellenes reproached them because they did not come to help, they said that they had manned sixty triremes, but had not been able to get past Malea owing to the Etesian Winds; therefore it was that they had not come to Salamis, nor was it by any want of courage on their part that they had been left of the sea–fight.

169. These then evaded the request of the Hellenes thus: but the Cretans, when those of the Hellenes who had been appointed to deal with these endeavoured to obtain their help, did thus, that is to say, they joined together and sent men to inquire of the god at Delphi whether it would be better for them if they gave assistance to Hellas: and the Pythian prophetess answered: "Ye fools, do ye think those woes too few,[160] which Minos sent upon you in his wrath,[161] because of the assistance that ye gave to Menelaos? seeing that, whereas they did not join with you in taking vengeance for his death in Camicos, ye nevertheless joined with them in taking vengeance for the woman who by a Barbarian was carried off from Sparta." When the Cretans heard this answer reported, they abstained from the giving of assistance. 170. For the story goes that Minos, having come to Sicania, which is now called Sicily, in search of Daidalos, died there by a violent death; and after a time the Cretans, urged thereto by a god, all except

the men of Polichne and Praisos, came with a great armament to Sicania and besieged for seven years the city of Camicos, which in my time was occupied by the Agrigentines; and at last not being able either to capture it or to remain before it, because they were hard pressed by famine, they departed and went away. And when, as they sailed, they came to be off the coast of Iapygia, a great storm seized them and cast them away upon the coast; and their vessels being dashed to pieces, they, since they saw no longer any way of coming to Crete, founded there the city of Hyria; and there they stayed and were changed so that they became instead of Cretans, Messapians of Iapygia, and instead of islanders, dwellers on the mainland: then from the city of Hyria they founded those other settlements which the Tarentines long afterwards endeavoured to destroy and suffer great disaster in that enterprise, so that this in fact proved to be the greatest slaughter of Hellenes that is known to us, and not only of the Tarentines themselves but of those citizens of Rhegion who were compelled by Mikythos the son of Choiros to go to the assistance of the Tarentines, and of whom there were slain in this manner three thousand men: of the Tarentines themselves however, who were slain there, there was no numbering made. This Mikythos, who was a servant of Anaxilaos, had been left by him in charge of Rhegion; and he it was who after being driven out of Rhegion took up his abode at Tegea of the Arcadians and dedicated those many statues at Olympia. 171. This of the men of Rhegion and of the Tarentines has been an episode[162] in my narrative: in Crete however, as the men of Praisos report, after it had been thus stripped of inhabitants, settlements were made by various nations, but especially by Hellenes; and in the next generation but one after the death of Minos came the Trojan war, in which the Cretans proved not the most contemptible of those who came to assist Menelaos. Then after this, when they had returned home from Troy, famine and pestilence came upon both the men and their cattle, until at last Crete was stripped of its inhabitants for the second time, and a third population of Cretans now occupy it together with those which were left of the former inhabitants. The Pythian prophetess, I say, by calling these things to their minds stopped them from giving assistance to the Hellenes, though they desired to do so.

172. As for the Thessalians, they at first had taken the side of the Persians against their will, and they gave proof that they were not pleased by that which the Aleuadai were designing; for so soon as they heard that the Persian was about to cross over into Europe, they sent envoys to the Isthmus: now at the Isthmus were assembled representatives of Hellas chosen by the cities which had the better mind about Hellas:

having come then to these, the envoys of the Thessalians said: "Hellenes, ye must guard the pass by Olympos, in order that both Thessaly and the whole of Hellas may be sheltered from the war. We are prepared to join with you in guarding it, but ye must send a large force as well as we; for if ye shall not send, be assured that we shall make agreement with the Persian; since it is not right that we, standing as outposts so far in advance of the rest of Hellas, should perish alone in your defence: and not being willing[163] to come to our help, ye cannot apply to us any force to compel inability;[164] but we shall endeavour to devise some means of safety for ourselves."
173. Thus spoke the Thessalians; and the Hellenes upon this resolved to send to Thessaly by sea an army of men on foot to guard the pass: and when the army was assembled it set sail through Euripos, and having come to Alos in the Achaian land, it disembarked there and marched into Thessaly leaving the ships behind at Alos, and arrived at Tempe, the pass which leads from lower Macedonia into Thessaly by the river Peneios, going between the mountains of Olympos and Ossa. There the Hellenes encamped, being assembled to the number of about ten thousand hoplites, and to them was added the cavalry of the Thessalians; and the commander of the Lacedemonians was Euainetos the son of Carenos, who had been chosen from the polemarchs,[165] not being of the royal house, and of the Athenians Themistocles the son of Neocles. They remained however but few days here, for envoys came from Alexander the son of Amyntas the Macedonian, who advised them to depart thence and not to remain in the pass and be trodden under foot by the invading host, signifying to them at the same time both the great numbers of the army and the ships which they had. When these gave them this counsel, they followed the advice, for they thought that the counsel was good, and the Macedonian was evidently well– disposed towards them. Also, as I think, it was fear that persuaded them to it, when they were informed that there was another pass besides this to the Thessalian land by upper Macedonia through the Perraibians and by the city of Gonnos, the way by which the army of Xerxes did in fact make its entrance. So the Hellenes went down to their ships again and made their way back to the Isthmus.

174. Such was the expedition to Thessaly, which took place when the king was about to cross over from Asia to Europe and was already at Abydos. So the Thessalians, being stripped of allies, upon this took the side of the Medes with a good will and no longer half–heartedly, so that in the course of events they proved very serviceable to the king.

175. When the Hellenes had returned to the Isthmus, they deliberated, having regard to that which had been said by Alexander, where and in what regions they should set the war on foot: and the opinion which prevailed was to guard the pass at Thermopylai; for it was seen to be narrower than that leading into Thessaly, and at the same time it was single,[166] and nearer also to their own land; and as for the path by means of which were taken those of the Hellenes who were taken by the enemy at Thermopylai, they did not even know of its existence until they were informed by the people of Trachis after they had come to Thermopylai. This pass then they resolved to guard, and not permit the Barbarian to go by into Hellas; and they resolved that the fleet should sail to Artemision in the territory of Histiaia: for these points are near to one another, so that each division of their forces could have information of what was happening to the other. And the places are so situated as I shall describe. 176. As to Artemision first, coming out of the Thracian Sea the space is contracted from great width to that narrow channel which lies between the island of Skiathos and the mainland of Magnesia; and after the strait there follows at once in Euboea the sea-beach called Artemision, upon which there is a temple of Artemis. Then secondly the passage into Hellas by Trechis is, where it is narrowest, but fifty feet wide: it is not here however that the narrowest part of this whole region lies, but in front of Thermopylai and also behind it, consisting of a single wheel- track only[167] both by Alpenoi, which lies behind Thermopylai and again by the river Phoinix near the town of Anthela there is no space but a single wheel-track only: and on the West of Thermopylai there is a mountain which is impassable and precipitous, rising up to a great height and extending towards the range of Oite, while on the East of the road the sea with swampy pools succeeds at once. In this passage there are hot springs, which the natives of the place call the "Pots,"[168] and an altar of Heracles is set up near them. Moreover a wall had once been built at this pass, and in old times there was a gate set in it; which wall was built by the Phokians, who were struck with fear because the Thessalians had come from the land of the Thesprotians to settle in the Aiolian land, the same which they now possess. Since then the Thessalians, as they supposed, were attempting to subdue them, the Phokians guarded themselves against this beforehand; and at that time they let the water of the hot springs run over the passage, that the place might be converted into a ravine, and devised every means that the Thessalians might not make invasion of their land. Now the ancient wall had been built long before, and the greater part of it was by that time in ruins from lapse of time; the Hellenes however resolved to set it up again, and at this spot to repel the Barbarian from Hellas: and very near the road there is a village called Alpenoi, from which the Hellenes counted on getting supplies.

177. These places then the Hellenes perceived to be such as their purpose required; for they considered everything beforehand and calculated that the Barbarians would not be able to take advantage either of superior numbers or of cavalry, and therefore they resolved here to receive the invader of Hellas: and when they were informed that the Persian was in Pieria, they broke up from the Isthmus and set forth for the campaign, some going to Thermopylai by land, and others making for Artemision by sea.

178. The Hellenes, I say, were coming to the rescue with speed, having been appointed to their several places: and meanwhile the men of Delphi consulted the Oracle of the god on behalf of themselves and on behalf of Hellas, being struck with dread; and a reply was given them that they should pray to the Winds, for these would be powerful helpers of Hellas in fight. So the Delphians, having accepted the oracle, first reported the answer which had been given them to those of the Hellenes who desired to be free; and having reported this to them at a time when they were in great dread of the Barbarian, they laid up for themselves an immortal store of gratitude: then after this the men of Delphi established an altar for the Winds in Thuia, where is the sacred enclosure of Thuia the daughter of Kephisos, after whom moreover this place has its name; and also they approached them with sacrifices.

179. The Delphians then according to the oracle even to this day make propitiary offerings to the Winds: and meanwhile the fleet of Xerxes setting forth from the city of Therma had passed over with ten of its ships, which were those that sailed best, straight towards Skiathos, where three Hellenic ships, a Troizenian, an Eginetan and an Athenian, were keeping watch in advance. When the crews of these caught sight of the ships of the Barbarians, they set off to make their escape: 180, and the ship of Troizen, of which Prexinos was in command, was pursued and captured at once by the Barbarians; who upon that took the man who was most distinguished by beauty among the fighting—men on board of her,[169] and cut his throat at the prow of the ship, making a good omen for themselves of the first of the Hellenes whom they had captured who was pre—eminent for beauty. The name of this man who was sacrificed was Leon, and perhaps he had also his name to thank in some degree for what befell him. 181. The ship of Egina however, of which Asonides was master, even gave them some trouble to capture it, seeing that Pytheas the son of Ischenoös served as a fighting—man on board of her, who proved himself a most valiant man on this day; for when the ship was being taken, he held out fighting until he was hacked all to pieces: and as when he had fallen he did not die, but had still breath in him, the Persians who

served as fighting—men on board the ships, because of his valour used all diligence to save his life, both applying unguents of myrrh to heal his wounds and also wrapping him up in bands of the finest linen; and when they came back to their own main body, they showed him to all the army, making a marvel of him and giving him good treatment; but the rest whom they had taken in this ship they treated as slaves. 182. Two of the three ships, I say, were captured thus; but the third, of which Phormos an Athenian was master, ran ashore in its flight at the mouth of the river Peneios; and the Barbarians got possession of the vessel but not of the crew; for so soon as the Athenians had run the ship ashore, they leapt out of her, and passing through Thessaly made their way to Athens.

183. Of these things the Hellenes who were stationed at Artemision were informed by fire—signals from Skiathos; and being informed of them and being struck with fear, they removed their place of anchorage from Atermision to Chalkis, intending to guard the Euripos, but leaving at the same time watchers by day[170] on the heights of Eubœa. Of the ten ships of the Barbarians three sailed up to the reef called Myrmex,[171] which lies between Skiathos and Magnesia; and when the Barbarians had there erected a stone pillar, which for that purpose they brought to the reef, they set forth with their main body[172] from Therma, the difficulties of the passage having now been cleared away, and sailed thither with all their ships, having let eleven days go by since the king set forth on his march from Therma. Now of this reef lying exactly in the middle of the fairway they were informed by Pammon of Skyros. Sailing then throughout the day the Barbarians accomplished the voyage to Sepias in Magnesia and to the sea—beach which is between the city of Casthanaia and the headland of Sepias.

184. So far as this place and so far as Thermopylai the army was exempt from calamity; and the number was then still, as I find by computation, this:—Of the ships which came from Asia, which were one thousand two hundred and seven, the original number of the crews supplied by the several nations I find to have been twenty—four myriads and also in addition to them one thousand four hundred,[173] if one reckons at the rate of two hundred men to each ship: and on board of each of these ships served as fighting—men,[174] besides the fighting—men belonging to its own nation in each case, thirty men who were Persians, Medes, or Sacans; and this amounts to three myriads six thousand two hundred and ten[175] in addition to the others. I will add also to this and to the former number the crews of the fifty—oared galleys, assuming

that there were eighty men, more or less,[176] in each one. Of these vessels there were gathered together, as was before said, three thousand: it would follow therefore that there were in them four–and–twenty myriads[177] of men. This was the naval force which came from Asia, amounting in all to fifty–one myriads and also seven thousand six hundred and ten in addition.[178] Then of the footmen there had been found to be a hundred and seventy myriads,[179] and of the horsemen eight myriads:[180] and I will add also to these the Arabian camel–drivers and the Libyan drivers of chariots, assuming them to amount to twenty thousand men. The result is then that the number of the ships' crews combined with that of the land–army amounts to two hundred and thirty–one myriads and also in addition seven thousand six hundred and ten.[181] This is the statement of the Army which was brought up out of Asia itself, without counting the attendants which accompanied it or the corn–transports and the men who sailed in these. 185. There is still to be reckoned, in addition to all this which has been summed up, the force which was being led from Europe; and of this we must give a probable estimate.[182] The Hellenes of Thrace and of the islands which lie off the coast of Thrace supplied a hundred and twenty ships; from which ships there results a sum of twenty–four thousand men: and as regards the land–force which was supplied by the Thracians, Paionians, Eordians, Bottiaians, the race which inhabits Chalkidike, the Brygians, Pierians, Macedonians, Perraibians, Enianians,[183] Dolopians, Magnesians, Achaians, and all those who dwell in the coast– region of Thrace, of these various nations I estimate that there were thirty myriads.[184] These myriads then added to those from Asia make a total sum of two hundred and sixty–four myriads of fighting men and in addition to these sixteen hundred and ten.[185] 186. Such being the number of this body of fighting–men,[186] the attendants who went with these and the men who were in the small vessels[187] which carried corn, and again in the other vessels which sailed with the army, these I suppose were not less in number but more than the fighting men. I assume them to be equal in number with these, and neither at all more nor less; and so, being supposed equal in number with the fighting body, they make up the same number of myriads as they. Thus five hundred and twenty–eight myriads three thousand two hundred and twenty[188] was the number of men whom Xerxes son of Dareios led as far as Sepias and Thermopylai. 187. This is the number of the whole army of Xerxes; but of the women who made bread for it, and of the concubines and eunuchs no man can state any exact number, nor again of the draught–animals and other beasts of burden or of the Indian hounds, which accompanied it, could any one state the number by reason of their multitude: so that it does not occur to me to wonder that the streams of some rivers should have failed them, but I wonder rather how the provisions were sufficient to feed so many myriads; for I find on computation that if each man received a quart[189] of wheat every day and nothing more, there would be expended every day eleven myriads of medimnoi[190] and three hundred and forty medimnoi besides: and here I am not reckoning anything for the women, eunuchs, baggage— animals, or dogs. Of all these men, amounting to so many myriads, not one was for beauty and stature more worthy than Xerxes himself to possess this power.

188. The fleet, I say, set forth and sailed: and when it had put in to land in the region of Magnesia at the beach which is between the city of Casthanaia and the headland of Sepias, the first of the ships which came lay moored by the land and the others rode at anchor behind them; for, as the beach was not large in extent, they lay at anchor with prows projecting[191] towards the sea in an order which was eight ships deep. For that night they lay thus; but at early dawn, after clear sky and windless calm, the sea began to be violently agitated and a great storm fell upon them with a strong East[192] Wind, that wind which they who dwell about those parts call Hellespontias. Now as many of them as perceived that the wind was rising and who were so moored that it was possible for them to do so, drew up their ships on land before the storm came, and both they and their ships escaped; but as for those of the ships which it caught out at sea, some it cast away at the place called Ipnoi[193] in Pelion and others on the beach, while some were wrecked on the headland of Sepias itself, others at the city of Meliboia, and others were thrown up on shore[194] at Casthanaia: and the violence of the storm could not be resisted. 189. There is a story reported that the Athenians had called upon Boreas to aid them, by suggestion of an oracle, because there had come to them another utterance of the god bidding them call upon their brother by marriage to be their helper. Now according to the story of the Hellenes Boreas has a wife who is of Attica, Oreithuia the daughter of Erechththeus. By reason of this affinity, I say, the Athenians, according to the tale which has gone abroad, conjectured that their "brother by marriage" was Boreas, and when they perceived the wind rising, as they lay with their ships at Chalkis in Eubœa, or even before that, they offered sacrifices and called upon Boreas and Oreithuia to assist them and to destroy the ships of the Barbarians, as they had done before round about mount Athos. Whether it was for this reason that the wind Boreas fell upon the Barbarians while they lay at anchor, I am not able to say; but however that may be, the Athenians report that Boreas had come to their help in former times, and that at this time he accomplished those things for them of which I speak; and when they had returned home they set up a temple dedicated to Boreas by the river Ilissos.

190. In this disaster the number of the ships which were lost was not less than four hundred, according to the report of those who state the number which is lowest, with men innumerable and an immense quantity of valuable things; insomuch that to Ameinocles the son of Cretines, a Magnesian who held lands about Sepias, this shipwreck proved very gainful; for he picked up many cups of gold which were thrown up afterwards on the shore, and many also of silver, and found treasure– chests[195] which had belonged to the Persians, and made acquisition of other things of gold[196] more than can be described. This man however, though he became very wealthy by the things which he found, yet in other respects was not fortunate; for he too suffered misfortune, being troubled by the slaying of a child.[197] 191. Of the corn–transplants and other vessels which perished there was no numbering made; and so great was the loss that the commanders of the fleet, being struck with fear lest the Thessalians should attack them now that they had been brought into an evil plight, threw round their camp a lofty palisade built of the fragments of wreck. For the storm continued during three days; but at last the Magians, making sacrifice of victims and singing incantations to appease the Wind by enchantments,[198] and in addition to this, offering to Thetis and the Nereïds, caused it to cease on the fourth day, or else for some other reason it abated of its own will. Now they offered sacrifice to Thetis, being informed by the Ionians of the story that she was carried off from the place by Peleus, and that the whole headland of Sepias belonged to her and to the other Nereïds. 192. The storm then had ceased on the fourth day; and meanwhile the day–watchers had run down from the heights of Euboea on the day after the first storm began, and were keeping the Hellenes informed of all that had happened as regards the shipwreck. They then, being informed of it, prayed first to Poseidon the Saviour and poured libations, and then they hastened to go back to Artemision, expecting that there would be but a very few ships of the enemy left to come against them. 193. They, I say, came for the second time and lay with their ships about Artemision: and from that time even to this they preserve the use of the surname "Saviour" for Poseidon. Meanwhile the Barbarians, when the wind had ceased and the swell of the sea had calmed down, drew their ships into the sea and sailed on along the shore of the mainland, and having rounded the extremity of Magnesia they sailed straight into the gulf which leads towards Pagasai. In this gulf of Magnesia there is a place where it is said that Heracles was left behind by Jason and his comrades, having been sent from the Argo to fetch water, at the time when they were sailing for the fleece to Aia in the land of Colchis: for from that place they designed, when they had taken in water, to loose[199] their ship into the open sea; and from this the place has come to have the name Aphetai. Here then the fleet of Xerxes took up its

moorings.

194. Now it chanced that fifteen of these ships put out to sea a good deal later than the rest, and they happened to catch sight of the ships of the Hellenes at Artemision. These ships the Barbarians supposed to be their own, and they sailed thither accordingly and fell among the enemy. Of these the commander was Sandokes the son of Thamasios, the governor of Kyme in Aiolia, whom before this time king Dareios had taken and crucified (he being one of the Royal Judges) for this reason,[199a] namely that Sandokes had pronounced judgment unjustly for money. So then after he was hung up, Dareios reckoned and found that more good services had been done by him to the royal house than were equal to his offences; and having found this, and perceived that he had himself acted with more haste than wisdom, he let him go. Thus he escaped from king Dareios, and did not perish but survived; now, however, when he sailed in toward the Hellenes, he was destined not to escape the second time; for when the Hellenes saw them sailing up, perceiving the mistake which was being made they put out against them and captured them without difficulty. 195. Sailing in one of these ships Aridolis was captured, the despot of Alabanda in Caria, and in another the Paphian commander Penthylos son of Demonoös, who brought twelve ships from Paphos, but had lost eleven of them in the storm which had come on by Sepias, and now was captured sailing in towards Artemision with the one which had escaped. These men the Hellenes sent away in bonds to the Isthmus of the Corinthians, after having inquired of them that which they desired to learn of the army of Xerxes.

196. The fleet of the Barbarians then, except the fifteen ships of which I said that Sandokes was in command, had arrived at Aphetai; and Xerxes meanwhile with the land−army, having marched through Thessalia and Achaia, had already entered the land of the Malians two days before,[200] after having held in Thessaly a contest for his own horses, making trial also of the Thessalian cavalry, because he was informed that it was the best of all among the Hellenes; and in this trial the horses of Hellas were far surpassed by the others. Now of the rivers in Thessalia the Onochonos alone failed to suffice by its stream for the drinking of the army; but of the rivers which flow in Achaia even that which is the largest of them, namely Epidanos, even this, I say, held out but barely.

197. When Xerxes had reached Alos of Achaia, the guides who gave him information of the way, wishing to inform him fully of everything, reported to him a legend of the

place, the things, namely, which have to do with the temple of Zeus Laphystios;[201] how Athamas the son of Aiolos contrived death for Phrixos, having taken counsel with Ino, and after this how by command of an oracle the Achaians propose to his descendants the following tasks to be performed:—whosoever is the eldest of this race, on him they lay an injunction that he is forbidden to enter the City Hall,[202] and they themselves keep watch; now the City Hall is called by the Achaians the "Hall of the People";[203] and if he enter it, it may not be that he shall come forth until he is about to be sacrificed. They related moreover in addition to this, that many of these who were about to be sacrificed had before now run away and departed to another land, because they were afraid; and if afterwards in course of time they returned to their own land and were caught, they were placed[204] in the City Hall: and they told how the man is sacrificed all thickly covered with wreaths, and with what form of procession he is brought forth to the sacrifice. This is done to the descendants of Kytissoros the son of Phrixos, because, when the Achaians were making of Athamas the son of Aiolos a victim to purge the sins of the land according to the command of an oracle, and were just about to sacrifice him, this Kytissoros coming from Aia of the Colchians rescued him; and having done so he brought the wrath of the gods upon his own descendants. Having heard these things, Xerxes, when he came to the sacred grove, both abstained from entering it himself, and gave the command to his whole army to so likewise; and he paid reverence both to the house and to the sacred enclosure of the descendants of Athamas.

198. These then are the things which happened in Thessalia and in Achaia; and from these regions he proceeded to the Malian land, going along by a gulf of the sea, in which there is an ebb and flow of the tide every day. Round about this gulf there is a level space, which in parts is broad but in other parts very narrow; and mountains lofty and inaccessible surrounding this place enclose the whole land of Malis and are called the rocks of Trachis. The first city upon this gulf as one goes from Achaia is Antikyra, by which the river Spercheios flowing from the land of the Enianians[205] runs out into the sea. At a distance of twenty furlongs[206] or thereabouts from this river there is another, of which the name is Dyras; this is said to have appeared that it might bring assistance to Heracles when he was burning: then again at a distance of twenty furlongs from this there is another river called Melas. 199. From this river Melas the city of Trachis is distant five furlongs; and here, in the parts where Trachis is situated, is even the widest portion of all this district, as regards the space from the mountains to the sea; for the plain has an extent of twenty-two thousand plethra.[207] In the

mountain—range which encloses the land of Trachis there is a cleft to the South of Trachis itself; and through this cleft the river Asopos flows, and runs along by the foot of the mountain. 200. There is also another river called Phoinix, to the South of the Asopos, of no great size, which flowing from these mountains runs out into the Asopos; and at the river Phoinix is the narrowest place, for here has been constructed a road with a single wheel—track only. Then from the river Phoinix it is a distance of fifteen furlongs to Thermopylai; and in the space between the river Phoinix and Thermopylai there is a village called Anthela, by which the river Asopos flows, and so runs out into the sea; and about this village there is a wide space in which is set up a temple dedicated to Demeter of the Amphictyons, and there are seats for the Amphictyonic councillors and a temple dedicated to Amphictyon himself.

201. King Xerxes, I say, was encamped within the region of Trachis in the land of the Malians, and the Hellenes within the pass. This place is called by the Hellenes in general Thermopylai, but by the natives of the place and those who dwell in the country round it is called Pylai. Both sides then were encamped hereabout, and the one had command of all that lies beyond Trachis[208] in the direction of the North Wind, and the others of that which tends towards the South Wind and the mid—day on this side of the continent.[209]

202. These were the Hellenes who awaited the attack of the Persian in this place:—of the Spartans three hundred hoplites; of the men of Tegea and Mantineia a thousand, half from each place, from Orchomenos in Arcadia a hundred and twenty, and from the rest of Arcadia a thousand,—of the Arcadians so many; from Corinth four hundred, from Phlius two hundred, and of the men of Mykene eighty: these were they who came from the Peloponnese; and from the Bœotians seven hundred of the Thespians, and of the Thebans four hundred. 203. In addition to these the Locrians of Opus had been summoned to come in their full force, and of the Phokians a thousand: for the Hellenes had of themselves sent a summons to them, saying by messengers that they had come as forerunners of the others, that the rest of the allies were to be expected every day, that their sea was safely guarded, being watched by the Athenians and the Eginetans and by those who had been appointed to serve in the fleet, and that they need fear nothing: for he was not a god, they said, who was coming to attack Hellas, but a man; and there was no mortal, nor would be any, with those fortunes evil had not been mingled at his very birth, and the greatest evils for the greatest men; therefore he also who was marching against them, being mortal, would be destined to fail of his

expectation. They accordingly, hearing this, came to the assistance of the others at Trachis.

204. Of these troops, although there were other commanders also according to the State to which each belonged, yet he who was most held in regard and who was leader of the whole army was the Lacedemonian Leonidas son of Anaxandrides, son of Leon, son of Eurycratides, son of Anaxander, son of Eurycrates, son of Polydoros, son of Alcamenes, son of Teleclos, son of Archelaos, son of Hegesilaos, son of Doryssos, son of Leobotes, son of Echestratos, son of Agis, son of Eurysthenes, son of Aristodemos, son of Aristomachos, son of Cleodaios, son of Hyllos, son of Heracles; who had obtained the kingdom of Sparta contrary to expectation. 205. For as he had two brothers each older than himself, namely Cleomenes and Dorieos, he had been far removed from the thought of becoming king. Since however Cleomenes had died without male child, and Dorieos was then no longer alive, but he also had brought his life to an end in Sicily,[210] thus the kingdom came to Leonidas, both because was of elder birth than Cleombrotos (for Cleombrotos was the youngest of the sons of Anaxandrides) and also because he had in marriage the daughter of Cleomenes. He then at this time went to Thermopylai, having chosen the three hundred who were appointed by law[211] and men who chanced to have sons; and he took with him besides, before he arrived, those Thebans whom I mentioned when I reckoned them in the number of the troops, of whom the commander was Leontiades the son of Eurymachos: and for this reason Leonidas was anxious to take up these with him of all the Hellenes, namely because accusations had been strongly brought against them that they were taking the side of the Medes; therefore he summoned them to the war, desiring to know whether they would send troops with them or whether they would openly renounce the alliance of the Hellenes; and they sent men, having other thoughts in their mind the while.

206. These with Leonidas the Spartans had sent out first, in order that seeing them the other allies might join in the campaign, and for fear that they also might take the side of the Medes, if they heard that the Spartans were putting off their action. Afterwards, however, when they had kept the festival, (for the festival of the Carneia stood in their way), they intended then to leave a garrison in Sparta and to come to help in full force with speed: and just so also the rest of the allies had thought of doing themselves; for it chanced that the Olympic festival fell at the same time as these events. Accordingly, since they did not suppose that the fighting in Thermopylai would so soon be decided,

they sent only the forerunners of their force. 207. These, I say, had intended to do thus: and meanwhile the Hellenes at Thermopylai, when the Persian had come near to the pass, were in dread, and deliberated about making retreat from their position. To the rest of the Peloponnesians then it seemed best that they should go to the Peloponnese and hold the Isthmus in guard; but Leonidas, when the Phokians and Locrians were indignant at this opinion, gave his vote for remaining there, and for sending at the same time messengers to the several States bidding them to come up to help them, since they were but few to repel the army of the Medes.

208. As they were thus deliberating, Xerxes sent a scout on horseback to see how many they were in number and what they were doing; for he had heard while he was yet in Thessaly that there had been assembled in this place a small force, and that the leaders of it were Lacedemonians together with Leonidas, who was of the race of Heracles. And when the horseman had ridden up towards their camp, he looked upon them and had a view not indeed of the whole of their army, for of those which were posted within the wall, which they had repaired and were keeping a guard, it was not possible to have a view, but he observed those who were outside, whose station was in front of the wall; and it chanced at that time that the Lacedemonians were they who were posted outside. So then he saw some of the men practising athletic exercises and some combing their long hair: and as he looked upon these things he marvelled, and at the same time he observed their number: and when he had observed all exactly, he rode back unmolested, for no one attempted to pursue him and he found himself treated with much indifference. And when he returned he reported to Xerxes all that which he had seen. 209. Hearing this Xerxes was not able to conjecture the truth about the matter, namely that they were preparing themselves to die and to deal death to the enemy so far as they might; but it seemed to him that they were acting in a manner merely ridiculous; and therefore he sent for Demaratos the son of Ariston, who was in his camp, and when he came, Xerxes asked him of these things severally, desiring to discover what this was which the Lacedemonians were doing: and he said: "Thou didst hear from my mouth at a former time, when we were setting forth to go against Hellas, the things concerning these men; and having heard them thou madest me an object of laughter, because I told thee of these things which I perceived would come to pass; for to me it is the greatest of all ends to speak the truth continually before thee, O king. Hear then now also: these men have come to fight with us for the passage, and this is it that they are preparing to do; for they have a custom which is as follows;—whenever they are about to put their lives in peril, then they attend to the arrangement of their

hair. Be assured however, that if thou shalt subdue these and the rest of them which remain behind in Sparta, there is no other race of men which will await thy onset, O king, or will raise hands against thee: for now thou art about to fight against the noblest kingdom and city of those which are among the Hellenes, and the best men." To Xerxes that which was said seemed to be utterly incredible, and he asked again a second time in what manner being so few they would fight with his host. He said; "O king, deal with me as with a liar, if thou find not that these things come to pass as I say."

210. Thus saying he did not convince Xerxes, who let four days go by, expecting always that they would take to flight; but on the fifth day, when they did not depart but remained, being obstinate, as he thought, in impudence and folly, he was enraged and sent against them the Medes and the Kissians, charging them to take the men alive and bring them into his presence. Then when the Medes moved forward and attacked the Hellenes, there fell many of them, and others kept coming up continually, and they were not driven back, though suffering great loss: and they made it evident to every man, and to the king himself not least of all, that human beings are many but men are few. This combat went on throughout the day: 211, and when the Medes were being roughly handled, then these retired from the battle, and the Persians, those namely whom the king called "Immortals," of whom Hydarnes was commander, took their place and came to the attack, supposing that they at least would easily overcome the enemy. When however these also engaged in combat with the Hellenes, they gained no more success than the Median troops but the same as they, seeing that they were fighting in a place with a narrow passage, using shorter spears than the Hellenes, and not being able to take advantage of their superior numbers. The Lacedemonians meanwhile were fighting in a memorable fashion, and besides other things of which they made display, being men perfectly skilled in fighting opposed to men who were unskilled, they would turn their backs to the enemy and make a pretence of taking to flight; and the Barbarians, seeing them thus taking a flight, would follow after them with shouting and clashing of arms: then the Lacedemonians, when they were being caught up, turned and faced the Barbarians; and thus turning round they would slay innumerable multitudes of the Persians; and there fell also at these times a few of the Spartans themselves. So, as the Persians were not able to obtain any success by making trial of the entrance and attacking it by divisions and every way, they retired back. 212. And during these onsets it is said that the king, looking on, three times leapt up from his seat, struck with fear for his army. Thus they contended then: and on the following

day the Barbarians strove with no better success; for because the men opposed to them were few in number, they engaged in battle with the expectation that they would be found to be disabled and would not be capable any longer of raising their hands against them in fight. The Hellenes however were ordered by companies as well as by nations, and they fought successively each in turn, excepting the Phokians, for these were posted upon the mountain to guard the path. So the Persians, finding nothing different from that which they had seen on the former day, retired back from the fight.

213. Then when the king was in a strait as to what he should do in the matter before him, Epialtes the son of Eurydemos, a Malian, came to speech with him, supposing that he would win a very great reward from the king; and this man told him of the path which leads over the mountain to Thermopylai, and brought about the destruction of those Hellenes who remained in that place. Afterwards from fear of the Lacedemonians he fled to Thessaly, and when he had fled, a price was proclaimed for his life by the Deputies,[212] when the Amphictyons met for their assembly at Pylai.[213] Then some time afterwards having returned to Antikyra he was slain by Athenades a man of Trachis. Now this Athenades killed Epialtes for another cause, which I shall set forth in the following part of the history,[214] but he was honoured for it none the less by the Lacedemonians. 214. Thus Epialtes after these events was slain: there is however another tale told, that Onetes the son of Phanagoras, a man of Carystos, and Corydallos of Antikyra were those who showed the Persians the way round the mountain; but this I can by no means accept: for first we must judge by this fact, namely that the Deputies of the Hellenes did not proclaim a price for the lives of Onetes and Corydallos, but for that of Epialtes the Trachinian, having surely obtained the most exact information of the matter; and secondly we know that Epialtes was an exile from his country to avoid this charge. True it is indeed that Onetes might know of this path, even though he were not a Malian, if he had had much intercourse with the country; but Epialtes it was who led them round the mountain by the path, and him therefore I write down as the guilty man.

215. Xerxes accordingly, being pleased by that which Epialtes engaged to accomplish, at once with great joy proceeded to send Hydarnes and the men of whom Hydarnes was commander;[215] and they set forth from the camp about the time when the lamps are lit. This path of which we speak had been discovered by the Malians who dwell in that land, and having discovered it they led the Thessalians by it against the Phokians, at the time when the Phokians had fenced the pass with a wall and thus were sheltered

from the attacks upon them: so long ago as this had the pass been proved by the Malians to be of no value.[216] And this path lies as follows:—it begins from the river Asopos, which flows through the cleft, and the name of this mountain and of the path is the same, namely Anopaia; and this Anopaia stretches over the ridge of the mountain and ends by the town of Alpenos, which is the first town of the Locrians towards Malis, and by the stone called Black Buttocks[217] and the seats of the Kercopes, where is the very narrowest part. 217. By this path thus situated the Persians after crossing over the Asopos proceeded all through the night, having on their right hand the mountains of the Oitaians and on the left those of the Trachinians: and when dawn appeared, they had reached the summit of the mountain. In this part of the mountain there were, as I have before shown, a thousand hoplites of the Phokians keeping guard, to protect their own country and to keep the path: for while the pass below was guarded by those whom I have mentioned, the path over the mountain was guarded by the Phokians, who had undertaken the business for Leonidas by their own offer. 218. While the Persians were ascending they were concealed from these, since all the mountain was covered with oak–trees; and the Phokians became aware of them after they had made the ascent as follows:—the day was calm, and not a little noise was made by the Persians, as was likely when leaves were lying spread upon the ground under their feet; upon which the Phokians started up and began to put on their arms, and by this time the Barbarians were close upon them. These, when they saw men arming themselves, fell into wonder, for they were expecting that no one would appear to oppose them, and instead of that they had met with an armed force. Then Hydarnes, seized with fear lest the Phokians should be Lacedemonians, asked Epialtes of what people the force was; and being accurately informed he set the Persians in order for battle. The Phokians however, when they were hit by the arrows of the enemy, which flew thickly, fled and got away at once to the topmost peak of the mountain, fully assured that it was against them that the enemy had designed to come,[218] and here they were ready to meet death. These, I say, were in this mind; but the Persians meanwhile with Epialtes and Hydarnes made no account of the Phokians, but descended the mountain with all speed.

219. To the Hellenes who were in Thermopylai first the soothsayer Megistias, after looking into the victims which were sacrificed, declared the death which was to come to them at dawn of day; and afterwards deserters brought the report[219] of the Persians having gone round. These signified it to them while it was yet night, and thirdly came the day–watchers, who had run down from the heights when day was

already dawning. Then the Hellenes deliberated, and their opinions were divided; for some urged that they should not desert their post, while others opposed this counsel. After this they departed from their assembly,[220] and some went away and dispersed each to their several cities, while others of them were ready to remain there together with Leonidas. 220. However it is reported also that Leonidas himself sent them away, having a care that they might not perish, but thinking that it was not seemly for himself and for the Spartans who were present to leave the post to which they had come at first to keep guard there. I am inclined rather to be of this latter opinion,[221] namely that because Leonidas perceived that the allies were out of heart and did not desire to face the danger with him to the end, he ordered them to depart, but held that for himself to go away was not honourable, whereas if he remained, a great fame of him would be left behind, and the prosperity of Sparta would not be blotted out: for an oracle had been given by the Pythian prophetess to the Spartans, when they consulted about this war at the time when it was being first set on foot, to the effect that either Lacedemon must be destroyed by the Barbarians, or their king must lose his life. This reply the prophetess gave them in hexameter verses, and it ran thus:

"But as for you, ye men who in wide-spaced Sparta inhabit, Either your glorious city is sacked by the children of Perses, Or, if it be not so, then a king of the stock Heracleian Dead shall be mourned for by all in the boundaries of broad Lacedemon. Him[222] nor the might of bulls nor the raging of lions shall hinder; For he hath might as of Zeus; and I say he shall not be restrained, Till one of the other of these he have utterly torn and divided."[223]

I am of opinion that Leonidas considering these things and desiring to lay up for himself glory above all the other Spartans,[224] dismissed the allies, rather than that those who departed did so in such disorderly fashion, because they were divided in opinion. 221. Of this the following has been to my mind a proof as convincing as any other, namely that Leonidas is known to have endeavoured to dismiss the soothsayer also who accompanied this army, Megistias the Acarnanian, who was said to be descended from Melampus, that he might not perish with them after he had declared from the victims that which was about to come to pass for them. He however when he was bidden to go would not himself depart, but sent away his son who was with him in the army, besides whom he had no other child.

222. The allies then who were dismissed departed and went away, obeying the word of Leonidas, and only the Thespians and the Thebans remained behind with the Lacedemonians. Of these the Thebans stayed against their will and not because they desired it, for Leonidas kept them, counting them as hostages; but the Thespians very willingly, for they said that they would not depart and leave Leonidas and those with him, but they stayed behind and died with them. The commander of these was Demophilos the son of Diadromes.

223. Xerxes meanwhile, having made libations at sunrise, stayed for some time, until about the hour when the market fills, and then made an advance upon them; for thus it had been enjoined by Epialtes, seeing that the descent of the mountain is shorter and the space to be passed over much less than the going round and the ascent. The Barbarians accordingly with Xerxes were advancing to the attack; and the Hellenes with Leonidas, feeling that they were going forth to death, now advanced out much further than at first into the broader part of the defile; for when the fence of the wall was being guarded,[225] they on the former days fought retiring before the enemy into the narrow part of the pass; but now they engaged with them outside the narrows, and very many of the Barbarians fell: for behind them the leaders of the divisions with scourges in their hands were striking each man, ever urging them on to the front. Many of them then were driven into the sea and perished, and many more still were trodden down while yet alive by one another, and there was no reckoning of the number that perished: for knowing the death which was about to come upon them by reason of those who were going round the mountain, they[226] displayed upon the Barbarians all the strength which they had, to its greatest extent, disregarding danger and acting as if possessed by a spirit of recklessness. 224. Now by this time the spears of the greater number of them were broken, so it chanced, in this combat, and they were slaying the Persians with their swords; and in this fighting fell Leonidas, having proved himself a very good man, and others also of the Spartans with him, men of note, of whose names I was informed as of men who had proved themselves worthy, and indeed I was told also the names of all the three hundred. Moreover of the Persians there fell here, besides many others of note, especially two sons of Dareios, Abrocomes and Hyperanthes, born to Dareios of Phratagune the daughter of Artanes: now Artanes was the brother of king Dareios and the son of Hystaspes, the son of Arsames; and he in giving his daughter in marriage to Dareios gave also with her all his substance, because she was his only child. 225. Two brothers of Xerxes, I say, fell here fighting; and meanwhile over the body of Leonidas there arose a great struggle between the Persians

and the Lacedemonians, until the Hellenes by valour dragged this away from the enemy and turned their opponents to flight four times. This conflict continued until those who had gone with Epialtes came up; and when the Hellenes learnt that these had come, from that moment the nature of the combat was changed; for they retired backwards to the narrow part of the way, and having passed by the wall they went and placed themselves upon the hillock,[227] all in a body together except only the Thebans: now this hillock is in the entrance, where now the stone lion is placed for Leonidas. On this spot while defending themselves with daggers, that is those who still had them left, and also with hands and with teeth, they were overwhelmed by the missiles of the Barbarians, some of these having followed directly after them and destroyed the fence of the wall, while others had come round and stood about them on all sides.

226. Such were the proofs of valour given by the Lacedemonians and Thespians; yet the Spartan Dienekes is said to have proved himself the best man of all, the same who, as they report, uttered this saying before they engaged battle with the Medes:—being informed by one of the men of Trachis that when the Barbarians discharged their arrows they obscured the light of the sun by the multitude of the arrows, so great was the number of their host, he was not dismayed by this, but making small account of the number of the Medes, he said that their guest from Trachis brought them very good news, for if the Medes obscured the light of the sun, the battle against them would be in the shade and not in the sun. 227. This and other sayings of this kind they report that Dienekes the Lacedemonian left as memorials of himself; and after him the bravest they say of the Lacedemonians were two brothers Alpheos and Maron, sons of Orsiphantos. Of the Thespians the man who gained most honour was named Dithyrambos son of Harmatides.

228. The men were buried were they fell; and for these, as well as for those who were slain before being sent away[228] by Leonidas, there is an inscription which runs thus:

"Here once, facing in fight three hundred myriads of foemen, Thousands four did contend, men of the Peloponnese."

This is the inscription for the whole body; and for the Spartans separately there is this:

"Stranger, report this word, we pray, to the Spartans, that lying Here in this spot we remain, faithfully keeping their laws."[229]

This, I say, for the Lacedemonians; and for the soothsayer as follows:

"This is the tomb of Megistias renowned, whom the Median foemen, Where Sperchios doth flow, slew when they forded the stream; Soothsayer he, who then knowing clearly the fates that were coming, Did not endure in the fray Sparta's good leaders to leave."

The Amphictyons it was who honoured them with inscriptions and memorial pillars, excepting only in the case of the inscription to the soothsayer; but that of the soothsayer Megistias was inscribed by Simonides the son of Leoprepes on account of guest–friendship.

229. Two of these three hundred, it is said, namely Eurystos and Aristodemos, who, if they had made agreement with one another, might either have come safe home to Sparta together (seeing that they had been dismissed from the camp by Leonidas and were lying at Alpenoi with disease of the eyes, suffering extremely), or again, if they had not wished to return home, they might have been slain together with the rest,—when they might, I say, have done either one of these two things, would not agree together; but the two being divided in opinion, Eurystos, it is said, when he was informed that the Persians had gone round, asked for his arms and having put them on ordered his Helot to lead him to those who were fighting; and after he had led him thither, the man who had led him ran away and departed, but Eurystos plunged into the thick of the fighting, and so lost his life: but Aristodemos was left behind fainting.[230] Now if either Aristodemos had been ill[231] alone, and so had returned home to Sparta, or the men had both of them come back together, I do not suppose that the Spartans would have displayed any anger against them; but in this case, as the one of them had lost his life and the other, clinging to an excuse which the first also might have used,[232] had not been willing to die, it necessarily happened that the Spartans had great indignation against Aristodemos. 230. Some say that Aristodemos came safe to Sparta in this manner, and on a pretext such as I have said; but others, that he had been sent as a messenger from the camp, and when he might have come up in time to find the battle going on, was not willing to do so, but stayed upon the road and so saved his life, while his fellow–messenger reached the battle and was slain. 213. When Aristodemos, I say, had returned home to Lacedemon, he had reproach and

dishonour;[233] and that which he suffered by way of dishonour was this,—no one of the Spartans would either give him light for a fire or speak with him, and he had reproach in that he was called Aristodemos the coward.[234] 232. He however in the battle at Plataia repaired all the guilt that was charged against him: but it is reported that another man also survived of these three hundred, whose name was Pantites, having been sent as a messenger to Thessaly, and this man, when he returned back to Sparta and found himself dishonoured, is said to have strangled himself.

233. The Thebans however, of whom the commander was Leontiades, being with the Hellenes had continued for some time to fight against the king's army, constrained by necessity; but when they saw that the fortunes of the Persians were prevailing, then and not before, while the Hellenes with Leonidas were making their way with speed to the hillock, they separated from these and holding out their hands came near to the Barbarians, saying at the same time that which was most true, namely that they were on the side of the Medes and that they had been among the first to give earth and water to the king; and moreover that they had come to Thermopylai constrained by necessity, and were blameless for the loss which had been inflicted upon the king: so that thus saying they preserved their lives, for they had also the Thessalians to bear witness to these words. However, they did not altogether meet with good fortune, for some had even been slain as they had been approaching, and when they had come and the Barbarians had them in their power, the greater number of them were branded by command of Xerxes with the royal marks, beginning with their leader Leontiades, the same whose son Eurymachos was afterwards slain by the Plataians, when he had been made commander of four hundred Thebans and had seized the city of the Plataians.[235]

234. Thus did the Hellenes at Thermopylai contend in fight; and Xerxes summoned Demaratos and inquired of him, having first said this: "Demaratos, thou art a good man; and this I conclude by the truth of thy words, for all that thou saidest turned out so as thou didst say. Now, however, tell me how many in number are the remaining Lacedemonians, and of them how many are like these in matters of war; or are they so even all of them?" He said: "O king, the number of all the Lacedemonians is great and their cities are many, but that which thou desirest to learn, thou shalt know. There is in Lacedemon the city of Sparta, having about eight thousand men; and these are all equal to those who fought here: the other Lacedemonians are not equal to these, but they are good men too." To this Xerxes said: "Demaratos, in what manner shall we with least

labour get the better of these men? Come set forth to us this; for thou knowest the courses of their counsels,[236] seeing that thou wert once their king." 235. He made answer: "O king, if thou dost in very earnest take counsel with me, it is right that I declare to thee the best thing. What if thou shouldest send three hundred ships from thy fleet to attack the Laconian land? Now there is lying near it an island named Kythera, about which Chilon, who was a very wise man among us, said that it would be a greater gain for the Spartans that it should be sunk under the sea than that it should remain above it; for he always anticipated that something would happen from it of such a kind as I am now setting forth to thee: not that he knew of thy armament beforehand, but that he feared equally every armament of men. Let thy forces then set forth from this island and keep the Lacedemonians in fear; and while they have a war of their own close at their doors, there will be no fear for thee from them that when the remainder of Hellas is being conquered by the land–army, they will come to the rescue there. Then after the remainder of Hellas has been reduced to subjection, from that moment the Lacedemonian power will be left alone and therefore feeble. If however thou shalt not do this, I will tell thee what thou must look for. There is a narrow isthmus leading to the Peloponnese, and in this place thou must look that other battles will be fought more severe than those which have taken place, seeing that all the Peloponnesians have sworn to a league against thee: but if thou shalt do the other thing of which I spoke, this isthmus and the cities within it will come over to thy side without a battle." 236. After him spoke Achaimenes, brother of Xerxes and also commander of the fleet, who chanced to have been present at this discourse and was afraid lest Xerxes should be persuaded to do this: "O king," he said, "I see that thou art admitting the speech of a man who envies thy good fortune, or is even a traitor to thy cause: for in truth the Hellenes delight in such a temper as this; they envy a man for his good luck, and they hate that which is stronger than themselves. And if, besides other misfortunes which we have upon us, seeing that four hundred of our ships[237] have suffered wreck, thou shalt send away another three hundred from the station of the fleet to sail round Peloponnese, then thy antagonists become a match for thee in fight; whereas while it is all assembled together our fleet is hard for them to deal with, and they will not be at all a match for thee: and moreover the whole sea– force will support the land–force and be supported by it, if they proceed onwards together; but if thou shalt divide them, neither wilt thou be of service to them nor they to thee. My determination is rather to set thy affairs in good order[238] and not to consider the affairs of the enemy, either where they will set on foot the war or what they will do or how many in number they are; for it is sufficient that they should themselves take thought for themselves, and we for ourselves likewise: and if the Lacedemonians come to stand against the Persians in fight, they will assuredly not heal the wound from which they are now suffering."[239] 237. To him Xerxes made answer as follows: "Achaimenes, I think that thou speakest well, and so will I do; but Demaratos speaks that which he believes to be best for me, though his opinion is defeated by thine: for I will not certainly admit that which thou saidest, namely that he is not well-disposed to my cause, judging both by what was said by him before this, and also by that which is the truth, namely that though one citizen envies another for his good fortune and shows enmity to him by his silence,[240] nor would a citizen when a fellow-citizen consulted him suggest that which seemed to him the best, unless he had attained to a great height of virtue, and such men doubtless are few; yet guest- friend to guest-friend in prosperity is well-disposed as nothing else on earth, and if his friend should consult him, he would give him the best counsel. Thus then as regards the evil-speaking against Demaratos, that is to say about one who is my guest-friend, I bid every one abstain from it in the future."

238. Having thus said Xerxes passed in review the bodies of the dead; and as for Leonidas, hearing that he had been the king and commander of the Lacedemonians he bade them cut off his head and crucify him. And it has been made plain to me by many proofs besides, but by none more strongly than by this, that king Xerxes was enraged with Leonidas while alive more than with any other man on earth; for otherwise he would never have done this outrage to his corpse; since of all the men whom I know, the Persians are accustomed most to honour those who are good men in war. They then to whom it was appointed to do these things, proceeded to do so.

239. I will return now to that point of my narrative where it remained unfinished.[241] The Lacedemonians had been informed before all others that the king was preparing an expedition against Hellas; and thus it happened that they sent to the Oracle at Delphi, where that reply was given them which I reported shortly before this. And they got this information in a strange manner; for Demaratos the son of Ariston after he had fled for refuge to the Medes was not friendly to the Lacedemonians, as I am of opinion and as likelihood suggests supporting my opinion; but it is open to any man to make conjecture whether he did this thing which follows in a friendly spirit or in malicious triumph over them. When Xerxes had resolved to make a campaign against Hellas, Demaratos, being in Susa and having been informed of this, had a desire to report it to the Lacedemonians. Now in no other way was he able to signify it, for there was

danger that he should be discovered, but he contrived thus, that is to say, he took a folding tablet and scraped off the wax which was upon it, and then he wrote the design of the king upon the wood of the tablet, and having done so he melted the wax and poured it over the writing, so that the tablet (being carried without writing upon it) might not cause any trouble to be given by the keepers of the road. Then when it had arrived at Lacedemon, the Lacedemonians were not able to make conjecture of the matter; until at last, as I am informed, Gorgo, the daughter of Cleomenes and wife of Leonidas, suggested a plan of which she had herself thought, bidding them scrape the wax and they would find writing upon the wood; and doing as she said they found the writing and read it, and after that they sent notice to the other Hellenes. These things are said to have come to pass in this manner.[242] ——————

NOTES TO BOOK VII

1. *kai ploia*, for transport of horses and also of provisions: however these words are omitted in some of the best MSS.

2. *all ei*: this is the reading of the better class of MSS. The rest have *alla*, which with *pressois* could only express a wish for success, and not an exhortation to action.

3. *outos men oi o logos en timoros*: the words may mean "this manner of discourse was helpful for his purpose."

4. *khresmologon e kai diatheten khresmon ton Mousaiou.*

5. *aphanizoiato*, representing the present tense *aphanizontai* in the oracle.

6. *ton thronon touton*: most MSS. have *ton thronon, touto.*

7. *epistasthe kou pantes*: the MSS. have *ta epistasthe kou pantes*, which is given by most Editors. In that case *oia erxan* would be an exclamation, "What evils they did to us, . . . things which ye all know well, I think."

8. *touton mentoi eineka*: it is hardly possible here to give *mentoi* its usual meaning: Stein in his latest edition reads *touton men toinun.*

9. *suneneike*: Stein reads *suneneike se*, "supposing that thou art worsted."

10. *ep andri ge eni*, as opposed to a god.

11. *akousesthai tina psemi ton k.t.l.*, "each one of those who are left behind."

12. *kai Kurou*, a conjectural emendation of *tou Kurou*. The text of the MSS. enumerates all these as one continuous line of ascent. It is clear however that the enumeration is in fact of two separate lines, which combine in Teïspes, the line of ascent through the father Dareios being, Dareios, Hystaspes, Arsames, Ariamnes, Teïspes, and through the mother, Atossa, Cyrus, Cambyses, Teïspes.

13. *kai mala*: perhaps, "even."

13a. Lit. "nor is he present who will excuse thee."

14. Lit. "my youth boiled over."

15. Lit. "words more unseemly than was right."

16. *all oude tauta esti o pai theia.*

17. *peplanesthai.*

18. *autai*: a correction of *autai.*

19. *se de epiphoitesei*: the better MSS. have *oude epiphoitesei*, which is adopted by Stein.

20. *pempto de etei anomeno.*

21. *ton Ionion.*

22. *kai oud ei eperai pros tautesi prosgenomenai*: some MSS. read *oud eterai pros tautesi genomenai*, which is adopted (with variations) by some Editors. The meaning would be "not all these, nor others which happened in addition to these, were equal to

this one."

23. *ama strateuomenoisi*: *ama* is omitted in some MSS.

24. *stadion*, and so throughout.

25. *entos Sanes*: some MSS. read *ektos Sanes*, which is adopted by Stein, who translates "beyond Sane, but on this side of Mount Athos": this however will not suit the case of all the towns mentioned, e.g. Acrothoon, and *ton Athen* just below clearly means the whole peninsula.

26. *leukolinou.*

27. *ton de on pleiston*: if this reading is right, *siton* must be understood, and some MSS. read *allon* for *alla* in the sentence above. Stein in his latest edition reads *siton* instead of *pleiston*.

28. Lit. "the name of which happens to be Catarractes."

29. i.e. 4,000,000.

30. The *stater dareikos* was of nearly pure gold (cp. iv. 166), weighing about 124 grains.

30a. *stele*, i.e. a square block of stone.

31. *athanato andri*, taken by some to mean one of the body of "Immortals."

32. *akte pakhea*: some inferior MSS. read *akte trakhea*, and hence some Editors have *akte trekhea*, "a rugged foreland."

33. *dolero*: some Editors read *tholero*, "turbid," by conjecture.

34. The meaning is much disputed. I understand Herodotus to state that though the vessels lay of course in the direction of the stream from the Hellespont, that is presenting their prows (or sterns) to the stream, yet this did not mean that they pointed

straight towards the Propontis and Euxine; for the stream after passing Sestos runs almost from North to South with even a slight tendency to the East (hence *eurou* a few lines further on), so that ships lying in the stream would point in a line cutting at right angles that of the longer axis (from East to West) of the Pontus and Propontis. This is the meaning of *epikarsios* elsewhere in Herodotus (i. 180 and iv. 101), and it would be rash to assign to it any other meaning here. It is true however that the expression *pros esperes* is used loosely below for the side toward the Egean. For *anakokheue* a subject must probably be supplied from the clause *pentekonterous—sunthentes*, "that it (i.e. the combination of ships) might support etc.," and *ton tonon ton oplon* may either mean as below "the stretched ropes," or "the tension of the ropes," which would be relieved by the support: the latter meaning seems to me preferable.

Mr. Whitelaw suggests to me that *epikarsios* (*epi kar*) may mean rather "head–foremost," which seems to be its meaning in Homer (Odyss. ix. 70), and from which might be obtained the idea of intersection, one line running straight up against another, which it has in other passages. In that case it would here mean "heading towards the Pontus."

35. *tas men pros tou Pontou tes eteres*. Most commentators would supply *gephures* with *tes eteres*, but evidently both bridges must have been anchored on both sides.

36. *eurou*: Stein adopts the conjecture *zephurou*.

37. *ton pentekonteron kai triereon trikhou*: the MSS. give *ton pentekonteron kai trikhou*, "between the fifty–oared galleys in as many as three places," but it is strange that the fifty–oared galleys should be mentioned alone, and there seems no need of *kai* with *trikhou*. Stein reads *ton pentekonteron kai triereon* (omitting *trikhou* altogether), and this may be right.

38. i.e. in proportion to the quantity: there was of course a greater weight altogether of the papyrus rope.

39. *autis epezeugnuon*.

40. *ekleipsin*: cp. *eklipon* above.

41. Or, according to some MSS., "Nisaian."

42. i.e. not downwards.

43. *tina autou sukhnon omilon*.

44. *to Priamou Pergamon*.

45. *en Abudo mese*: some inferior authorities (followed by most Editors) omit *mese*: but the district seems to be spoken of, as just above.

46. *proexedre lothou leukou*: some kind of portico or loggia seems to be meant.

47. *daimonie andoon*.

48. *ena auton*.

49. *to proso aiei kleptomenos*: "stealing thy advance continually," i.e. "advancing insensibly further." Some take *kleptomenos* as passive, "insensibly lured on further."

50. *neoteron ti poiesein*.

51. Or, according to some MSS., "the Persian land."

52. Lit. "the name of which happens to be Agora."

53. i.e. 1,700,000.

54. *sunnaxantes*: a conjectural emendation very generally adopted of *sunaxantes* or *sunapsantes*.

55. *apageas*, i.e. not stiffly standing up; the opposite to *pepeguias* (ch. 64).

56. *lepidos siderees opsin ikhthueideos*: many Editors suppose that some words have dropped out. The *kithon* spoken of may have been a coat of armour, but elsewhere the body armour *thorex* is clearly distinguished from the *kithon*, see ix. 22.

57. *gerra*: cp. ix. 61 and 102.

58. Cp. i. 7.

59. *mitrephoroi esan*: the *mitre* was perhaps a kind of turban.

60. *tesi Aiguptiesi*, apparently *makhairesi* is meant to be supplied: cp. ch. 91.

61. *eklethesan*, "were called" from the first.

62. These words are by some Editors thought to be an interpolation. The Chaldeans in fact had become a caste of priests, cp. i. 181.

63. *kurbasias*: supposed to be the same as the tiara (cp. v. 49), but in this case stiff and upright.

64. i.e. Areians, cp. iii. 93.

65. *sisurnas*: cp. iv. 109.

66. *akinakas*.

67. *sisurnophoroi*.

68. *zeiras*.

69. *toxa palintona*.

70. *spathes*, which perhaps means the stem of the leaf.

71. *gupso*, "white chalk."

72. *milto*, "red ochre."

73. Some words have apparently been lost containing the name of the nation to which the following description applies. It is suggested that this might be either the

Chalybians or the Pisidians.

74. *lukioergeas*, an emendation from Athenæus of *lukoergeas* (or *lukergeas*), which might perhaps mean "for wolf–hunting."

75. *anastpastous*: cp. iii. 93.

76. Some Editors place this clause before the words: "and Smerdomenes the son of Otanes," for we do not hear of Otanes or Smerdomenes elsewhere as brother and nephew of Dareios. On the other hand Mardonios was son of the sister of Dareios.

77. *tukhe*, "hits."

78. *keletas*, "single horses."

79. This name is apparently placed here wrongly. It has been proposed to read *Kaspeiroi* or *Paktues*.

80. *ippeue*: the greater number of MSS. have *ippeuei* here as at the beginning of ch. 84, to which this is a reference back, but with a difference of meaning. There the author seemed to begin with the intention of giving a full list of the cavalry force of the Persian Empire, and then confined his account to those actually present on this occasion, whereas here the word in combination with *mouna* refers only to those just enumerated.

81. i.e. 80,000.

82. *Suroisi*, see note on ii. 104.

83. *tukous*, which appears to mean ordinarily a tool for stone– cutting.

84. *mitresi*, perhaps "turbans."

85. *kithonas*: there is some probability in the suggestion of *kitarias* here, for we should expect mention of a head–covering, and the word *kitaris* (which is explained to mean the same as *tiara*), is quoted by Pollux as occurring in Herodotus.

86. *kithonas.*

87. *drepana,* "reaping–hooks," cp. v. 112.

88. See i. 171.

89. *Pelasgoi Aigialees.*

90. *kerkouroi.*

91. *makra:* some MSS. and editions have *smikra,* "small."

92. Or "Mapen."

93. Or "Seldomos."

94. *metopedon.*

95. *me oentes arthmioi.* This is generally taken to mean, "unless they were of one mind together"; but that would very much weaken the force of the remark, and *arthmios* elsewhere is the opposite of *polemios,* cp. vi. 83 and ix. 9, 37. Xerxes professes enmity only against those who had refused to give the tokens of submission.

96. *men mounoisi:* these words are omitted in some good MSS., and *mounoisi* has perhaps been introduced from the preceding sentence. The thing referred to in *touto* is the power of fighting in single combat with many at once, which Demaratos is supposed to have claimed for the whole community of the Spartans.

97. *stergein malista.*

98. *oudamoi ko.*

99. Or, "Strauos."

100. Or, "Compsatos."

101. *tas epeirotidas polis*: it is not clear why these are thus distinguished. Stein suggests *Thasion tas epeirotidas polis*, cp. ch. 118; and if that be the true reading *ion* is probably a remnant of *Thasion* after *khoras*.

102. Or, "Pistiros."

103. *oi propheteountes*, i.e. those who interpret the utterances of the Oracle, cp. viii. 36.

104. *promantis*.

105. *kai ouden poikiloteron*, an expression of which the meaning is not quite clear; perhaps "and the oracles are not at all more obscure," cp. Eur. Phœn. 470 and Hel. 711 (quoted by Bähr).

106. "Ennea Hodoi."

107. Cp. iii. 84.

108. The "royal cubit" is about 20 inches; the *daktulos*, "finger's breadth," is rather less than ¾ inch.

109. Or, "Cape Canastraion."

110. Or "Echeidoros": so it is usually called, but not by any MS. here, and by a few only in ch. 127.

111. *pro mesogaian tamnon tes odou*: cp. iv. 12 and ix. 89.

112. Cp. ch. 6 and 174: but it does not appear that the Aleuadai, of whom Xerxes is here speaking, ever thought of resistance, and perhaps *gnosimakheontes* means, "when they submitted without resistance."

113. Some MSS. have *Ainienes* for *Enienes*.

114. *dekateusai*: there is sufficient authority for this rendering of *dekateuein*, and it seems better here than to understand the word to refer only to a "tithing" of goods.

115. *es to barathron*, the place of execution at Athens.

116. "undesirable thing."

117. *ouk ex isou*: i.e. it is one–sided, because the speaker has had experience of only one of the alternatives.

118. Cp. ch. 143 (end), and viii. 62.

119. *teikheon kithones*, a poetical expression, quoted perhaps from some oracle; and if so, *kithon* may here have the Epic sense of a "coat of mail," equivalent to *thorex* in i. 181: see ch. 61, note 56.

120. *to megaron*.

121. The form of address changes abruptly to the singular number, referring to the Athenian people.

122. *azela*, probably for *aionla*, which has been proposed as a correction: or possibly "wretched."

123. *oxus Ares*.

124. i.e. Assyrian, cp. ch. 63.

125. *min*, i.e. the city, to which belong the head, feet, and body which have been mentioned.

126. *kakois d' epikidnate thumon*: this might perhaps mean (as it is taken by several Editors), "show a courageous soul in your troubles," but that would hardly suit with the discouraging tone of the context.

127. *onax*, cp. iv. 15.

128. *ouros*: the word might of course be for *oros*, "mountain," and *Kekropos ouros* would then mean the Acropolis (so it is understood by Stein and others), but the combination with Kithairon makes it probable that the reference is to the boundaries of Attica, and this seems more in accordance with the reference to it in viii. 53.

129. *Demeteros*.

130. *sustas*, "having been joined" cp. viii. 142.

131. *ton peri ten Ellada Ellenon ta ameino phroneonton*: the MSS. have *ton* also after *Ellenon*, which would mean "those of the Hellenes in Hellas itself, who were of the better mind;" but the expression *ton ta ameino phroneouseon peri ten Ellada* occurs in ch. 172. Some Editors omit *Ellenon* as well as *ton*.

132. *egkekremenoi* (from *egkerannumi*, cp. v. 124), a conjectural emendation (by Reiske) of *egkekhremenoi*. Others have conjectured *egkekheiremenoi* or *egegermenoi*.

133. *te ge alle*: many Editors adopt the conjecture *tede alle* "is like the following, which he expressed on another occasion."

134. See vi. 77. This calamity had occurred about fourteen years before, and it was not in order to recover from this that the Argives wished now for a thirty years' truce; but warned by this they desired (they said) to guard against the consequence of a similar disaster in fighting with the Persians, against whom, according to their own account, they were going to defend themselves independently. So great was their fear of this that, "though fearing the oracle," they were willing to disobey it on certain conditions.

135. *probalaion*, cp. *probolous*, ch. 76.

136. *es tous pleunas*.

137. Cp. v. 53.

138. *ethelousi*: this is omitted in most of the MSS., but contained in several of the best. Many Editors have omitted it.

139. *ta oikeia kaka* seems to mean the grievances which each has against his neighbours, "if all the nations of men should bring together into one place their own grievances against their neighbours, desiring to make a settlement with them, each people, when they had examined closely the grievances of others against themselves, would gladly carry away back with them those which they had brought," judging that they had offended others more than they had suffered themselves.

140. *oiketor o en Gele*: some Editors read by conjecture *oiketor eon Geles*, others *oiketor en Gele*.

141. *iropsantai ton khthonion theon*: cp. vi. 134.

142. i.e. by direct inspiration.

143. *en dorupsoros*: the MSS. have *os en dorupsoros*. Some Editors mark a lacuna.

144. *gamorous*, the name given to the highest class of citizens.

145. Or, "Killyrians." They were conquered Sicanians, in the position of the Spartan Helots.

146. *pakheas*: cp. v. 30.

147. *gar*: inserted conjecturally by many Editors.

148. See v. 46.

149. *e ke meg oimexeie*, the beginning of a Homeric hexameter, cp. Il. vii. 125.

150. Or, "since your speech is so adverse."

151. See Il. ii. 552.

152. Some Editors mark this explanation "Now this is the meaning— year," as interpolated.

153. *purannida.*

154. *es meson Kooisi katatheis ten arkhen.*

155. *para Samion*: this is the reading of the best MSS.: others have *meta Samion*, "together with the Samians," which is adopted by many Editors. There can be little doubt however that the Skythes mentioned in vi. 23 was the father of this Cadmos, and we know from Thuc. vi. 4 that the Samians were deprived of the town soon after they had taken it, by Anaxilaos, who gave it the name of Messene, and no doubt put Cadmos in possession of it, as the son of the former king.

156. Cp. ch. 154.

157. i.e. 300,000.

159. The MSS. add either *os Karkhedonioi*, or *os Karkhedonioi kai Surekosioi*, but the testimony of the Carthaginians has just been given, *os Phoinikes legousi*, and the Syracusans professed to be unable to discover anything of him at all. Most of the Editors omit or alter the words.

160. *epimemphesthe*: some Editors have tried corrections, e.g. *ou ti memnesthe*, "do ye not remember," or *epimemnesthe*, "remember"; but cp. viii. 106, *oste se me mempsasthai ten . . . diken.*

161. *osa umin . . . Minos epempse menion dakrumata.* The oracle would seem to have been in iambic verse.

162. *parentheke.*

163. *ou boulomenoi*, apparently equivalent to *me boulemenoi.*

164. Cp. viii. 111.

165. i.e. the six commanders of divisions *morai* in the Spartan army.

166. *mia*: for this most MSS. have *ama*. Perhaps the true reading is *ama mia.*

167. *amaxitos moune*, cp. ch. 200.

168. *Khutrous.*

169. *ton epibateon autes.*

170. *emeroskopous*: perhaps simply "scouts," cp. ch. 219, by which it would seem that they were at their posts by night also, though naturally they would not see much except by day.

171. i.e. "Ant."

172. *autoi.*

173. i.e. 241,400.

174. *epebateuon.*

175. 36,210.

176. *o ti pleon en auton e elasson.* In ch. 97, which is referred to just above, these ships are stated to have been of many different kinds, and not only fifty–oared galleys.

177. 240,000.

178. 517,610.

179. 1,700,000: see ch. 60.

180. 80,000.

181. 2,317,610.

182. *dokesin de dei legein.*

183. Some MSS. have *Ainienes* for *Enienes.*

184. 300,000.

185. 2,641,610.

186. *tou makhimou toutou*.

187. *akatoisi*.

188. 5,283,220.

189. *khoinika*, the usual daily allowance.

190. The *medimnos* is about a bushel and a half, and is equal to 48 *khoinikes*. The reckoning here of 110,340 *medimnoi* is wrong, owing apparently to the setting down of some numbers in the quotient which were in fact part of the dividend.

191. *prokrossai ormeonto es ponton*: the meaning of *prokrossai* is doubtful, but the introduction of the word is probably due to a reminiscence of Homer, Il. xiv. 35, where the ships are described as drawn up in rows one behind the other on shore, and where *prokrossas* is often explained to mean *klimakedon*, i.e. either in steps one behind the other owing to the rise of the beach, or in the arrangement of the quincunx. Probably in this passage the idea is rather of the prows projecting in rows like battlements *krossai*, and this is the sense in which the word is used by Herodotus elsewhere (iv. 152). The word *krossai* however is used for the successively rising stages of the pyramids (ii. 125), and *prokrossos* may mean simply "in a row," or "one behind the other," which would suit all passages in which it occurs, and would explain the expression *prokrossoi pheromenoi epi ton kindunon*, quoted by Athenæus.

192. *apeliotes*. Evidently, from its name *Ellespontias* and from its being afterwards called *Boreas*, it was actually a North–East Wind.

193. i.e. "Ovens."

194. *exebrassonto*.

195. *thesaurous*.

196. The word *khrusea*, "of gold," is omitted by some Editors.

197. "in his case also *kai touton* there was an unpleasing misfortune of the slaying of a child *paidophonos* which troubled him," i.e. he like others had misfortunes to temper his prosperity.

198. *goesi*, (from a supposed word *goe*): a correction of *geosi*, "by enchanters," which is retained by Stein. Some read *khoesi*, "with libations," others *boesi*, "with cries."

199. *aphesein*, whence the name *Aphetai* was supposed to be derived.

199a. Or, "had crucified . . . having convicted him of the following charge, namely," etc. Cp. iii. 35 (end).

200. *tritaios*. According to the usual meaning of the word the sense should be "on the third day after" entering Thessaly, but the distance was much greater than a two–days' march.

201. i.e. "the Devourer."

202. *Prutaneiou*, "Hall of the Magistrates."

203. *leiton*.

204. *estellonto*: many Editors, following inferior MSS., read *eselthontes* and make changes in the rest of the sentence.

205. Some MSS. have *Ainienon* for *Enienon*.

206. *stadion*.

207. *diskhilia te gar kai dismuria plethra tou pediou esti*. If the text is right, the *plethron* must here be a measure of area. The amount will then be about 5000 acres.

208. *mekhri Trekhinos*, "up to Trachis," which was the Southern limit.

209. *to epi tautes tes epeirou*. I take *to epi tautes* to be an adverbial expression like *tes eteres* in ch. 36, for I cannot think that the rendering "towards this continent" is satisfactory.

210. See v. 45.

211. *tous katesteotas*. There is a reference to the body of 300 so called *ippeis* (cp. i. 67), who were appointed to accompany the king in war; but we must suppose that on special occasions the king made up this appointed number by selection, and that in this case those were preferred who had sons to keep up the family. Others (including Grote) understand *tous katesteotas* to mean "men of mature age."

212. *ton Pulagoron*.

213. *es ten Pulaien*.

214. An indication that the historian intended to carry his work further than the year 479.

215. See ch. 83.

216. *ek te tosou de katededekto eousa ouden khreste Melieusi*, i.e. *e esbole*.

217. *Melampugon*.

218. Lit. "had set out to go at first."

219. Lit. "and afterwards deserters were they who reported."

220. *diakrithentes*.

221. *taute kai mallon te gnome pleistos eimi*.

222. i.e. the Persian.

223. *prin tond eteron dia panta dasetai*: i.e. either the city or the king.

224. *mounon Spartieteon*: some Editors (following Plutarch) read *mounon Spartieteon*, "lay up for the Spartans glory above all other nations."

225. *to men gar eruma tou teikheos ephulasseto, oi de k.t.l.*

226. i.e. the Lacedemonians.

227. *izonto epi ton kolonon.*

228. Some Editors insert *tous* after *e*, "before those who were sent away by Leonidas had departed."

229. *remasi.*

230. *leipopsukheonta*, a word which refers properly to bodily weakness. It has been proposed to read *philopsukheonta*, "loving his life," cp. vi. 29.

231. *algesanta*: some good MSS. have *alogesanta*, which is adopted by Stein, "had in his ill–reckoning returned alone."

232. *tes autes ekhomenou prophasios.*

233. *atimien.*

234. *o tresas.*

235. Thuc. ii. 2 ff.

236. *tas diexodous ton bouleumaton*, cp. iii. 156.

237. *ton vees k.t.l.*: some Editors insert *ek* before *ton*, "by which four hundred ships have suffered shipwreck."

238. *ta seoutou de tithemenos eu gnomen ekho*: for *ekho* some inferior MSS. have *ekhe*, which is adopted by several Editors, "Rather set thy affairs in good order and determine not to consider," etc.

239. *to pareon troma*, i.e. their defeat.

240. *kai esti dusmenes te sige*. Some commentators understand *te sige* to mean "secretly," like *sige*, viii. 74.

241. See ch. 220.

242. Many Editors pronounce the last chapter to be an interpolation, but perhaps with hardly sufficient reason.

BOOK VIII. THE EIGHTH BOOK OF THE HISTORIES, CALLED URANIA

1. Those of the Hellenes who had been appointed to serve in the fleet were these:—the Athenians furnished a hundred and twenty–seven ships, and the Plataians moved by valour and zeal for the service, although they had had no practice in seamanship, yet joined with the Athenians in manning their ships. The Corinthians furnished forty ships, the Megarians twenty; the Chalkidians manned twenty ships with which the Athenians furnished them;[1] the Eginetans furnished eighteen ships, the Sikyonians twelve, the Lacedemonians ten, the Epidaurians eight, the Eretrians seven, the Troizenians five, the Styrians two, the Keïans two ships[2] and two fifty–oared galleys, while the Locrians of Opus came also to the assistance of the rest with seven fifty–oared galleys.

2. These were those who joined in the expedition to Artemision, and I have mentioned them according to the number[3] of the ships which they severally supplied: so the number of the ships which were assembled at Artemision was (apart from the fifty–oared galleys) two hundred and seventy–one: and the commander who had the supreme power was furnished by the Spartans, namely Eurybiades son of Eurycleides, since the allies said that they would not follow the lead of the Athenians, but unless a Lacedemonian were leader they would break up the expedition which was to be made: 3, for it had come to be said at first, even before they sent to Sicily to obtain allies, that the fleet ought to be placed in the charge of the Athenians. So as the allies opposed this, the Athenians yielded, having it much at heart that Hellas should be saved, and perceiving that if they should have disagreement with one another about the leadership,

Hellas would perish: and herein they judged rightly, for disagreement between those of the same race is worse than war undertaken with one consent by as much as war is worse than peace. Being assured then of this truth, they did not contend, but gave way for so long time as they were urgently in need of the allies; and that this was so their conduct proved; for when, after repelling the Persian from themselves, they were now contending for his land and no longer for their own, they alleged the insolence of Pausanias as a pretext and took away the leadership from the Lacedemonians. This however took place afterwards. 4. But at this time these Hellenes also who had come to Artemision,[4] when they saw that a great number of ships had put in to Aphetai and that everything was filled with their armament, were struck with fear, because the fortunes of the Barbarians had different issue from that which they expected, and they deliberated about retreating from Artemision to the inner parts of Hellas. And the Euboeans perceiving that they were so deliberating, asked Eurybiades to stay there by them for a short time, until they should have removed out of their land their children, and their households; and as they did not persuade him, they went elsewhere and persuaded Themistocles the commander of the Athenians by a payment of thirty talents, the condition being that the fleet should stay and fight the sea–battle in front of Euboea. 5. Themistocles then caused the Hellenes to stay in the following manner:—to Eurybiades he imparted five talents of the sum with the pretence that he was giving it from himself; and when Eurybiades had been persuaded by him to change his resolution, Adeimantos son of Okytos, the Corinthian commander, was the only one of all the others who still made a struggle, saying that he would sail away from Artemision and would not stay with the others: to him therefore Themistocles said with an oath: "Thou at least shalt not leave us, for I will give thee greater gifts than the king of the Medes would send to thee, if thou shouldest desert thy allies." Thus he spoke, and at the same time he sent to the ship of Adeimantos three talents of silver. So these all[5] had been persuaded by gifts to change their resolution, and at the same time the request of the Euboeans had been gratified and Themistocles himself gained money; and it was not known that he had the rest of the money, but those who received a share of this money were fully persuaded that it had come from the Athenian State for this purpose.

6. Thus they remained in Euboea and fought a sea–battle; and it came to pass as follows:—when the Barbarians had arrived at Aphetai about the beginning of the afternoon, having been informed even before they came that a few ships of the Hellenes were stationed about Artemision and now seeing them for themselves, they

were eager to attack them, to see if they could capture them. Now they did not think it good yet to sail against them directly for this reason,—for fear namely that the Hellenes, when they saw them sailing against them, should set forth to take flight and darkness should come upon them in their flight; and so they were likely (thought the Persians)[6] to get away; whereas it was right, according to their calculation, that not even the fire–bearer[7] should escape and save his life. 7. With a view to this then they contrived as follows:—of the whole number of their ships they parted off two hundred and sent them round to sail by Caphereus and round Geriastos to the Euripos, going outside Skiathos so that they might not be sighted by the enemy as they sailed round Eubœa: and their purpose was that with these coming up by that way, and blocking the enemies' retreat, and themselves advancing against them directly, they might surround them on all sides. Having formed this plan they proceeded to send off the ships which were appointed for this, and they themselves had no design of attacking the Hellenes on that day nor until the signal agreed upon should be displayed to them by those who were sailing round, to show that they had arrived. These ships, I say, they were sending round, and meanwhile they were numbering the rest at Aphetai.

8. During this time, while these were numbering their ships, it happened thus:—there was in that camp a man of Skione named Skyllias, as a diver the best of all the men of that time, who also in the shipwreck which took place by Pelion had saved for the Persians many of their goods and many of them also he had acquired for himself: this Skyllias it appears had had an intention even before this of deserting to the side of the Hellenes, but it had not been possible for him to do so then. In what manner after this attempt he did actually come to the Hellenes, I am not able to say with certainty, but I marvel if the tale is true which is reported; for it is said that he dived into the sea at Aphetai and did not come up till he reached Artemision, having traversed here somewhere about eighty furlongs through the sea. Now there are told about this man several other tales which seem likely to be false, but some also which are true: about this matter however let it be stated as my opinion that he came to Artemision in a boat. Then when he had come, he forthwith informed the commanders about the shipwreck, how it had come to pass, and of the ships which had been sent away to go round Eubœa. 9. Hearing this the Hellenes considered the matter with one another; and after many things had been spoken, the prevailing opinion was that they should remain there that day and encamp on shore, and then, when midnight was past, they should set forth and go to meet those ships which were sailing round. After this however, as no one sailed out to attack them, they waited for the coming of the late hours of the afternoon

and sailed out themselves to attack the Barbarians, desiring to make a trial both of their manner of fighting and of the trick of breaking their line.[8] 10. And seeing them sailing thus against them with few ships, not only the others in the army of Xerxes but also their commanders judged them to be moved by mere madness, and they themselves also put out their ships to sea, supposing that they would easily capture them: and their expectation was reasonable enough, since they saw that the ships of the Hellenes were few, while theirs were many times as numerous and sailed better. Setting their mind then on this, they came round and enclosed them in the middle. Then so many of the Ionians as were kindly disposed to the Hellenes and were serving in the expedition against their will, counted it a matter of great grief to themselves when they saw them being surrounded and felt assured that not one of them would return home, so feeble did they think the power of the Hellenes to be; while those to whom that which was happening was a source of pleasure, were vying with one another, each one endeavouring to be the first to take an Athenian ship and receive gifts from the king: for in their camps there was more report of the Athenians than of any others. 11. The Hellenes meanwhile, when the signal was given, first set themselves with prows facing the Barbarians and drew the sterns of their ships together in the middle; and when the signal was given a second time, although shut off in a small space and prow against prow,[9] they set to work vigorously; and they captured thirty ships of the Barbarians and also Philaon the son of Chersis, the brother of Gorgos kind of the Salaminians, who was a man of great repute in the army. Now the first of the Hellenes who captured a ship of the enemy was an Athenian, Lycomedes the son of Aischraios, and he received the prize for valour. So these, as they were contending in this sea–fight with doubtful result, were parted from one another by the coming on of night. The Hellenes accordingly sailed away to Artemision and the Barbarians to Aphetai, the contest having been widely different from their expectation. In this sea–fight Antidoros of Lemnos alone of the Hellenes who were with the king deserted to the side of the Hellenes, and the Athenians on account of this deed gave him a piece of land in Salamis.

12. When the darkness had come on, although the season was the middle of summer, yet there came on very abundant rain, which lasted through the whole of the night, with crashing thunder[10] from Mount Pelion; and the dead bodies and pieces of wreck were cast up at Aphetai and became entangled round the prows of the ships and struck against the blades of the oars: and the men of the army who were there, hearing these things became afraid, expecting that they would certainly perish, to such troubles had

they come; for before they had had even breathing space after the shipwreck and the storm which had arisen off Mount Pelion, there had come upon them a hard sea–fight, and after the sea–fight a violent storm of rain and strong streams rushing to the sea and crashing thunder. 13. These then had such a night as I have said; and meanwhile those of them who had been appointed to sail round Euboea experienced the very same night, but against them it raged much more fiercely, inasmuch as it fell upon them while they were making their course in the open sea. And the end of it proved distressful[11] to them; for when the storm and the rain together came upon them as they sailed, being then off the "Hollows" of Euboea,[12] they were borne by the wind not knowing by what way they were carried, and were cast away upon the rocks. And all this was being brought about by God in order that the Persian force might be made more equal to that of the Hellenes and might not be by very much the larger. 14. These then, I say, were perishing about the Hollows of Euboea, and meanwhile the Barbarians at Aphetai, when day had dawned upon them, of which they were glad, were keeping their ships quiet, and were satisfied in their evil plight to remain still for the present time; but to the Hellenes there came as a reinforcement three–and–fifty Athenian ships. The coming of these gave them more courage, and at the same time they were encouraged also by a report that those of the Barbarians who had been sailing round Euboea had all been destroyed by the storm that had taken place. They waited then for the same time of day as before, and then they sailed and fell upon some Kilikian ships; and having destroyed these, they sailed away when the darkness came on, and returned to Artemision.

15. On the third day the commanders of the Barbarians, being exceedingly indignant that so small a number of ships should thus do them damage, and fearing what Xerxes might do, did not wait this time for the Hellenes to begin the fight, but passed the word of command and put out their ships to sea about the middle of the day. Now it so happened that these battles at sea and the battles on land at Thermopylai took place on the same days; and for those who fought by sea the whole aim of the fighting was concerned with the channel of Euripos, just as the aim of Leonidas and of his band was to guard the pass: the Hellenes accordingly exhorted one another not to let the Barbarians go by into Hellas; while these cheered one another on to destroy the fleet of the Hellenes and to get possession of the straits. 16. Now while the forces of Xerxes were sailing in order towards them, the Hellenes kept quiet at Artemision; and the Barbarians, having made a crescent of their ships that they might enclose them, were endeavouring to surround them. Then the Hellenes put out to sea and engaged with

them; and in this battle the two sides were nearly equal to one another; for the fleet of Xerxes by reason of its great size and numbers suffered damage from itself, since the ships were thrown into confusion and ran into one another: nevertheless it stood out and did not give way, for they disdained to be turned to flight by so few ships. Many ships therefore of the Hellenes were destroyed and many men perished, but many more ships and men of the Barbarians. Thus contending they parted and went each to their own place. 17. In this sea—fight the Egyptians did best of the men who fought for Xerxes; and these, besides other great deeds which they displayed, captured five ships of the Hellenes together with their crews: while of the Hellenes those who did best on this day were the Athenians, and of the Athenians Cleinias the son of Alkibiades, who was serving with two hundred man and a ship of his own, furnishing the expense at his own proper cost.

18. Having parted, both sides gladly hastened to their moorings; and after they had separated and got away out of the sea—fight, although the Hellenes had possession of the bodies of the dead and of the wrecks of the ships, yet having suffered severely[13] (and especially the Athenians, of whose ships half had been disabled), they were deliberating now about retreating to the inner parts of Hellas. 19. Themistocles however had conceived that if there should be detached from the force of the Barbarians the Ionian and Carian nations, they would be able to overcome the rest; and when the people of Eubœa were driving their flocks down to that sea,[14] he assembled the generals and said to them that he thought he had a device by which he hoped to cause the best of the king's allies to leave him. This matter he revealed to that extent only; and with regard to their present circumstances, he said that they must do as follows:—every one must slaughter of the flocks of the Eubœans as many as he wanted, for it was better that their army should have them than the enemy; moreover he advised that each one should command his own men to kindle a fire: and as for the time of their departure he would see to it in such wise that they should come safe to Hellas. This they were content to do, and forthwith when they had kindled a fire they turned their attention to the flocks. 20. For in fact the Eubœans, neglecting the oracle of Bakis as if it had no meaning at all, had neither carried away anything from their land nor laid in any store of provisions with a view to war coming upon them, and by their conduct moreover they had brought trouble upon themselves.[15] For the oracle uttered by Bakis about these matters runs as follows:

"Mark, when a man, a Barbarian, shall yoke the Sea with papyrus, Then do thou plan to remove the loud—bleating goats from Euboea."

In the evils which at this time were either upon them or soon to be expected they might feel not a little sorry that they had paid no attention to these lines.

21. While these were thus engaged, there came to them the scout from Trachis: for there was at Artemision a scout named Polyas, by birth of Antikyra, to whom it had been appointed, if the fleet should be disabled,[16] to signify this to those at Thermopylai, and he had a vessel equipped and ready for this purpose; and similarly there was with Leonidas Abronichos son of Lysicles, an Athenian, ready to carry news to those at Artemision with a thirty—oared galley, if any disaster should happen to the land—army. This Abronichos then had arrived, and he proceeded to signify to them that which had come to pass about Leonidas and his army; and then when they were informed of it no longer put off their retreat, but set forth in the order in which they were severally posted, the Corinthians first and the Athenians last. 22. Themistocles however selected those ships of the Athenians which sailed best, and went round to the springs of drinking—water, cutting inscriptions on the stones there, which the Ionians read when they came to Artemision on the following day. These inscriptions ran thus: "Ionians, ye act not rightly in making expedition against the fathers of your race and endeavouring to enslave Hellas. Best of all were it that ye should come and be on our side; but if that may not be done by you, stand aside even now from the combat against us and ask the Carians to do the same as ye. If however neither of these two things is possible to be done, and ye are bound down by too strong compulsion to be able to make revolt, then in the action, when we engage battle, be purposely slack, remember that ye are descended from us and that our quarrel with the Barbarian took its rise at the first from you." Themistocles wrote thus, having, as I suppose, two things together in his mind, namely that either the inscriptions might elude the notice of the king and cause the Ionians to change and come over to the side on which he was, or that having been reported and denounced to Xerxes they might cause the Ionians to be distrusted by him, and so he might keep them apart from the sea— fights.

Themistocles then had set these inscriptions: and to the Barbarians there came immediately after these things a man of Histaia in a boat bringing word of the retreat of the Hellenes from Artemision. They however, not believing it, kept the messenger under guard and sent swift—sailing ships to look on before. Then these having reported the facts, at last as daylight was spreading over the sky, the whole armament sailed in a body to Artemision; and having stayed at this place till mid-day, after this they sailed to Histaia, and there arrived they took possession of the city of Histaia and overran all the villages which lie along the coast in the region of Ellopia, which is the land of Histaia.

24. While they were there, Xerxes, after he had made his dispositions with regard to the bodies of the dead, sent a herald to the fleet: and the dispositions which he made beforehand were as follows:—for all those of his army who were lying dead at Thermopylai, (and there were as many as twenty thousand in all), with the exception of about a thousand whom he left, he dug trenches and buried them, laying over them leaves and heaping earth upon them, that they might not be seen by the men of the fleet. Then when the herald had gone over to Histaia, he gathered an assembly of the whole force and spoke these words: "Allies, king Xerxes grants permission to any one of you who desires it, to leave his post and to come and see how he fights against those most senseless men who looked to overcome the power of the king." 25. When the herald had proclaimed this, then boats were of all things most in request, so many were they who desired to see this sight; and when they had passed over they went through the dead bodies and looked at them: and every one supposed that those who were lying there were all Lacedemonians or Thespians, though the Helots also were among those that they saw: however, they who had passed over did not fail to perceive that Xerxes had done that which I mentioned about the bodies of his own dead; for in truth it was a thing to cause laughter even: on the one side there were seen a thousand dead bodies lying, while the others lay all gathered together in the same place, four thousand[17] of them. During this day then they busied themselves with looking, and on the day after this they sailed back to the ships at Histaia, while Xerxes and his army set forth upon their march.

26. There had come also to them a few deserters from Arcadia, men in want of livelihood and desiring to be employed. These the Persians brought into the king's presence and inquired about the Hellenes, what they were doing; and one man it was who asked them this for all the rest. They told them that the Hellenes were keeping the Olympic festival and were looking on at a contest of athletics and horsemanship. He then inquired again, what was the prize proposed to them, for the sake of which they contended; and they told them of the wreath of olive which is given. Then Tigranes[18] the son of Artabanos uttered a thought which was most noble, though

thereby he incurred from the king the reproach of cowardice: for hearing that the prize was a wreath and not money, he could not endure to keep silence, but in the presence of all he spoke these words: "Ah! Mardonios, what kind of men are these against whom thou hast brought us to fight, who make their contest not for money but for honour!" Thus was it spoken by this man.

27. In the meantime, so soon as the disaster at Thermopylai had come about, the Thessalians sent a herald forthwith to the Phokians, against whom they had a grudge always, but especially because of the latest disaster which they had suffered: for when both the Thessalians themselves and their allies had invaded the Phokian land not many years before this expedition of the king, they had been defeated by the Phokians and handled by them roughly. For the Phokians had been shut up in Mount Parnassos having with them a soothsayer, Tellias the Eleian; and this Tellias contrived for them a device of the following kind:—he took six hundred men, the best of the Phokians, and whitened them over with chalk, both themselves and their armour, and then he attacked the Thessalians by night, telling the Phokians beforehand to slay every man whom they should see not coloured over with white. So not only the sentinels of the Thessalians, who saw these first, were terrified by them, supposing it to be something portentous and other than it was, but also after the sentinels the main body of their army; so that the Phokians remained in possession of four thousand bodies of slain men and shields; of which last they dedicated half at Abai and half at Delphi; and from the tithe of booty got by this battle were made the large statues which are contending for the tripod in front of the temple[19] at Delphi, and others similar to these are dedicated as an offering at Abai. 28. Thus had the Phokians done to the Thessalian footmen, when they were besieged by them; and they had done irreparable hurt to their cavalry also, when this had invaded their land: for in the pass which is by Hyampolis they had dug a great trench and laid down in it empty wine-jars; and then having carried earth and laid it on the top and made it like the rest of the ground, they waited for the Thessalians to invade their land. These supposing that they would make short work with the Phokians,[20] riding in full course fell upon the wine-jars; and there the legs of their horses were utterly crippled. 29. Bearing then a grudge for both of these things, the Thessalians sent a herald and addressed them thus: "Phokians, we advise you to be more disposed now to change your minds and to admit that ye are not on a level with us: for in former times among the Hellenes, so long as it pleased us to be on that side, we always had the preference over you, and now we have such great power with the Barbarian that it rests with us to cause you to be deprived of your land and to be sold

into slavery also. We however, though we have all the power in our hands, do not bear malice, but let there be paid to us fifty talents of silver in return for this, and we will engage to avert the dangers which threaten to come upon your land." 30. Thus the Thessalians proposed to them; for the Phokians alone of all the people in those parts were not taking the side of the Medes, and this for no other reason, as I conjecture, but only because of their enmity with the Thessalians; and if the Thessalians had supported the cause of the Hellenes, I am of opinion that the Phokians would have been on the side of the Medes. When the Thessalians proposed this, they said that they would not give the money, and that it was open to them to take the Median side just as much as the Thessalians, if they desired it for other reasons; but they would not with their own will be traitors to Hellas.

31. When these words were reported, then the Thessalians, moved with anger against the Phokians, became guides to the Barbarian to show him the way: and from the land of Trachis they entered Doris; for a narrow strip[21] of the Dorian territory extends this way, about thirty furlongs in breadth, lying between Malis and Phokis, the region which was in ancient time called Dryopis; this land is the mother–country of the Dorians in Peloponnese. Now the Barbarians did not lay waste this land of Doris when they entered it, for the people of it were taking the side of the Medes, and also the Thessalians did not desire it. 32. When however from Doris they entered Phokis, they did not indeed capture the Phokians themselves; for some of them had gone up to the heights of Parnassos,—and that summit of Parnassos is very convenient to receive a large number, which lies by itself near the city of Neon, the name of it being Tithorea,—to this, I say, some of them had carried up their goods and gone up themselves; but most of them had conveyed their goods out to the Ozolian Locrians, to the city of Amphissa, which is situated above the Crissaian plain. The Barbarians however overran the whole land of Phokis, for so the Thessalians led their army, and all that they came to as they marched they burned or cut down, and delivered to the flames both the cities and the temples: 33, for they laid everything waste, proceeding this way by the river Kephisos, and they destroyed the city of Drymos by fire, and also the following, namely Charadra, Erochos, Tethronion, Amphikaia, Neon, Pedieis, Triteis, Elateia, Hyampolis, Parapotamioi and Abai, at which last–named place there was a temple of Apollo, wealthy and furnished with treasuries and votive offerings in abundance; and there was then, as there is even now, the seat of an Oracle there: this temple they plundered and burnt. Some also of the Phokians they pursued and captured upon the mountains, and some women they did to death by repeated outrage.

34. Passing by Parapotamioi the Barbarians came to Panopeus, and from this point onwards their army was separated and went different ways. The largest and strongest part of the army, proceeding with Xerxes himself against Athens, entered the land of the Bœotians, coming into the territory of Orchomenos. Now the general body of the Bœotians was taking the side of the Medes, and their cities were being kept by Macedonians appointed for each, who had been sent by Alexander; and they were keeping them this aim, namely in order to make it plain to Xerxes that the Bœotians were disposed to be on the side of the Medes. 35. These, I say, of the Barbarians took their way in this direction; but others of them with guides had set forth to go to the temple at Delphi, keeping Parnassos on their right hand: and all the parts of Phokis over which these marched they ravaged; for they set fire to the towns of Panopeus and Daulis and Aiolis. And for this reason they marched in that direction, parted off from the rest of the army, namely in order that they might plunder the temple at Delphi and deliver over the treasures there to king Xerxes: and Xerxes was well acquainted with all that there was in it of any account, better, I am told, than with the things which he had left in his own house at home, seeing that many constantly reported of them, and especially of the votive offerings of Crœsus the son of Alyattes. 36. Meanwhile the Delphians, having been informed of this, had been brought to extreme fear; and being in great terror they consulted the Oracle about the sacred things, whether they should bury them in the earth or carry them forth to another land; but the god forbade them to meddle with these, saying that he was able by himself to take care of his own. Hearing this they began to take thought for themselves, and they sent their children and women over to Achaia on the other side of the sea, while most of the men themselves ascended up towards the summits of Parnassos and carried their property to the Corykian cave, while others departed for refuge to Amphissa of the Locrians. In short the Delphians had all left the town excepting sixty men and the prophet of the Oracle.[22] 37. When the Barbarians had come near and could see the temple, then the prophet, whose name was Akeratos, saw before the cell[23] arms lying laid out, having been brought forth out of the sanctuary,[24] which were sacred and on which it was not permitted to any man to lay hands. He then was going to announce the portent to those of the Delphians who were stil there, but when the Barbarians pressing onwards came opposite the temple of Athene Pronaia, there happened to them in addition portents yet greater than that which had come to pass before: for though that too was a marvel, that arms of war should appear of themselves laid forth outside the cell, yet this, which happened straightway after that, is worthy of marvel even beyond all other prodigies. When the Barbarians in their approach were opposite the temple of Athene Pronaia, at this point

of time from the heaven there fell thunderbolts upon them, and from Parnassos two crags were broken away and rushed down upon them with a great crashing noise falling upon many of them, while from the temple of Pronaia there was heard a shout, and a battle–cry was raised. 38. All these things having come together, there fell fear upon the Barbarians; and the Delphians having perceived that they were flying, came down after them and slew a great number of them; and those who survived fled straight to Bœotia. These who returned of the Barbarians reported, as I am informed, that in addition to this which we have said they saw also other miraculous things; for two men (they said) in full armour and of stature more than human followed them slaying and pursuing. 39. These two the Delphians say were the native heroes Phylacos and Autonoös, whose sacred enclosures are about the temple, that of Phylacos being close by the side of the road above the temple of Pronaia and that of Autonoös near Castalia under the peak called Hyampeia. Moreover the rocks which fell from Parnassos were still preserved even to my time, lying in the sacred enclosure of Athene Pronaia, into which they fell when they rushed through the ranks of the Barbarians. Such departure had these men from the temple.

40. Meanwhile the fleet of the Hellenes after leaving Artemision put in to land at Salamis at the request of the Athenians: and for this reason the Athenians requested them to put in to Salamis, namely in order that they might remove out of Attica to a place of safety their children and their wives, and also deliberate what they would have to do; for in their present case they meant to take counsel afresh, because they had been deceived in their expectation. For they had thought to find the Peloponnesians in full force waiting for the Barbarians in Bœotia; they found however nothing of this, but they were informed on the contrary that the Peloponnesians were fortifying the Isthmus with a wall, valuing above all things the safety of the Peloponnese and keeping this in guard; and that they were disposed to let all else go. Being informed of this, the Athenians therefore made request of them to put in to Salamis. 41. The others then put in their ships to land at Salamis, but the Athenians went over to their own land; and after their coming they made a proclamation that every one of the Athenians should endeavour to save his children and household as best he could. So the greater number sent them to Troizen, but others to Egina, and others to Salamis, and they were urgent to put these out of danger, both because they desired to obey the oracle and also especially for another reason, which was this:—the Athenians say that a great serpent lives in the temple[25] and guards the Acropolis; and they not only say this, but also they set forth for it monthly offerings, as if it were really there; and the offering

consists of a honey-cake. This honey-cake, which before used always to be consumed, was at this time left untouched. When the priestess had signified this, the Athenians left the city much more and with greater eagerness than before, seeing that the goddess also had (as they supposed) left the Acropolis. Then when all their belongings had been removed out of danger, they sailed to the encampment of the fleet.

42. When those who came from Artemision had put their ships in to land at Salamis, the remainder of the naval force of the Hellenes, being informed of this, came over gradually to join them[26] from Troizen: for they had been ordered beforehand to assemble at Pogon, which is the harbour of the Troizenians. There were assembled accordingly now many more ships than those which were in the sea-fight at Artemision, and from more cities. Over the whole was set as admiral the same man as at Artemision, namely Eurybiades the son of Eurycleides, a Spartan but not of the royal house; the Athenians however supplied by far the greatest number of ships and those which sailed the best. 43. The following were those who joined the muster:—From Peloponnese the Lacedemonians furnishing sixteen ships, the Corinthians furnishing the same complement as at Artemision, the Sikyonians furnishing fifteen ships, the Epidaurians ten, the Troizenians five, the men of Hermion[26a] three, these all, except the Hermionians, being of Doric and Makednian[27] race and having made their last migration from Erineos and Pindos and the land of Dryopis;[28] but the people of Hermion are Dryopians, driven out by Heracles and the Malians from the land which is now called Doris. 44. These were the Peloponnesians who joined the fleet, and those of the mainland outside the Peloponnese were as follows:—the Athenians, furnishing a number larger than all the rest,[29] namely one hundred and eighty ships, and serving alone, since the Plataians did not take part with the Athenians in the sea-fight at Salamis, because when the Hellenes were departing from Artemision and come near Chalkis, the Plataians disembarked on the opposite shore of Bœotia and proceeded to the removal of their households. So being engaged in saving these, they had been left behind. As for the Athenians, in the time when the Pelasgians occupied that which is now called Hellas, they were Pelasgians, being named Cranaoi, and in the time of king Kecrops they came to be called Kecropidai; then when Erechtheus had succeeded to his power, they had their name changed to Athenians; and after Ion the son of Xuthos became commander[30] of the Athenians, they got the name from him of Ionians. 45. The Megarians furnished the same complement as at Artermision; the Amprakiots came to the assistance of the rest with seven ships, and the Leucadians with three,

these being by race Dorians from Corinth. 46. Of the islanders the Eginetans furnished thirty; these had also other ships manned, but with them they were guarding their own land, while with the thirty which sailed best they joined in the sea—fight at Salamis. Now the Eginetans are Dorians from Epidauros, and their island had formerly the name of Oinone. After the Eginetans came the Chalkidians with the twenty ships which were at Artemision, and the Eretrians with their seven: these are Ionians. Next the Keïans, furnishing the same as before and being by race Ionians from Athens. The Naxians furnished four ships, they having been sent out by the citizens of their State to join the Persians, like the other islanders; but neglecting these commands they had come to the Hellenes, urged thereto by Democritos, a man of repute among the citizens and at that time commander of a trireme. Now the Naxians are Ionians coming originally from Athens. The Styrians furnished the same ships as at Artemision, and the men of Kythnos one ship and one fifty—oared galley, these both being Dryopians. Also the Seriphians, the Siphnians and the Melians served with the rest; for they alone of the islanders had not given earth and water to the Barbarian. 47. These all who have been named dwelt inside the land of the Thesprotians and the river Acheron; for the Thesprotians border upon the land of the Amprakiots and Leucadians, and these were they who came from the greatest distance to serve: but of those who dwell outside these limits the men of Croton were the only people who came to the assistance of Hellas in her danger; and these sent one ship, of whom the commander was Phaÿlos, a man who had three times won victories at the Pythian games. Now the men of Croton are by descent Achaians. 48. All the rest who served in the fleet furnished triremes, but the Melians, Siphnian and Seriphians fifty—oared galleys: the Melians, who are by descent from Lacedemon, furnished two, the Siphnians and Seriphians, who are Ionians from Athens, each one. And the whole number of the ships, apart from the fifty—oared galleys, was three hundred and seventy—eight.[31]

49. When the commanders had assembled at Salamis from the States which have been mentioned, they began to deliberate, Eurybiades having proposed that any one who desired it should declare his opinion as to where he thought it most convenient to fight a sea—battle in those regions of which they had command; for Attica had already been let go, and he was now proposing the question about the other regions. And the opinions of the speakers for the most part agreed that they should sail to the Isthmus and there fight a sea—battle in defence of the Peloponnese, arguing that if they should be defeated in the sea— battle, supposing them to be at Salamis they would be blockaded in an island, where no help would come to them, but at the Isthmus they

would be able to land where their own men were. 50. While the commanders from the Peloponnese argued thus, an Athenian had come in reporting that the Barbarians were arrived in Attica and that all the land was being laid waste with fire. For the army which directed its march through Bœotia in company with Xerxes, after it had burnt the city of the Thespians (the inhabitants having left it and gone to the Peloponnese) and that of the Plataians likewise, had now come to Athens and was laying waste everything in those regions. Now he had burnt Thespiai[31a] and Plataia because he was informed by the Thebans that these were not taking the side of the Medes. 51. So in three months from the crossing of the Hellespont, whence the Barbarians began their march, after having stayed there one month while they crossed over into Europe, they had reached Attica, in the year when Calliades was archon of the Athenians. And they took the lower city, which was deserted, and then they found that there were still a few Athenians left in the temple, either stewards of the temple or needy persons, who had barred the entrance to the Acropolis with doors and with a palisade of timber and endeavoured to defend themselves against the attacks of the enemy, being men who had not gone out to Salamis partly because of their poverty, and also because they thought that they alone had discovered the meaning of the oracle which the Pythian prophetess had uttered to them, namely that the "bulwark of wood" should be impregnable, and supposed that this was in fact the safe refuge according to the oracle, and not the ships. 52. So the Persians taking their post upon the rising ground opposite the Acropolis, which the Athenians call the Hill of Ares,[32] proceeded to besiege them in this fashion, that is they put tow round about their arrows and lighted it, and then shot them against the palisade. The Athenians who were besieged continued to defend themselves nevertheless, although they had come to the extremity of distress and their palisade had played them false; nor would they accept proposals for surrender, when the sons of Peisistratos brought them forward: but endeavouring to defend themselves they contrived several contrivances against the enemy, and among the rest they rolled down large stones when the Barbarians approached the gates; so that for a long time Xerxes was in a difficulty, not being able to capture them. 53. In time however there appeared for the Barbarians a way of approach after their difficulties, since by the oracle it was destined that all of Attica which is on the mainland should come to be under the Persians. Thus then it happened that on the front side[33] of the Acropolis behind the gates and the way up to the entrance, in a place where no one was keeping guard, nor would one have supposed that any man could ascend by this way, here men ascended by the temple of Aglauros the daughter of Kecrops, although indeed the place is precipitous: and when the Athenians saw that they had ascended up to the Acropolis, some of them threw themselves down from the wall and perished, while others took refuge in the sanctuary[34] of the temple. Then those of the Persians who had ascended went first to the gates, and after opening these they proceeded to kill the suppliants; and when all had been slain by them, they plundered the temple and set fire to the whole of the Acropolis.

54. Then Xerxes, having fully taken possession of Athens, sent to Susa a mounted messenger to report to Artabanos the good success which they had. And on the next day after sending the herald he called together the exiles of the Athenians who were accompanying him, and bade them go up to the Acropolis and sacrifice the victims after their own manner; whether it was that he had seen some vision of a dream which caused him to give this command, or whether perchance he had a scruple in his mind because he had set fire to the temple. The Athenian exiles did accordingly that which was commanded them: 55, and the reason why I made mention of this I will here declare:—there is in this Acropolis a temple[35] of Erechtheus, who is said to have been born of the Earth, and in this there is an olive–tree and a sea, which (according to the story told by the Athenians) Poseidon and Athene, when they contended for the land, set as witnesses of themselves. Now it happened to this olive–tree to be set on fire with the rest of the temple by the Barbarians; and on the next day after the conflagration those of the Athenians who were commanded by the king to offer sacrifice, saw when they had gone up to the temple that a shoot had run up from the stock of the tree about a cubit in length. These then made report of this.

56. The Hellenes meanwhile at Salamis, when it was announced to them how it had been as regards the Acropolis of the Athenians, were disturbed so greatly that some of the commanders did not even wait for the question to be decided which had been proposed, but began to go hastily to their ships and to put up their sails, meaning to make off with speed; and by those of them who remained behind it was finally decided to fight at sea in defence of the Isthmus. So night came on, and they having been dismissed from the council were going to their ships: 57, and when Themistocles had come to his ship, Mnesiphilos an Athenian asked him what they had resolved; and being informed by him that it had been determined to take out the ships to the Isthmus and fight a battle by sea in defence of the Peloponnese, he said: "Then, if they set sail with the ships from Salamis, thou wilt not fight any more sea–battles at all for the fatherland, for they will all take their way to their several cities and neither Eurybiades nor any other man will be able to detain them or to prevent the fleet from being

dispersed: and Hellas will perish by reason of evil counsels. But if there by any means, go thou and try to unsettle that which has been resolved, if perchance thou mayest persuade Eurybiades to change his plans, so as to stay here." 58. This advice very much commended itself to Themistocles; and without making any answer he went to the ship of Eurybiades. Having come thither he said that he desired to communicate to him a matter which concerned the common good; and Eurybiades bade him come into his ship and speak, if he desired to say anything. Then Themistocles sitting down beside him repeated to him all those things which he had heard Mnesiphilos say, making as if they were his own thoughts, and adding to them many others; until at last by urgent request he persuaded him to come out of his ship and gather the commanders to the council. 59. So when they were gathered together, before Eurybiades proposed the discussion of the things for which he had assembled the commanders, Themistocles spoke with much vehemence[36] being very eager to gain his end; and as he was speaking, the Corinthian commander, Adeimantos the son of Okytos, said: "Themistocles, at the games those who stand forth for the contest before the due time are beaten with rods." He justifying himself said: "Yes, but those who remain behind are not crowned." 60. At that time he made answer mildly to the Corinthian; and to Eurybiades he said not now any of those things which he had said before, to the effect that if they should set sail from Salamis they would disperse in different directions; for it was not seemly for him to bring charges against the allies in their presence: but he held to another way of reasoning, saying: "Now it is in thy power to save Hellas, if thou wilt follow my advice, which is to stay here and here to fight a sea–battle, and if thou wilt not follow the advice of those among these men who bid thee remove the ships to the Isthmus. For hear both ways, and then set them in comparison. If thou engage battle at the Isthmus, thou wilt fight in an open sea, into which it is by no means convenient for us that we go to fight, seeing that we have ships which are heavier and fewer in number than those of the enemy. Then secondly thou wilt give up to destruction Salamis and Megara and Egina, even if we have success in all else; for with their fleet will come also the land–army, and thus thou wilt thyself lead them to the Peloponnese and wilt risk the safety of all Hellas. If however thou shalt do as I say, thou wilt find therein all the advantages which I shall tell thee of:—in the first place by engaging in a narrow place with few ships against many, if the fighting has that issue which it is reasonable to expect, we shall have very much the better; for to fight a sea–fight in a narrow space is for our advantage, but to fight in a wide open space is for theirs. Then again Salamis will be preserved, whither our children and our wives have been removed for safety; and moreover there is this also secured thereby, to which ye are most of all attached, namely that by remaining here thou wilt fight in defence of the Peloponnese as much as if the fight were at the Isthmus; and thou wilt not lead the enemy to Peloponnese, if thou art wise. Then if that which I expect come to pass and we gain a victory with our ships, the Barbarians will not come to you at the Isthmus nor will they advance further than Attica, but they will retire in disorder; and we shall be the gainers by the preservation of Megara and Egina and Salamis, at which place too an oracle tells us that we shall get the victory over our enemies.[37] Now when men take counsel reasonably for themselves, reasonable issues are wont as a rule to come, but if they do not take counsel reasonably, then God is not wont generally to attach himself to the judgment of men." 61. When Themistocles thus spoke, the Corinthian Adeimantos inveighed against him for the second time, bidding him to be silent because he had no native land, and urging Eurybiades not to put to the vote the proposal of one who was a citizen of no city; for he said that Themistocles might bring opinions before the council if he could show a city belonging to him, but otherwise not. This objection he made against him because Athens had been taken and was held by the enemy. Then Themistocles said many evil things of him and of the Corinthians both, and declared also that he himself and his countrymen had in truth a city and a land larger than that of the Corinthians, so long as they had two hundred ships fully manned; for none of the Hellenes would be able to repel the Athenians if they came to fight against them. 62. Signifying this he turned then to Eurybiades and spoke yet more urgently: "If thou wilt remain here, and remaining here wilt show thyself a good man, well; but if not, thou wilt bring about the overthrow of Hellas, for upon the ships depends all our power in the war. Nay, but do as I advise. If, however, thou shalt not do so, we shall forthwith take up our households and voyage to Siris in Italy, which is ours already of old and the oracles say that it is destined to be colonised by us; and ye, when ye are left alone and deprived of allies such as we are, will remember my words." 63. When Themistocles thus spoke, Eurybiades was persuaded to change his mind; and, as I think, he changed his mind chiefly from fear lest the Athenians should depart and leave them, if he should take the ships to the Isthmus; for if the Athenians left them and departed, the rest would be no longer able to fight with the enemy. He chose then this counsel, to stay in that place and decide matters there by a sea–fight.

64. Thus those at Salamis, after having skirmished with one another in speech, were making preparations for a sea–fight there, since Eurybiades had so determined: and as day was coming on, at the same time when the sun rose there was an earthquake felt both on the land and on the sea: and they determined to pray to the gods and to call

upon the sons of Aiacos to be their helpers. And as they had determined, so also they did; for when they had prayed to all the gods, they called Ajax and Telamon to their help from Salamis, where the fleet was,[38] and sent a ship to Egina to bring Aiacos himself and the rest of the sons of Aiacos.

65. Moreover Dicaios the son of Theokydes, an Athenian, who was an exile and had become of great repute among the Medes at this time, declared that when the Attic land was being ravaged by the land—army of Xerxes, having been deserted by the Athenians, he happened then to be in company with Demaratos the Lacedemonian in the Thriasian plain; and he saw a cloud of dust going up from Eleusis, as if made by a company of about thirty thousand men, and they wondered at the cloud of dust, by what men it was caused. Then forthwith they heard a sound of voices, and Dicaios perceived that the sound was the mystic cry Iacchos; but Demaratos, having no knowledge of the sacred rites which are done at Eleusis, asked him what this was that uttered the sound, and he said: "Demaratos, it cannot be but that some great destruction is about to come to the army of the king: for as to this, it is very manifest, seeing that Attica is deserted, that this which utters the sound is of the gods, and that it is going from Eleusis to help the Athenians and their allies: if then it shall come down in the Peloponnese, there is danger for the king himself and for the army which is upon the mainland, but if it shall direct its course towards the ships which are at Salamis, the king will be in danger of losing his fleet. This feast the Athenians celebrate every year to the Mother and the Daughter;[39] and he that desires it, both of them and of the other Hellenes, is initiated in the mysteries; and the sound of voices which thou hearest is the cry Iacchos which they utter at this feast." To this Demaratos said: "Keep silence and tell not this tale to any other man; for if these words of thine be reported to the king, thou wilt surely lose thy head, and neither I nor any other man upon earth will be able to save thee: but keep thou quiet, and about this expedition the gods will provide." He then thus advised, and after the cloud of dust and the sound of voices there came a mist which was borne aloft and carried towards Salamis to the camp of the Hellenes: and thus they learnt (said he) that the fleet of Xerxes was destined to be destroyed. Such was the report made by Dicaios the son of Theodykes, appealing to Demaratos and others also as witnesses.

66. Meanwhile those who were appointed to serve in the fleet of Xerxes, having gazed in Trachis upon the disaster of the Lacedemonians and having passed over from thence to Histiaia, after staying three days sailed through Euripos, and in other three days they

had reached Phaleron. And, as I suppose, they made their attack upon Athens not fewer in number both by land and sea than when they had arrived at Sepias and at Thermopylai: for against those of them who perished by reason of the storm and those who were slain at Thermopylai and in the sea—fights at Artemision, I will set those who at that time were not yet accompanying the king, the Malians, Dorians, Locrians, and Bœotians (who accompanied him in a body, except the Thespians and Plataians), and moreover those of Carystos, Andros, and Tenos, with all the other islanders except the five cities of which I mentioned the names before; for the more the Persian advanced towards the centre of Hellas, the more nations accompanied him.

67. So then, when all these had come to Athens except the Parians (now the Parians had remained behind at Kythnos waiting to see how the war would turn out),—when all the rest, I say, had come to Phaleron, then Xerxes himself came down to the ships desiring to visit them and to learn the opinions of those who sailed in them: and when he had come and was set in a conspicuous place, then those who were despots of their own nations or commanders of divisions being sent for came before him from their ships, and took their seats as the king had assigned rank to each one, first the king of Sidon, then he of Tyre, and after them the rest: and when they were seated in due order, Xerxes sent Mardonios and inquired, making trial of each one, whether he should fight a battle by sea. 68. So when Mardonios went round asking them, beginning with the king of Sidon, the others gave their opinions all to the same effect, advising him to fight a battle by sea, but Artemisia spoke these words:—(a) "Tell the king I pray thee, Mardonios, that I, who have proved myself not to be the worst in the sea—fights which have been fought near Eubœa, and have displayed deeds not inferior to those of others, speak to him thus: Master, it is right that I set forth the opinion which I really have, and say that which I happen to think best for thy cause: and this I say,—spare thy ships and do not make a sea—fight; for the men are as much stronger than thy men by sea, as men are stronger than women. And why must thou needs run the risk of sea—battles? Hast thou not Athens in thy possession, for the sake of which thou didst set forth on thy march, and also the rest of Hellas? and no man stands in thy way to resist, but those who did stand against thee came off as it was fitting that they should. (b) Now the manner in which I think the affairs of thy adversaries will have their issue, I will declare. If thou do not hasten to make a sea—fight, but keep thy ships here by the land, either remaining here thyself or even advancing on to the Peloponnese, that which thou hast come to do, O master, will easily be effected; for the Hellenes are not able to hold out against thee for any long time, but thou wilt soon

disperse them and they will take flight to their several cities: since neither have they provisions with them in this island, as I am informed, nor is it probable that if thou shalt march thy land−army against the Peloponnese, they who have come from thence will remain still; for these will have no care to fight a battle in defence of Athens. (c) If however thou hasten to fight forthwith, I fear that damage done to the fleet may ruin the land−army also. Moreover, O king, consider also this, that the servants of good men are apt to grow bad, but those of bad men good; and thou, who art of all men the best, hast bad servants, namely those who are reckoned as allies, Egyptians and Cyprians and Kilikians and Pamphylians, in whom there is no profit." 69. When she thus spoke to Mardonios, those who were friendly to Artemisia were grieved at her words, supposing that she would suffer some evil from the king because she urged him not to fight at sea; while those who had envy and jealousy of her, because she had been honoured above all the allies, were rejoiced at the opposition,[40] supposing that she would now be ruined. When however the opinions were reported to Xerxes, he was greatly pleased with the opinion of Artemisia; and whereas even before this he thought her excellent, he commended her now yet more. Nevertheless he gave orders to follow the advice of the greater number, thinking that when they fought by Eubœa they were purposely slack, because he was not himself present with them, whereas now he had made himself ready to look on while they fought a sea−battle.

70. So when they passed the word to put out to sea, they brought their ships out to Salamis and quietly ranged themselves along the shore in their several positions. At that time the daylight was not sufficient for them to engage battle, for night had come on; but they made their preparations to fight on the following day. Meanwhile the Hellenes were possessed by fear and dismay, especially those who were from Peloponnese: and these were dismayed because remaining in Salamis they were to fight a battle on behalf of the land of the Athenians, and being defeated they would be cut off from escape and blockaded in an island, leaving their own land unguarded. And indeed the land−army of the Barbarians was marching forward during that very night towards the Peloponnese. 71. Yet every means had been taken that the Barbarians might not be able to enter Peloponnesus by land: for as soon as the Peloponnesians heard that Leonidas and his company had perished at Thermopylai, they came together quickly from the cities and took post at the Isthmus, and over them was set as commander Cleombrotos, the son of Anaxandrides and brother of Leonidas. These being posted at the Isthmus had destroyed the Skironian way, and after this (having so determined in counsel with one another) they began to build a wall across the Isthmus;

and as they were many myriads[41] and every man joined in the work, the work proceeded fast; for stones and bricks and pieces of timber and baskets full of sand were carried to it continually, and they who had thus come to help paused not at all in their work either by night or by day. 72. Now those of the Hellenes who came in full force to the Isthmus to help their country were these,—the Lacedemonians, the Arcadians of every division, the Eleians, Corinthians, Sikyonians, Epidaurians, Phliasians, Troizenians and Hermionians. These were they who came to the help of Hellas in her danger and who had apprehension for her, while the rest of the Peloponnesians showed no care: and the Olympic and Carneian festivals had by this time gone by. 73. Now Peloponnesus is inhabited by seven races; and of these, two are natives of the soil and are settled now in the place where they dwelt of old, namely the Arcadians and the Kynurians; and one race, that of the Achaians, though it did not remove from the Peloponnese, yet removed in former time from its own land and dwells now in that which was not its own. The remaining races, four in number, have come in from without, namely the Dorians, Aitolians, Dryopians and Lemnians. Of the Dorians there are many cities and of great renown; of the Aitolians, Elis alone; of the Dryopians, Hermion[42] and Asine, which latter is opposite Cardamyle in the Laconian land; and of the Lemnians, all the Paroreatai. The Kynurians, who are natives of the soil, seem alone to be Ionians, but they have become Dorians completely because they are subject to the Argives and by lapse of time, being originally citizens of Orneai or the dwellers in the country round Orneai.[43] Of these seven nations the remaining cities, except those which I enumerated just now, stood aside and did nothing; and if one may be allowed to speak freely, in thus standing aside they were in fact taking the side of the Medes.

74. Those at the Isthmus were struggling with the labour which I have said, since now they were running a course in which their very being was at stake, and they did not look to have any brilliant success with their ships: while those who were at Salamis, though informed of this work, were yet dismayed, not fearing so much for themselves as for Peloponnesus. For some time then they spoke of it in private, one man standing by another, and they marvelled at the ill-counsel of Eurybiades; but at last it broke out publicly. A meeting accordingly was held, and much was spoken about the same points as before, some saying that they ought to sail away to Peloponnesus and run the risk in defence of that, and not stay and fight for a land which had been captured by the enemy, while the Athenians, Eginetans and Megarians urged that they should stay there and defend themselves. 75. Then Themistocles, when his opinion was like to be

defeated by the Peloponnesians, secretly went forth from the assembly, and having gone out he sent a man to the encampment of the Medes in a boat, charging him with that which he must say: this man's name was Sikinnos, and he was a servant of Themistocles and tutor to his children; and after these events Themistocles entered him as a Thespian citizen, when the Thespians were admitting new citizens, and made him a wealthy man. He at this time came with a boat and said to the commanders of the Barbarians these words: "The commander of the Athenians sent me privately without the knowledge of the other Hellenes (for, as it chances, he is disposed to the cause of the king, and desires rather that your side should gain the victory than that of the Hellenes), to inform you that the Hellenes are planning to take flight, having been struck with dismay; and now it is possible for you to execute a most noble work, if ye do not permit them to flee away: for they are not of one mind with one another and they will not stand against you in fight, but ye shall see them fighting a battle by sea with one another, those who are disposed to your side against those who are not." 76. He then having signified to them this, departed out of the way; and they, thinking that the message deserved credit, landed first a large number of Persians in the small island of Psyttaleia, which lies between Salamis and the mainland; and then, as midnight came on, they put out the Western wing of their fleet to sea, circling round towards Salamis, and also those stationed about Keos and Kynosura put out their ships to sea; and they occupied all the passage with their ships as far as Munychia. And for this reason they put out their ships, namely in order that the Hellenes might not even be permitted to get away, but being cut off in Salamis might pay the penalty for the contests at Artemision: and they disembarked men of the Persians on the small island called Psyttaleia for this reason, namely that when the fight should take place, these might save the men of one side and destroy those of the other, since there especially it was likely that the men and the wrecks of ships would be cast up on shore, for the island lay in the way of the sea–fight which was to be. These things they did in silence, that the enemy might not have information of them.

77. They then were making their preparations thus in the night without having taken any sleep at all: and with regard to oracles, I am not able to make objections against them that they are not true, for I do not desire to attempt to overthrow the credit of them when they speak clearly, looking at such matters as these which here follow:

"But when with ships they shall join the sacred strand of the goddess, Artemis golden–sword–girded, and thee, wave–washed Kynosura, Urged by a maddening hope,[44] having given rich Athens to plunder, Then shall Justice divine quell Riot, of Insolence first—born,[45] Longing to overthrow all things[46] and terribly panting for bloodhshed: Brass shall encounter with brass, and Ares the sea shall empurple, Tinging its waves with the blood: then a day of freedom for Hellas Cometh from wide—seeing Zeus[47] and from Victory, lady and mother."[48]

Looking to such things as this, and when Bakis speaks so clearly, I do not venture myself to make any objections about oracles, nor can I admit them from others.

78. Now between the commanders that were at Salamis there came to be great contention of speech and they did not yet know that the Barbarians were surrounding them with their ships, but they thought that they were still in their place as they saw them disposed in the day. 79. Then while the commanders were engaged in strife, there came over from Egina Aristeides the son of Lysimachos, an Athenian who had been ostracised by the people, a man whom I hold (according to that which I hear of his character) to have been the best and most upright of all Athenians. This man came into the council and called forth Themistocles, who was to him not a friend, but an enemy to the last degree; but because of the greatness of the present troubles he let those matters be forgotten and called him forth, desiring to communicate with him. Now he had heard beforehand that the Peloponnesians were pressing to take the ships away to the Isthmus. So when Themistocles came forth to him, Aristeides spoke these words: "Both at other times when occasion arises, and also especially at this time we ought to carry on rivalry as to which of us shall do more service to our country. And I tell thee now that it is indifferent whether the Peloponnesians say many words or few about sailing away from hence; for having been myself an eye—witness I tell thee that now not even if the Corinthians and Eurybiades himself desire to sail out, will they be able; for we are encompassed round by the enemy. Go thou in then, and signify this to them." 80. He made answer as follows: "Thou advisest very well,[49] and also the news which thou hast brought is good, since thou art come having witnessed with thine own eyes that which I desired might come to pass: for know that this which is being done by the Medes is of my suggestion; because, when the Hellenes would not come to a battle of their own will, it was necessary to bring them over to us against their will. Do thou however, since thou art come bearing good news, thyself report it to them; for if I say these things, I shall be thought to speak that which I have myself invented, and I shall not persuade them, but they will think that the Barbarians are not doing so. Do thou thyself however come forward to speak, and declare to them how things are; and

when thou hast declared this, if they are persuaded, that will be the best thing, but if this is not credible to them, it will be the same thing so far as concerns us, for they will no longer be able to take to flight, if we are encompassed on all sides, as thou sayest." 81. Aristeides accordingly came forward and told them this, saying that he had come from Egina and had with difficulty escaped without being perceived by those who were blockading them; for the whole encampment of the Hellenes was encompassed by the ships of Xerxes; and he counselled them to get ready to defend themselves. He then having thus spoken retired, and among them again there arose dispute, for the greater number of the commanders did not believe that which was reported to them: 83, and while these were doubting, there came a trireme manned by Tenians, deserting from the enemy, of which the commander was Panaitios the son of Sosimenes, which brought them the whole truth. For this deed the Tenians were inscribed at Delphi on the tripod among those who had conquered the Barbarians. With the ship which deserted at Salamis and the Lemnian ship which deserted before and came to Artemision, the naval force of the Hellenes was completed to the number of three hundred and eighty ships, for before this two ships were yet wanting to make up this number.

83. The Hellenes then, since they believed that which was said by the Tenians, were preparing for a sea–fight: and as the dawn appeared, they made an assembly of those who fought on board the ships[50] and addressed them, Themistocles making a speech which was eloquent beyond the rest; and the substance of it was to set forth all that is better as opposed to that which is worse, of the several things which arise in the nature and constitution of man; and having exhorted them to choose the better,[51] and thus having wound up his speech, he bade them embark in their ships. These then proceeded to embark, and there came in meanwhile the trireme from Egina which had gone away to bring the sons of Aiacos. 84. Then the Hellenes put out all their ships, and while they were putting out from shore, the Barbarians attacked them forthwith. Now the other Hellenes began backing their ships and were about to run them aground, but Ameinias of Pallene, an Athenian, put forth with his ship and charged one of the enemy; and his ship being entangled in combat and the men not being able to get away, the others joined in the fight to assist Ameinias. The Athenians say that the beginning of the battle was made thus, but the Eginetans say that the ship which went away to Egina to bring the sons of Aiacos was that which began the fight. It is also reported that an apparition of a woman was seen by them, and that having appeared she encouraged them to the fight so that the whole of the army of the Hellenes heard it,

first having reproached them in these words: "Madmen,[52] how far will ye yet back your ships?"

85. Opposite the Athenians had been ranged the Phenicians, for these occupied the wing towards Eleusis and the West, and opposite the Lacedemonians were the Ionians, who occupied the wing which extended to the East and to Piræus. Of them however a few were purposely slack in the fight according to the injunctions of Themistocles,[53] but the greater number were not so. I might mention now the names of many captains of ships who destroyed ships of the Hellenes, but I will make no use of their names except in the case of Theomestor, the son of Androdamas and Phylacos the son of Histiaios, of Samos both: and for this reason I make mention of these and not of the rest, because Theomestor on account of this deed became despot of Samos, appointed by the Persians, and Phylacos was recorded as a benefactor of the king and received much land as a reward. Now the benefactors of the king are called in the Persian tongue orosangai. 86. Thus it was with these; but the greater number of their ships were disabled at Salamis, being destroyed some by the Athenians and others by the Eginetans: for since the Hellenes fought in order and ranged in their places, while the Barbarians were no longer ranged in order nor did anything with design, it was likely that there would be some such result as in fact followed. Yet on this day they surpassed themselves much more than when they fought by Eubœa, every one being eager and fearing Xerxes, and each man thinking that the king was looking especially at him. 87. As regards the rest I cannot speak of them separately, or say precisely how the Barbarians or the Hellenes individually contended in the fight; but with regard to Artemisia that which happened was this, whence she gained yet more esteem than before from the king.—When the affairs of the king had come to great confusion, at this crisis a ship of Artemisia was being pursued by an Athenian ship; and as she was not able to escape, for in front of her were other ships of her own side, while her ship, as it chanced, was furthest advanced towards the enemy, she resolved what she would do, and it proved also much to her advantage to have done so. While she was being pursued by the Athenian ship she charged with full career against a ship of her own side manned by Calyndians and in which the king of the Calyndians Damasithymos was embarked. Now, even though it be true that she had had some strife with him before, while they were still about the Hellespont, yet I am not able to say whether she did this by intention, or whether the Calyndian ship happened by chance to fall in her way. Having charged against it however and sunk it, she enjoyed good fortune and got for herself good in two ways; for first the captain of the Athenian ship, when he saw

her charge against a ship manned by Barbarians, turned away and went after others, supposing that the ship of Artemisia was either a Hellenic ship or was deserting from the Barbarians and fighting for the Hellenes, 88,—first, I say, it was her fortune to have this, namely to escape and not suffer destruction; and then secondly it happened that though she had done mischief, she yet gained great reputation by this thing with Xerxes. For it is said that the king looking on at the fight perceived that her ship had charged the other; and one of those present said: "Master, dost thou see Artemisia, how well she is fighting, and how she sank even now a ship of the enemy?" He asked whether this was in truth the deed of Artemisia, and they said that it was; for (they declared) they knew very well the sign of her ship: and that which was destroyed they thought surely was one of the enemy; for besides other things which happened fortunately for her, as I have said, there was this also, namely that not one of the crew of the Calyndian ship survived to become her accuser. And Xerxes in answer to that which was said to him is reported to have uttered these words: "My men have become women, and my women men." Thus it is said that Xerxes spoke. 89. And meanwhile in this struggle there was slain the commander Ariabignes, son of Dareios and brother of Xerxes, and there were slain too many others of note of the Persians and Medes and also of the allies; and of the Hellenes on their part a few; for since they knew how to swim, those whose ships were destroyed and who were not slain in hand—to—hand conflict swam over to Salamis; but of the Barbarians the greater number perished in the sea, not being able to swim. And when the first ships turned to flight, then it was that the largest number perished, for those who were stationed behind, while endeavouring to pass with their ships to the front in order that they also might display some deed of valour for the king to see, ran into the ships of their own side as they fled.

90. It happened also in the course of this confusion that some of the Phenicians, whose ships had been destroyed, came to the king and accused the Ionians, saying that by means of them their ships had been lost, and that they had been traitors to the cause. Now it so came about that not only the commanders of the Ionians did not lose their lives, but the Phenicians who accused them received a reward such as I shall tell. While these men were yet speaking thus, a Samothrakian ship charged against an Athenian ship: and as the Athenian ship was being sunk by it, an Eginetan ship came up against the Samothrakian vessel and ran it down. Then the Samothrakians, being skilful javelin— throwers, by hurling cleared off the fighting—men from the ship which had wrecked theirs and then embarked upon it and took possession of it. This event saved the Ionians from punishment; for when Xerxes saw that they had performed a

great exploit, he turned to the Phenicians (for he was exceedingly vexed and disposed to find fault with all) and bade cut off their heads, in order that they might not, after having been cowards themselves, accuse others who were better men than they. For whensoever Xerxes (sitting just under the mountain opposite Salamis, which is called Aigaleos) saw any one of his own side display a deed of valour in the sea-fight, he inquired about him who had done it, and the scribes recorded the name of the ship's captain with that of his father and the city from whence he came. Moreover also Ariaramnes, a Persian who was present, shared[54] the fate of the Phenicians, being their friend. They[55] then proceeded to deal with the Phenicians.

91. In the meantime, as the Barbarians turned to flight and were sailing out towards Phaleron, the Eginetans waited for them in the passage and displayed memorable actions: for while the Athenians in the confused tumult were disabling both those ships which resisted and those which were fleeing, the Eginetans were destroying those which attempted to sail away; and whenever any escaped the Athenians, they went in full course and fell among the Eginetans. 92. Then there met one another the ship of Themistocles, which was pursuing a ship of the enemy, and that of Polycritos the son of Crios the Eginetan. This last had charged against a ship of Sidon, the same that had taken the Eginetan vessel which was keeping watch in advance at Skiathos,[56] and in which sailed Pytheas the son of Ischenoös, whom the Persians kept in their ship, all cut to pieces as he was, making a marvel of his valour. The Sidonian ship then was captured bearing with it this man as well as the Persians of whom I spoke, so that Pytheas thus came safe to Egina. Now when Polycritos looked at the Athenian vessel he recognised when he saw it the sign of the admiral's ship, and shouting out he addressed Themistocles with mockery about the accusation brought against the Eginetans of taking the side of the Medes,[57] and reproached him. This taunt Polycritos threw out against Themistocles after he had charged against the ship of Sidon. And meanwhile those Barbarians whose ships had escaped destruction fled and came to Phaleron to be under cover of the land-army.

93. In this sea-fight the Eginetans were of all the Hellenes the best reported of, and next to them the Athenians; and of the individual men the Eginetan Polycritos and the Athenians Eumenes of Anagyrus and Ameinias of Pallene, the man who had pursued after Artemisia. Now if he had known that Artemisia was sailing in this ship, he would not have ceased until either he had taken her or had been taken himself; for orders had been given to the Athenian captains, and moreover a prize was offered of ten thousand

drachmas for the man who should take her alive; since they thought it intolerable that a woman should make an expedition against Athens. She then, as has been said before, had made her escape; and the others also, whose ships had escaped destruction, were at Phaleron.

94. As regards Adeimantos the commander of the Corinthians, the Athenians say that forthwith at the beginning when the ships were engaging in the fight, being struck with panic and terror he put up his sails and fled away; and the Corinthians, when they saw the admiral's ship fleeing, departed likewise: and after this, as the story goes, when they came in their flight opposite to the temple of Athene Skiras in the land of Salamis, there fell in with them by divine guidance a light vessel,[58] which no one was ever found to have sent, and which approached the Corinthians at a time when they knew nothing of that which was happening with the fleet. And by this it is conjectured[59] that the matter was of the Deity; for when they came near to the ships, the men in the light vessel said these words: "Adeimantos, thou hast turned thy ships away and hast set forth to flee, deserting the cause of the Hellenes, while they are in truth gaining a victory and getting the better of their foes as much as they desired." When they said this, since Adeimantos doubted of it, they spoke a second time and said that they might be taken as hostages and slain, if the Hellenes should prove not to be gaining the victory. Then he turned his ship back, he and the others with him, and they reached the camp when the work was finished. Such is the report spread by the Athenians against these: the Corinthians however do not allow this to be so, but hold that they were among the first in the sea–fight; and the rest of Hellas also bears witness on their side.

95. Aristeides moreover the son of Lysimachos, the Athenian, of whom I made mention also shortly before this as a very good man, he in this tumult which had arisen about Salamis did as follows:—taking with him a number of the hoplites of Athenian race who had been ranged along the shore of the land of Salamis, with them he disembarked on the island of Psyttaleia; and these slew all the Persians who were in this islet.

96. When the sea–fight had been broken off, the Hellenes towed in to Salamis so many of the wrecks as chanced to be still about there, and held themselves ready for another sea–fight, expecting that the king would yet make use of the ships which remained unhurt; but many of the wrecks were taken by the West Wind and borne to that strand in Attica which is called Colias; so as to fulfil[60] not only all that other oracle which

was spoken about this sea–fight by Bakis and Musaios, but also especially, with reference to the wrecks cast up here, that which had been spoken in an oracle many years before these events by Lysistratos, an Athenian who uttered oracles, and which had not been observed by any of the Hellenes:

"Then shall the Colian women with firewood of oars roast barley."[61]

This was destined to come to pass after the king had marched away.

97. When Xerxes perceived the disaster which had come upon him, he feared lest some one of the Ionians should suggest to the Hellenes, or they should themselves form the idea, to sail to the Hellespont and break up the bridges; and so he might be cut off in Europe and run the risk of perishing utterly: therefore he began to consider about taking flight. He desired however that his intention should not be perceived either by the Hellenes or by those of his own side; therefore he attempted to construct a mole going across to Salamis, and he bound together Phenician merchant vessels in order that they might serve him both for a bridge and a wall, and made preparations for fighting as if he were going to have another battle by sea. Seeing him do so, all the rest made sure that he had got himself ready in earnest and intended to stay and fight; but Mardonios did not fail to perceive the true meaning of all these things, being by experience very well versed in his way of thinking.

98. While Xerxes was doing thus, he sent a messenger to the Persians, to announce the calamity which had come upon them. Now there is nothing mortal which accomplishes a journey with more speed than these messengers, so skilfully has this been invented by the Persians: for they say that according to the number of days of which the entire journey consists, so many horses and men are set at intervals, each man and horse appointed for a day's journey. These neither snow nor rain nor heat nor darkness of night prevents from accomplishing each one the task proposed to him, with the very utmost speed. The first then rides and delivers the message with which he is charged to the second, and the second to the third; and after that it goes through them handed from one to the other,[62] as in the torch–race among the Hellenes, which they perform for Hephaistos. This kind of running of their horses the Persians call angareion. 99. The first message then which came to Susa, announcing that Xerxes had Athens in his possession, so greatly rejoiced the Persians who had been left behind, that they strewed all the ways with myrtle boughs and offered incense perpetually, and themselves

continued in sacrifices and feasting. The second message however, which came to them after this, so greatly disturbed them that they all tore their garments and gave themselves up to crying and lamentation without stint, laying the blame upon Mardonios: and this the Persians did not so much because they were grieved about the ships, as because they feared for Xerxes himself.

100. As regards the Persians this went on for all the time which intervened, until the coming of Xerxes himself caused them to cease: and Mardonios seeing that Xerxes was greatly troubled by reason of the sea–fight, and suspecting that he was meaning to take flight from Athens, considered with regard to himself that he would have to suffer punishment for having persuaded the king to make an expedition against Hellas, and that it was better for him to run the risk of either subduing Hellas or ending his own life honourably, placing his safety in suspense for a great end,[63] though his opinion was rather that he would subdue Hellas;—he reckoned up these things, I say, and addressed his speech to the king as follows: "Master, be not thou grieved, nor feel great trouble on account of this thing which has come to pass; for it is not upon a contest of timbers that all our fortunes depend, but of men and of horses: and none of these who suppose now that all has been achieved by them will attempt to disembark from the ships and stand against thee, nor will any in this mainland do so; but those who did stand against us paid the penalty. If therefore thou thinkest this good to do, let us forthwith attempt the Peloponnese, or if thou thinkest good to hold back, we may do that. Do not despond however, for there is no way of escape for the Hellenes to avoid being thy slaves, after they have first given an account of that which they did to thee both now and at former times. Thus it were best to do; but if thou hast indeed resolved to retire thyself and to withdraw thy army, I have another counsel to offer for that case too. Do not thou, O king, let the Persians be an object of laughter to the Hellenes; for none of thy affairs have suffered by means of the Persians, nor wilt thou be able to mention any place where we proved ourselves cowards: but if Phenicians or Egyptians or Cyprians or Kilikians proved themselves cowards, the calamity which followed does not belong to the Persians in any way. Now therefore, since it is not the Persians who are guilty towards thee, follow my counsel. If thou hast determined not to remain here, retire thou to thine own abode, taking with thee the main body of the army, and it must then be for me to deliver over to thee Hellas reduced to subjection, choosing for this purpose thirty myriads[64] from the army." 101. Hearing this Xerxes was rejoiced and delighted so far as he might be after his misfortunes,[65] and to Mardonios he said that when he had taken counsel he would reply and say which of these two things he would

do. So when he was taking counsel with those of the Persians who were called to be his advisers,[66] it seemed good to him to send for Artemisia also to give him counsel, because at the former time she alone had showed herself to have perception of that which ought to be done. So when Artemisia had come, Xerxes removed from him all the rest, both the Persian councillors and also the spearmen of the guard and spoke to her thus: "Mardonios bids me stay here and make an attempt on the Peloponnese, saying that the Persians and the land– army are not guilty of any share in my calamity, and that they would gladly give me proof of this. He bids me therefore either do this or, if not, he desires himself to choose thirty myriads from the army and to deliver over to me Hellas reduced to subjection; and he bids me withdraw with the rest of the army to my own abode. Do thou therefore, as thou didst well advise about the sea–fight which was fought, urging that we should not bring it on, so also now advise me which of these things I shall do, that I may succeed in determining well." 102. He thus consulted her, and she spoke these words: "O king, it is hard for me to succeed in saying the best things when one asks me for counsel; yet it seems good to me at the present that thou shouldest retire back and leave Mardonios here, if he desires it and undertakes to do this, together with those whom he desires to have: for on the one hand if he subdue those whom he says that he desires to subdue, and if those matters succeed well which he has in mind when he thus speaks, the deed will after all be thine, master, seeing that thy slaves achieved it: and on the other hand if the opposite shall come to pass of that which Mardonios intends, it will be no great misfortune, seeing that thou wilt thyself remain safe, and also the power in those parts[67] which concerns thy house:[68] for if thou shalt remain safe with thy house, many contests many times over repeated will the Hellenes have to pass through for their own existence.[69] Of Mardonios however, if he suffer any disaster, no account will be made; and if the Hellenes conquer they gain a victory which is no victory, having destroyed one who is but thy slave. Thou however wilt retire having done that for which thou didst make thy march, that is to say, having delivered Athens to the fire."

103. With this advice Xerxes was greatly delighted, since she succeeded in saying that very thing which he himself was meaning to do: for not even if all the men and all the women in the world had been counselling him to remain, would he have done so, as I think, so much had he been struck with terror. He commended Artemisia therefore and sent her away to conduct his sons to Ephesos, for there were certain bastard sons of his which accompanied him. 104. With these sons he sent Hermotimos to have charge of them, who was by race of Pedasa and was in the estimation of the king second to none

of the eunuchs. [Now the Pedasians dwell above Halicarnassos, and at this Pedasa a thing happens as follows:—whenever to the whole number of those who dwell about this city some trouble is about to come within a certain time, then the priestess of Athene in that place gets a long beard; and this has happened to them twice before now. 105. Of these Pedasians was Hermotimos.][70] And this man of all persons whom we know up to this time obtained the greatest revenge for a wrong done to him. For he had been captured by enemies and was being sold, and Panionios a man of Chios bought him, one who had set himself to gain his livelihood by the most impious practices; for whenever he obtained boys who possessed some beauty, he would make eunuchs of them, and then taking them to Sardis or Ephesos sold them for large sums of money, since with the Barbarians eunuchs are held to be of more value for all matters of trust than those who are not eunuchs. Panionios then, I say, made eunuchs of many others, since by this he got his livelihood, and also of this man about whom I speak: and Hermotimos, being not in everything unfortunate, was sent from Sardis to the king with other gifts, and as time went on he came to be honoured more than all the other eunuchs in the sight of Xerxes. 106. And when the king, being at that time in Sardis, was setting the Persian army in motion to march against Athens, then Hermotimos, having gone down for some business to that part of Mysia which the Chians occupy and which is called Atarneus, found there Panionios: and having recognised him he spoke to him many friendly words, first recounting to him all the good things which he had by his means, and next making promises in return for this, and saying how many good things he would do for him, if he would bring his household and dwell in that land; so that Panionios gladly accepting his proposals brought his children and his wife. Then, when he had caught him together with his whole house, Hermotimos spoke as follows: "O thou, who of all men that ever lived up to this time didst gain thy substance by the most impious deeds, what evil did either I myself or any of my forefathers do either to thee or to any of thine, that thou didst make me to be that which is nought instead of a man? Didst thou suppose that thou wouldest escape the notice of the gods for such things as then thou didst devise? They however following the rule of justice delivered[71] thee into my hands, since thou hadst done impious deeds; so that thou shalt not have reason to find fault with the penalty which shall be inflicted upon thee by me." When he had thus reproached him, the man's sons were brought into his presence and Panionios was compelled to make eunuchs of his own sons, who were four in number, and being compelled he did so; and then when he had so done, the sons were compelled to do the same thing to him. Thus vengeance by the hands of Hermotimos[72] overtook Panionios.

107. When Xerxes had entrusted his sons to Artemisia to carry them back to Ephesos, he called Mardonios and bade him choose of the army whom he would, and make his deeds, if possible, correspond to his words. During this day then things went so far; and in the night on the command of the king the leaders of the fleet began to withdraw their ships from Phaleron to the Hellespont, as quickly as they might each one, to guard the bridges for the king to pass over. And when the Barbarians were near Zoster as they sailed, then seeing the small points of rock which stretch out to sea from this part of the mainland, they thought that these were ships and fled for a good distance. In time however, perceiving that they were not ships but points of rock, they assembled together again and continued on their voyage.

108. When day dawned, the Hellenes, seeing that the land–army was staying still in its place, supposed that the ships also were about Phaleron; and thinking that they would fight another sea–battle, they made preparations to repel them. When however they were informed that the ships had departed, forthwith upon this they thought it good to pursue after them. They pursued therefore as far as Andros, but did not get a sight of the fleet of Xerxes; and when they had come to Andros, they deliberated what they should do. Themistocles then declared as his opinion that they should take their course through the islands and pursue after the ships, and afterwards sail straight to the Hellespont to break up the bridges; but Eurybiades expressed the opposite opinion to this, saying that if they should break up the floating–bridges, they would therein do[73] the greatest possible evil to Hellas: for if the Persian should be cut off and compelled to remain in Europe, he would endeavour not to remain still, since if he remained still, neither could any of his affairs go forward, nor would any way of returning home appear; but his army would perish of hunger: whereas if he made the attempt and persevered in it, all Europe might be brought over to him, city by city and nation by nation, the inhabitants being either conquered[74] or surrendering on terms before they were conquered: moreover they would have for food the crops of the Hellenes which grew year by year. He thought however that conquered in the sea–fight the Persian would not stay in Europe, and therefore he might be allowed to flee until in his flight he came to his own land. Then after that they might begin the contest for the land which belonged to the Persian. To this opinion the commanders of the other Peloponnesians adhered also. 109. When Themistocles perceived that he would not be able to persuade them, or at least the greater number of them, to sail to the Hellespont, he changed his counsel[75] and turning to the Athenians (for these were grieved most at the escape of the enemy and were anxious to sail to the Hellespont even by

themselves alone,[76] if the others were not willing) to them he spoke as follows: "I myself also have been present before now on many occasions, and have heard of many more, on which something of this kind came to pass, namely that men who were forced into great straits, after they had been defeated fought again and repaired their former disaster: and as for us, since we have won as a prize from fortune the existence of ourselves and of Hellas by repelling from our land so great a cloud of men, let us not pursue enemies who flee from us: for of these things not we were the doers, but the gods and heroes, who grudged that one man should become king of both Asia and of Europe, and he a man unholy and presumptuous, one who made no difference between things sacred and things profane,[77] burning and casting down the images of the gods, and who also scourged the Sea and let down into it fetters. But as things are at present, it is well that we should now remain in Hellas and look after ourselves and our households; and let each man repair his house, and have a care for sowing his land, after he has completely driven away the Barbarian: and then at the beginning of the spring let us sail down towards the Hellespont and Ionia." Thus he spoke, intending to lay up for himself a store of gratitude with the Persian, in order that if after all any evil should come upon him at the hands of the Athenians, he might have a place of refuge: and this was in fact that which came to pass.

110. Themistocles then speaking thus endeavoured to deceive them, and the Athenians followed his advice: for he had had the reputation even in former times of being a man of ability[78] and he had now proved himself to be in truth both able and of good judgment; therefore they were ready in every way to follow his advice when he spoke. So when these had been persuaded by him, forthwith after this Themistocles sent men with a vessel, whom he trusted to keep silence, to whatever test they might be brought, of that which he himself charged them to tell the king; and of them Sikinnos his servant again was one. When these came to Attica, the rest stayed behind in the ship, while Sikinnos went up to Xerxes and spoke these words: "Themistocles the son of Neocles sent me, who is commander of the Athenians, and of all the allies the best and ablest man, to tell thee that Themistocles the Athenian, desiring to be of service to thee, held back the Hellenes when they were desirous to pursue after thy ships and to destroy the bridges on the Hellespont. Now therefore thou mayest make thy way home quite undisturbed." They having signified this sailed away again.

111. The Hellenes meanwhile, having resolved not to pursue after the ships of the Barbarians further, nor to sail to the Hellespont to break up the passage, were investing

Andros intending to take it: for the Andrians were the first of the islanders who, being asked by Themistocles for money, refused to give it: and when Themistocles made proposals to them and said that the Athenians had come having on their side two great deities, Persuasion and Compulsion, and therefore they must by all means give them money, they replied to this that not without reason, as it now appeared, was Athens great and prosperous, since the Athenians were well supplied with serviceable deities; but as for the Andrians, they were poor,[79] having in this respect attained to the greatest eminence, and there were two unprofitable deities which never left their island but always remained attached to the place, Poverty, namely, and Helplessness: and the Andrians being possessed of these deities would not give money; for never could the power of the Athenians get the better of their inability.[80] 112. These, I say, having thus made answer and having refused to give the money, were being besieged: and Themistocles not ceasing in his desire for gain sent threatening messages to the other islands and asked them for money by the same envoys, employing those whom he had before sent to the king;[81] and he said that if they did not give that which was demanded of them, he would bring the fleet of the Hellenes against them to besiege and take them. Thus saying he collected great sums of money from the Carystians and the Parians, who being informed how Andros was being besieged, because it had taken the side of the Medes, and how Themistocles was held in more regard than any of the other commanders, sent money for fear of this. Whether any others of the islanders also gave money I am not able to say, but I think that some others gave and not these alone. Yet to the Carystians at least there was no respite from the evil on this account, but the Parians escaped the attack, because they propitiated Themistocles with money. Thus Themistocles with Andros as his starting–point was acquiring sums of money for himself from the men of the islands without the knowledge of the other commanders.

113. Xerxes meanwhile with his army stayed for a few days after the sea–fight, and then they all began to march forth towards Bœotia by the same way by which they had come: for Mardonios thought both that it was well for him to escort the king on his way, and also that it was now too late in the year to carry on the war; it was better, he thought, to winter in Thessaly and then at the beginning of spring to attempt the Peloponnese. When he came to Thessaly, then Mardonios chose out for himself first all those Persians who are called "Immortals," except only their commander Hydarnes (for Hydarnes said that he would not be left behind by the king), and after them of the other Persians those who wore cuirasses, and the body of a thousand horse: also the Medes, Sacans, Bactrians and Indians, foot and horsemen both.[82] These nations he chose in

the mass,[83] but from the other allies he selected by few at a time, choosing whose who had fine appearance of those of whom he knew that they had done good service. From the Persians he chose more than from any other single nation, and these wore collars of twisted metal and bracelets; and after them came the Medes, who in fact were not inferior in number to the Persians, but only in bodily strength. The result was that there were thirty myriads in all, including cavalry.

114. During this time, while Mardonios was selecting his army and Xerxes was in Thessaly, there had come an oracle from Delphi to the Lacedemonians, bidding them ask satisfaction from Xerxes for the murder of Leonidas and accept that which should be given by him. The Spartans therefore sent a herald as quickly as possible, who having found the whole army still in Thessaly came into the presence of Xerxes and spoke these words: "O king of the Medes, the Lacedemonians and the sons of Heracles of Sparta demand of thee satisfaction for murder, because thou didst kill their king, fighting in defence of Hellas." He laughed and then kept silence some time, and after that pointing to Mardonios, who happened to be standing by him, he said: "Then Mardonios here shall give them satisfaction, such as is fitting for them to have." 115. The herald accordingly accepted the utterance and departed; and Xerxes leaving Mardonios in Thessaly went on himself in haste to the Hellespont and arrived at the passage where the crossing was in five—and—thirty days, bringing back next to nothing, as one may say,[84] of his army: and whithersoever they came on the march and to whatever nation, they seized the crops of that people and used them for provisions; and if they found no crops, then they took the grass which was growing up from the earth, and stripped off the bark from the trees and plucked down the leaves and devoured them, alike of the cultivated trees and of those growing wild; and they left nothing behind them: thus they did by reason of famine. Then plague too seized upon the army and dysentery, which destroyed them by the way, and some of them also who were sick the king left behind, laying charge upon the cities where at the time he chanced to be in his march, to take care of them and support them: of these he left some in Thessaly, and some at Siris in Paionia, and some in Macedonia. In these parts too he had left behind him the sacred chariot of Zeus, when he was marching against Hellas; but on his return he did not receive it back: for the Paionians had given it to the Thracians, and when Xerxes asked for it again, they said that the mares while at pasture had been carried off by the Thracians of the upper country, who dwelt about the source of the Strymon. 116. Here also a Thracian, the king of the Bisaltians and of the Crestonian land, did a deed of surpassing horror; for he had said that he would not

himself be subject to Xerxes with his own will and had gone away up to Mount Rhodope, and also he had forbidden his sons to go on the march against Hellas. They however, either because they cared not for his command, or else because a desire came upon them to see the war, went on the march with the Persian: and when they returned all unhurt, being six in number, their father plucked out their eyes for this cause. 117. They then received this reward: and as to the Persians, when passing on from Thrace they came to the passage, they crossed over the Hellespont in haste to Abydos by means of the ships, for they did not find the floating–bridges still stretched across but broken up by a storm. While staying there for a time they had distributed to them an allowance of food more abundant than they had had by the way, and from satisfying their hunger without restraint and also from the changes of water there died many of those in the army who had remained safe till then. The rest arrived with Xerxes at Sardis.

118. There is also another story reported as follows, namely that when Xerxes on his march away from Athens came to Eïon on the Strymon, from that point he did not continue further to make marches by road, but delivered his army to Hydarnes to lead back to the Hellespont, while he himself embarked in a Phenician ship and set forth for Asia; and as he sailed he was seized by a wind from the Strymon,[85] violent and raising great waves; and since he was tossed by the storm more and more, the ship being heavily laden (for there were upon the deck great numbers of Persians, those namely who went with Xerxes), the king upon that falling into fear shouted aloud and asked the pilot whether there were for them any means of safety. He said: "Master, there are none, unless some way be found of freeing ourselves of the excessive number of passengers." Then it is said that Xerxes, when he heard this, spoke thus: "Persians, now let each one of you show that he has care for the king; for my safety, as it seems, depends upon you." He, they say, thus spoke, and they made obeisance to him and leapt out into the sea; and so the ship being lightened came safe to Asia. As soon as they had landed Xerxes, they say, first presented the pilot with a wreath of gold, because he had saved the life of the king, and then cut off his head, because he had caused the death of many of the Persians. 119. This other story, I say, is reported about the return of Xerxes, but I for my part can by no means believe it, either in other respects or as regards this which is said to have happened to the Persians; for if this which I have related had in truth been said by the pilot to Xerxes, not one person's opinion in ten thousand will differ from mine that the king would have done some such thing as this, that is to say, he would have caused those who were upon the deck to go

down below into the hold, seeing that they were Persians of the highest rank among the Persians; and of the rowers, who were Phenicians, he would have thrown out into the sea a number equal to the number of those. In fact however, as I have said before, he made his return to Asia together with the rest of the army by road. 120. And this also which follows is a strong witness that it was so; for Xerxes is known to have come to Abdera on his way back, and to have made with them a guest–friendship and presented them with a Persian sword of gold and a gold–spangled tiara: and as the men of Abdera themselves say (though I for my part can by no means believe it), he loosed his girdle for the first time during his flight back from Athens, considering himself to be in security. Now Abdera is situated further towards the Hellespont than the river Strymon and Eïon, from which place the story says that he embarked in the ship.

121. The Hellenes meanwhile, when it proved that they were not able to conquer Andros, turned towards Carystos, and having laid waste the land of that people they departed and went to Salamis. First then for the gods they chose out first–fruits of the spoil, and among them three Persian triremes, one to be dedicated as an offering at the Isthmus, which remained there still up to my time, another at Sunion, and the third to Ajax in Salamis where they were. After this they divided the spoil among themselves and sent the first–fruits[86] to Delphi, of which was made a statue holding in its hand the beak of a ship and in height measuring twelve cubits. This statue stood in the same place with the golden statue of Alexander the Macedonian. 122. Then when the Hellenes had sent first–fruits to Delphi, they asked the god on behalf of all whether the first–fruits which he had received were fully sufficient and acceptable to him. He said that from the Hellenes he had received enough, but not from the Eginetans, and from them he demanded the offering of their prize of valour for the sea– fight at Salamis. Hearing this the Eginetans dedicated golden stars, three in number, upon a ship's mast of bronze, which are placed in the corner[87] close to the mixing–bowl of Crœsus. 123. After the division of the spoil the Hellenes sailed to the Isthmus, to give the prize of valour to him who of all the Hellenes had proved himself the most worthy during this war: and when they had come thither and the commanders distributed[88] their votes at the altar of Poseidon, selecting from the whole number the first and the second in merit, then every one of them gave in his vote for himself, each man thinking that he himself had been the best; but for the second place the greater number of votes came out in agreement, assigning that to Themistocles. They then were left alone in their votes, while Themistocles in regard to the second place surpassed the rest by far: 124, and although the Hellenes would not give decision of this by reason of envy, but sailed

away each to their own city without deciding, yet Themistocles was loudly reported of and was esteemed throughout Hellas to be the man who was the ablest[89] by far of the Hellenes: and since he had not received honour from those who had fought at Salamis, although he was the first in the voting, he went forthwith after this to Lacedemon, desiring to receive honour there; and the Lacedemonians received him well and gave him great honours. As a prize of valour they gave to Eurybiades a wreath of olive; and for ability and skill they gave to Themistocles also a wreath of olive, and presented him besides with the chariot which was judged to be the best in Sparta. So having much commended him, they escorted him on his departure with three hundred picked men of the Spartans, the same who are called the "horsemen,"[90] as far as the boundaries of Tegea: and he is the only man of all we know to whom the Spartans ever gave escort on his way. 125. When however he had come to Athens from Lacedemon, Timodemos of Aphidnai, one of the opponents of Themistocles, but in other respects not among the men of distinction, maddened by envy attacked him, bringing forward against him his going to Lacedemon, and saying that it was on account of Athens that he had those marks of honour which he had from the Lacedemonians, and not on his own account. Then, as Timodemos continued ceaselessly to repeat this, Themistocles said: "I tell thee thus it is:—if I had been a native of Belbina[91] I should never have been thus honoured by the Spartans; but neither wouldest thou, my friend, for all that thou art an Athenian." So far then went these matters.

126. Artabazos meanwhile the son of Pharnakes, a man who was held in esteem among the Persians even before this and came to be so yet more after the events about Plataia, was escorting the king as far as the passage with six myriads[92] of that army which Mardonios had selected for himself; and when the king was in Asia and Artabazos on his march back came near to Pallene, finding that Mardonios was wintering in Thessaly and Macedonia and was not at present urgent with him to come and join the rest of the army, he thought it not good to pass by without reducing the Potidaians to slavery, whom he had found in revolt: for the men of Potidaia, when the king had marched by them and when the fleet of the Persians had departed in flight from Salamis, had openly made revolt from the Barbarians; and so also had the others done who occupy Pallene. 127. So upon this Artabazos began to besiege Potidaia, and suspecting that the men of Olynthos also were intending revolt from the king, he began to besiege this city too, which was occupied by Bottiaians who had been driven away from the Thermaian gulf by the Macedonians. So when he had taken these men by siege, he brought them forth to a lake and slew them[93] there; and the city he

delivered to Critobulos of Torone to have in charge, and to the natives of Chalkidike; and thus it was that the Chalkidians got possession of Olynthos. 128. Having taken this city Artabazos set himself to attack Potidaia with vigour, and as he was setting himself earnestly to this work, Timoxeinos the commander of the troops from Skione concerted with him to give up the town by treachery. Now in what manner he did this at the first, I for my part am not able to say, for this is not reported; at last however it happened as follows. Whenever either Timoxeinos wrote a paper wishing to send it to Artabazos, or Artabazos wishing to send one to Timoxeinos, they wound it round by the finger–notches[94] of an arrow, and then, putting feathers over the paper, they shot it to a place agreed upon between them. It came however to be found out that Timoxeinos was attempting by treachery to give up Potidaia; for Artabazos, shooting an arrow at the place agreed upon, missed this spot and struck a man of Potidaia in the shoulder; and when he was struck, a crowd came about him, as is apt to happen when there is fighting, and they forthwith took the arrow and having discovered the paper carried it to the commanders. Now there was present an allied force of the other men of Pallene also. Then when the commanders had read the paper and discovered who was guilty of the treachery, they resolved not openly to convict[95] Timoxeinos of treachery, for the sake of the city of Skione, lest the men of Skione should be esteemed traitors for all time to come. 129. He then in such a manner as this had been discovered; and when three months had gone by while Artabazos was besieging the town, there came to be a great ebb of the sea backwards, which lasted for a long time; and the Barbarians, seeing that shallow water had been produced, endeavoured to get by into the peninsula of Pallene,[96] but when they had passed through two fifth–parts of the distance, and yet three– fifths remained, which they must pass through before they were within Pallene, then there came upon them a great flood–tide of the sea, higher than ever before, as the natives of the place say, though high tides come often. So those of them who could not swim perished, and those who could were slain by the men of Potidaia who put out to them in boats. The cause of the high tide and flood and of that which befell the Persians was this, as the Potidaians say, namely that these same Persians who perished by means of the sea had committed impiety towards the temple of Poseidon and his image in the suburb of their town; and in saying that this was the cause, in my opinion they say well. The survivors of his army Artabazos led away to Thessaly to join Mardonios. Thus it fared with these who escorted the king on his way.

130. The fleet of Xerxes, so much of it as remained, when it had touched Asia in its flight from Salamis, and had conveyed the king and his army over from the Chersonese

to Abydos, passed the winter at Kyme: and when spring dawned upon it, it assembled early at Samos, where some of the ships had even passed the winter; and most of the Persians and Medes still served as fighting-men on board of them.[97] To be commanders of them there came Mardontes the son of Bagaios, and Artaÿntes the son of Artachaies, and with them also Ithamitres was in joint command, who was brother's son to Artaÿntes and had been added by the choice of Artaÿntes himself. They then, since they had suffered a heavy blow, did not advance further up towards the West, nor did any one compel them to do so; but they remained still in Samos and kept watch over Ionia, lest it should revolt, having three hundred ships including those of the Ionians; and they did not expect that the Hellenes on their part would come to Ionia, but thought that it would satisfy them to guard their own land, judging from the fact that they had not pursued after them in their flight from Salamis but were well contented then to depart homewards. As regards the sea then their spirit was broken, but on land they thought that Mardonios would get much the advantage. So they being at Samos were taking counsel to do some damage if they could to their enemies, and at the same time they were listening for news how the affairs of Mardonios would fall out.

131. The Hellenes on their part were roused both by the coming on of spring and by the presence of Mardonios in Thessaly. Their land-army had not yet begun to assemble, when the fleet arrived at Egina, in number one hundred and ten ships, and the commander and admiral was Leotychides, who was the son of Menares, the son of Hegesilaos, the son of Hippocratides, the son of Leotychides, the son of Anaxilaos, the son of Archidemos, the son of Anaxandriddes, the son of Theopompos, the son of Nicander, the son of Charilaos,[98] the son of Eunomos, the son of Polydectes, the son of Prytanis, the son of Euryphon,[99] the son of Procles, the son of Aristodemos, the son of Aristomachos, the son of Cleodaios, the son of Hyllos, the son of Heracles, being of the other royal house.[100] These all, except the two[101] enumerated first after Leotychides, had been kings of Sparta. And of the Athenians the commander was Xanthippos the son of Ariphon. 132. When all the ships had arrived at Egina, there came Ionian envoys to the camp of the Hellenes, who also came a short time before this to Sparta and asked the Lacedemonians to set Ionia free; and of them one was Herodotus the son of Basileides. These had banded themselves together and had plotted to put to death Strattis the despot of Chios, being originally seven in number; but when one of those who took part with them gave information of it and they were discovered to be plotting against him, then the remaining six escaped from Chios and

came both to Sparta and also at this time to Egina, asking the Hellenes to sail over to Ionia: but they with difficulty brought them forward as far as Delos; for the parts beyond this were all fearful to the Hellenes, since they were without experience of those regions and everything seemed to them to be filled with armed force, while their persuasion was that it was as long a voyage to Samos as to the Pillars of Heracles. Thus at the same time it so chanced that the Barbarians dared sail no further up towards the West than Samos, being smitten with fear, and the Hellenes no further down towards the East than Delos, when the Chians made request of them. So fear was guard of the space which lay between them.

133. The Hellenes, I say, sailed to Delos; and Mardonios meanwhile had been wintering in Thessaly. From thence he sent round a man, a native of Europos, whose name was Mys, to the various Oracles, charging him to go everywhere to consult,[102] wherever they[103] were permitted to make trial of the Oracles. What he desired to find out from the Oracles when he gave this charge, I am not able to say, for that is not reported; but I conceive for my part that he sent to consult about his present affairs and not about other things. 134. This Mys is known to have come to Lebadeia and to have persuaded by payment of money one of the natives of the place to go down to Trophonios, and also he came to the Oracle at Abai of the Phokians; and moreover when he came for the first time to Thebes, he not only consulted the Ismenian Apollo,— there one may consult just as at Olympia with victims,—but also by payment he persuaded a stranger who was not a Theban, and induced him to lie down to sleep in the temple of Amphiaraos. In this temple no one of the Thebans is permitted to seek divination, and that for the following reason:—Amphiaraos dealing by oracles bade them choose which they would of these two things, either to have him as a diviner or else as an ally in war, abstaining from the other use; and they chose that he should be their ally in war: for this reason it is not permitted to any of the Thebans to lie down to sleep in that temple. 135. After this a thing which to me is a very great marvel is said by the Thebans to have come to pass:—it seems that this man Mys of Europos, as he journeyed round to all the Oracles, came also to the sacred enclosure of the Ptoan Apollo. This temple is called "Ptoon," and belongs to the Thebans, and it lies above the lake Copaïs at the foot of the mountains, close to the town of Acraiphia. When the man called Mys came to this temple with three men chosen from the citizens[104] in his company, who were sent by the public authority to write down that which the god should utter in his divination, forthwith it is said the prophet[105] of the god began to give the oracle in a Barbarian tongue; and while those of the Thebans

who accompanied him were full of wonder, hearing a Barbarian instead of the Hellenic tongue, and did not know what to make of the matter before them, it is said that the man of Europos, Mys, snatched from them the tablet which they bore and wrote upon it that which was being spoken by the prophet; and he said that the prophet was giving his answer in the Carian tongue: and then when he had written it, he went away and departed to Thessaly.

136. Mardonios having read that which the Oracles uttered, whatever that was, after this sent as an envoy to Athens Alexander the son of Amyntas, the Macedonian, both because the Persians were connected with him by marriage, (for Gygaia the sister of Alexander and daughter of Amyntas had been married to a Persian Bubares,[106] and from her had been born to him that Amyntas who lived in Asia, having the name of his mother's father, to whom the king gave Alabanda,[107] a great city of Phrygia, to possess), and also Mardonios was sending him because he was informed that Alexander was a public guest–friend and benefactor of the Athenians; for by this means he thought that he would be most likely to gain over the Athenians to his side, about whom he heard that they were a numerous people and brave in war, and of whom he knew moreover that these were they who more than any others had brought about the disasters which had befallen the Persians by sea. Therefore if these should be added to him, he thought that he should easily have command of the sea (and this in fact would have been the case), while on land he supposed himself to be already much superior in force. Thus he reckoned that his power would be much greater than that of the Hellenes. Perhaps also the Oracles told him this beforehand, counselling him to make the Athenian his ally, and so he was sending in obedience to their advice.

137. Now of this Alexander the seventh ancestor[108] was that Perdiccas who first became despot of the Macedonians, and that in the manner which here follows:—From Argos there fled to the Illyrians three brothers of the descendents of Temenos, Gauanes, Aëropos, and Perdiccas; and passing over from the Illyrians into the upper parts of Macedonia they came to the city of Lebaia. There they became farm– servants for pay in the household of the king, one pasturing horses, the second oxen, and the youngest of them, namely Perdiccas, the smaller kinds of cattle; for[109] in ancient times even those who were rulers over men[110] were poor in money, and not the common people only; and the wife of the king cooked for them their food herself. And whenever she baked, the loaf of the boy their servant, namely Perdiccas, became double as large as by nature it should be. When this happened constantly in the same

manner, she told it to her husband, and he when he heard it conceived forthwith that this was a portent and tended to something great. He summoned the farm—servants therefore, and gave notice to them to depart out of his land; and they said that it was right that before they went forth they should receive the wages which were due. Now it chanced that the sun was shining into the house down through the opening which received the smoke, and the king when he heard about the wages said, being infatuated by a divine power: "I pay you then this for wages, and it is such as ye deserve," pointing to the sunlight. So then Gauanes and Aëropos the elder brothers stood struck with amazement when they heard this, but the boy, who happened to have in his hand a knife, said these words: "We accept, O king, that which thou dost give;" and he traced a line with his knife round the sunlight on the floor of the house, and having traced the line round he thrice drew of the sunlight into his bosom, and after that he departed both himself and his fellows. 138. They then were going away, and to the king one of those who sat by him at table told what manner of thing the boy had done, and how the youngest of them had taken that which was given with some design: and he hearing this and being moved with anger, sent after them horsemen to slay them. Now there is a river in this land to which the descendents of these men from Argos sacrifice as a saviour. This river, so soon as the sons of Temenos had passed over it, began to flow with such great volume of water that the horsemen became unable to pass over. So the brothers, having come to another region of Macedonia, took up their dwelling near the so—called gardens of Midas the son of Gordias, where roses grow wild which have each one sixty petals and excel all others in perfume. In these gardens too Silenos was captured, as is reported by the Macedonians: and above the gardens is situated a mountain called Bermion, which is inaccessible by reason of the cold. Having taken possession of that region, they made this their starting—point, and proceeded to subdue also the rest of Macedonia. 139. From this Perdiccas the descent of Alexander was as follows:—Alexander was the son of Amyntas, Amyntas was the son of Alketes, the father of Alketes was Aëropos, of him Philip, of Philip Argaios, and of this last the father was Perdiccas, who first obtained the kingdom.

140. Thus then, I say, Alexander the son of Amyntas was descended; and when he came to Athens sent from Mardonios, he spoke as follows: (a) "Athenians, Mardonios speaks these words:—There has come to me a message from the king which speaks in this manner:—To the Athenians I remit all the offences which were committed against me: and now, Mardonios, thus do,—first give them back their own land; then let them choose for themselves another in addition to this, whichsoever they desire, remaining

independent; and set up for them again all their temples, which I set on fire, provided that they consent to make a treaty with me. This message having come to me, it is necessary for me to do so, unless by your means I am prevented: and thus I speak to you now:—Why are ye so mad as to raise up war against the king? since neither will ye overcome him, nor are ye able to hold out against him for ever: for ye saw the multitude of the host of Xerxes and their deeds, and ye are informed also of the power which is with me at the present time; so that even if ye overcome and conquer us (of which ye can have no hope if ye are rightly minded), another power will come many times as large. Do not ye then desire to match yourselves with the king, and so to be both deprived of your land and for ever running a course for your own lives; but make peace with him: and ye have a most honourable occasion to make peace, since the king has himself set out upon this road: agree to a league with us then without fraud or deceit, and remain free. (b) These things Mardonios charged me to say to you, O Athenians; and as for me, I will say nothing of the goodwill towards you on my part, for ye would not learn that now for the first time; but I ask of you to do as Mardonios says, since I perceive that ye will not be able to war with Xerxes for ever,—if I perceived in you ability to do this, I should never have come to you speaking these words,—for the power of the king is above that of a man and his arm is very long. If therefore ye do not make an agreement forthwith, when they offer you great things as the terms on which they are willing to make a treaty, I have fear on your behalf, seeing that ye dwell more upon the highway than any of your allies, and are exposed ever to destruction alone, the land which ye possess being parted off from the rest and lying between the armies which are contending together.[111] Nay, but be persuaded, for this is a matter of great consequence to you, that to you alone of the Hellenes the great king remits the offences committed and desires to become a friend."

141. Thus spoke Alexander; and the Lacedemonians having been informed that Alexander had come to Athens to bring the Athenians to make a treaty with the Barbarians, and remembering the oracles, who it was destined that they together with the other Dorians should be driven forth out of the Peloponnese by the Medes and the Athenians combined, had been very greatly afraid lest the Athenians should make a treaty with the Persians; and forthwith they had resolved to send envoys. It happened moreover that they were introduced at the same time with Alexander;[112] for the Athenians had waited for them, protracting the time, because they were well assured that the Lacedemonians would hear that an envoy had come from the Barbarians to make a treaty, and that having heard it they would themselves send envoys with all

speed. They acted therefore of set purpose, so as to let the Lacedemonians see their inclination. 142. So when Alexander had ceased speaking, the envoys from Sparta followed him forthwith and said: "As for us, the Lacedemonians sent us to ask of you not to make any change in that which concerns Hellas, nor to accept proposals from the Barbarian; since this is not just in any way nor honourable for any of the Hellenes to do, but least of all for you, and that for many reasons. Ye were they who stirred up this war, when we by no means willed it; and the contest came about for your dominion, but now it extends even to the whole of Hellas. Besides this it is by no means to be endured that ye Athenians, who are the authors of all this, should prove to be the cause of slavery to the Hellenes, seeing that ye ever from ancient time also have been known as the liberators of many. We feel sympathy however with you for your sufferings and because ye were deprived of your crops twice and have had your substance ruined now for a long time. In compensation for this the Lacedemonians and their allies make offer to support your wives and all those of your households who are unfitted for war, so long as this war shall last: but let not Alexander the Macedonian persuade you, making smooth the speech of Mardonios; for these things are fitting for him to do, since being himself a despot he is working in league with a despot: for you however they are not fitting to do, if ye chance to be rightly minded; for ye know that in Barbarians there is neither faith nor truth at all."

Thus spoke the envoys: 143, and to Alexander the Athenians made answer thus: "Even of ourselves we know so much, that the Mede has a power many times as numerous as ours; so that there is no need for thee to cast this up against us. Nevertheless because we long for liberty we shall defend ourselves as we may be able: and do not thou endeavour to persuade us to make a treaty with the Barbarian, for we on our part shall not be persuaded. And now report to Mardonios that the Athenians say thus:—So long as the Sun goes on the same course by which he goes now, we will never make an agreement with Xerxes; but we will go forth to defend ourselves[113] against him, trusting in the gods and the heroes as allies, for whom he had no respect when he set fire to their houses and to their sacred images. And in the future do not thou appear before the Athenians with any such proposals as these, nor think that thou art rendering them good service in advising them to do that which is not lawful; for we do not desire that thou shouldest suffer anything unpleasant at the hands of the Athenians, who art their public guest and friend." 144. To Alexander they thus made answer, but to the envoys from Sparta as follows: "That the Lacedemonians should be afraid lest we should make a treaty with the Barbarian was natural no doubt;[114] but it seems to be an unworthy fear for men who know so well the spirit of the Athenians, namely that there is neither so great quantity of gold anywhere upon the earth, nor any land so much excelling in beauty and goodness, that we should be willing to accept it and enslave Hellas by taking the side of the Medes. For many and great are the reasons which hinder us from doing this, even though we should desire it; first and greatest the images and houses of the gods set on fire or reduced to ruin, which we must necessarily avenge to the very utmost rather than make an agreement with him who did these deeds; then secondly there is the bond of Hellenic race, by which we are of one blood and of one speech, the common temples of the gods and the common sacrifices, the manners of life which are the same for all; to these it would not be well that the Athenians should become traitors. And be assured of this, if by any chance ye were not assured of it before, that so long as one of the Athenians remains alive, we will never make an agreement with Xerxes. We admire however the forethought which ye had with regard to us, in that ye took thought for us who have had our substance destroyed, and are willing to support the members of our households; and so far as ye are concerned, the kindness has been fully performed: but we shall continue to endure as we may, and not be a trouble in any way to you. Now therefore, with full conviction this is so, send out an army as speedily as ye may: for, as we conjecture, the Barbarian will be here invading our land at no far distant time but so soon as he shall be informed of the message sent, namely that we shall do none of those things which he desired of us. Therefore before he arrives here in Attica, it is fitting that ye come to our rescue quickly in Bœotia." Thus the Athenians made answer, and upon that the envoys went away back to Sparta. ―――――

NOTES TO BOOK VIII

1. See v. 77.

2. i.e. triremes.

3. *os to plethos ekastoi ton neon pareikhonto*: some read by conjecture *oson to plethos k.t.l.*

4. Perhaps "also" refers to the case of those who had come to Thermopylai, cp. vii. 207. Others translate, "these Hellenes who had come after all to Artemision," i.e. after all the doubt and delay.

5. *pantes*: some MSS. have *plegentes*, which is adopted by most Editors, "smitten by bribes."

6. *dethen*, with ironical sense.

7. *mede purphoron*: the *purphoros* had charge of the fire brought for sacrifices from the altar of Zeus Agetor at Sparta, and ordinarily his person would be regarded as sacred; hence the proverb *oude purphoros esothe*, used of an utter defeat.

8. *tou diekploou*.

9. *kata stoma*.

10. *sklerai brontai*: the adjective means "harsh−sounding."

11. *akhari*.

12. *ta Koila tes Euboies*.

13. "having been roughly handled."

14. *epi ten thalassan tauten*: some MSS. read *taute* for *tauten*, which is to be taken with *sullexas*, "he assembled the generals there."

15. *peripetea epoiesanto sphisi autoisi ta pregmata*.

16. *paleseie*, a word which does not occur elsewhere, and is explained by Hesychius as equivalent to *diaphtharein*. Various emendations have been proposed, and Valla seems to have had the reading *apelaseie*, for he says discessisset. Stein explains *paleseie* (as from *pale*) "should contend."

17. Some suppose the number "four thousand" is interpolated by misunderstanding of the inscription in vii. 228; and it seems hardly possible that the dead were so many as four thousand, unless at least half were Helots.

18. Some MSS. have "Tritantaichmes," which is adopted by many Editors.

19. *neou.*

20. *os anarpasomenoi tous Phokeas*: cp. ix. 60.

21. *podeon steinos*, like the neck of a wineskin; cp. ii. 121, note 102.

22. *tou propheten*, the interpreter of the utterances of the *promantis.*

23. *neou.*

24. *megarou.*

25. i.e. of Athene Polias, the Erechtheion; so throughout this account.

26. *sunerree*, "kept flowing together."

26a. Or, "Hermione."

27. See i. 56.

28. See ch. 31.

29. *pros pantas tous allous*, "in comparison with all the rest," cp. iii. 94.

30. *stratarkheo*: a vague expression, because being introduced after Kecrops he could not have the title of king.

31. The number obtained by adding up the separate contingents is 366. Many Editors suppose that the ships with which the Eginetans were guarding their own coast (ch. 46) are counted here, and quote the authority of Pausanias for the statement that the Eginetans supplied more ships than any others except the Athenians. Stein suggests the insertion of the number twelve in ch. 46.

31a. Or, "Thespeia."

32. i.e. "Areopagus."

33. i.e. the North side.

34. *megaron.*

35. *neos.*

36. *pollos en en tois logois*: cp. ix. 91.

37. See vii. 141–143.

38. *autothen ik Salaminos.*

39. *te Metri kai te Koure*, Demeter and Persephone.

40. *te anakrisi*: cp. *anakrinomenous*, ix. 56. Some Editors, following inferior MSS., read *te krisi*, "at the judgment expressed."

41. *muriadon*, "ten thousands."

42. Or, "Hermione."

43. *oi perioikoi*: some Editors omit the article and translate "and these are the so-called Orneates or dwellers round (Argos)," Orneates being a name for the *perioikoi* of Argos, derived from the conquered city of Orneai.

44. *elpidi mainomene*, "with a mad hope."

45. *krateron Koron Ubrios uion.*

46. *dokeunt ana panta tithesthai*: the MSS. have also *pithesthai*. Possibly *tithesthai* might stand, though *anatithesthai* is not found elsewhere in this sense. Stein adopts in his last edition the conjecture *piesthai*, "swallow up."

47. *Kronides.*

48. *potnia Nike.*

49. i.e. about rivalry.

50. *ton epibateon.*

51. Many Editors reading *osa de* and *parainesas de,* make the stop after *antitithemena*: "and in all that is produced in the nature and constitution of man he exhorted them to choose the better."

52. *o daimonioi,* "strange men."

53. See ch. 22.

54. *pros de eti kai proselabeto*: the MSS. have *prosebaleto.* Most Editors translate, "Moreover Ariamnes . . . contributed to the fate of the Phenicians, being a friend (of the Ionians);" but this does not seem possible unless we read *philos eon Iosi* (or *Ionon*). Valla translates nearly as I have done. (It does not appear that *prosballesthai* is found elsewhere in the sense of *sumballesthai.*)

55. i.e. they who were commanded to execute them.

56. See vii. 179, 181.

57. See vi. 49, etc., and 73.

58. *keleta.*

59. *sumballontai*: the Athenians apparently are spoken of, for they alone believed the story.

60. *apoplesai*: this is the reading of the MSS.; but many Editors adopt corrections (*apoplesthai* or *apoplesthenai*). The subject to *apoplesai* is to be found in the preceding sentence and the connexion with *ton te allon panta k.t.l.* is a loose one. This in fact is added as an afterthought, the idea being originally to call attention simply to the fulfilment of the oracle of Lysistratos.

61. *phruxousi*: a conjectural emendation, adopted by most Editors, of *phrixousi*, "will shudder (at the sight of oars)."

62. *kat allon kai allon*: the MSS. have *kat allon*, but Valla's rendering is "alium atque alium."

63. *uper megalon aiorethenta.*

64. i.e. 300,000.

65. *os ek kakon*: some translate, "thinking that he had escaped from his troubles."

66. *toisi epikletoisi*, cp. vii. 8 and ix. 42.

67. i.e. Asia, as opposed to "these parts."

68. Stein would take *peri oikon ton son* with *oudemia sumphore*, but the order of words is against this.

69. *pollous pollakis agonas drameontai peri spheon auton.*

70. See i. 175. The manner of the repetition and some points in the diction raise suspicion that the passage is interpolated here; and so it is held to be by most Editors. In i. 175 we find *tris* instead of *dis*.

71. *upegagon*, cp. vi. 72, with the idea of bringing before a court for punishment, not "by underhand means," as it is understood by Larcher and Bähr.

72. "vengeance and Hermotimos."

73. *spheis . . . ergasaiato*: the MSS. read *sphi* (one *spheas*) and *ergasaito*, and this is retained by some Editors.

74. "taken."

75. *metabalon*: others translate, "he turned from them to the Athenians"; but cp. vii. 52. The words *pros tous Athenaious* are resumed by *sphi* with *elege*.

76. *kai epi spheon auton balomenoi*, "even at their own venture," cp. iii. 71.

77. *ta idia*, "things belonging to private persons."

78. *sophos.*

79. *geopeinas*, "poor in land."

80. It seems necessary to insert *an* with *einai*. For the sentiment cp. vii. 172.

81. *khreomenos toisi kai pros basilea ekhresato*. This is the reading of the best MSS.: the rest have *khreomenos logoisi toisi kai pros Andrious ekhresato*, "using the same language as he had before used to the Andrians."

82. *kai ten allen ippon*: some MSS. omit *allen*.

83. *ola*, i.e. not the whole number of them, but great masses without individual selection.

84. *ouden meros os eipein.*

85. *anemon Strumonien*, "the wind called Strymonias."

86. *ta akrothinia*, i.e. the tithe.

87. i.e. the corner of the entrance–hall, *epi tou proneiou tes gonies*, i. 51.

88. *dienemon*: some understand this to mean "distributed the voting tablets," and some MSS. read *dienemonto*, "distributed among themselves," which is adopted by many Editors.

89. *sophotatos.*

90. See i. 67.

91. A small island near Attica, taken here as the type of insignificance. To suppose that Timodemos was connected with it is quite unnecessary. The story in Plutarch about the Seriphian is different.

92. i.e. 60,000.

93. *katesphaxe*, "cut their throats."

94. *para tas gluphidas*: some Editors read *peri tas gluphidas* on the authority of Æneas Tacticus. The *gluphides* are probably notches which give a hold for the fingers as they draw back the string.

95. *kataplexai*, "strike down" by the charge.

96. The way was shut against them ordinarily by the town of Potidaia, which occupied the isthmus.

97. i.e. most of those who before served as *epibatai* (vii. 96) continued to serve still. The sentence is usually translated, "of those who served as fighting–men in them the greater number were Persians or Medes," and this may be right.

98. The MSS. have "Charilos" or "Charillos."

99. Some Editors read "Eurypon," which is the form found elsewhere.

100. Cp. vii. 204.

101. *duon*. It seems certain that the number required here is seven and not two, and the emendation *epta* for *duon* (*z* for *b*) is approved by several Editors.

102. *khresomenon*: the best MSS. read *khresamenon*, which is retained by Stein, with the meaning "charging him to consult the Oracles everywhere . . . and then return."

103. i.e. Mardonios and the Persians.

104. i.e. Theban citizens.

105. *promantin*: he is afterwards called *prophetes*.

106. Cp. v. 21.

107. Some Editors would read "Alabastra." Alabanda was a Carian town.

108. Counting Alexander himself as one.

109. *esan gar*: this is the reading of the best MSS.: others have *esan de*. Stein (reading *esan gar*) places this clause after the next, "The wife of the king herself baked their bread, for in ancient times, etc." This transposition is unnecessary; for it would be easy to understand it as a comment on the statement that three members of the royal house of Argos became farm−servants.

110. *ai turannides ton anthropon*.

111. *exaireton metaikhmion te ten gun ektemenon*: there are variations of reading and punctuation in the MSS.

112. *sunepipte oste omou spheon ginesthai ten katastasin*, i.e. their introduction before the assembly, cp. iii. 46.

113. *epeximen amunomenoi*, which possibly might be translated, "we will continue to defend ourselves."

114. *karta anthropeion*.

BOOK IX. THE NINTH BOOK OF THE HISTORIES, CALLED CALLIOPE

1. Mardonios, when Alexander had returned back and had signified to him that which was said by the Athenians, set forth from Thessaly and began to lead his army with all diligence towards Athens: and to whatever land he came, he took up with him the

people of that land. The leaders of Thessaly meanwhile did not repent of all that which had been done already, but on the contrary they urged on the Persian yet much more; and Thorax of Larissa had joined in escorting Xerxes in his flight and at this time he openly offered Mardonios passage to invade Hellas. 2. Then when the army in its march came to Bœotia, the Thebans endeavoured to detain Mardonios, and counselled him saying that there was no region more convenient for him to have his encampment than that; and they urged him not to advance further, but to sit down there and endeavour to subdue to himself the whole of Hellas without fighting: for to overcome the Hellenes by open force when they were united, as at the former time they were of one accord together,[1] was a difficult task even for the whole world combined, "but," they proceeded, "if thou wilt do that which we advise, with little labour thou wilt have in thy power all their plans of resistance.[2] Send money to the men who have power in their cities, and thus sending thou wilt divide Hellas into two parties: after that thou wilt with ease subdue by the help of thy party those who are not inclined to thy side." 3. Thus they advised, but he did not follow their counsel; for there had instilled itself into him a great desire to take Athens for the second time, partly from obstinacy[3] and partly because he meant to signify to the king in Sardis that he was in possession of Athens by beacon-fires through the islands. However he did not even at this time find the Athenians there when he came to Attica; but he was informed that the greater number were either in Salamis or in the ships, and he captured the city finding it deserted. Now the capture of the city by the king had taken place ten months before the later expedition of Mardonios against it.

4. When Mardonios had come to Athens, he sent to Salamis Morychides a man of the Hellespont, bearing the same proposals as Alexander the Macedonian had brought over to the Athenians. These he sent for the second time, being aware beforehand that the dispositions of the Athenians were not friendly, but hoping that they would give way and leave their obstinacy, since the Attic land had been captured by the enemy and was in his power. 5. For this reason he sent Morychides to Salamis; and he came before the Council[4] and reported the words of Mardonios. Then one of the Councillors, Lykidas, expressed the opinion that it was better to receive the proposal which Morychides brought before them and refer it to the assembly of the people.[5] He, I say, uttered this opinion, whether because he had received money from Mardonios, or because this was his own inclination: however the Athenians forthwith, both those of the Council and those outside, when they heard of it, were very indignant, and they came about Lykidas and stoned him to death; but the Hellespontian Morychides they

dismissed unhurt. Then when there had arisen much uproar in Salamis about Lykidas, the women of the Athenians heard of that which was being done, and one woman passing the word to another and one taking another with her, they went of their own accord to the house of Lykidas and stoned his wife and his children to death.

6. The Athenians had passed over to Salamis as follows:—So long as they were looking that an army should come from the Peloponnese to help them, they remained in Attica; but as those in Peloponnesus acted very slowly and with much delay, while the invader was said to be already in Bœotia, they accordingly removed everything out of danger, and themselves passed over to Salamis; and at the same time they sent envoys to Lacedemon to reproach the Lacedemonians for having permitted the Barbarian to invade Attica and for not having gone to Bœotia to meet him in company with them, and also to remind them how many things the Persian had promised to give the Athenians if they changed sides; bidding the envoys warn them that if they did not help the Athenians, the Athenians would find some shelter[6] for themselves. 7. For the Lacedemonians in fact were keeping a feast during this time, and celebrating the Hyakinthia; and they held it of the greatest consequence to provide for the things which concerned the god, while at the same time their wall which they had been building at the Isthmus was just at this moment being completed with battlements. And when the envoys from the Athenians came to Lacedemon, bringing with them also envoys from Megara and Plataia, they came in before the Ephors and said as follows: "The Athenians sent us saying that the king of the Medes not only offers to give us back our land, but also desires to make us his allies on fair and equal terms without deceit or treachery,[7] and is desirous moreover to give us another land in addition to our own, whichsoever we shall ourselves choose. We however, having respect for Zeus of the Hellenes and disdaining to be traitors to Hellas, did not agree but refused, although we were unjustly dealt with by the other Hellenes and left to destruction, and although we knew that it was more profitable to make a treaty with the Persian than to carry on war: nor shall we make a treaty at any future time, if we have our own will. Thus sincerely is our duty done towards the Hellenes:[8] but as for you, after having come then to great dread lest we should make a treaty with the Persian, so soon as ye learnt certainly what our spirit was, namely that we should never betray Hellas, and because your wall across the Isthmus is all but finished, now ye make no account of the Athenians, but having agreed with us to come to Bœotia to oppose the Persian, ye have now deserted us, and ye permitted the Barbarian moreover to make invasion of Attica. For the present then the Athenians have anger against you, for ye did not do as

was fitting to be done: and now they bid[9] you with all speed send out an army together with us, in order that we may receive the Barbarian in the land of Attica; for since we failed of Bœotia, the most suitable place to fight in our land is the Thriasian plain." 8. When the Ephors heard this they deferred their reply to the next day, and then on the next day to the succeeding one; and this they did even for ten days, deferring the matter from day to day, while during this time the whole body of the Peloponnesians were building the wall over the Isthmus with great diligence and were just about to complete it. Now I am not able to say why, when Alexander the Macedonian had come to Athens, they were so very anxious lest the Athenians should take the side of the Medes, whereas now they had no care about it, except indeed that their wall over the Isthmus had now been built, and they thought they had no need of the Athenians any more; whereas when Alexander came to Attica the wall had not yet been completed, but they were working at it in great dread of the Persians. 9. At last however the answer was given and the going forth of the Spartans took place in the following manner:—on the day before that which was appointed for the last hearing of the envoys, Chileos a man of Tegea, who of all strangers had most influence in Lacedemon, heard from the Ephors all that which the Athenians were saying; and he, it seems, said to them these words: "Thus the matter stands, Ephors:—if the Athenians are not friendly with us but are allies of the Barbarian, then though a strong wall may have been built across the Isthmus, yet a wide door has been opened for the Persian into Peloponnesus. Listen to their request, however, before the Athenians resolve upon something else tending to the fall of Hellas." 10. Thus he counselled them, and they forthwith took his words to heart; and saying nothing to the envoys who had come from the cities, while yet it was night they sent out five thousand Spartans, with no less than seven of the Helots set to attend upon each man of them,[9a] appointing Pausanias the son of Cleombrotos to lead them forth. Now the leadership belonged to Pleistarchos the son of Leonidas; but he was yet a boy, and the other was his guardian and cousin: for Cleombrotos, the father of Pausanias and son of Anaxandrides, was no longer alive, but when he had led home from the Isthmus the army which had built the wall, no long time after this he died. Now the reason why Cleombrotos led home the army from the Isthmus was this:—as he was offering sacrifice for fighting against the Persian, the sun was darkened in the heaven. And Pausanias chose as commander in addition to himself Euryanax the son of Dorieos, a man of the same house. 11. So Pausanias with his army had gone forth out of Sparta; and the envoys, when day had come, not knowing anything of this going forth, came in before the Ephors meaning to depart also, each to his own State: and when they had come in before them they said these words: "Ye, O Lacedemonians, are remaining here and celebrating this Hyakinthia and disporting yourselves, having left your allies to destruction; and the Athenians being wronged by you and for want of allies will make peace with the Persians on such terms as they can: and having made peace, evidently we become allies of the king, and therefore we shall join with him in expeditions against any land to which the Persians may lead us; and ye will learn then what shall be the issue for you of this matter." When the envoys spoke these words, the Ephors said and confirmed it with an oath, that they supposed by this time the men were at Orestheion on their way against the strangers: for they used to call the Barbarians "strangers."[10] So they, not knowing of the matter, asked the meaning of these words, and asking they learnt all the truth; so that they were struck with amazement and set forth as quickly as possible in pursuit; and together with them five thousand chosen hoplites of the Lacedemonian "dwellers in the country round"[11] did the same thing also.

12. They then, I say, were hastening towards the Isthmus; and the Argives so soon as they heard that Pausanias with his army had gone forth from Sparta, sent as a herald to Attica the best whom they could find of the long–distance runners,[12] because they had before of their own motion engaged for Mardonios that they would stop the Spartans from going forth: and the herald when he came to Athens spoke as follows: "Mardonios, the Argives sent me to tell thee that the young men have gone forth from Lacedemon, and that the Argives are not able to stop them from going forth: with regard to this therefore may it be thy fortune to take measures well."[13] 13. He having spoken thus departed and went back; and Mardonios was by no means anxious any more to remain in Attica when he heard this message. Before he was informed of this he had been waiting, because he desired to know the news from the Athenians as to what they were about to do; and he had not been injuring or laying waste the land of Attica, because he hoped always that they would make a treaty with him; but as he did not persuade them, being now informed of everything he began to retire out of the country before the force of Pausanias arrived at the Isthmus, having first set fire to Athens and cast down and destroyed whatever was left standing of the walls, houses or temples. Now he marched away for this cause, namely first because Attica was not a land where horsemen could act freely, and also because, if he should be defeated in a battle in Attica, there was no way of retreat except by a narrow pass, so that a few men could stop them. He intended therefore to retreat to Thebes, and engage battle near to a friendly city and to a country where horsemen could act freely.

14. Mardonios then was retiring out of the way, and when he was already upon a road a message came to him saying that another body of troops in advance of the rest[14] had come to Megara, consisting of a thousand Lacedemonians. Being thus informed he took counsel with himself, desiring if possible first to capture these. Therefore he turned back and proceeded to lead his army towards Megara, and the cavalry going in advance of the rest overran the Megaran land: this was the furthest land in Europe towards the sun–setting to which this Persian army came. 15. After this a message came to Mardonios that the Hellenes were assembled at the Isthmus; therefore he marched back by Dekeleia, for the chiefs of Bœotia[15] had sent for those of the Asopians who dwelt near the line of march, and these were his guides along the road to Sphendaleis and thence to Tanagra. So having encamped for the night at Tanagra and on the next day having directed his march to Scolos, he was within the land of the Thebans. Then he proceeded to cut down the trees in the lands of the Thebans, although they were on the side of the Medes, moved not at all by enmity to them, but pressed by urgent necessity both to make a defence for his camp, and also he was making it for a refuge, in case that when he engaged battle things should not turn out for him as he desired. Now the encampment of his army extended from Erythrai along by Hysiai and reached the river Asopos: he was not however making the wall to extend so far as this, but with each face measuring somewhere about ten furlongs.[16]

16. While the Barbarians were engaged upon this work, Attaginos the son of Phyrnon, a Theban, having made magnificent preparations invited to an entertainment Mardonios himself and fifty of the Persians who were of most account; and these being invited came; and the dinner was given at Thebes. Now this which follows I heard from Thersander, an Orchomenian and a man of very high repute in Orchomenos. This Thersander said that he too was invited by Attaginos to this dinner, and there were invited also fifty men of the Thebans, and their host did not place them to recline[17] separately each nation by themselves, but a Persian and a Theban upon every couch. Then when dinner was over, as they were drinking pledges to one another,[18] the Persian who shared a couch with him speaking in the Hellenic tongue asked him of what place he was, and he answered that he was of Orchomenos. The other said: "Since now thou hast become my table– companion and the sharer of my libation, I desire to leave behind with thee a memorial of my opinion, in order that thou thyself also mayest know beforehand and be able to take such counsels for thyself as may be profitable. Dost thou see these Persians who are feasting here, and the army which we left behind encamped upon the river? Of all these, when a little time has gone by, thou

shalt see but very few surviving." While the Persian said these words he shed many tears, as Thersander reported; and he marvelling at his speech said to him: "Surely then it is right to tell Mardonios and to those of the Persians who after him are held in regard." He upon this said: "Friend, that which is destined to come from God, it is impossible for a man to avert; for no man is willing to follow counsel, even when one speaks that which is reasonable. And these things which I say many of us Persians know well; yet we go with the rest being bound in the bonds of necessity: and the most hateful grief of all human griefs is this, to have knowledge of the truth but no power over the event."[19] These things I heard from Thersander of Orchomenos, and in addition to them this also, namely that he told them to various persons forthwith, before the battle took place at Plataia.

17. Mardonios then being encamped in Bœotia, the rest of the Hellenes who lived in these parts and took the side of the Medes were all supplying troops and had joined in the invasion of Attica, but the Phokians alone had not joined in the invasion,—the Phokians, I say, for these too were now actively[20] taking the side of the Medes, not of their own will however, but by compulsion. Not many days however after the arrival of Mardonios at Thebes, there came of them a thousand hoplites, and their leader was Harmokydes, the man who was of most repute among their citizens. When these too came to Thebes, Mardonios sent horsemen and bade the Phokians take up their position by themselves in the plain. After they had so done, forthwith the whole cavalry appeared; and upon this there went a rumour[21] through the army of Hellenes which was with the Medes that the cavalry was about to shoot them down with javelins, and this same report went through the Phokians themselves also. Then their commander Harmokydes exhorted them, speaking as follows: "Phokians, it is manifest that these men are meaning to deliver us to a death which we may plainly foresee,[22] because we have been falsely accused by the Thessalians, as I conjecture: now therefore it is right that every one of you prove himself a good man; for it is better to bring our lives to an end doing deeds of valour and defending ourselves, than to be destroyed by a dishonourable death offering ourselves for the slaughter. Let each man of them learn that they are Barbarians and that we, against whom they contrived murder, are Hellenes." 18. While he was thus exhorting them, the horsemen having encompassed them round were riding towards them as if to destroy them; and they were already aiming their missiles as if about to discharge them, nay some perhaps did discharge them: and meanwhile the Phokians stood facing them gathered together and with their ranks closed as much as possible every way. Then the horsemen turned and

rode away back. Now I am not able to say for certain whether they came to destroy the Phokians at the request of the Thessalians, and then when they saw them turn to defence they feared lest they also might suffer some loss, and therefore rode away back, for so Mardonios had commanded them; or whether on the other hand he desired to make trial of them and to see if they had in them any warlike spirit. Then, when the horsemen had ridden away back, Mardonios sent a herald and spoke to them as follows: "Be of good courage, Phokians, for ye proved yourselves good men, and not as I was informed. Now therefore carry on this way with zeal, for ye will not surpass in benefits either myself or the king." Thus far it happened as regards the Phokians.

19. When the Lacedemonians came to the Isthmus they encamped upon it, and hearing this the rest of the Peloponnesians who favoured the better cause, and some also because they saw the Spartans going out, did not think it right to be behind the Lacedemonians in their going forth. So from the Isthmus, when the sacrifices had proved favourable, they marched all together and came to Eleusis; and having performed sacrifices there also, when the signs were favourable they marched onwards, and the Athenians together with them, who had passed over from Salamis and had joined them at Eleusis. And then they had come to Erythrai in Bœotia, then they learnt that the Barbarians were encamping on the Asopos, and having perceived this they ranged themselves over against them on the lower slopes of Kithairon. 20. Then Mardonios, as the Hellenes did not descend into the plain, sent towards them all his cavalry, of which the commander was Masistios (by the Hellenes called Makistios), a man of reputation among the Persians, who had a Nesaian horse with a bridle of gold and in other respects finely caparisoned. So when the horsemen had ridden up to the Hellenes they attacked them by squadrons, and attacking[23] they did them much mischief, and moreover in contempt they called them women. 21. Now it happened by chance that the Megarians were posted in the place which was the most assailable of the whole position and to which the cavalry could best approach: so as the cavalry were making their attacks, the Megarians being hard pressed sent a herald to the commanders of the Hellenes, and the herald having come spoke these words: "The Megarians say:—we, O allies, are not able by ourselves to sustain the attacks of the Persian cavalry, keeping this position where we took post at the first; nay, even hitherto by endurance and valour alone have we held out against them, hard pressed as we are: and now unless ye shall send some others to take up our position in succession to us, know that we shall leave the position in which we now are." The herald brought report to them thus; and upon this Pausanias made trial of the Hellenes, whether any

others would voluntarily offer to go to this place and post themselves there in succession to the Megarians: and when the rest were not desirous to go, the Athenians undertook the task, and of the Athenians those three hundred picked men of whom Olympidoros the son of Lampon was captain. 22. These they were who undertook the task and were posted at Erythrai in advance of the other Hellenes who ere there present, having chosen to go with them the bow–men also. For some time then they fought, and at last an end was set to the fighting in the following manner:—while the cavalry was attacking by squadrons, the horse of Masistios, going in advance of the rest, was struck in the side by an arrow, and feeling pain he reared upright and threw Masistios off; and when he had fallen, the Athenians forthwith pressed upon him; and his horse they took and himself, as he made resistance, they slew, though at first they could not, for his equipment was of this kind,—he wore a cuirass of gold scales underneath, and over the cuirass he had put on a crimson tunic. So as they struck upon the cuirass they could effect nothing, until some one, perceiving what the matter was, thrust into his eye. Then at length he fell and died; and by some means the other men of the cavalry had not observed this take place, for they neither saw him when he had fallen from his horse nor when he was being slain, and while the retreat and the turn[24] were being made, they did not perceive that which was happening; but when they had stopped their horses, then at once they missed him, since there was no one to command them; and when they perceived what had happened, they passed the word to one another and all rode together, that they might if possible recover the body. 23. The Athenians upon that, seeing that the cavalry were riding to attack them no longer by squadrons but all together, shouted to the rest of the army to help them. Then while the whole number of those on foot were coming to their help, there arose a sharp fight for the body; and so long as the three hundred were alone they had much the worse and were about to abandon the body, but when the mass of the army came to their help, then the horsemen no longer sustained the fight, nor did they succeed in recovering the body; and besides him they lost others of their number also. Then they drew off about two furlongs away and deliberated what they should do; and it seemed good to them, as they had no commander, to ride back to Mardonios. 24. When the cavalry arrived at the camp, the whole army and also Mardonios made great mourning for Masistios, cutting off their own hair and that of their horses and baggage–animals and giving way to lamentation without stint; for all Bœotia was filled with the sound of it, because one had perished who after Mardonios was of the most account with the Persians and with the king. 25. The Barbarians then were paying honours in their own manner to Masistios slain: but the Hellenes, when they had sustained the attack of the cavalry and having sustained it had driven them back, were much more encouraged; and first they put the dead body in a cart and conveyed it along their ranks; and the body was a sight worth seeing for its size and beauty, wherefore also the men left their places in the ranks and went one after the other[25] to gaze upon Masistios. After this they resolved to come down further towards Plataia; for the region of Plataia was seen to be much more convenient for them to encamp in than that of Erythrai, both for other reasons and because it is better watered. To this region then and to the spring Gargaphia, which is in this region, they resolved that they must come, and encamp in their several posts. So they took up their arms and went by the lower slopes of Kithairon past Hysiai to the Plataian land; and having there arrived they posted themselves according to their several nations near the spring Gargaphia and the sacred enclosure of Androcrates the hero, over low hills or level ground.

26. Then in the arranging of the several posts there arose a contention of much argument[25a] between the Tegeans and the Athenians; for they each claimed to occupy the other wing of the army[26] themselves, alleging deeds both new and old. The Tegeans on the one hand said as follows: "We have been always judged worthy of this post by the whole body of allies in all the common expeditions which the Peloponnesians have made before this, whether in old times or but lately, ever since that time when the sons of Heracles endeavoured after the death of Eurystheus to return to the Peloponnese. This honour we gained at that time by reason of the following event:—When with the Achaians and the Ionians who were then in Peloponnesus we had come out to the Isthmus to give assistance and were encamped opposite those who desired to return, then it is said that Hyllos made a speech saying that it was not right that the one army should risk its safety by engaging battle with the other, and urging that that man of the army of the Peloponnesians whom they should judge to be the best of them should fight in single combat with himself on terms concerted between them. The Peloponnesians then resolved that this should be done; and they made oath with one another on this condition,—that if Hyllos should conquer the leader of the Peloponnesians, then the sons of Heracles should return to their father's heritage; but he should be conquered, then on the other hand the sons of Heracles should depart and lead away their army, and not within a hundred years attempt to return to the Peloponnese. There was selected then of all the allies, he himself making a voluntary offer, Echemos the son of Aëropos, the son of Phegeus,[27] who was our commander and king: and he fought a single combat and slew Hyllos. By reason of this deed we obtained among the Peloponnesians of that

time, besides many other great privileges which we still possess, this also of always leading the other wing of the army, when a common expedition is made. To you, Lacedemonians, we make no opposition, but we give you freedom of choice, and allow you to command whichever wing ye desire; but of the other we say that it belongs to us to be the leaders as in former time: and apart from this deed which has been related, we are more worthy than the Athenians to have this post; for in many glorious contests have we contended against you, O Spartans, and in many also against others. Therefore it is just that we have the other wing rather than the Athenians; for they have not achieved deeds such as ours, either new or old." 27. Thus they spoke, and the Athenians replied as follows: "Though we know that this gathering was assembled for battle with the Barbarian and not for speech, yet since the Tegean has proposed to us as a task to speak of things both old and new, the deeds of merit namely which by each of our two nations have been achieved in all time, it is necessary for us to point out to you whence it comes that to us, who have been brave men always, it belongs as a heritage rather than to the Arcadians to have the chief place. First as to the sons of Heracles, whose leader they say that they slew at the Isthmus, these in the former time, when they were driven away by all the Hellenes to whom they came flying from slavery under those of Mykene, we alone received; and joining with them we subdued the insolence of Eurystheus. having conquered in fight those who then dwelt in Peloponnesus. Again when the Argives who with Polyneikes marched against Thebes, had been slain and were lying unburied, we declare that we marched an army against the Cadmeians and recovered the dead bodies and gave them burial in our own land at Eleusis. We have moreover another glorious deed performed against the Amazons who invaded once the Attic land, coming from the river Thermodon: and in the toils of Troy we were not inferior to any. But it is of no profit to make mention of these things; for on the one hand, though we were brave men in those times, we might now have become worthless, and on the other hand even though we were then worthless, yet now we might be better. Let it suffice therefore about ancient deeds; but if by us no other deed has been displayed (as many there have been and glorious, not less than by any other people of the Hellenes), yet even by reason of the deed wrought at Marathon alone we are worthy to have this privilege and others besides this, seeing that we alone of all the Hellenes fought in single combat with the Persian, and having undertaken so great a deed we overcame and conquered six−and−forty nations.[28] Are we not worthy then to have this post by reason of that deed alone? However, since at such a time as this it is not fitting to contend for post, we are ready to follow your saying, O Lacedemonians, as to where ye think it most convenient that we should stand and opposite to whom; for wheresoever we are posted, we shall endeavour to be brave men. Prescribe to us therefore and we shall obey." They made answer thus; and the whole body of the Lacedemonians shouted aloud that the Athenians were more worthy to occupy the wing than the Arcadians. Thus the Athenians obtained the wing, and overcame the Tegeans.

28. After this the Hellenes were ranged as follows, both those of them who came in continually afterwards[29] and those who had come at the first. The right wing was held by ten thousand Lacedemonians; and of these the five thousand who were Spartans were attended by thirty-five thousand Helots serving as light-armed troops, seven of them appointed for each man.[30] To stand next to themselves the Spartans chose the Tegeans, both to do them honour and also because of their valour; and of these there were one thousand five hundred hoplites. After these were stationed five thousand Corinthians, and they had obtained permission from Pausanias that the three hundred who were present of the men of Potidaia in Pallene should stand by their side. Next to these were stationed six hundred Arcadians of Orchomenos; and to these three thousand Sikyonians. Next after these were eight hundred Epidaurians: by the side of these were ranged a thousand Troizenians: next to the Troizenians two hundred Lepreates: next to these four hundred of the men of Mikene and Tiryns; and then a thousand Phliasians. By the side of these stood three hundred Hermionians; and next to the Hermionians were stationed six hundred Eretrians and Styrians; next to these four hundred Chalkidians; and to these five hundred men of Amprakia. After these stood eight hundred Leucadians and Anactorians; and next to them two hundred from Pale in Kephallenia. After these were ranged five hundred Eginetans; by their side three thousand Megarians; and next to these six hundred Plataians. Last, or if you will first, were ranged the Athenians, occupying the left wing, eight thousand in number, and the commander of them was Aristeides the son of Lysimachos. 29. These all, excepting those who were appointed to attend the Spartans, seven for each man, were hoplites, being in number altogether three myriads eight thousand and seven hundred.[31] This was the whole number of hoplites who were assembled against the Barbarian; and the number of the light-armed was as follows:—of the Spartan division thirty-five thousand men, reckoning at the rate of seven for each man, and of these every one was equipped for fighting; and the light-armed troops of the rest of the Lacedemonians and of the other Hellenes, being about one for each man, amounted to thirty-four thousand five hundred. 30. Of the light- armed fighting men the whole number then was six myriads nine thousand and five hundred;[32] and of the whole Hellenic force which

assembled at Plataia the number (including both the hoplites and the light–armed fighting men) was eleven myriads[33] all but one thousand eight hundred men; and with the Thespians who were present the number of eleven myriads was fully made up; for there were present also in the army those of the Thespians who survived, being in number about one thousand eight hundred, and these too were without heavy arms.[34] These then having been ranged in order were encamped on the river Asopos.

31. Meanwhile the Barbarians with Mardonios, when they had sufficiently mourned for Masistios, being informed that the Hellenes were at Plataia came themselves also to that part of the Asopos which flows there; and having arrived there, they were ranged against the enemy by Mardonios thus:—against the Lacedemonians he stationed the Persians; and since the Persians were much superior in numbers, they were arrayed in deeper ranks than those, and notwithstanding this they extended in front of the Tegeans also: and he ranged them in this manner,—all the strongest part of that body he selected from the rest and stationed it opposite to the Lacedemonians, but the weaker part he ranged by their side opposite to the Tegeans. This he did on the information and suggestion of the Thebans. Then next to the Persians he ranged the Medes; and these extended in front of the Corinthians, Potidaians, Orchomenians and Sikyonians. Next to the Medes he ranged the Bactrians; and these extended in front of the Epidaurians, Troizenians, Lepreates, Tirynthians, Mykenians and Phliasians. After the Bactrians he stationed the Indians; and these extended in front of the Hermionians, Eretrians, Styrians and Chalkidians. Next to the Indians he ranged the Sacans, who extended in front of the men of Amprakia, the Anactorians, Leucadians, Palians and Eginetans. Next to the Sacans and opposite to the Athenians, Plataians and Megarians, he ranged the Bœotians, Locrians, Malians, Thessalians, and the thousand men of the Phokians: for not all the Phokians had taken the side of the Medes, but some of them were even supporting the cause of the Hellenes, being shut up in Parnassos; and setting out from thence they plundered from the army of Mardonios and from those of the Hellenes who were with him. He ranged the Macedonians also and those who dwell about the borders of Thessaly opposite to the Athenians. 32. These which have been named were the greatest of the nations who were arrayed in order by Mardonios, those, I mean, which were the most renowned and of greatest consideration: but there were in his army also men of several other nations mingled together, of the Phrygians, Thracians, Mysians, Paionians, and the rest; and among them also some Ethiopians, and of the Egyptians those called Hermotybians and Calasirians,[35] carrying knives,[36] who of all the Egyptians are the only warriors. These men, while he was

yet at Phaleron, he had caused to disembark from the ships in which they served as fighting-men; for the Egyptians had not been appointed to serve in the land-army which came with Xerxes to Athens. Of the Barbarians then there were thirty myriads,[37] as has been declared before; but of the Hellenes who were allies of Mardonios no man knows what the number was, for they were not numbered; but by conjecture I judge that these were assembled to the number of five myriads. These who were placed in array side by side were on foot; and the cavalry was ranged apart from them in a separate body.

33. When all had been drawn up by nations and by divisions, then on the next day they offered sacrifice on both sides. For the Hellenes Tisamenos the son of Antiochos was he who offered sacrifice, for he it was who accompanied this army as diviner. This man the Lacedemonians had made to be one of their own people, being an Eleian and of the race of the Iamidai:[38] for when Tisamenos was seeking divination at Delphi concerning issue, the Pythian prophetess made answer to him that he should win five of the greatest contests. He accordingly, missing the meaning of the oracle, began to attend to athletic games, supposing that he should win contests of athletics; and he practised for the "five contests"[39] and came within one fall of winning a victory at the Olympic games,[40] being set to contend with Hieronymos of Andros. The Lacedemonians however perceived that the oracle given to Tisamenos had reference not to athletic but to martial contests, and they endeavoured to persuade Tisamenos by payment of money, and to make him a leader in their wars together with the kings of the race of Heracles. He then, seeing that the Spartans set much store on gaining him over as a friend, having perceived this, I say, he raised his price and signified to them that he would do as they desired, if they would make him a citizen of their State and give him full rights, but for no other payment. The Spartans at first when they heard this displayed indignation and altogether gave up their request, but at last, when great terror was hanging over them of this Persian armament, they gave way[41] and consented. He then perceiving that they had changed their minds, said that he could not now be satisfied even so, nor with these terms alone; but it was necessary that his brother Hegias also should be made a Spartan citizen on the same terms as he himself became one. 34. By saying this he followed the example of Melampus in his request,[42] if one may compare royal power with mere citizenship; for Melampus on his part, when the women in Argos had been seized by madness, and the Argives endeavoured to hire him to come from Pylos and to cause their women to cease from the malady, proposed as payment for himself the half of the royal power; and the

Argives did not suffer this, but departed: and afterwards, when more of their women became mad, at length they accepted that which Melampus had proposed, and went to offer him this: but he then seeing that they had changed their minds, increased his demand, and said that he would not do that which they desired unless they gave to his brother Bias also the third share in the royal power.[43] And the Argives, being driven into straits, consented to this also. 35. Just so the Spartans also, being very much in need of Tisamenos, agreed with him on any terms which he desired: and when the Spartans had agreed to this demand also, then Tisamenos the Eleian, having become a Spartan, had part with them in winning five of the greatest contests as their diviner: and these were the only men who ever were made fellow– citizens of the Spartans. Now the five contests were these: one and the first of them was this at Plataia; and after this the contest at Tegea, which took place with the Tegeans and the Argives; then that at Dipaieis against all the Arcadians except the Mantineians; after that the contest with the Messenians at Ithome;[44] and last of all that which took place at Tanagra against the Athenians and Argives. This, I say, was accomplished last of the five contests.

36. This Tisamenos was acting now as diviner for the Hellenes in the Plataian land, being brought by the Spartans. Now to the Hellenes the sacrifices were of good omen if they defended themselves only, but not if they crossed the Asopos and began a battle; 37, and Mardonios too, who was eager to begin a battle, found the sacrifices not favourable to this design, but they were of good omen to him also if he defended himself only; for he too used the Hellenic manner of sacrifice, having as diviner Hegesistratos an Eleian and the most famous of the Telliadai, whom before these events the Spartans had taken and bound, in order to put him to death, because they had suffered much mischief from him. He then being in this evil case, seeing that he was running a course for his life and was likely moreover to suffer much torment before his death, had done a deed such as may hardly be believed. Being made fast on a block bound with iron, he obtained an iron tool, which in some way had been brought in, and contrived forthwith a deed the most courageous of any that we know: for having first calculated how the remaining portion of his foot might be got out of the block, he cut away the flat of his own foot,[45] and after that, since he was guarded still by warders, he broke through the wall and so ran away to Tegea, travelling during the nights and in the daytime entering a wood and resting there; so that, though the Lacedemonians searched for him in full force, he arrived at Tegea on the third night; and the Lacedemonians were possessed by great wonder both at his courage, when

they saw the piece of the foot that was cut off lying there, and also because they were not able to find him. So he at that time having thus escaped them took refuge at Tegea, which then was not friendly with the Lacedemonians; and when he was healed and had procured for himself a wooden foot, he became an open enemy of the Lacedemonians. However in the end the enmity into which he had fallen with the Lacedemonians was not to his advantage; for he was caught by them while practising divination in Zakynthos, and was put to death.

38. However the death of Hegesistratos took place later than the events at Plataia, and he was now at the Asopos, having been hired by Mardonios for no mean sum, sacrificing and displaying zeal for his cause both on account of his enmity with the Lacedemonians and on account of the gain which he got: but as the sacrifices were not favourable for a battle either for the Persians themselves or for those Hellenes who were with them (for these also had a diviner for themselves, Hippomachos a Leucadian), and as the Hellenes had men constantly flowing in and were becoming more in number, Timagenides the son of Herpys, a Theban, counselled Mardonios to set a guard on the pass of Kithairon, saying that the Hellenes were constantly flowing in every day and that he would thus cut off large numbers. 39. Eight days had now passed while they had been sitting opposite to one another, when he gave this counsel to Mardonios; and Mardonios, perceiving that the advice was good, sent the cavalry when night came on to the pass of Kithairon leading towards Plataia, which the Bœotians call the "Three Heads"[46] and the Athenians the "Oak Heads."[47] Having been thus sent, the cavalry did not come without effect, for they caught five hundred baggage–animals coming out into the plain, which were bearing provisions from Peloponnesus to the army, and also the men who accompanied the carts: and having taken this prize the Persians proceeded to slaughter them without sparing either beast or man; and when they were satiated with killing they surrounded the rest and drove them into the camp to Mardonios.

40. After this deed they spent two days more, neither side wishing to begin a battle; for the Barbarians advanced as far as the Asopos to make trial of the Hellenes, but neither side would cross the river. However the cavalry of Mardonios made attacks continually and did damage to the Hellenes; for the Thebans, being very strong on the side of the Medes, carried on the war with vigour, and always directed them up to the moment of fighting; and after this the Persians and Medes took up the work and were they who displayed valour in their turn.

41. For ten days then nothing more was done than this; but when the eleventh day had come, while they still sat opposite to one another at Plataia, the Hellenes having by this time grown much more numerous and Mardonios being greatly vexed at the delay of action, then Mardonios the son of Gobryas and Artabazos the son of Pharnakes, who was esteemed by Xerxes as few of the Persians were besides, came to speech with one another; and as they conferred, the opinions they expressed were these,—that of Artabazos, that they must put the whole army in motion as soon as possible and go to the walls of the Thebans, whither great stores of corn had been brought in for them and fodder for their beasts; and that they should settle there quietly and get their business done as follows:—they had, he said, great quantities of gold, both coined and uncoined, and also of silver and of drinking– cups; and these he advised they should send about to the Hellenes without stint, more especially to those of the Hellenes who were leaders in their several cities; and these, he said, would speedily deliver up their freedom: and he advised that they should not run the risk of a battle. His opinion then was the same as that of the Thebans,[48] for he as well as they had some true foresight: but the opinion of Mardonios was more vehement and more obstinate, and he was by no means disposed to yield; for he said that he thought their army far superior to that of the Hellenes, and he gave as his opinion that they should engage battle as quickly as possible and not allow them to assemble in still greater numbers than were already assembled; and as for the sacrifices of Hegesistratos, they should leave them alone and not endeavour to force a good sign, but follow the custom of the Persians and engage battle. 42. When he so expressed his judgment, none opposed him, and thus his opinion prevailed; for he and not Artabazos had the command of the army given him by the king. He summoned therefore the commanders of the divisions and the generals of those Hellenes who were with him, and asked whether they knew of any oracle regarding the Persians, which said that they should be destroyed in Hellas; and when those summoned to council[49] were silent, some not knowing the oracles and others knowing them but not esteeming it safe to speak, Mardonios himself said: "Since then ye either know nothing or do not venture to speak, I will tell you, since I know very well. There is an oracle saying that the Persians are destined when they come to Hellas to plunder the temple at Delphi, and having plundered it to perish every one of them. We therefore, just because we know this, will not go to that temple nor will we attempt to plunder it; and for this cause we shall not perish. So many of you therefore as chance to wish well to the Persians, have joy so far as regards this matter, and be assured that we shall overcome the Hellenes." Having spoken to them thus, he next commanded to prepare everything and to set all in order, since at dawn of the next day

a battle would be fought.

43. Now this oracle, which Mardonios said referred to the Persians, I know for my part was composed with reference with the Illyrians and the army of the Enchelians, and not with reference to the Persians at all. However, the oracle which was composed by Bakis with reference to this battle,

"The gathering of Hellenes together and cry of Barbarian voices, Where the Thermodon flows, by the banks of grassy Asopos; Here very many shall fall ere destiny gave them to perish, Medes bow–bearing in fight, when the fatal day shall approach them,"—

these sayings, and others like them composed by Musaios, I know had reference to the Persians. Now the river Thermodon flows between Tanagra and Glisas.

44. After the inquiry about the oracles and the exhortation given by Mardonios night came on and the guards were set: and when night was far advanced, and it seemed that there was quiet everywhere in the camps, and that the men were in their deepest sleep, then Alexander the son of Amyntas, commander and king of the Macedonians, rode his horse up to the guard–posts of the Athenians and requested that he might have speech with their generals. So while the greater number of the guards stayed at their posts, some ran to the generals, and when they reached them they said that a man had come riding on a horse out of the camp of the Medes, who discovered nothing further, but only named the generals and said that he desired to have speech with them. 45. Having heard this, forthwith they accompanied the men to the guard–posts, and when they had arrived there, Alexander thus spoke to them: "Athenians, I lay up these words of mine as a trust to you, charging you to keep them secret and tell them to no one except only to Pausanias, lest ye bring me to ruin: for I should not utter them if I did not care greatly for the general safety of Hellas, seeing that I am a Hellene myself by original descent and I should not wish to see Hellas enslaved instead of free. I say then that Mardonios and his army cannot get the offerings to be according to their mind,[50] for otherwise ye would long ago have fought. Now however he has resolved to let the offerings alone and to bring on a battle at dawn of day; for, as I conjecture, he fears lest ye should assemble in greater numbers. Therefore prepare yourselves; and if after all Mardonios should put off the battle and not bring it on, stay where ye are and hold out patiently; for they have provisions only for a few days remaining. And if this way shall

have its issue according to your mind, then each one of you ought to remember me also concerning liberation,[51] since I have done for the sake of the Hellenes so hazardous a deed by reason of my zeal for you, desiring to show you the design of Mardonios, in order that the Barbarians may not fall upon you when ye are not as yet expecting them: and I am Alexander the Macedonian." Thus having spoken he rode away back to the camp and to his own position.

46. Then the generals of the Athenians came to the right wing and told Pausanias that which they had heard from Alexander. Upon this saying he being struck with fear of the Persians spoke as follows: "Since then at dawn the battle comes on, it is right that ye, Athenians, should take your stand opposite to the Persians, and we opposite to the Bœotians and those Hellenes who are now posted against you; and for this reason, namely because ye are acquainted with the Medes and with their manner of fighting, having fought with them at Marathon, whereas we have had no experience of these men and are without knowledge of them; for not one of the Spartans has made trial of the Medes in fight, but of the Bœotians and Thessalians we have had experience. It is right therefore that ye should take up your arms and come to this wing of the army, and that we should go to the left wing." In answer to this the Athenians spoke as follows: "To ourselves also long ago at the very first, when we saw that the Persians were being ranged opposite to you, it occurred to us to say these very things, which ye now bring forward before we have uttered them; but we feared lest these words might not be pleasing to you. Since however ye yourselves have made mention of this, know that your words have caused us pleasure, and that we are ready to do this which ye say." 47. Both then were content to do this, and as dawn appeared they began to change their positions with one another: and the Bœotians perceiving that which was being done reported it to Mardonios, who, when he heard it, forthwith himself also endeavoured to change positions, bringing the Persians along so as to be against the Lacedemonians: and when Pausanias learnt that this was being done, he perceived that he was not unobserved, and he led the Spartans back again to the right wing; and just so also did Mardonios upon his left.

48. When they had been thus brought to their former positions, Mardonios sent a herald to the Spartans and said as follows: "Lacedemonians, ye are said forsooth by those who are here to be very good men, and they have admiration for you because ye do not flee in war nor leave your post, but stay there and either destroy your enemies or perish yourselves. In this however, as it now appears, there is no truth; for before we

engaged battle and came to hand–to– hand conflict we saw you already flee and leave your station, desiring to make the trial with the Athenians first, while ye ranged yourselves opposite to our slaves. These are not at all the deeds of good men in war, but we were deceived in you very greatly; for we expected by reason of your renown that ye would send a herald to us, challenging us and desiring to fight with the Persians alone; but though we on our part were ready to do this, we did not find that ye said anything of this kind, but rather that ye cowered with fear. Now therefore since ye were not the first to say this, we are the first. Why do we not forthwith fight,[52] ye on behalf of the Hellenes, since ye have the reputation of being the best, and we on behalf of the Barbarians, with equal numbers on both sides? and if we think it good that the others should fight also, then let them fight afterwards; and if on the other hand we should not think it good, but think it sufficient that we alone should fight, then let us fight it out to the end, and whichsoever of us shall be the victors, let these be counted as victorious with their whole army." 49. The herald having thus spoken waited for some time, and then, as no one made him any answer, he departed and went back; and having returned he signified to Mardonios that which had happened to him. Mardonios then being greatly rejoiced and elated by his empty[53] victory, sent the cavalry to attack the Hellenes: and when the horsemen had ridden to attack them, they did damage to the whole army of the Hellenes by hurling javelins against them and shooting with bows, being mounted archers and hard therefore to fight against: and they disturbed and choked up the spring Gargaphia, from which the whole army of the Hellenes was drawing its water. Now the Lacedemonians alone were posted near this spring, and it was at some distance from the rest of the Hellenes, according as they chanced to be posted, while the Asopos was near at hand; but when they were kept away from the Asopos, then they used to go backwards and forwards to this spring; for they were not permitted by the horsemen and archers to fetch water from the river. 50. Such then being the condition of things, the generals of the Hellenes, since the army had been cut off from its water and was being harassed by the cavalry, assembled to consult about these and other things, coming to Pausanias upon the right wing: for other things too troubled them yet more than these of which we have spoken, since they no longer had provisions, and their attendants who had been sent to Peloponnese for the purpose of getting them had been cut off by the cavalry and were not able to reach the camp. 51. It was resolved then by the generals in council with one another, that if the Persians put off the battle for that day, they would go to the Island. This is distant ten furlongs[54] from the Asopos and the spring Gargaphia, where they were then encamped, and is in front of the city of the Plataians: and if it be asked how there can be an island on the mainland, thus it is[55]:— the river parts in two above, as it flows from Kithairon down to the plain, keeping a distance of about three furlongs between its streams, and after that it joins again in one stream; and the name of it is Oëroe, said by the natives of the country to be the daughter of Asopos. To this place of which I speak they determined to remove, in order that they might be able to get an abundant supply of water and that the cavalry might not do them damage, as now when they were right opposite. And they proposed to remove when the second watch of the night should have come, so that the Persians might not see them set forth and harass them with the cavalry pursuing. They proposed also, after they had arrived at this place, round which, as I say, Oëroe the daughter of Asopos flows, parting into two streams[56] as she runs from Kithairon, to send half the army to Kithairon during this same night, in order to take up their attendants who had gone to get the supplies of provisions; for these were cut off from them in Kithairon.

52. Having thus resolved, during the whole of that day they had trouble unceasingly, while the cavalry pressed upon them; but when the day drew to a close and the attacks of the cavalry had ceased, then as it was becoming night and the time had arrived at which it had been agreed that they should retire from their place, the greater number of them set forth and began to retire, not however keeping it in mind to go to the place which had been agreed upon; but on the contrary, when they had begun to move, they readily took occasion to flee[57] from the cavalry towards the city of the Plataians, and in their flight they came as far as the temple of Hera, which temple is in front of the city of the Plataians at a distance of twenty furlongs from the spring Gargaphia; and when they had there arrived they halted in front of the temple. 53. These then were encamping about the temple of Hera; and Pausanias, seeing that they were retiring from the camp, gave the word to the Lacedemonians also to take up their arms and go after the others who were preceding them, supposing that these were going to the place to which they had agreed to go. Then, when all the other commanders were ready to obey Pausanias, Amompharetos the son of Poliades, the commander of the Pitanate division,[58] said that he would not flee from the strangers, nor with his own will would he disgrace Sparta; and he expressed wonder at seeing that which was being done, not having been present at the former discussion. And Pausanias and Euryanax were greatly disturbed that he did not obey them and still more that they should be compelled to leave the Pitanate division behind, since he thus refused;[59] for they feared that if they should leave it in order to do that which they had agreed with the other Hellenes, both Amompharetos himself would perish being left behind and also

the men with him. With this thought they kept the Lacedemonian force from moving, and meanwhile they endeavoured to persuade him that it was not right for him to do so. 54. They then were exhorting Amompharetos, who had been left behind alone of the Lacedemonians and Tegeans; and meanwhile the Athenians were keeping themselves quiet in the place where they had been posted, knowing the spirit of the Lacedemonians, that they were apt to say otherwise than they really meant;[60] and when the army began to move, they sent a horseman from their own body to see whether the Spartans were attempting to set forth, or whether they had in truth no design at all to retire; and they bade him ask Pausanias what they ought to do. 55. So when the herald came to the Lacedemonians, he saw that they were still in their place and that the chiefs of them had come to strife with one another: for when Euryanax and Pausanias both exhorted Amompharetos not to run the risk of remaining behind with his men, alone of all the Lacedemonians, they did not at all persuade him, and at last they had come to downright strife; and meanwhile the herald of the Athenians had arrived and was standing by them. And Amompharetos in his contention took a piece of rock in both his hands and placed it at the feet of Pausanias, saying that with this pebble he gave his vote not to fly from the strangers, meaning the Barbarians.[61] Pausanias then, calling him a madman and one who was not in his right senses, bade tell the state of their affairs to the Athenian herald,[62] who was asking that which he had been charged to ask; and at the same time he requested the Athenians to come towards the Lacedemonians and to do in regard to the retreat the same as they did. 56. He then went away back to the Athenians; and as the dawn of day found them yet disputing with one another, Pausanias, who had remained still throughout all this time, gave the signal, and led away all the rest over the low hills, supposing that Amonpharetos would not stay behind when the other Lacedemonians departed (in which he was in fact right); and with them also went the Tegeans. Meanwhile the Athenians, following the commands which were given them, were going in the direction opposite to that of the Lacedemonians; for these were clinging to the hills and the lower slope of Kithairon from fear of the cavalry, while the Athenians were marching below in the direction of the plain. 57. As for Amonpharetos, he did not at first believe that Pausanias would ever venture to leave him and his men behind, and he stuck to it that they should stay there and not leave their post; but when Pausanias and his troops were well in front, then he perceived that they had actually left him behind, and he made his division take up their arms and led them slowly towards the main body. This, when it had got away about ten furlongs, stayed for the division of Amompharetos, halting at the river Moloeis and the place called Argiopion, where also there stands a temple of the Eleusinian Demeter: and it stayed there for this reason, namely in order that of Amonpharetos and his division should not leave the place where they had been posted, but should remain there, it might be able to come back to their assistance. So Amompharetos and his men were coming up to join them, and the cavalry also of the Barbarians was at the same time beginning to attack them in full force: for the horsemen did on this day as they had been wont to do every day; and seeing the place vacant in which the Hellenes had been posted on the former days, they rode their horses on continually further, and as soon as they came up with them they began to attack them.

58. Then Mardonios, when he was informed that the Hellenes had departed during the night, and when he saw their place deserted, called Thorax of Larissa and his brothers Eurypylos and Thrasydeios, and said: "Sons of Aleuas, will ye yet say anything,[63] now that ye see these places deserted? For ye who dwell near them were wont to say that the Lacedemonians did not fly from a battle, but were men unsurpassed in war; and these men ye not only saw before this changing from their post, but now we all of us see that they have run away during the past night; and by this they showed clearly, when the time came for them to contend in battle with those who were in truth the best of all men, that after all they were men of no worth, who had been making a display of valour among Hellenes, a worthless race. As for you, since ye had had no experience of the Persians, I for my part was very ready to excuse you when ye praised these, of whom after all ye knew something good; but much more I marvelled at Artabazos that he should have been afraid of the Lacedemonians, and that having been afraid he should have uttered that most cowardly opinion, namely that we ought to move our army away and go to the city of the Thebans to be besieged there,—an opinion about which the king shall yet be informed by me. Of these things we will speak in another place; now however we must not allow them to act thus, but we must pursue them until they are caught and pay the penalty to us for all that they did to the Persians in time past." 59. Thus having spoken he led on the Persians at a run, after they had crossed the Asopos, on the track of the Hellenes, supposing that these were running away from him; and he directed his attack upon the Lacedemonians and Tegeans only, for the Athenians, whose march was towards the plain, he did not see by reason of the hills. Then the rest of the commanders of the Barbarian divisions, seeing that the Persians had started to pursue the Hellenes, forthwith all raised the signals for battle and began to pursue, each as fast as they could, not arranged in any order or succession of post. 60. These then were coming on with shouting and confused numbers, thinking to make

short work of[64] the Hellenes; and Pausanias, when the cavalry began to attack, sent to the Athenians a horseman and said thus: "Athenians, now that the greatest contest is set before us, namely that which has for its issue the freedom or the slavery of Hellas, we have been deserted by our allies, we Lacedemonians and ye Athenians, seeing that they have run away during the night that is past. Now therefore it is determined what we must do upon this, namely that we must defend ourselves and protect one another as best we may. If then the cavalry had set forth to attack you at the first, we and the Tegeans, who with us refuse to betray the cause of Hellas, should have been bound to go to your help; but as it is, since the whole body has come against us, it is right that ye should come to that portion of the army which is hardest pressed, to give aid. If however anything has happened to you which makes it impossible for you to come to our help, then do us a kindness by sending to us the archers; and we know that ye have been in the course of this present war by far the most zealous of all, so that ye will listen to our request in this matter also." 61. When the Athenians heard this they were desirous to come to their help and to assist them as much as possible; and as they were already going, they were attacked by those of the Hellenes on the side of the king who had been ranged opposite to them, so that they were no longer able to come to the help of the Lacedemonians, for the force that was attacking them gave them much trouble. Thus the Lacedemonians and Tegeans were left alone, being in number, together with light−armed men, the former fifty thousand and the Tegeans three thousand; for these were not parted at all from the Lacedemonians: and they began to offer sacrifice, meaning to engage battle with Mardonios and the force which had come against them. Then since their offerings did not prove favourable, and many of them were being slain during this time and many more wounded,—for the Persians had made a palisade of their wicker−work shields[65] and were discharging their arrows in great multitude and without sparing,—Pausanias, seeing that the Spartans were hard pressed and that the offerings did not prove favourable, fixed his gaze upon the temple of Hera of the Plataians and called upon the goddess to help, praying that they might by no means be cheated of their hope: 62, and while he was yet calling upon her thus, the Tegeans started forward before them and advanced against the Barbarians, and forthwith after the prayer of Pausanias the offerings proved favourable for the Lacedemonians as they sacrificed. So when this at length came to pass, then they also advanced against the Persians; and the Persians put away their bows and came against them. Then first there was fighting about the wicker−work shields, and when these had been overturned, after that the fighting was fierce by the side of the temple of Demeter, and so continued for a long time, until at last they came to justling; for the Barbarians would take hold of the spears and break them off. Now in courage and in strength the Persians were not inferior to the others, but they were without defensive armour,[66] and moreover they were unversed in war and unequal to their opponents in skill; and they would dart out one at a time or in groups of about ten together, some more and some less, and fall upon the Spartans and perish. 63. In the place where Mardonios himself was, riding on a white horse and having about him the thousand best men of the Persians chosen out from the rest, here, I say, they pressed upon their opponents most of all: and so long as Mardonios survived, they held out against them, and defending themselves they cast down many of the Lacedemonians; but when Mardonios was slain and the men who were ranged about his person, which was the strongest portion of the whole army, had fallen, then the others too turned and gave way before the Lacedemonians; for their manner of dress, without defensive armour, was a very great cause of destruction to them, since in truth they were contending light–armed against hoplites. 64. Then the satisfaction for the murder of Leonidas was paid by Mardonios according to the oracle given to the Spartans,[67] and the most famous victory of all those about which we have knowledge was gained by Pausanias the son of Cleombrotos, the son of Anaxandrides; of his ancestors above this the names have been given for Leonidas,[68] since, as it happens, they are the same for both. Now Mardonios was slain by Arimnestos,[69] a man of consideration in Sparta, who afterwards, when the Median wars were over, with three hundred men fought a battle against the whole army of the Messenians, then at war with the Lacedemonians, at Stenycleros, and both he was slain and also the three hundred. 65. When the Persians were turned to flight at Plataia by the Lacedemonians, they fled in disorder to their own camp and to the palisade which they had made in the Theban territory:[70] and it is a marvel to me that, whereas they fought by the side of the sacred grove of Demeter, not one of the Persians was found to have entered the enclosure or to have been slain within it, but round about the temple in the unconsecrated ground fell the greater number of the slain. I suppose (if one ought to suppose anything about divine things) that the goddess herself refused to receive them, because they had set fire to the temple, that is to say the "palace"[71] at Eleusis.

66. Thus far then had this battle proceeded: but Artabazos the son of Pharnakes had been displeased at the very first because Mardonios remained behind after the king was gone; and afterwards he had been bringing forward objections continually and doing nothing, but had urged them always not to fight a battle: and for himself he acted as follows, not being pleased with the things which were being done by Mardonios.—The

men of whom Artabazos was commander (and he had with him no small force but one which was in number as much as four myriads[72] of men), these, when the fighting began, being well aware what the issue of the battle would be, he led carefully,[73] having first given orders that all should go by the way which he should lead them and at the same pace at which they should see him go. Having given these orders he led his troops on pretence of taking them into battle; and when he was well on his way, he saw the Persians already taking flight. Then he no longer led his men in the same order as before, but set off at a run, taking flight by the quickest way not to the palisade nor yet to the wall of the Thebans, but towards Phokis, desiring as quickly as possible to reach the Hellespont. 67. These, I say, were thus directing their march: and in the meantime, while the other Hellenes who were on the side of the king were purposely slack in the fight,[74] the Bœotians fought with the Athenians for a long space; for those of the Thebans who took the side of the Medes had no small zeal for the cause, and they fought and were not slack, so that three hundred of them, the first and best of all, fell there by the hands of the Athenians: and when these also turned to flight, they fled to Thebes, not to the same place as the Persians: and the main body of the other allies fled without having fought constantly with any one or displayed any deeds of valour. 68. And this is an additional proof to me that all the fortunes of the Barbarians depended upon the Persians, namely that at that time these men fled before they had even engaged with the enemy, because they saw the Persians doing so. Thus all were in flight except only the cavalry, including also that of the Bœotians; and this rendered service to the fugitives by constantly keeping close to the enemy and separating the fugitives of their own side from the Hellenes. 69. The victors then were coming after the troops of Xerxes, both pursuing them and slaughtering them; and during the time when this panic arose, the report was brought to the other Hellenes who had posted themselves about the temple of Hera and had been absent from the battle, that a battle had taken place and that the troops of Pausanias were gaining the victory. When they heard this, then without ranging themselves in any order the Corinthians and those near them turned to go by the skirts of the mountain and by the low hills along the way which led straight up to the temple of Demeter, while the Megarians and Phliasians and those near them went by the plain along the smoothest way. When however the Megarians and Phliasians came near to the enemy, the cavalry of the Thebans caught sight of them from a distance hurrying along without any order, and rode up to attack them, the commander of the cavalry being Asopodoros the son of Timander; and having fallen upon them they slew six hundred of them, and the rest they pursued and drove to Kithairon.

70. These then perished thus ingloriously;[75] and meanwhile the Persians and the rest of the throng, having fled for refuge to the palisade, succeeded in getting up to the towers before the Lacedemonians came; and having got up they strengthened the wall of defence as best they could. Then when the Lacedemonians[76] came up to attack it, there began between them a vigorous[77] fight for the wall: for so long as the Athenians were away, they defended themselves and had much the advantage over the Lacedemonians, since these did not understand the art of fighting against walls; but when the Athenians came up to help them, then there was a fierce fight for the wall, lasting for a long time, and at length by valour and endurance the Athenians mounted up on the wall and made a breach in it, through which the Hellenes poured in. Now the Tegeans were the first who entered the wall, and these were they who plundered the tent of Mardonios, taking, besides the other things which were in it, also the manger of his horse, which was all of bronze and a sight worth seeing. This manger of Mardonios was dedicated by the Tegeans as an offering in the temple of Athene Alea,[78] but all the other things which they took, they brought to the common stock of the Hellenes. The Barbarians however, after the wall had been captured, no longer formed themselves into any close body, nor did any of them think of making resistance, but they were utterly at a loss,[79] as you might expect from men who were in a panic with many myriads of them shut up together in a small space: and the Hellenes were able to slaughter them so that out of an army of thirty myriads,[80] if those four be subtracted which Artabazos took with him in his flight, of the remainder not three thousand men survived. Of the Lacedemonians from Sparta there were slain in the battle ninety–one in all, of the Tegeans sixteen, and of the Athenians two–and–fifty.

71. Among the Barbarians those who proved themselves the best men were, of those on foot the Persians, and of the cavalry the Sacans, and for a single man Mardonios it is said was the best. Of the Hellenes, though both the Tegeans and the Athenians proved themselves good men, yet the Lacedemonians surpassed them in valour. Of this I have no other proof (for all these were victorious over their opposites), but only this, that they fought against the strongest part of the enemy's force and overcame it. And the man who proved himself in my opinion by much the best was that Aristodemos who, having come back safe from Thermopylai alone of the three hundred, had reproach and dishonour attached to him. After him the best were Poseidonios and Philokyon and Amompharetos the Spartan.[81] However, when there came to be conversation as to which of them had proved himself the best, the Spartans who were present gave it as their opinion that Aristodemos had evidently wished to be slain in

consequence of the charge which lay against him, and so, being as it were in a frenzy and leaving his place in the ranks, he had displayed great deeds, whereas Poseidonios had proved himself a good man although he did not desire to be slain; and so far he was the better man of the two. This however they perhaps said from ill–will; and all these whose names I mentioned among the men who were killed in this battle, were specially honoured, except Aristodemos; but Aristodemos, since he desired to be slain on account of the before–mentioned charge, was not honoured.

72. These obtained the most renown of those who fought at Plataia, for as for Callicrates, the most beautiful who came to the camp, not of the Lacedemonians alone, but also of all the Hellenes of his time, he was not killed in the battle itself; but when Pausanias was offering sacrifice, he was wounded by an arrow in the side, as he was sitting down in his place in the ranks; and while the others were fighting, he having been carried out of the ranks was dying a lingering death: and he said to Arimnestos[82] a Plataian that it did not grieve him to die for Hellas, but it grieved him only that he had not proved his strength of hand, and that no deed of valour had been displayed by him worthy of the spirit which he had in him to perform great deeds.[83]

73. Of the Athenians the man who gained most glory is said to have been Sophanes the son of Eutychides of the deme of Dekeleia,—a deme of which the inhabitants formerly did a deed that was of service to them for all time, as the Athenians themselves report. For when of old the sons of Tyndareus invaded the Attic land with a great host, in order to bring home Helen, and were laying waste the demes, not knowing to what place of hiding Helen had been removed, then they say that the men of Dekeleia, or as some say Dekelos himself, being aggrieved by the insolence of Theseus and fearing for all the land of the Athenians, told them the whole matter and led them to Aphidnai, which Titakos who was sprung from the soil delivered up by treachery to the sons of Tyndareus. In consequence of this deed the Dekeleians have had continually freedom from dues in Sparta and front seats at the games,[84] privileges which exist still to this day; insomuch that even in the war which many years after these events arose between the Athenians and the Peloponnesians, when the Lacedemonians laid waste all the rest of Attica, they abstained from injury to Dekeleia. 74. To this deme belonged Sophanes, who showed himself the best of all the Athenians in this battle; and of him there are two different stories told: one that he carried an anchor of iron bound by chains of bronze to the belt of his corslet; and this he threw whensoever he came up with the enemy, in order, they say, that the enemy when they came forth out of their ranks

might not be able to move him from his place; and when a flight of his opponents took place, his plan was to take up the anchor first and then pursue after them. This story is reported thus; but the other of the stories, disputing the truth of that which has been told above, is reported as follows, namely that upon his shield, which was ever moving about and never remaining still, he bore an anchor as a device, and not one of iron bound to his corslet. 75. There was another illustrious deed done too by Sophanes; for when the Athenians besieged Egina he challenged to a fight and slew Eurybates the Argive,[85] one who had been victor in the five contests[86] at the games. To Sophanes himself it happened after these events that when he was general of the Athenians together with Leagros the son of Glaucon, he was slain after proving himself a good man by the Edonians at Daton, fighting for the gold mines.

76. When the Barbarians had been laid low by the Hellenes at Plataia, there approached to these a woman, the concubine of Pharandates the son of Teaspis a Persian, coming over of her own free will from the enemy, who when she perceived that the Persians had been destroyed and that the Hellenes were the victors, descended from her carriage and came up to the Lacedemonians while they were yet engaged in the slaughter. This woman had adorned herself with many ornaments of gold, and her attendants likewise, and she had put on the fairest robe of those which she had; and when she saw that Pausanias was directing everything there, being well acquainted before with his name and with his lineage, because she had heard it often, she recognised Pausanias and taking hold of his knees she said these words: "O king of Sparta, deliver me thy suppliant from the slavery of the captive: for thou hast also done me service hitherto in destroying these, who have regard neither for demigods nor yet for gods.[87] I am by race of Cos, the daughter of Hegetorides the son of Antagoras; and the Persian took me by force in Cos and kept me a prisoner." He made answer in these words: "Woman, be of good courage, both because thou art a suppliant, and also if in addition to this it chances that thou art speaking the truth and art the daughter of Hegetorides the Coan, who is bound to me as a guest−friend more than any other of the men who dwell in those parts." Having thus spoken, for that time her gave her in charge to those Ephors who were present, and afterwards he sent her away to Egina, whither she herself desired to go.

77. After the arrival of the woman, forthwith upon this arrived the Mantineians, when all was over; and having learnt that they had come too late for the battle, they were greatly grieved, and said that they deserved to be punished: and being informed that

the Medes with Artabazos were in flight, they pursued after them as far as Thessaly, though the Lacedemonians endeavoured to prevent them from pursuing after fugitives.[88] Then returning back to their own country they sent the leaders of their army into exile from the land. After the Mantineians came the Eleians; and they, like the Mantineians, were greatly grieved by it and so departed home; and these also when they had returned sent their leaders into exile. So much of the Mantineians and Eleians.

78. At Plataia among the troops of the Eginetans was Lampon the son of Pytheas, one of the leading men of the Eginetans, who was moved to go to Pausanias with a most impious proposal, and when he had come with haste, he said as follows: "Son of Cleombrotos, a deed has been done by thee which is of marvellous greatness and glory, and to thee God has permitted by rescuing Hellas to lay up for thyself the greatest renown of all the Hellenes about whom we have any knowledge. Do thou then perform also that which remains to do after these things, in order that yet greater reputation may attach to thee, and also that in future every one of the Barbarians may beware of being the beginner of presumptuous deeds towards the Hellenes. For when Leonidas was slain at Thermopylai, Mardonios and Xerxes cut off his head and crucified him: to him therefore do thou repay like with like, and thou shalt have praise first from all the Spartans and then secondly from the other Hellenes also; for if thou impale the body of Mardonios, thou wilt then have taken vengeance for Leonidas thy father's brother." 79. He said this thinking to give pleasure; but the other made him answer in these words: "Stranger of Egina, I admire thy friendly spirit and thy forethought for me, but thou hast failed of a good opinion nevertheless: for having exalted me on high and my family and my deed, thou didst then cast me down to nought by advising me to do outrage to a dead body, and by saying that if I do this I shall be better reported of. These things it is more fitting for Barbarians to do than for Hellenes; and even with them we find fault for doing so. However that may be, I do not desire in any such manner as this to please either Eginetans or others who like such things; but it is enough for me that I should keep from unholy deeds, yea and from unholy speech also, and so please the Spartans. As for Leonidas, whom thou biddest me avenge, I declare that he has been greatly avenged already, and by the unnumbered lives which have been taken of these men he has been honoured, and not he only but also the rest who brought their lives to an end at Thermopylai. As for thee however, come not again to me with such a proposal, nor give me such advice; and be thankful moreover that thou hast no punishment for it now."

80. He having heard this went his way; and Pausanias made a proclamation that none should lay hands upon the spoil, and he ordered the Helots to collect the things together. They accordingly dispersed themselves about the camp and found tents furnished with gold and silver, and beds overlaid with gold and overlaid with silver, and mixing–bowls of gold, and cups and other drinking vessels. They found also sacks laid upon waggons, in which there proved to be caldrons both of gold and of silver; and from the dead bodies which lay there they stripped bracelets and collars, and also their swords[89] if they were of gold, for as to embroidered raiment, there was no account made of it. Then the Helots stole many of the things and sold them to the Eginetans, but many things also they delivered up, as many of them as they could not conceal; so that the great wealth of the Eginetans first came from this, that they bought the gold from the Helots making pretence that it was brass. 81. Then having brought the things together, and having set apart a tithe for the god of Delphi, with which the offering was dedicated of the golden tripod which rests upon the three–headed serpent of bronze and stands close by the altar, and also[90] for the god at Olympia, with which they dedicated the offering of a bronze statue of Zeus ten cubits high, and finally for the god at the Isthmus, with which was made a bronze statue of Poseidon seven cubits high,—having set apart these things, they divided the rest, and each took that which they ought to have, including the concubines of the Persians and the gold and the silver and the other things, and also the beasts of burden. How much was set apart and given to those of them who had proved themselves the best men at Plataia is not reported by any, though for my part I suppose that gifts were made to these also; Pausanias however had ten of each thing set apart and given to him, that is women, horses, talents, camels, and so also of the other things.

82. It is said moreover that this was done which here follows, namely that Xerxes in his flight from Hellas had left to Mardonios the furniture of his own tent, and Pausanias accordingly seeing the furniture of Mardonios furnished[91] with gold and silver and hangings of different colours ordered the bakers and the cooks to prepare a meal as they were used to do for Mardonios. Then when they did this as they had been commanded, it is said that Pausanias seeing the couches of gold and of silver with luxurious coverings, and the tables of gold and silver, and the magnificent apparatus of the feast, was astonished at the good things set before him, and for sport he ordered his own servants to prepare a Laconian meal; and as, when the banquet was served, the difference between the two was great, Pausanias laughed and sent for the commanders of the Hellenes; and when these had come together, Pausanias said, pointing to the

preparation of the two meals severally: "Hellenes, for this reason I assembled you together, because I desired to show you the senselessness of this leader of the Medes, who having such fare as this, came to us who have such sorry fare as ye see here, in order to take it away from us." Thus it is said that Pausanias spoke to the commanders of the Hellenes.

83. However,[92] in later time after these events many of the Plataians also found chests of gold and of silver and of other treasures; and moreover afterwards this which follows was seen in the case of the dead bodies here, after the flesh had been stripped off from the bones; for the Plataians brought together the bones all to one place:—there was found, I say, a skull with no suture but all of one bone, and there was seen also a jaw–bone, that is to say the upper part of the jaw, which had teeth joined together and all of one bone, both the teeth that bite and those that grind; and the bones were seen also of a man five cubits high. 84. The body of Mardonios however had disappeared[93] on the day after the battle, taken by whom I am not able with certainty to say, but I have heard the names of many men of various cities who are said to have buried Mardonios, and I know that many received gifts from Artontes the son of Mardonios for having done this: who he was however who took up and buried the body of Mardonios I am not able for certain to discover, but Dionysophanes an Ephesian is reported with some show of reason to have been he who buried Mardonios. 85. He then was buried in some such manner as this: and the Hellenes when they had divided the spoil at Plataia proceeded to bury their dead, each nation apart by themselves. The Spartans made for themselves three several burial–places, one in which they buried the younger Spartans,[94] of whom also were Poseidonios, Amompharetos, Philokyon and Callicrates,—in one of the graves, I say, were laid the younger men, in the second the rest of the Spartans, and in the third the Helots. These then thus buried their dead; but the Tegeans buried theirs all together in a place apart from these, and the Athenians theirs together; and the Megarians and Phliasians those who had been slain by the cavalry. Of all these the burial–places had bodies laid in them, but as to the burial–places of other States which are to be seen at Plataia, these, as I am informed, are all mere mounds of earth without any bodies in them, raised by the several peoples on account of posterity, because they were ashamed of their absence from the fight; for among others there is one there called the burial–place of the Eginetans, which I hear was raised at the request of the Eginetans by Cleades the son of Autodicos, a man of Plataia who was their public guest–friend,[95] no less than ten years after these events.

86. When the Hellenes had buried their dead at Plataia, forthwith they determined in common council to march upon Thebes and to ask the Thebans to surrender those who had taken the side of the Medes, and among the first of them Timagenides and Attaginos, who were leaders equal to the first; and if the Thebans did not give them up, they determined not to retire from the city until they had taken it. Having thus resolved, they came accordingly on the eleventh day after the battle and began to besiege the Thebans, bidding them give the men up: and as the Thebans refused to give them up, they began to lay waste their land and also to attack their wall. 87. So then, as they did not cease their ravages, on the twentieth day Timagenides spoke as follows to the Thebans: "Thebans, since it has been resolved by the Hellenes not to retire from the siege until either they have taken Thebes or ye have delivered us up to them, now therefore let not the land of Bœotia suffer[96] any more for our sakes, but if they desire to have money and are demanding our surrender as a colour for this, let us give them money taken out of the treasury of the State; for we took the side of the Medes together with the State and not by ourselves alone: but if they are making the siege truly in order to get us into their hands, then we will give ourselves up for trial."[97] In this it was thought that he spoke very well and seasonably, and the Thebans forthwith sent a herald to Pausanias offering to deliver up the men. 88. After they had made an agreement on these terms, Attaginos escaped out of the city; and when his sons were delivered up to Pausanias, he released them from the charge, saying that the sons had no share in the guilt of taking the side of the Medes. As to the other men whom the Thebans delivered up, they supposed that they would get a trial,[98] and they trusted moreover to be able to repel the danger by payment of money; but Pausanias, when he had received them, suspecting this very thing, first dismissed the whole army of allies, and then took the men to Corinth and put them to death there. These were the things which happened at Plataia and at Thebes.

89. Artabazos meanwhile, the son of Pharnakes, in his flight from Plataia was by this time getting forward on his way: and the Thessalians, when he came to them, offered him hospitality and inquired concerning the rest of the army, not knowing anything of that which had happened at Plataia; and Artabazos knowing that if he should tell them the whole truth about the fighting, he would run the risk of being destroyed, both himself and the whole army which was with him, (for he thought that they would all set upon him if they were informed of that which had happened),—reflecting, I say, upon this he had told nothing of it to the Phokians, and now to the Thessalians he spoke as follows: "I, as you see, Thessalians, am earnest to march by the shortest way

to Thracia; and I am in great haste, having been sent with these men for a certain business from the army; moreover Mardonios himself and his army are shortly to be looked for here, marching close after me. To him give entertainment and show yourselves serviceable, for ye will not in the end repent of so doing." Having thus said he continued to march his army with haste through Thessaly and Macedonia straight for Thracia, being in truth earnest to proceed and going through the land by the shortest possible way:[99] and so he came to Byzantion, having left behind him great numbers of his army, who had either been cut down by the Thracians on the way or had been overcome by hunger and fatigue;[100] and from Byzantion he passed over in ships. He himself[101] then thus made his return back to Asia.

90. Now on the same day on which the defeat took place at Plataia, another took place also, as fortune would have it, at Mycale in Ionia. For when the Hellenes who had come in the ships with Leotychides the Lacedemonian, were lying at Delos, there came to them as envoys from Samos Lampon the son of Thrasycles and Athenagoras the son of Archestratides and Hegesistratos the son of Aristagoras, who had been sent by the people of Samos without the knowledge either of the Persians or of the despot Theomestor the son of Androdamas, whom the Persians had set up to be despot of Samos. When these had been introduced before the commanders, Hegesistratos spoke at great length using arguments of all kinds, and saying that so soon as the Ionians should see them they would at once revolt from the Persians, and that the Barbarians would not wait for their attack; and if after all they did so, then the Hellenes would take a prize such as they would never take again hereafter; and appealing to the gods worshipped in common he endeavoured to persuade them to rescue from slavery men who were Hellenes and to drive away the Barbarian: and this he said was easy for them to do, for the ships of the enemy sailed badly and were no match for them in fight. Moreover if the Hellenes suspected that they were endeavouring to bring them on by fraud, they were ready to be taken as hostages in their ships. 91. Then as the stranger of Samos was urgent in his prayer, Leotychides inquired thus, either desiring to hear for the sake of the omen or perhaps by a chance which Providence brought about: "Stranger of Samos, what is thy name?" He said "Hegesistratos."[102] The other cut short the rest of the speech, stopping all that Hegesistratos had intended to say further, and said: "I accept the augury given in Hegesistratos, stranger of Samos. Do thou on thy part see that thou give us assurance, thou and the men who are with thee, that the Samians will without fail be our zealous allies, and after that sail away home." 92. Thus he spoke and to the words he added the deed; for forthwith the Samians gave

assurance and made oaths of alliance with the Hellenes, and having so done the others sailed away home, but Hegesistratos he bade sail with the Hellenes, considering the name to be an augury of good success. Then the Hellenes after staying still that day made sacrifices for success on the next day, their diviner being Deïphonos the son of Euenios an Apolloniate, of that Apollonia which lies in the Ionian gulf.[102a] 93. To this man's father Euenios it happened as follows:—There are at this place Apollonia sheep sacred to the Sun, which during the day feed by a river[103] running from Mount Lacmon through the land of Apollonia to the sea by the haven of Oricos; and by night they are watched by men chosen for this purpose, who are the most highly considered of the citizens for wealth and noble birth, each man having charge of them for a year; for the people of Apollonia set great store on these sheep by reason of an oracle: and they are folded in a cave at some distance from the city. Here at the time of which I speak this man Euenios was keeping watch over them, having been chosen for that purpose; and it happened one night that he fell asleep during his watch, and wolves came by into the cave and killed about sixty of the sheep. When he perceived this, he kept it secret and told no one, meaning to buy others and substitute them in the place of those that were killed. It was discovered however by the people of Apollonia that this had happened; and when they were informed of it, they brought him up before a court and condemned him to be deprived of his eyesight for having fallen asleep during his watch. But when they had blinded Euenios, forthwith after this their flocks ceased to bring forth young and their land to bear crops as before. Then prophesyings were uttered to them both at Dodona and also at Delphi, when they asked the prophets the cause of the evil which they were suffering, and they told them[104] that they had done unjustly in depriving of his sight Euenios the watcher of the sacred sheep; for the gods of whom they inquired had themselves sent the wolves to attack the sheep; and they would not cease to take vengeance for him till the men of Apollonia should have paid to Euenios such satisfaction as he himself should choose and deem sufficient; and this being fulfilled, the gods would give to Euenios a gift of such a kind that many men would think him happy in that he possessed it. 94. These oracles then were uttered to them, and the people of Apollonia, making a secret of it, proposed to certain men of the citizens to manage the affair; and they managed it for them thus:—when Euenios was sitting on a seat in public, they came and sat by him, and conversed about other matters, and at last they came to sympathising with him in his misfortune; and thus leading him on they asked what satisfaction he should choose, if the people of Apollonia should undertake to give him satisfaction for that which they had done. He then, not having heard the oracle, made choice and said that if there should be given him the lands belonging to certain citizens, naming those whom he knew to possess the two best lots of land in Apollonia, and a dwelling—house also with these, which he knew to be the best house in the city,—if he became the possessor of these, he said, he would have no anger against them for the future, and this satisfaction would be sufficient for him if it should be given. Then as he was thus speaking, the men who sat by him said interrupting him: "Euenios, this satisfaction the Apolloniates pay to thee for thy blinding in accordance with the oracles which have been given to them." Upon this he was angry, being thus informed of the whole matter and considering that he had been deceived; and they bought the property from those who possessed it and gave him that which he had chosen. And forthwith after this he had a natural gift of divination,[105] so that he became very famous. 95. Of this Euenios, I say, Deïphonos was the son, and he was acting as diviner for the army, being brought by the Corinthians. I have heard however also that Deïphonos wrongly made use of the name of Euenios, and undertook work of this kind about Hellas, not being really the son of Euenios.

96. Now when the sacrifices were favourable to the Hellenes, they put their ships to sea from Delos to go to Samos; and having arrived off Calamisa[106] in Samos, they moored their ships there opposite the temple of Hera which is at this place, and made preparations for a sea—fight; but the Persians, being informed that they were sailing thither, put out to sea also and went over to the mainland with their remaining ships, (those of the Phenicians having been already sent away to sail home): for deliberating of the matter they thought it good not to fight a battle by sea, since they did not think that they were a match for the enemy. And they sailed away to the mainland in order that they might be under the protection of their land—army which was in Mycale, a body which had stayed behind the rest of the army by command of Xerxes and was keeping watch over Ionia: of this the number was six myriads[107] and the commander of it was Tigranes, who in beauty and stature excelled the other Persians. The commanders of the fleet then had determined to take refuge under the protection of this army, and to draw up their ships on shore and put an enclosure round as a protection for the ships and a refuge for themselves. 97. Having thus determined they began to put out to sea; and they came along by the temple of the "Revered goddesses"[107a] to the Gaison and to Scolopoeis in Mycale, where there is a temple of the Eleusinian Demeter, which Philistos the son of Pasicles erected when he had accompanied Neileus the son of Codros for the founding of Miletos; and there they drew up their ships on shore and put an enclosure round them of stones and timber, cutting down

fruit-trees for this purpose, and they fixed stakes round the enclosure and made their preparations either for being besieged or for gaining a victory, for in making their preparations they reckoned for both chances.

98. The Hellenes however, when they were informed that the Barbarians had gone away to the mainland, were vexed because they thought that they had escaped; and they were in a difficulty what they should do, whether they should go back home, or sail down towards the Hellespont. At last they resolved to do neither of these two things, but to sail on to the mainland. Therefore when they had prepared as for a sea-fight both boarding-bridges and all other things that were required, they sailed towards Mycale; and when they came near to the camp and no one was seen to put out against them, but they perceived ships drawn up within the wall and a large land-army ranged along the shore, then first Leotychides, sailing along in his ship and coming as near to the shore as he could, made proclamation by a herald to the Ionians, saying: "Ionians, those of you who chance to be within hearing of me, attend to this which I say: for the Persians will not understand anything at all of that which I enjoin to you. When we join battle, each one of you must remember first the freedom of all, and then the watchword 'Hebe'; and this let him also who has not heard know from him who has heard." The design in this act was the same as that of Themistocles at Artemision; for it was meant that either the words uttered should escape the knowledge of the Barbarians and persuade the Ionians, or that they should be reported to the Barbarians and make them distrustful of the Hellenes.[108]

99. After Leotychides had thus suggested, then next the Hellenes proceeded to bring their ships up to land, and they disembarked upon the shore. These then were ranging themselves for fight; and the Persians, when they saw the Hellenes preparing for battle and also that they had given exhortation to the Ionians, in the first place deprived the Samians of their arms, suspecting that they were inclined to the side of the Hellenes; for when the Athenian prisoners, the men whom the army of Xerxes had found left behind in Attica, had come in the ships of the Barbarians, the Samians had ransomed these and sent them back to Athens, supplying them with means for their journey; and for this reason especially they were suspected, since they had ransomed five hundred persons of the enemies of Xerxes. Then secondly the Persians appointed the Milesians to guard the passes which lead to the summits of Mycale, on the pretext that they knew the country best, but their true reason for doing this was that they might be out of the camp. Against these of the Ionians, who, as they suspected, would make some hostile

move[109] if they found the occasion, the Persians sought to secure themselves in the manner mentioned; and they themselves then brought together their wicker–work shields to serve them as a fence.

100. Then when the Hellenes had made all their preparations, they proceeded to the attack of the Barbarians; and as they went, a rumour came suddenly[110] to their whole army, and at the same time a herald's staff was found lying upon the beach; and the rumour went through their army to this effect, namely that the Hellenes were fighting in Bœotia and conquering the army of Mardonios. Now by many signs is the divine power seen in earthly things, and by this among others, namely that now, when the day of the defeat at Plataia and of that which was about to take place at Mycale happened to be the same, a rumour came to the Hellenes here, so that the army was encouraged much more and was more eagerly desirous to face the danger. 101. Moreover this other thing by coincidence happened besides, namely that there was a sacred enclosure of the Eleusinian Demeter close by the side of both the battle–fields; for not only in the Plataian land did the fight take place close by the side of the temple of Demeter, as I have before said, but also in Mycale it was to be so likewise. And whereas the rumour which came to them said that a victory had been already gained by the Hellenes with Pausanias, this proved to be a true report; for that which was done at Plataia came about while it was yet early morning, but the fighting at Mycale took place in the afternoon; and that it happened on the same day of the same month as the other became evident to them not long afterwards, when they inquired into the matter. Now they had been afraid before the rumour arrived, not for themselves so much as for the Hellenes generally, lest Hellas should stumble and fall over Mardonios; but when this report had come suddenly to them, they advanced on the enemy much more vigorously and swiftly than before. The Hellenes then and the Barbarians were going with eagerness into the battle, since both the islands and the Hellespont were placed before them as prizes of the contest.

102. Now for the Athenians and those who were ranged next to them, to the number perhaps of half the whole army, the road lay along the sea– beach and over level ground, while the Lacedemonians and those ranged in order by these were compelled to go by a ravine and along the mountain side: so while the Lacedemonians were yet going round, those upon the other wing were already beginning the fight; and as long as the wicker–work shields of the Persians still remained upright, they continued to defend themselves and had rather the advantage in the fight; but when the troops of the

Athenians and of those ranged next to them, desiring that the achievement should belong to them and not to the Lacedemonians, with exhortations to one another set themselves more vigorously to the work, then from that time forth the fortune of the fight was changed; for these pushed aside the wicker–work shields and fell upon the Persians with a rush all in one body, and the Persians sustained their first attack and continued to defend themselves for a long time, but at last they fled to the wall; and the Athenians, Corinthians, Sikyonians and Troizenians, for that was the order in which they were ranged, followed close after them and rushed in together with them to the space within the wall: and when the wall too had been captured, then the Barbarians no longer betook themselves to resistance, but began at once to take flight, excepting only the Persians, who formed into small groups and continued to fight with the Hellenes as they rushed in within the wall. Of the commanders of the Persians two made their escape and two were slain; Artaÿntes and Ithamitres commanders of the fleet escaped, while Mardontes and the commander of the land–army, Tigranes, were slain. 103. Now while the Persians were still fighting, the Lacedemonians and those with them arrived, and joined in carrying through the rest of the work; and of the Hellenes themselves many fell there and especially many of the Sikyonians, together with their commander Perilaos. And those of the Samians who were serving in the army, being in the camp of the Medes and having been deprived of their arms, when they saw that from the very first the battle began to be doubtful,[111] did as much as they could, endeavouring to give assistance to the Hellenes; and the other Ionians seeing that the Samians had set the example, themselves also upon that made revolt from the Persians and attacked the Barbarians. 104. The Milesians too had been appointed to watch the passes of the Persians[112] in order to secure their safety, so that if that should after all come upon them which actually came, they might have guides and so get safe away to the summits of Mycale,—the Milesians, I say, had been appointed to do this, not only for that end but also for fear that, if they were present in the camp, they might make some hostile move:[113] but they did in fact the opposite of that which they were appointed to do; for they not only directed them in the flight by other than the right paths, by paths indeed which led towards the enemy, but also at last they themselves became their worst foes and began to slay them. Thus then for the second time Ionia revolted from the Persians.

105. In this battle, of the Hellenes the Athenians were the best men, and of the Athenians Hermolycos the son of Euthoinos, a man who had trained for the pancration. This Hermolycos after these events, when there was war between the Athenians and

the Carystians, was killed in battle at Kyrnos in the Carystian land near Geraistos, and there was buried. After the Athenians the Corinthians, Troizenians and Sikyonians were the best.

106. When the Hellenes had slain the greater number of the Barbarians, some in the battle and others in their flight, they set fire to the ships and to the whole of the wall, having first brought out the spoil to the sea-shore; and among the rest they found some stores of money. So having set fire to the wall and to the ships they sailed away; and when they came to Samos, the Hellenes deliberated about removing the inhabitants of Ionia, and considered where they ought to settle them in those parts of Hellas of which they had command, leaving Ionia to the Barbarians: for it was evident to them that it was impossible on the one hand for them to be always stationed as guards to protect the Ionians, and on the other hand, if they were not stationed to protect them, they had no hope that the Ionians would escape with impunity from the Persians. Therefore it seemed good to those of the Peloponnesians that were in authority that they should remove the inhabitants of the trading ports which belonged to those peoples of Hellas who had taken the side of the Medes, and give that land to the Ionians to dwell in; but the Athenians did not think it good that the inhabitants of Ionia should be removed at all, nor that the Peloponnesians should consult about Athenian colonies; and as these vehemently resisted the proposal, the Peloponnesians gave way. So the end was that they joined as allies to their league the Samians, Chians, Lesbians, and the other islanders who chanced to be serving with the Hellenes, binding them by assurance and by oaths to remain faithful and not withdraw from the league: and having bound these by oaths they sailed to break up the bridges, for they supposed they would find them still stretched over the straits.

These then were sailing towards the Hellespont; 107, and meanwhile those Barbarians who had escaped and had been driven to the heights of Mycale, being not many in number, were making their way to Sardis: and as they went by the way, Masistes the son of Dareios, who had been present at the disaster which had befallen them, was saying many evil things of the commander Artaÿntes, and among other things he said that in respect of the generalship which he had shown he was worse than a woman, and that he deserved every kind of evil for having brought evil on the house of the king. Now with the Persians to be called worse than a woman is the greatest possible reproach. So he, after he had been much reviled, at length became angry and drew his sword upon Masistes, meaning to kill him; and as he was running upon him,

Xeinagoras the son of Prexilaos, a man of Halicarnassos, perceived it, who was standing just behind Artaÿntes; and this man seized him by the middle and lifting him up dashed him upon the ground; and meanwhile the spearmen of Masistes came in front to protect him. Thus did Xeinagoras, and thus he laid up thanks for himself both with Masistes and also with Xerxes for saving the life of his brother; and for this deed Xeinagoras became ruler of all Kilikia by the gift of the king. Nothing further happened than this as they went on their way, but they arrived at Sardis.

Now at Sardis, as it chanced, king Xerxes had been staying ever since that time when he came thither in flight from Athens, after suffering defeat in the sea–fight. 108. At that time, while he was in Sardis, he had a passionate desire, as it seems, for the wife of Masistes, who was also there: and as she could not be bent to his will by his messages to her, and he did not wish to employ force because he had regard for his brother Masistes and the same consideration withheld the woman also, for she well knew that force would not be used towards her), then Xerxes abstained from all else, and endeavoured to bring about the marriage of his own son Dareios with the daughter of this woman and of Masistes, supposing that if he should do so he would obtain her more easily. Then having made the betrothal and done all the customary rites, he went away to Susa; and when he had arrived there and had brought the woman into his own house for Dareios, then he ceased from attempting the wife of Masistes and changing his inclination he conceived a desire for the wife of Dareios, who was daughter of Masistes, and obtained her: now the name of this woman was Artaÿnte. 109. However as time went on, this became known in the following manner:—Amestris the wife of Xerxes had woven a mantle, large and of various work and a sight worthy to be seen, and this she gave to Xerxes. He then being greatly pleased put it on and went to Artaÿnte; and being greatly pleased with her too, he bade her ask what she would to be given to her in return for the favours which she had granted to him, for she should obtain, he said, whatsoever she asked: and she, since it was destined that she should perish miserably with her whole house, said to Xerxes upon this: "Wilt thou give me whatsoever I ask thee for?" and he, supposing that she would ask anything rather than that which she did, promised this and swore to it. Then when he had sworn, she boldly asked for the mantle; and Xerxes tried every means of persuasion, not being willing to give it to her, and that for no other reason but only because he feared Amestris, lest by her, who even before this had some inkling of the truth, he should thus be discovered in the act; and he offered her cities and gold in any quantity, and an army which no one else should command except herself. Now this of an army is a thoroughly Persian gift.

Since however he did not persuade her, he gave her the mantle; and she being overjoyed by the gift wore it and prided herself upon it. 110. And Amestris was informed that she had it; and having learnt that which was being done, she was not angry with the woman, but supposing that her mother was the cause and that she was bringing this about, she planned destruction for the wife of Masistes. She waited then until her husband Xerxes had a royal feast set before him:—this feast is served up once in the year on the day on which the king was born, and the name of this feast is in Persian tycta, which in the tongue of the Hellenes means "complete"; also on this occasion alone the king washes his head,[114] and he makes gifts then to the Persians:—Amestris, I say, waited for this day and then asked of Xerxes that the wife of Masistes might be given to her. And he considered it a strange and untoward thing to deliver over to her his brother's wife, especially since she was innocent of this matter; for he understood why she was making the request. 111. At last however as she continued to entreat urgently and he was compelled by the rule, namely that it is impossible among them that he who makes request when a royal feast is laid before the king should fail to obtain it, at last very much against his will consented; and in delivering her up he bade Amestris do as she desired, and meanwhile he sent for his brother and said these words: "Masistes, thou art the son of Dareios and my brother, and moreover in addition to this thou art a man of worth. I say to thee, live no longer with this wife with whom thou now livest, but I give thee instead of her my daughter; with her live as thy wife, but the wife whom thou now hast, do not keep; for it does not seem good to me that thou shouldest keep her." Masistes then, marvelling at that which was spoken, said these words: "Master, how unprofitable a speech is this which thou utterest to me, in that thou biddest me send away a wife by whom I have sons who are grown up to be young men, and daughters one of whom even thou thyself didst take as a wife for thy son, and who is herself, as it chances, very much to my mind,—that thou biddest me, I say, send away her and take to wife thy daughter! I, O king, think it a very great matter that I am judged worthy of thy daughter, but nevertheless I will do neither of these things: and do not thou urge me by force to do such a thing as this: but for thy daughter another husband will be found not in any wise inferior to me, and let me, I pray thee, live still with my own wife." He returned answer in some such words as these; and Xerxes being stirred with anger said as follows: "This then, Masistes, is thy case,—I will not give thee my daughter for thy wife, nor yet shalt thou live any longer with that one, in order that thou mayest learn to accept that which is offered thee." He then when he heard this went out, having first said these words: "Master, thou hast not surely brought ruin upon me?"[115] 112. During this interval of time, while Xerxes was conversing with his brother, Amestris had sent the spearmen of Xerxes to bring the wife of Masistes, and she was doing to her shameful outrage; for she cut away her breasts and threw them to dogs, and she cut off her nose and ears and lips and tongue, and sent her back home thus outraged. 113. Then Masistes, not yet having heard any of these things, but supposing that some evil had fallen upon him, came running to his house; and seeing his wife thus mutilated, forthwith upon this he took counsel with his sons and set forth to go to Bactria together with his sons and doubtless some others also, meaning to make the province of Bactria revolt and to do the greatest possible injury to the king: and this in fact would have come to pass, as I imagine, if he had got up to the land of the Bactrians and Sacans before he was overtaken, for they were much attached to him, and also he was the governor of the Bactrians: but Xerxes being informed that he was doing this, sent after him an army as he was on his way, and slew both him and his sons and his army. So far of that which happened about the passion of Xerxes and the death of Masistes.

114. Now the Hellenes who had set forth from Mycale to the Hellespont first moored their ships about Lecton, being stopped from their voyage by winds; and thence they came to Abydos and found that the bridges had been broken up, which they thought to find still stretched across, and on account of which especially they had come to the Hellespont. So the Peloponnesians which Leotychides resolved to sail back to Hellas, while the Athenians and Xanthippos their commander determined to stay behind there and to make an attempt upon the Chersonese. Those then sailed away, and the Athenians passed over from Abydos to the Chersonese and began to besiege Sestos. 115. To this town of Sestos, since it was the greatest stronghold of those in that region, men had come together from the cities which lay round it, when they heard that the Hellenes had arrived at the Hellespont, and especially there had come from the city of Cardia Oiobazos a Persian, who had brought to Sestos the ropes of the bridges. The inhabitants of the city were Aiolians, natives of the country, but there were living with them a great number of Persians and also of their allies. 116. And of the province Artaÿctes was despot, as governor under Xerxes, a Persian, but a man of desperate and reckless character, who also had practised deception upon the king on his march against Athens, in taking away from Elaius the things belonging to Protesilaos the son of Iphiclos. For at Elaius in the Chersonese there is the tomb of Protesilaos with a sacred enclosure about it, where there were many treasures, with gold and silver cups and bronze and raiment and other offerings, which things Artaÿctes carried off as plunder, the king having granted them to him. And he deceived Xerxes by saying to

him some such words as these: "Master, there is here the house of a man, a Hellene, who made an expedition against thy land and met with his deserts and was slain: this man's house I ask thee to give to me, that every one may learn not to make expeditions against thy land." By saying this it was likely that he would easily enough persuade Xerxes to give him a man's house, not suspecting what was in his mind: and when he said that Protesilaos had made expedition against the land of the king, it must be understood that the Persians consider all Asia to be theirs and to belong to their reigning king. So when the things had been given him, he brought them from Elaius to Sestos, and he sowed the sacred enclosure for crops and occupied it as his own; and he himself, whenever he came to Elaius, had commerce with women in the inner cell of the temple.[116] And now he was being besieged by the Athenians, when he had not made any preparation for a siege nor had been expecting that the Hellenes would come; for they fell upon him, as one may say, inevitably.[117] 117. When however autumn came and the siege still went on, the Athenians began to be vexed at being absent from their own land and at the same time not able to conquer the fortress, and they requested their commanders to lead them away home; but these said that they would not do so, until either they had taken the town or the public authority of the Athenians sent for them home: and so they endured their present state.[118] 118. Those however who were within the walls had now come to the greatest misery, so that they boiled down the girths of their beds and used them for food; and when they no longer had even these, then the Persians and with them Artaÿctes and Oiobazos ran away and departed in the night, climbing down by the back part of the wall, where the place was left most unguarded by the enemy; and when day came, the men of the Chersonese signified to the Athenians from the towers concerning that which had happened, and opened the gates to them. So the greater number of them went in pursuit, and the rest occupied the city. 119. Now Oiobazos, as he was escaping[119] into Thrace, was caught by the Apsinthian Thracians and sacrificed to their native god Pleistoros with their rites, and the rest who were with him they slaughtered in another manner: but Artaÿctes with his companions, who started on their flight later and were overtaken at a little distance above Aigospotamoi, defended themselves for a considerable time and were some of them killed and others taken alive: and the Hellenes had bound these and were bringing them to Sestos, and among them Artaÿctes also in bonds together with his son. 120. Then, it is said by the men of the Chersonese, as one of those who guarded them was frying dried fish, a portent occurred as follows,—the dried fish when laid upon the fire began to leap and struggle just as if they were fish newly caught: and the others gathered round and were marvelling at the portent, but Artaÿctes seeing it called to the man who was frying the fish and said: "Stranger of Athens, be not at all afraid of this portent, seeing that it has not appeared for thee but for me. Protesilaos who dwells at Elaius signifies thereby that though he is dead and his body is dried like those fish,[120] yet he has power given him by the gods to exact vengeance from the man who does him wrong. Now therefore I desire to impose this penalty for him,[121]—that in place of the things which I took from the temple I should pay down a hundred talents to the god, and moreover as ransom for myself and my son I will pay two hundred talents to the Athenians, if my life be spared." Thus he engaged to do, but he did not prevail upon the commander Xanthippos; for the people of Elaius desiring to take vengeance for Protesilaos asked that he might be put to death, and the inclination of the commander himself tended to the same conclusion. They brought him therefore to that headland to which Xerxes made the passage across, or as some say to the hill which is over the town of Madytos, and there they nailed him to boards[122] and hung him up; and they stoned his son to death before the eyes of Artaÿctes himself. 121. Having so done, they sailed away to Hellas, taking with them, besides other things, the ropes also of the bridges, in order to dedicate them as offerings in the temples: and for that year nothing happened further than this.

122. Now a forefather of this Artaÿctes who was hung up, was that Artembares who set forth to the Persians a proposal which they took up and brought before Cyrus, being to this effect: "Seeing that Zeus grants to the Persians leadership, and of all men to thee, O Cyrus, by destroying Astyages, come, since the land we possess is small and also rugged, let us change from it and inhabit another which is better: and there are many near at hand, and many also at a greater distance, of which if we take one, we shall have greater reverence and from more men. It is reasonable too that men who are rulers should do such things; for when will there ever be a fairer occasion than now, when we are rulers of many nations and of the whole of Asia?" Cyrus, hearing this and not being surprised at the proposal,[123] bade them do so if they would; but he exhorted them and bade them prepare in that case to be no longer rulers but subjects; "For," said he, "from lands which are not rugged men who are not rugged are apt to come forth, since it does not belong to the same land to bring forth fruits of the earth which are admirable and also men who are good in war." So the Persians acknowledged that he was right and departed from his presence, having their opinion defeated by that of Cyrus; and they chose rather to dwell on poor land and be rulers, than to sow crops in a level plain and be slaves to others. ————————

NOTES TO BOOK IX

1. "the same who at the former time also were of one accord together."

2. *ta ekeinon iskhura bouleumata*: some good MSS. omit *iskhura*, and so many Editors.

3. *up agnomosunes.*

4. *boulen.*

5. *exeneikai es ton dumon.*

6. *aleoren.*

7. Cp. viii. 140 (a).

8. *to men ap emeon outo akibdelon nemetai epi tous Ellenas*, "that which we owe to the Hellenes is thus paid in no counterfeit coin.

9. *ekeleusan*, i.e. "their bidding was" when they sent us.

9a. This clause, "with no less—each man of them," is omitted in some MSS. and considered spurious by several Editors.

10. Cp. ch. 55.

11. *perioikon.*

12. *ton emerodromon*, cp. vi. 105.

13. *tugkhane eu bouleoumenos*: perhaps, "endeavour to take measures well."

14. *prodromon*, a conjectural emendation of *prodromos*.

15. *boiotarkhai*, i.e. the heads of the Bœotian confederacy.

16. *os epi deka stadious malista ke.*

17. *klinai*: several Editors have altered this, reading *klithenai* or *klinenai*, "they were made to recline."

18. *diapinonton*, cp. v. 18.

19. *polla phroneonta medenos krateein.*

20. *sphodra*: not quite satisfactory with *emedizon*, but it can hardly go with *ouk ekontes*, as Krüger suggests.

21. *pheme*, as in ch. 100.

22. *proopto thanato.*

23. *prosballontes*: most of the MSS. have *prosbalontes*, and so also in ch. 21 and 22 they have *prosbalouses.*

24. i.e. the retreat with which each charge ended and the turn from retreat in preparation for a fresh charge. So much would be done without word of command, before reining in their horses.

25. *ephoiteon.*

25a. Or, according to some MSS., "much contention in argument."

26. i.e. the left wing.

27. The name apparently should be Kepheus, but there is no authority for changing the text.

28. This is the number of nations mentioned in vii. 61–80 as composing the land–army of Xerxes.

29. *oi epiphoiteontes.*

30. *peri andra ekaston.*

31. i.e. 38,700.

32. i.e. 69,500.

33. i.e. 110,000.

34. *opla de oud outoi eikhon*: i.e. these too must be reckoned with the light–armed.

35. Cp. ii. 164.

36. *makhairophoroi*: cp. vii. 89.

37. i.e. 300,000: see viii. 113.

38. *geneos tou Iamideon*: the MSS. have *Klutiaden* after *Iamideon*, but the Clytiadai seem to have been a distinct family of soothsayers.

39. *pentaethlon.*

40. *para en palaisma edrame nikan Olumpiada.* The meaning is not clear, because the conditions of the *pentaethlon* are not known: however the wrestling *pale* seems to have been the last of the five contests, and the meaning may be that both Tisamenos and Hieronymos had beaten all the other competitors and were equal so far, when Tisamenos failed to win two out of three falls in the wrestling.

41. *metientes*: some MSS. have *metiontes*, "they went to fetch him.'

42. *aiteomenos*: this is the reading of the MSS., but the conjecture *aiteomenous* (or *aiteomenon*) seems probable enough: "if one may compare the man who asked for royal power with him who asked only for citizenship."

43. i.e. instead of half for himself, he asks for two–thirds to be divided between himself and his brother.

44. *o pros Ithome*: a conjectural emendation of *o pros Isthmo*.

45. *ton tarson eoutou*.

46. *Treis Kephalas*.

47. *Druos Kephalas*.

48. See ch. 2.

49. *ton epikleton*: cp. vii. 8.

50. *Mardonio te kai te stratie ta sphagia ou dunatai katathumia genesthai*.

51. He asks for their help to free his country also from the Persian yoke.

52. *emakhesametha*.

53. *psukhre*, cp. vi. 108.

54. *deka stadious*.

55. *nesos de outo an eie en epeiro*.

56. *periskhizetai*.

57. *epheugon asmenoi*.

58. *tou Pitaneteon lokhou*, called below *ton lokhon ton Pitaneten*. Evidently *lokhos* here is a division of considerable size.

59. *anainomenou*: some MSS. and many Editors read *nenomenou*, "since he was thus minded."

60. *os alla phroneonton kai alla legonton*.

61. Cp. ch. 11.

62. The structure of the sentence is rather confused, and perhaps some emendation is required.

63. *eti ti lexete*. The MSS. and most Editors read *ti*, "what will ye say after this?" The order of the words is against this.

64. *anarpasomenoi*: cp. viii. 28.

65. *phraxantes ta gerra*: cp. ch. 99.

66. *anoploi*, by which evidently more is meant than the absence of shields; cp. the end of ch. 63, where the equipment of the Persians is compared to that of light–armed troops.

67. See viii. 114.

68. *es Leoniden*: this is ordinarily translated "as far as Leonidas;" but to say "his ancestors above Anaxandrides have been given as far as Leonidas" (the son of Anaxandrides), is hardly intelligible. The reference is to vii. 204.

69. Most of the MSS. call him Aeimnestos (with some variation of spelling), but Plutarch has Arimnestos.

70. See ch. 15. There is no sharp distinction here between camp and palisade, the latter being merely the fortified part of the encampment.

71. *anaktoron*, a usual name for the temple of Demeter and Persephone at Eleusis.

72. i.e. 40,000.

73. *ege katertemenos*: the better MSS. have *eie* for *ege*, which is retained by some Editors (*toutous* being then taken with *inai pantas*): for *katertemenos* we find as variations *katertemenos* and *katertismenos*. Many Editors read *katertismenos* ("well prepared"), following the Aldine tradition.

74. *ephelokakeonton.*

75. *en oudeni logo apolonto.*

76. Stein proposes to substitute "Athenians" for "Lacedemonians" here, making the comparative *erremenestere* anticipate the account given in the next few clauses.

77. *erromenestere.*

78. Cp. i. 66.

79. *aluktazon,* a word of doubtful meaning which is not found elsewhere.

80. i.e. 300,000.

81. *o Spartietes*: it has been proposed to read *Spartietai,* for it can hardly be supposed that the other two were not Spartans also.

82. One MS. at least calls him Aeimenstos, cp. ch. 64. Thucydides (iii. 52) mentions Aeimnestos as the name of a Plataian citizen, the father of Lacon. Stein observes that in any case this cannot be that Arimnestos who is mentioned by Plutarch as commander of the Plataian contingent.

83. *eoutou axion prophumeumenou apodexasthai.*

84. *atelein te kai proedrin.*

85. vi. 92.

86. *andra pentaethlon.*

87. *oute daimonon oute theon*: heroes and in general divinities of the second order are included under the term *daimonon.*

88. Most of the commentators (and following them the historians) understand the imperfect *ediokon* to express the mere purpose to attempt, and suppose that this

purpose was actually hindered by the Lacedemonians. but for a mere half-formed purpose the expression *mekhri Thessalies* seems to definite, and Diodorus states that Artabazos was pursued. I think therefore that Krüger is right in understanding *eon* of an attempt to dissuade which was not successful. The alternative version would be "they were for pursuing them as far as Thessaly, but the Lacedemonians prevented them from pursuing fugitives."

89. *akinakas.*

90. Whether three tithes were taken or only one is left uncertain.

91. "furniture furnished" is hardly tolerable; perhaps Herodotus wrote *skenen* for *kataskeuen* here.

92. The connexion here is not satisfactory, and the chapter is in part a continuation of chapter 81. It is possible that ch. 82 may be a later addition by the author, thrown in without much regard to the context.

93. "Whereas however the body of Mardonios had disappeared on the day after the battle (taken by whom I am not able to say . . . .), it is reported with some show of reason that Dionysophanes, an Ephesian, was he who buried it." The construction however is irregular and broken by parentheses: possibly there is some corruption of text.

94. *tous irenas.* Spartans between twenty and thirty years old were so called. The MSS. have *ireas.*

95. *proxeinon.*

96. "fill up more calamities," cp. v. 4.

97. *es antilogien.*

98. *antilogies kuresein.*

99. *ten mesogaian tamnon tes odou*, cp. vii. 124. The expression seems almost equivalent to *tamnon ten mesen odon*, apart from any question of inland or coast roads.

100. *limo sustantas kai kamato*, "having struggled with hunger and fatigue."

101. *autos*: some MSS. read *outos*. If the text is right, it means Artabazos as distinguished from his troops.

102. i.e. "leader of the army."

102a. *en to Ionio kolpo.*

103. Stein reads *para Khona potamon*, "by the river Chon," a conjecture derived from Theognostus.

104. It is thought by some Editors that "the prophets" just above, and these words, "and they told them," are interpolated.

105. *emphuton mantiken*, as opposed to the *entekhnos mantike* possessed for example by Melampus, cp. ii. 49.

106. Or possibly "Calamoi."

107. i.e. 60,000.

107a. *ton Potneion*, i.e. either the Eumenides or Demeter and Persephone.

108. *apistous toisi Ellesi*. Perhaps the last two words are to be rejected, and *apistous* to be taken in its usual sense, "distrusted"; cp. viii. 22.

109. *neokhmon an ti poieein.*

110. *pheme eseptato.*

111. *eteralkea*, cp. viii. 11.

112. *ton Perseon*: perhaps we should read *ek ton Perseon*, "appointed by the Persians to guard the passes."

113. *ti neokhmon poieoien*.

114. *ten kephalen smatai*: the meaning is uncertain.

115. *Pou de kou me apolesas*: some Editors read *ko* for *kou* (by conjecture), and print the clause as a statement instead of a question, "not yet hast thou caused by ruin."

116. *en to aduto*.

117. *aphuktos*: many Editors adopt the reading *aphulakto* from inferior MSS., "they fell upon him when he was, as one may say, off his guard."

118. *estergon ta pareonta*.

119. *ekpheugonta*: many Editors have *ekphugonta*, "after he had escaped."

120. *tarikhos eon*. The word *tarikhos* suggests the idea of human bodies embalmed, as well as of dried or salted meat.

121. *oi*: some Editors approve the conjecture *moi*, "impose upon myself this penalty."

122. *sanidas*: some read by conjecture *sanidi*, or *pros sanida*: cp. vii. 33.

123. Or, "when he had heard this, although he did not admire the proposal, yet bade them do so if they would."

Printed in the United States
48909LVS00003B/68